Rebirthed in Heaven's Light

Revised Edition © Sarah Heart, 2024.
First published (2023) as 'Ever-Now Christmas in my soul.'
All Rights Reserved.

Paperback Colour Edition ISBN 978-1-0687841-0-1
Paperback Black & White Edition ISBN 978-1-0687841-2-5

This publication includes some narrations from the private revelations of privileged Catholic Church religious, who lived lives of extraordinary virtue. Ecclesiastical authorities have positively judged these works as divine, granting them the *Nihil Obstat* and *Imprimatur* [Latin: *"Let it be printed"*], as testimonial to their orthodoxy in matters of Christian and Catholic faith, and moral doctrine. The entirely of the works cannot, however, be guaranteed free from error. These accounts do not replace the essentials and obligations of the Catholic faith found in Sacred Scripture, or taught by the Magisterium of the Church. Scriptural quotations mostly drawn from World English Bible [Catholic] and Catholic Public Domain version. Quotations from other sources do not exceed permission levels. Quotes from Church saints and mystics predominantly derived from public domain sources, or fall below threshold for permission. See also p. xxvi.

> *"There are also many other things which Jesus did, which if they would all be written, I suppose that even the world itself, wouldn't have room for the books that would be written."*
>
> John 21:25.

This book is dedicated to our Brother, Master, and Saviour Jesus Christ,
Who descended amongst us from on High,
And was wrapped in the perishable rags of poor man's will,
To Live and to Die pure and expansive suffering Love,
Swallowing up mortal death,
And issuing forth an ocean of Love and Mercy,
Re-opening the Way once closed, to carry us back up on High,
Restoring Cosmic order, and
Recovering for poor man,
The imperishable and refulgent Light-garment of Eternal Life.

Sweetest Jesus, Lamb of God,
Mighty Jesus, Lion of Judah,
Thank you for Loving us,
Thank you for freeing us.
Amen.

"What home will you build for Me;
what place can be My resting place?"

Isaiah 66:1.

Contents

Useful Terms 1
Introduction 31
The Nuptial Light-ring of the Homeland 37
Thankfulness, Gratitude & Relationship 44
Faithfulness, Courage & Compassion 51
Joy Like No Other 58
Eternity is Ever-Now 63
Light-fire & Victory in Jesus Christ 68
The Alpha and the Omega 73
The Blessed Virgin Mary 85
The Tree of Life 96
Adam and Eve 102
The Lamb of God 113
The Scales of Justice 119
Fiat 135
The Holy Spirit 145
The Mass 156
The Eucharist 168
    Holy Hour 177
Water 184
Prayer 191
Agape 226
The Garden of the Soul 245
Journey to Bethlehem 257

King of kings	266
The Maji	273
Gifts	281
Charity	294
The Holy Angels	315
The Nativity of Jesus Christ	333
New Advent	348
Appendix 1: Paradise Lost	i
Hell: The Infernal Fire	ix
Appendix 2: Spiritual Discernment	xiv
Appendix 3: The Golden Maxims of St. John of the Cross	xviii
Appendix 4: The Three Stages of Spiritual Growth	xix
Appendix 5: The Three Degrees of Prayer	xxi
Appendix 6: Suggested Reading	xxiv

Useful Terms

Blessed: meaning *"happy", "joyous", "delighted", "contented",* and *"fortunate",* in Aramaic and Hebrew. The best a person can be or has to offer, in all Spiritual prosperity and well-being [God-being, John 10:34]. Man was created to be blessed by God, and to be the blessing of God upon all [Romans 12:14]. The Hebrew expression of the word can also mean *"to kneel",* signifying man's reverence for, and praise of God, from whom all blessings come. Jesus opens the Beatitudes with the words: *"Blessed are the poor in spirit, for theirs is the kingdom of Heaven"* Matthew 5:3, confirming that the gifts of God are primarily Spiritual, and are conferred upon those who are most free from the fleeting desires, expectations, fears, and gatherings of the flesh [carnal-ego self] and the old world, in favour of Eternal things. See 'Detachment', 'Glory' and 'Poor in Spirit'.

Body: the body is made by God, as a living image of God, and is intrinsically good. Its purpose is to serve the soul of man, purified and re-ordered to the operation of the Spirit, who re-integrates [re-centres] and re-creates [re-births] him anew in Jesus Christ. The fulfilment of this divinely creative work in time, is the reception of the transfigured wholeness [holiness and all-perfection] of the divinely-human person in Eternity. Man's regard for his body, and that of other persons, should be to treat it as a *living* temple of the Holy Spirit [Romans 12:1; 1 Corinthians 3:16; 6:19], consecrated to God for the purpose of the indwelling of the Most Holy Trinity. See 'Flesh', 'Holiness', 'New man' and 'Re-creation [re-birth]'.

Charity: God is Spirit and action, and Charity is His Love [*"Agape"*] in action [in His Divine Will]. Enshrined in the first two commandments, to Love God above all else, and one's neighbour as oneself, Charity is the Light of faith made operable by and in Jesus Christ [Galatians 5:6]. Faith without works [Charity] is dead, says James 2:26. Flowing in every act [of thought, word, and deed], Charity is the supreme aim and purpose of every man who is the true seed of, and heir to, the Kingdom of Heaven. For the very nature of God is Charity [1 John 4:8], demonstrated in Jesus Christ's Coming to earth as God and man, to Live and Die for created man; destroying death that we might rise again to Eternal Life in Him. It is in operating in God's own Perfect [Whole and All-Perfect] Love in His Divine Will, that man realizes his God-being [John 10:34] and Good-being, while assisting everyone and everything. Pure Charity is the full substance and depth of God's own work in and through the consenting soul, that operates in Jesus Christ. See 'Love', 'religion', 'self-forgetting' and Chapter on St. Nicholas.

Chastity: holy purity [cleanliness and clarity] of heart, or purity of desire for God, which is desire for the re-ordering, re-integration [re-centring], and re-creation [re-birth] of our being, and that of others, in the primordial Wholeness [Holiness and All-Perfection] of God. Chastity is reflected in the entirety of one's being [in spirit, soul, and body], and flows through every act [of thought, word, and deed], by upright governance of the five senses, and the mind bowed in the heart. Fundamental in all blessed life-states which serve God's Plan, chastity is divine wisdom, preserving or recovering the [self-empty and transcendent] virgin element of the soul, which is the substance-essence of God-likeness, and the space in which God unites Himself with man. Perpetual chastity, for Love of God and the sake of the Kingdom [Matthew 19:12], is the God-given state of virginity. In this state, the soul's desire is for God alone [in all things] as it acts and rests in Him, for Love of Him and for everyone and everything in Him. Chastity is one of the three Evangelical Counsels [virtuous dispositions and practices] which includes Poverty ['Poorness of Spirit'] and Obedience [co-operation with God in His Love and Divine Will], and which purify and safeguard the soul, drawing it upwards and out of itself, to participate in the higher Life of the *"Fiat"*. Chastity is essential to our ascent to the company of Heaven [Matthew 5:8]. See 'Holiness', 'Perfection', and 'Poor in Spirit'.

Concupiscence: St. John the Apostle [1 John: 2:16] identifies three kinds of concupiscence or covetness which are sin:
1) Lust of the eyes and **2)** Lust of the body [both of which are carnal]; and **3)** Pride of life [which refers to the ego-self and materiality].
In the wider sense, concupiscence refers not to actual sin, but to any desire for inordinate pleasures of the five senses, as well as the general inclination towards excessive sense pleasure that leads to sin.

Contemplation: mystical knowledge of God, communicated by Him to the soul by way of Love. See 'Agape'.

Culture [Jesus Christ]: meaning *"to cultivate or "to till", "to inhabit",* or *"to worship"* in Latin. More recent definitions refer to patterns of meaning [symbolism or worldview] and strategies for action, including language, social structures, laws [human ordinances], the arts, technologies etc. Man is a semiovore [meaning maker] and a worshipping being, constantly processing and navigating subjective societal ideas, cues, norms, values, and ideals, which change over time. In His Life, Death and Resurrection, Jesus subverted human culture, and confirmed that He is the Locus and Blueprint for all meaning and action, which should be done through Him, with Him and in Him. In Jesus Christ, all meaning and action - every cause-and-effect relationship, is purified, re-ordered, and elevated to the Divine Design, which is the order, peace, harmony, and beatitude of the Kingdom of God, flowing within and through the re-created [re-birthed] soul. See 'The World' and Chapter on 'The Maji'.

Darkness: from the Hebrew word *"hoshech"* signifying a dense and dis-ordered, and chaotic and violent force, that seeks to operate out of harmony with everything. Genesis 1:2 tells us that in the beginning, God breathed Light into the darkness. See 'Light' and 'Satan'.

Detachment: interior *and* exterior freedom from desires, expectations, fears, and possessions; from perceptions of identity and possession; at the level of the flesh [carnal ego-self] and the old world, in both material and Spiritual matters. A state of non-resistance and non-attachment, that allows the interior virgin space [self-emptiness] in which God [in Jesus Christ] can be conceived and birthed in and through the consenting soul. Genuine detachment [non-attachment] means freedom from people-pleasing co-dependence; from all duplicity and insincerity that gives false witness. See 'I-dentity', 'Poor in Spirit', and 'Possess'.

Eternal rest: the souls return to its original primordial state of being, in a way that completes its dynamic re-union with God. It is the unfixed and dynamic resting point [place without struggle], of all potentiality and possibility; where God rests in the soul and the soul rests in God.

Existence-ignorance: is the absence of knowledge of Truth in one capable of finding it and accepting it, and/or the absence of realizing [making real] Truth, by conceiving and birthing it as *an entire way of being*. To accept Truth, and not conceive it as a *living and active* way of Life, is to remain unknown to God [in Jesus Christ], and to who we really are [in Him], in the Light of hallowed reality. We cannot know with perfect accuracy, the degree of responsibility, capability, or culpability of another person, because this can reflect both the divine ordering of all things, as well as the works of evil. Similarly, we cannot judge another's purity of motivation or intention. While even in our own case, we can only come to a judgement of moral or practical certainty, in fidelity to the teachings and standards of the Church. See 'Indifferentism'.

Faith: Light. The measure of the Light of sanctifying grace, that is the presence of Jesus Christ birthed through the centre of our being, when we abandon back to God. Faith allows us to believe [not in ourselves, but] in God living with us, within us, and through us, as the One absolute reality. Faith implies relationship and self-forgetting awareness, because without God, we can do nothing [John 15:5]. See 'Charity', 'Light', 'self-forgetting', and p. 195 in Chapter on 'Prayer'.

Fasting: usually thought of as abstinence from [excess, novelty, or luxury] food and drink, but includes moderating or abstaining from all carnal passions and appetites that incline man towards lower [old worldly and material], rather than higher [Spiritual] meaning and ways, and lead him to sin. It includes thoughts, words, deeds, products, and ways that pollute and corrupt man, and his neighbour, and which plunder and pollute the earth. Fasting may be undertaken as an act of penance [reparation for sin], or as an act of self-sacrifice [governance of the senses, tongue, mind, and heart], for the purpose of self-control [control of the human will], and to facilitate Spiritual freedom, growth, and enrichment. Fasting and all self-sacrifice and good works, should be done in the knowledge that they are enabled by grace for the Love and glory of God. Offered in union with Jesus Christ, they merit not only oneself, but serve as acts of reparation for the benefit of everyone and everything. The Church advises due moderation in all aesthetic practices as befits one's life-state, office, and soul-condition. Jesus did not teach severe ascetism and penitential practices, but that all self-offering should be done in Love; in the knowledge that genuine detachment from [non-attachment to] the flesh [carnal ego-self] and materiality, is the key to higher Life in the Spirit. See 'Concupiscence', 'Flesh', 'Good works', 'Penance' and 'Self-sacrifice'.

Fear [Holy]: awe-filled awareness of, and reverence for who God is, what He has done for us, and our requirement to be in right relationship with Him [and everyone and everything else in Him]. Resting in humility and trust [positive abandonment], and driven by Love of God in His Divine Will, rather than by natural fear, guilt, or anxiety about earthly or Eternal loss.

Flesh: as distinct from the body, is the natural carnal ego-self [Romans 8:5-7; 1 Peter 2:11]. **Rooted in self-love, it is the mortal element of the soul** that defines ['knows' only] itself [self-consciousness], and conducts itself dis-united [by degree of estrangement] from the Life-breath of the Holy Spirit, while borrowing from, and existing upon Him. Tending to operate according to [untransformed] human nature [the corporeal senses, and natural intellect] and the conceptual old world, the flesh element of man is the dis-ordered, unstable, and mis-governed *"old man"*, whose relationship with himself and all things, is afflicted by the mark of the serpent [Satan]. This mark is the interior worm of dark fire [Mark 9:48 and Isaiah 66:24], which traps him in a feverous and vicious cycle of unrest and blind desires; of curiosities, expectations, and sorrows, within the narrow circumference of the carnal ego-self. Ruled by fear and pride, and with a superiority [self-aggrandizement], inferiority [inverted ego] or hidden ego [false humility] complex, it wants to want and to have, of itself, and from others, to satisfy its individual ideals of self-actualization and gratification. Straining, reacting, competing, resisting, and struggling; and knowing, judging, and relating to itself and to others according to unreliable and false standards and appearances, it mistakenly perceives that the more man 'has' in terms of possession [from the Latin word *"power"*] and self-identity, the more [esteemed and accomplished] he is in himself. Man's God-given task and purpose is to overcome [cast off] the old world, the flesh, and the devil [Satan], by abandoning back [consenting] to the creative work of the Spirit, in respect of *both* outer earthly and interior Spiritual matters. Only this continuity of inner and outer being truly liberates and restores the native purity, nobility, and unity of his body and soul, in right relationship with God, and all creation in Him. **The creative work of the Holy Spirit transforms individuals [pseudo-personalities] of flesh into fully human and fully divine *persons*, united in the Divine-Human Personhood of Jesus Christ.** *"For those who are Christ's have crucified their flesh, along with its vices and desires"* Galatians 5:24. See "I-dentity', 'Incarnation', 'Man', and 'self-forgetting'.

Glory: the blissful magnificence of God in the fullness of His divine nobility, creative power, and splendour, in which is contained the infinity of divine goods, joys, beauties, harmonies, and contentment's of Paradise. In speaking of the many rooms in His Father's house [John 14:2], Jesus spoke of degrees of glory or fields of Light-consciousness [Light-freedom and bliss]; an infinity of higher and more refined states of being [vibrations] in the hierarchy of fields or realms, that is the Kingdom of Heaven. See 'Blessed' and 'Light'.

Good works: works of prayer, fasting, penance, and self-sacrifice; participation in the sacraments and Church life; and all pure acts of Charity that together express the higher Life of the *"Fiat"*. Participation in Church life includes attending Holy Hour, Spiritual reading, and Evangelization. Good works should be done in the knowledge that they are enabled by grace, for the Love and glory of God [and all things in Him]. Offered in union with Jesus Christ, they serve as reparation not only for one's own sins but make reparation for the sins of others. The Church advises due moderation in all aesthetic practices, as befits one's life-state, office, and soul-condition. See 'Fasting', 'Penance', 'Repentance' and 'Self-sacrifice'.

Grace: Light [Light-consciousness or Light relationship] of Divine Life. Grace is the gift of the Light-presence of God within the soul, by which alone the *"old man"* is healed and re-created [re-birthed] anew to the primordial state of the *"new man"* in Jesus Christ. There are two forms of grace: actual grace and sanctifying grace.

> **Actual grace -** is transient, brightening the mind, and moving and strengthening the human will [heart's desire], in order to enable man to do good and avoid evil.

Sanctifying [or deifying] grace - is the Divine Life [Light] Substance-Energies* that recover man, in time; strengthening, healing, and re-creating [re-birthing] him anew; and allowing him to conceive Eternal Truth by way of the unerring Spiritual intellect. **Operating beyond natural human reason, feelings and emotions, the Light of sanctifying grace facilitates man's discernment between value judgements of relative good and provisional reality [in the flesh and the old world], and original and actual standards of absolute good and hallowed reality.** In finding his movement towards, and in God by way of grace, man grows capable of receiving the gift of the indwelling of the Most Holy Trinity. This is his primordial Edenic state of innocence and justice; of Eternal Beatitude of God-being, John 10:34 and Good-being; which is received by degree of Light-union in and for all Eternity. See 'Light' and 'Spiritual Intellect'.

[*Church saints, such as Thomas Aquinas, teach us that God's Essence is synonymous with His Substance, which is Love. *"God is Love"* says 1 John 4:8. His Energies signify His Ever-creative, divine acts or actions, which is the operation of His Divine Will. The life (substance-energies) of the human soul, and the Life (Substance-Energies) of God although distinctly different become as One, by the soul's intuitive participation in God, in Jesus Christ, through the witness of the Holy Spirit].

Holy/Holiness: meaning *"whole"* [wholeness or whole-heartedness], *"fulfilled"* [fulfilment], or *"complete"* [completeness] in Aramaic. Also *"set apart"*, *"hallowed" "sacred"* or *"sanctified"* in Greek and Hebrew. All definitions of holiness point to [spirit-bearing] sanctity; to that which God is, and that which man is restored to, in the Perfect [Whole and All-Perfect] Cosmic Personhood of Jesus Christ. Holiness is not inherent in man, but is received as gift from God, in the measure of his abandoning back [giving the consent of] his human will [heart's desire] to the operation of the Love and Divine Will of God. **To be holy, is to be wholly and authentically alive in the Light [consciousness and relationship] of Jesus Christ.** In Jesus Christ, man is saved [preserved in Truth]; he is Spiritualized and restored to his primordial power and purpose of being, as mediator between God and all His living creatures and creation. See 'Perfection', 'Religion' and 'Will'.

Humility: self-forgetting freedom of being that allows God's purely creative work within and through the soul. Humility first requires awareness and knowledge of man's fallen human condition, in light of the glory of hallowed reality. We can only begin to get into right relationship with God, and with everyone and everything in Him, when we have conceived a sense of Truth [Light], which allows us to see in a correct perspective. Practising **humility, means living from this real knowledge of self**, which sees through the illusions and evils of the old world, the flesh [carnal ego-self], and the devil [Satan]. Humility safeguards the soul from pride, self-righteousness, self-aggrandisement, and selfishness, in respect of natural or Spiritual knowledge, reputation and wealth. It means thinking less, and less often of oneself, and more of God [Jesus Christ] in our own soul, and in every other soul. The more humble [and meek] the soul, the more it is capable of turning back and moving towards God with trusting abandonment [consent], knowing that without Him, we can do nothing [John 15:5]. *"For if My Head is pierced and bowed down on the Cross for thee, thy head should be inclined to humility"* Jesus speaks to St. Bridget of Sweden. See 'Meek', 'Poor in Spirit' and 'self-forgetting'.

i-dentity: the 'i' within the 'I AM'. The fullness and uniqueness of man's divine-human personhood in God. Man is healed and re-created [re-birthed] anew in time, by the purification, re-ordering, and re-integration [re-centring] of his being, in the Perfect [Whole and All-Perfecting] Cosmic Divine-Human Personhood of Jesus Christ. **This All-unity with his Life-source, and with all created life, is God's original Divine Ideal for the divinely-human person, fully Spiritualized in Him.** Re-birthing this primordial way of being, is not an experience of the [individual] carnal ego-self, but is the dynamic expression of the *"new man's"* uniquely divine-human personhood, participating in the All-unity [communion of relationship] of the Most Holy Trinity. It is man's wholeness [holiness and all-perfection] of personality and being in Jesus Christ, which according to the degree realized on earth, holds the promise of the Beatific Vision [direct and immediate sight of God], and the glorious [blissfully magnificent] reality of Paradise. See 'Detachment', 'Love', 'New man' and 'self-forgetting'.

Immortality of the Soul: that quality or attribute of the soul as Spiritual substance-energies, by reason of which it cannot die, but will exist Eternally after mortal death.

Incarnation: the entirety and Perfection [Wholeness and All-Perfection] of God, made human in Jesus Christ for the purpose of redeeming fallen man from the kingdom of Satan, and restoring him to his native i-dentity in the transfigured Kingdom of Heaven. The Greek translation of the Latin word *"incarnatio"*, defines the Incarnation of Jesus Christ as the *"enhumanment"* of God, which recognizes that He took on human nature in every way but sin, and avoids the issue with the Latin translation of the word as *"enfleshment"*. The idea that Jesus took flesh, jars with the upward call [invitation] to overcome the flesh, which is synonymous with the carnal ego-self in common English. See 'Identity'.

Indifferentism: is an attitude of mind which denies or disregards man's most fundamental task and responsibility of recognizing God's absolute claim upon him, and striving to live in accordance with the teachings and standards of His Church on earth. See 'Existence-ignorance'.

Inherit/Inheritance: to repent [meaning *"to turn back"* or *"come back"* in Aramaic and Hebrew] and abandon back to [awaken to, welcome, surrender to, consent to, or give in to] the Kingdom of God within the soul, which wants to be conceived and birthed through in time. To realize [make real] Eternal Life, which is Now. While imperfect and largely imperceptible in time, the Kingdom will be attained according to the degree of Light reaped [conceived and birthed] by the soul, during its appointed time on earth. See 'Light', 'Perfection' and 'Repentance'.

Light: figuratively Light is the Three-Fold Spirit of God [1 John 1:6]. It is the All-pure Substance-Energies*, that is the dynamic *Livingness* of God in His Love and Divine Will, and which is the perpetual Light-union of Divine Life [of the Most Holy Trinity]. **Offered to man as sanctifying grace, the Light-radiance of God warms, burns, purifies, and transfigures and ennobles everything that is in it.** Light is Holiness [Wholeness and All-Perfection] and Truth [uncreated knowledge and wisdom]. It is *real Life and purpose* [Eternal Life] in Jesus Christ; the Ever-creative and blissful Divine Life-state to which man is called [invited] to participate in beyond the natural intellect and sense perception in time, to receive in due measure of fullness in Eternity. Those found capable of penetrating the Light-union of Heaven, will be the *"Children of Light"* Luke 16:18; John 12:36; Ephesians 5:8; 1 Thessalonians 5:5. The souls who wisely and diligently committed their time on earth to reaping [conceiving and birthing] this Light, which draws the soul into a dynamic relationship of Light-union with God, and with everyone and everything in its circle. The degree of Light reaped determines the soul's strength and capacity for being consumed in, and ever-discovering and enjoying the Light-freedom of Paradise; the glorious infinity of divine goods, joys, beauties, harmonies, and contentment's of Ever-lasting Life. *"This Light permeates the soul, and lifts it above the turmoil of temporal things, to rest in God. The soul cannot progress except with the Light which God has given it as a nuptial gift; Love works the likeness of God into the soul"* says Meister Eckhart. See 'Glory', 'Grace – *footnote', 'Light-union' and 'Perfection'. Also, Chapter on 'Holy Joy'.

Light-union: the dynamic *Livingness* of the Divine Life of the Most Holy Trinity, that is the Kingdom of Heaven. Also referred to as **Light-consciousness, Light-being, Light-relationship, Light-community, Light-freedom, and Light-glory** throughout this book. See 'Light'.

Love: capitalized throughout this book, and referred to as the Greek *"Agape"* in the New Testament, is God's own All-powerful, Whole-Hearted, and super-abundant Divine Love, which operates in His Divine Will. Proceeding from and governed by the Spirit, it is the completely Self-giving [Eucharistic and Self-sacrificial] Love that is the mutual Life of the Most Holy Trinity. In His own Life, Passion, Death, and Resurrection Jesus Christ identifies Himself as the living embodiment of *"Agape*; the suffering Love of God in pursuit of Oneness with His bride, the *living* Church on earth. On the night before He died, Jesus declared that this highest Love would be the mark of His *true* followers [John 13:34-35]. See 'Charity', 'Self-Love' and 'Will [Divine]'.

Man: the created human being or person; man, woman, child, person, or people; referred to as 'man' throughout this book. Man, in the mirror of the divine image and likeness [similitude], is a trinity of spirit, soul and body [with a mind and heart]. His spirit flows from, and he is held in being by, the Trinitarian Spirit of God. His soul [Spiritual nature] consists of a memory, will and intellect, and his body [human nature] operates with five senses, a mind and heart. **Man is a creative being - not in himself, but as a mediator of divine power,** operating at three levels which are corporal - sense man; rational - interior man; and Spiritual - supernatural man. See 'Soul'.

> **Old man [insular]:** the term used by St. Paul to describe the human person under the influence of original sin, which is washed away in the sacrament of Baptism. After Baptism, the evil effects of original sin revive through self-will and weakness, as dis-ordered and dis-integrated natural man tends to walk in the flesh by way of the carnal senses and natural intellect. In this mode, and by degree of estrangement, he tends to judge and perceive by appearances, and the light of natural reason, feelings, and emotions, rather than in the self-empty and Light-enriched way of the Spirit. The effort and aversion experienced by the insular *"old man"* in relinquishing self-interest and impressions, and doing what is good, right, and healthful on God's terms [in His Love and Divine Will] is confirmation of his Spiritual [Light-] poverty; the dark voids within his soul [memory, will and intellect] which operates as a confused, and ever-changing and restless community of voices, that wants to want and to have [victory] on its own agenda, rather than in Truth. For this reason, the teachings, sacraments, and provisions of the Church are necessary to purify, re-order, re-integrate [re-centre], re-create [re-birth], and preserve the *"new man"* in Jesus Christ [Romans 6:3-8; Ephesians 4:22-24; Colossians 3:1-17]. Only the Holy Spirit can do the creative work of purifying and transfiguring the 'graven image' of the *"old man"* into the Life-bearing *"new man"* by way of his Life-releasing death and re-birth [re-creation] in Jesus Christ. Natural man can only perceive good and evil relative to his soul-condition, which tends to be dis-ordered to temporal and provisional [earthly] judgements of what is good and real, rather than the transcendent [Heavenly] standard of absolute good and hallowed reality. Further, **without the power of the Holy Spirit, he cannot perceive the hidden treachery of pure evil, nor the authenticity of pure good, which operate at the Spiritual level**, while all shades of good and evil are enmeshed in the earthly realm. *"Owing to anthropomorphism...the majority of souls judge all things, and even of God, in relation to themselves, whereas*

they ought to consider everything and themselves in relation to God" says St. Elizabeth of the Trinity. See 'Flesh', 'Original sin' and 'Spiritual poverty'.

New man [Eucharistic]: The human person who has been healed and re-created [re-birthed] anew, to the power and privilege of *real Life and purpose* [Eternal Life] in Jesus Christ. St. Paul refers some eighty times in Sacred Scripture to being **re-created** *"in Christ."* This work of transformation, from self-centredness to God-centredness, involves the healing and re-creation [re-birth] of man in the Love and Divine Will of God. It requires the vigilant abandonment [consent] of his human will [heart's desire], to the divine initiative [Cosmic Divine Will], in every moment of his life. In this creative work of grace, the dis-integrated mind [the seat of knowledge and wisdom] and heart [the seat of emotions] of the *"old man"*, which project from his soul [memory, will and intellect] and body, as directed by his senses, are re-ordered in the Light of the Spirit. When the Spirit purifies, illuminates, and re-unites man's mind and heart to govern his soul, and direct his five senses, he experiences a re-ordering and re-integration [re-centring] of his being [spirit, soul, and body] in the Supreme Light-Being of God. His soul [memory, will and intellect] comes to rest in the single voice of the Cosmic Divine Will, and the natural reasoning, and desires of the flesh [carnal ego-self], and its associated feelings, emotions, and attachments are re-dimensioned, and become serenely and zealously attendant to re-hearing and re-seeing in this Light. Guided by the Spiritual Intellect and walking upright in knowledge and in wisdom, the Eucharistic *"new man"* experiences a celestial strength, peace, and joy, that enables him to overcome self-love and co-operate with and participate in God, from a pure motive of Love of Him, and of everyone and everything in Him, in His Divine Will. **No longer impressible nor impressionable by the void standards [projections, judgements, and neediness] of the flesh [carnal ego-self] and the old world, he is capable of looking beyond words and appearances, to the substance-essence [absolute Truth] of things. He is capable of protecting and taking best care of his mind, [in his] heart, and the entirety of his being as the glory [blissful magnificence] of God. He is also conscious and capable of assisting, and not thwarting others.** 'Poor in Spirit' and strong in interior silence and solitude, the self-forgetting and aware *"new man"* is capable of a dialogue of *living* prayer and *living* silence; of actively participating in God, in the abolition of evil and the reinstatement of the Kingdom. While not perceived or received in full at the natural level on earth, this dynamic preparation is man's restoration to the blissful All-unity [community] of Eternal Life in God. It is his return to holiness [whole-hearted fullness of being]; to the character and stature [Ephesians 4:11] of his primordial divine-human nature and personhood, in the Perfect [Whole and All-Perfect] Cosmic Divine-Human Personhood of Jesus Christ. See 'Poor in Spirit', 'self-forgetting', 'Will [Divine]' and 'Will [Human]'.

Meek: usually misunderstood to mean timid, the Aramaic and Hebrew translations of the word *"meek"*, give us a true sense of what Jesus was saying when He describes Himself as *"meek and humble of heart"* Matthew 11:29, and says [in the second beatitude] *"Blessed are the meek, for they shall inherit the earth"* Matthew 5:4. For the word *"meek"* in Aramaic suggests softening of what is rigid, both within and without, which is to say the flesh [carnal ego-mask] with all its interior and exterior perceptions, desires, expectations, fears and sorrows. The Hebrew translation of the word offers similar interpretation, suggesting gentleness, modesty, and humility; balance, patience, and harmony, borne of a humble and tranquil conscience. The meaning of this beatitude in these language frames, is then to say that blessed are those who have positively abandoned back [consented] or assented, to a state of unknowing at the natural level, and who co-operate with and participate in God in His Love and Divine Will, for they shall receive the strength and vigour of Eternal Life. See 'Humility' and 'Poor in Spirit'.

Neighbour: primarily the human person, because it is man who is made in God's image and likeness [Genesis 1:26-27], and it is in and through man [in Jesus Christ], that the Kingdom of God is seeded, centred, and restored. However, while Hebrew and Greek conceptions of the word, *"neighbour"* give it to mean *"a person that is near or close"*, the Aramaic word *"kareb"* expresses it as anyone who is either physically *or* mentally close [present] to us, which means anyone that we think of, or focus our attention upon. It includes those who have passed from this world [into Purgatory], or even those who have yet to come. This broader conception of *"neighbour"*, can be yet further expanded and aligned with Sacred Scripture teachings, by looking to the Hebrew and Aramaic meaning of the word *"self"*, in the context of the first two and greatest commandments, to *"...Love the Lord your God with all your heart, with all your soul, with all your mind"* Matthew 22:37; Mark 12:30, and to *"Love [in "Agape"] your neighbour as yourself"* Matthew 22:39; Mark 12:31 For the word *"self"*, [*"nephesh"*] in Hebrew, used interchangeably to mean *"soul"* or *"spirit"*, speaks of the living Spirit [and Soul] of God in all living beings with life in the blood. While the equivalent word [*"nafsha"* or *"naphsha"*] in Aramaic, also used interchangeably to mean *"soul"* or *"being"*, speaks of the *"self"* as the *"breath of life"*. In these frames, to 'Love our neighbour as our *"self"*', as One with Loving God above all else with the entirety of our being, is to Love the living Spirit [and Soul] of God in all living beings, in the One Cosmic Life-breath [or consciousness] of the Holy Spirit. **Our *"neighbour"* in the complete sense, then encompasses not only ourselves, and all people, but all living [conscious] creatures.** For as all were present in the ecological Paradise of Eden, and were entrusted to man's care and keep [meaning *"to exercise great care over"* in Hebrew], the healthfulness of man's relationship with God cannot be separated from the healthfulness of his relationship with *His* living creatures [Genesis 1:26,28; 2:15; 9:1-2]. **Nor, can it be separated from his diligent care of the plant life and ecological systems on which all life depends.** Declared *"good"* Genesis 1:21,25,31, and blessed, all God's creatures are part of the One living Spirit and beating Heart of creation. While distinctly different from man, and without the privilege of a free will [e.g., not understanding self-sacrifice], thus rendering them **innocent** of all transgressions; all are imbued with a beating heart, a living soul [memory, will and intellect], and with intelligence and purpose. All share in God's Covenant of Love [Luke 12:6, Matthew 6:26;10:29], and all have life in Jesus Christ through whom, and for whom all things are made [John 1:1]. All have a future in the new Heaven and new earth where *"No hurt shall be done; no life taken"* Isaiah 11:9. During His time on earth, Jesus taught about God's Love and providential care for all His living creatures [Luke 12:6, Matthew 6:26;10:29], as well as man's duty of care towards them [Luke 13:15; 14:5]. An obligation, which, as instructed from early in the Old Testament, requires not only avoiding passive neglect and mistreatment of them, but proactively stepping up to assist them. All His creatures play an essential role in the health and success of the planet, the climate, and ultimately man, and his purpose, privilege, and responsibility on earth [as to be fit for Heaven]. **The earth is only man's in so far as he is appointed by God as a delegated caretaker, to keep it, while treading most gently upon it, and co-operating with God to return to his primordial state of God-being [John 10:34].** In this two-fold work, man fulfils his creative potential as mediator between God and all His creation, because as he is Spiritualized in Jesus Christ, he Spiritualizes all creation by offering it back to God in Jesus Christ. To Love our neighbour is therefore to avoid the legalistic misunderstanding that it is the means to saving our soul. Love [*"Agape"*] is the gracious radiating creative energy that is Truth and Life; freely received and freely given, by co-operating with and participating in the Divine Being who is the source of all that is.

[In understanding who our neighbour is, in the complete sense of the word, is to first accept that God comes to meet man where he is. In the beginning, and before the fall, God declares to Adam that He has given Him every herb-bearing seed, and every seed-bearing tree upon the face of the earth for food. *"And God said: "Behold, I have given you every seed-bearing plant upon the earth, and all the trees that have in themselves the ability to sow their own kind, to be food for you""* Genesis 1:29. **After the fall (because of man's sin), God had to make clothing for Adam and Eve out of animal skins (Genesis 3:21).** While throughout the Old Testament, He undertakes the work of gradually teaching man again about the sacredness of life, and the right treatment of His living creatures. This is strikingly notable when after the Flood, God says to Noah that he can eat of everything *"Except that flesh with blood you shall not eat" Genesis* 9:4 (Leviticus 7:26). **In the New Testament, Jesus replaces all previous laws, customs, and practices with the law of Love [Charity] in Himself, but makes no direct comment or command regarding eating meat.** He does however instruct the outwardly scrupulous Pharisees, in response to a complaint about the disciples' eating without washing their hands that *"That which enters into the mouth doesn't defile the man…But the things which proceed out of the mouth come out of the heart, and they defile the man"* Matthew 15:11,18. With these words, He confirms that purity (cleanliness and clarity) of heart is primary before God, who looks to whether man is motivated by Love of Him, and all things in Him, for the sake of the Kingdom. **Outward acts must then be accompanied by right interior disposition, as not to be found empty before Him.** As confirmation of this teaching, Jesus urges His followers tasked with spreading the Gospel to *"eat the things that are set before you"* Luke 10:8. He calls fisherman to be his apostles, and He feeds fish to the five thousand. He helps the apostles improve their haul of fish after His Resurrection, and is described as eating with them. Therefore, while Sacred Scripture states that man in the Oneness of his divinely-human ideal form was created to be vegetarian, his Spiritual growth and transfiguration has many levels in the ordering of Divine Providence, that must be anchored in *interior revolution*. The Church does not teach that it is wrong or shameful to eat flesh meat, but teaches abstinence on certain days in the calendar year. While many Church saints have demonstrated great Love for and extraordinary ability to communicate with animals; healing them, keeping company with them, and tending towards vegetarianism or pescetarianism].

Obedience: willingly and attentively listening to God, and learning what he wants us to do in His Love and Divine Will, and acting accordingly. **Jesus did nothing by Himself, but operated always in perfect Oneness with the Father [John 5:19].** We must first and always actively listen to God by cultivating *living* silence, which is consciousness of the unspoken primordial voice of God, as the rooted Light-centre of our being. This supernatural state of presence is essential to co-operating with and participating in Him. See 'Love' and 'Will [Divine]'.

Parish [Parishioner]: from the Greek word *"pariki"* meaning *"beside [or outside] the house"*, or *"paroikos"* meaning *"sojourner"*, or *"temporary resident"*, a parishioner is a travelling exile without a permanent home. See Acts 7:6 and 1 Peter 2:11. A parish is a community of pilgrim souls living within a boundary, who are ministered to by a Priest, while journeying as outsiders towards citizenship of the Heavenly Homeland.

Passion [of Christ]: from the Latin word *"pati"* meaning *"to suffer,"* or *"to endure"*, refers to the divine and human suffering Love [*"Agape"*] of Jesus Christ; most particularly His agony in the Garden, to His death on Calvary. Modern day carnal interpretations of the word *"passion"*, which arose in the 13th Century, have no relation to its original meaning. God is without human *"passions"*, while His Passion for souls, is the expression of His Whole-Hearted and Self-less Charity. See 'Charity', 'Love' and 'Suffering'.

Peace: at the natural level of understanding, peace denotes freedom from fear, distress, and conflict. It means the forgiveness [releasing] of sin, which restores our relationship with God, and with all people and creation in Him. Sacred Scripture however, as well as the Aramaic [*"shlama"*] and Hebrew [*"shalom"*] words for peace, point to a celestial peace which is much more profound than that which is understood at the natural level. While Sacred Scripture advises us to: *"Have salt in yourselves, and have peace among yourselves"* Mark 9:50. In these frames, the word *"peace"* speaks of **celestial harmony that abides in Truth**, and is preserved in Truth. This is the *"peace"* which contains all possibilities and potentialities; all surrender, deliverance, and fulfilment. It is *"the peace of God, which surpasses all understanding, [and] will guard your hearts and your thoughts in Christ Jesus"* Philippians 4:7.

Crucially, Church saints warn of the counterfeit peace offered to the soul by the old world, and the devil [Satan], which is pleasing to the flesh [carnal ego-self], but detrimental to the spirit of man. **St. Teresa of Avila [in her Meditations on the Song of Songs] speaks of nine kinds of false peace offered by Satan, who *does not wage war* against those who agree or abide with him [in soul-slumber or in revolt against God], and who inspire or assist others in doing the same.**

Penance: repentance in action. Penance is the expression or act of the soul's *"turning back"* or *"coming back"* to God [in Aramaic and Hebrew] to demonstrate repentance for sin, by way of prayer and reparation. Penance is expressed both by way of one's interior disposition, and outer way of living, and includes sacramental penance [Confession] and nonsacramental penitential practices. Nonsacramental practices involve acts that purify our interior *and* exterior way of being; namely fasting, praying and self-sacrifice; acts that increase humility, such as apologizing for one's conduct, or graciously accepting unmerited tasks; and acts that express our Love for our neighbour, in Charity [Love in action]. Penance and all good works, should be done in the knowledge that they are enabled by grace, for the Love and glory of God [and for the sake of our glory in God]. Offered in union with Jesus Christ, they serve as reparation not only for one's own sins but for the sins of others. The Church advises due moderation in all aesthetic practices, as befits one's life-state, office, and soul-condition. See 'Fasting', 'Repentance' and 'Self-sacrifice'. Also 'The Golden Maxims of St. John of the Cross' in Appendix 3.

Perfection: meaning *"complete"* [completeness], *"whole"* [wholeness or whole-heartedness], *"holy"*, *"thorough"*, or *"all-encompassing"* in Aramaic and Hebrew. God is Perfect - He is Whole [Holy] and All-Perfect, and desires to restore natural man to the wholeness and all-perfection of his being in Him [Matthew 5:48]. Sacred Scripture tells us that Jesus Christ was made *"perfect through suffering"* so that he could bring *"many children to glory"* Hebrews 2:10. A soul may be 'perfect' or 'whole' at different levels or stages of Spiritual growth or degrees of Light-union [Light-glory], in the Father's divine ordering of the entire human family. The level of perfection or holiness [whole-hearted fullness of being] that is sufficient for admittance into the lower degrees of Light-union [Light-freedom], is very different to that which is required for entry into the higher realms of glory and bliss. While the Light-realm of the highest Heaven [Deuteronomy 10:14; 2 Corinthians 12:2] admits only the purest, and most refined Spirit brides and Spirit brides-men. This is the Holy of Holies, and the immediate dwelling place of Almighty God. *"I learned in the Heart of Jesus, that in Heaven itself, there is a Heaven to which not all, but only chosen souls have access...Souls are penetrated by His divinity and pass from brightness to brightness; an unchanging Light but never monotonous, always new, though never changing"* says St. Faustina [Divine Mercy]. It is each person's personal privilege and responsibility to correspond with the maturing of their soul, according to the height of Light-union which they are willing and capable of realizing. In this creative work, the soul will not be taken beyond its capacity for suffering, detachment, and expansion, known only to God. **Perfection can be understood, not a fixed point or destination, or personal achievement, but as a state of perpetual becoming; of seeing and relationship; enabled, grown, and preserved by grace alone. It is the soul's flight in the self-forgetting freedom of Charity. This is its Spiritual ascent to Light-union in the earthly realm, which determines its strength and capacity for penetrating [journeying in] the infinite Light-fields [vibrations or realms] of the Homeland.** See 'Holy/Holiness' and 'self-forgetting'.

Poor in Spirit: graceful [grace-filled] simplicity of desire. The soul-condition of humble persons who are sufficiently empty [free] of the illusions and desires of the flesh [carnal ego-self] and the old world, and the works of the devil [Satan], to realize purity of hunger [heart], by which they abandon back [give the consent of] their human will [heart's desire] to the operation of the Divine Will. Poorness in Spirit both draws and guards the Spiritual riches of the Kingdom within the soul. It is the opposite of Spiritual poverty, which is the Light-starved condition of the insular *"old man"*, who tends to be mis-governed by the flesh [carnal ego-self] and the old world, rather than governed by the Spirit. **Poorness in Spirit before God should also be man's disposition before his fellowman, in recognition that all true good, is the Charity of God operating within and through the consenting soul.** See 'Humility', 'Meek' and 'Soul economy'.

Poverty: the two sides of poverty identified in Sacred Scripture are that of Spiritual [Light-] poverty, and material poverty - in the sense of abject, and essential need. While Light-poverty is ultimately the greater ill, mis-leading man in the ways of the flesh [canal ego-self] and the old world, and ultimately to Eternal [Spiritual] death, both sides of poverty are inextricably linked. **The Holy Family's perfect example of Spiritual wealth, invigorated and safeguarded by voluntary, ungrasping material simplicity and glad sharing with others, sets the standard for walking upright in [the Charity of] Jesus Christ.** See 'Poor in Spirit' and Chapter on 'Charity'.

Possess: from the Latin word *"power"*, in modern English, meaning to take ownership of, or to keep in one's possession; carrying connotations of power and control. The biblical sense of the word however, is profoundly different. Meaning *"to dwell in"*, or *"hold in occupancy"* in Hebrew, it implies man's **selfless participation and sharing in the Life of God** according to his willingness and capacity for Light-union [1 Corinthians 12:12-13]. Man is absorbed in the Light-consciousness and Light-community of God, by way of the exchange of his no-thingness with the All-ness of God [God-being, John 10:34]. See 'Detachment'.

Reality [Hallowed]: is the relationship of Light between God and the soul. Every perception and act [of thought, word, or deed] in darkness or in Light, becomes man's state of being in Christ or anti-Christ consciousness. See 'Light' and 'Truth'.

Real Presence: the Church teaching, that the sacrament of the Eucharist contains really, substantially, and completely, and not only in symbol, sign, or virtue, the Body and Blood; and Soul and Divinity of Jesus Christ.

Re-creation: re-birth in Jesus Christ. Made actual in Baptism and strengthened in Confirmation, man's task and responsibility is to be healed and restored to the original planned purpose, privilege, and power of his being, through the purification, re-ordering, and re-integration [re-centring] of his personhood in the Perfect [Whole and All-Perfecting] Cosmic Divine-Human Personhood Jesus Christ. Man is re-birthed to *real Life and purpose* [Eternal Life] in Jesus Christ [Romans 6:3-8; Ephesians 4:22-24; Colossians 3:1-17], by way of the teachings, sacraments, and provisions of His Church on earth. See 'Work'.

Religion: from the 1st century Latin word *"religio"* meaning *"bind-back"*. Christianity is supernatural religion, based upon divine revelation from God the Father in Jesus Christ. In the Old Testament God calls Israel His *"first-born son"* Exodus 4:22 and *"the offspring [seed] of Abraham"* Isaiah 41:8, while in the New Testament, St. Paul calls Abraham's offspring *"One... which is Christ"* Galatians 3:16, who is *"the firstborn of every creature"* Colossians 1:15. **Jesus Christ is the *living* embodiment of religion. He is the unbroken continuity between God and man, and man and God. Going out from the Father, and returning to Him in the Holy Spirit, as in a circle, while enclosing the entire Universe in Himself, He is our *living* relationship with, and way back [*"binding back"*] to God our Father, and the Spiritual state of the Kingdom [John 14:6].** In Jesus Christ, we are found clean and undefiled before God the Father [James 1:27]. Every baptised person has received the [Three-in-One] gift of the Light-seed of Jesus Christ within their being. They are a consecrated person, with a vocation to religious life, which is the Life-releasing death of the *"old man"*, and the creative manifestation of *real Life and purpose* in Jesus Christ [Romans 6:3-5]. To be religious, is to *'put on Jesus Christ'*. It is to be created anew [re-birthed] by Him and in Him. In Jesus Christ, man fulfils his creative potential as mediator between God and all His creation, because as he is Spiritualized in Jesus Christ, he returns to the state of mediator and creator, Spiritualizing all creation and offering it back to the Father in Jesus Christ. See 'Holy/Holiness' and 'Re-creation'.

Repentance: meaning to *"turn back"* **or** *"come back"* **to [face] God** in Aramaic and Hebrew, thus giving the sense of circling back to the beginning, which is the original purpose of ones being, living in perfect [whole and all-perfect] union with God. Repentance is the opening of the interior Spiritual eye to the Light of Truth, which allows man to see and desire to return to, who he is called [invited] to be in Jesus Christ. Repentance requires awareness of, and sorrow for, our waywardness and separation from God [and God-being, John 10:34], and the desire to return to Him. **Repentance is the essential means to man's healing and re-creation [re-birth] in time [Luke 13:1-5], which restores him to the exalted Edenic state.** One who is truly repentant is penitent, and inspired to do penance, which is repentance in action. See 'Inherit/Inheritance', 'Penance' and 'Re-creation'.

Righteous [Upright]: to be aware of Truth, and to live one's life in the best interests of everyone and everything, in its Light alone. To walk upright, is to walk in Truth; in the Love and Divine Will of God our Father in Jesus Christ, through the witness of the Holy Spirit.

Satan: appearing in Sacred Scripture in Hebrew, Greek, and Aramaic and meaning *"adversary"*, *"accuser"* or *"a being divided against itself"*. The word can mean the mark of the serpent of fire or inner worm [Mark 9:48 and Isaiah 66:24], which is man's interior struggle and fragmentation [division] between Light and darkness. It can also mean Satan or demons [malevolent spiritual beings] in general. With no creative power, but only the will to destroy, the 'powers' of evil are injurious and destructive spiritual 'powers' that prey upon [tempt, afflict, and oppress, either directly or indirectly, and more rarely possess] the soul, causing it to turn or fall away from God, and into mis-creating sin and evil. While Satan and evil are realities, we should not dwell upon them, nor address them directly, but focus on our restoration to a *living* relationship with God our Father in Jesus Christ. See 'Religion'.

Before his rebellion against God, Satan was known in Heaven as the mighty Angel, Lucifer the *"shining one [day star], son of the dawn"* Isaiah 14:12. This Latin name, meaning 'Light Bearer' in English, is derived from the original Hebrew word *"helel"*, interpreted as *"day star"* or similar in Isaiah. However, this word can also be interpreted as *"to howl"* or *"to lament"*, which means that Isaiah 14:12 can too read, *"Howl [lament], son of dawn"*, representing Satan's great vexation of spirit [Isaiah 65:14] at being cast down from original glory. The traditionally accepted name Lucifer, then denotes the exceptional brilliance from which Satan fell, as well as his vehement fury at his fall. Jesus Christ is the One true *"Light of the world"* John 8:12 and 9:5, while Satan is the imitative false 'Light Bearer', disguised in elaborate slyness and appealing ways, that man deficient of sanctifying grace can neither detect nor understand.

Search: meaning *"to look for"* or *"examine into"*. In the Hebrew imperative form, this takes the form of an invitation to come alive to who God is, and turn back to [face] Him [Isaiah 59:2]. To reciprocate His One Cosmic Heart's desire to reconcile with us [Romans 5:8-9]

self-Love: God commands man to Love his neighbour as himself [Matthew 22:39]. Together with the first and greatest commandment, which requires him to Love God supremely and above all else, with the entirety of his being, the first two commandments are those on which the whole of the law [centred and personified in Jesus Christ] depend [Matthew 22:37,40]. In contrast to ego-self-love, **true self-Love is Spiritualized Love [*"Agape"*],** encapsulated in the teachings, sacraments, and provisions of the Church, which guide and provide man with what is needed to realize [make real] and preserve, his true i-dentity in Jesus Christ. See 'I-dentity', 'Love', and 'self-forgetting'.

self-forgetting [awareness]: forgetting the flesh [carnal ego-self] and re-centring in Spiritualized self-awareness, and awareness of others in Jesus Christ. While the human conscious naturally works on the principle of contradiction; that something cannot be true and untrue at the same time; this is not the case at the Spiritual level. Self-forgetting awareness does not mean neglecting one's personal needs, but operating at a higher level [in Jesus Christ-consciousness], which means keen awareness of and attention to, one's own and other's *true* needs.

self-sacrifice: acts of self-giving or self-renunciation, in respect of the appetites, desires, understanding and ways of the *"old man"*, for the purpose of Spiritual freedom, growth, and enrichment, and ultimately re-union with God. **Self-sacrifice motivated by Love of God, and desire for re-union with Him, is the essential means of bringing the human will into harmony with the Cosmic Divine Will in Jesus Christ [Luke 9:23].** Interior acts of self-giving discipline [and release] involve the human will and understanding, while exterior acts involve fasting from the carnal passions and appetites. Both necessitate control of the five senses [particularly the eyes and ears], tongue, mind, and heart, and the renunciation of all that does not give glory to God. Acts of self-sacrifice offered in union with the Life and sufferings of Jesus Christ are dynamic acts of reparation, which benefit not only the soul, but everyone and everything. While the more the soul gives [back] to God, the more He increases its capacity for giving. Like all good works, acts of self-sacrifice should be done in secret where possible, and in the knowledge that all is enabled by grace, for the Love and glory of God, and all things in Him. The Church advises due moderation in all aesthetic practices as befits one's life-state, office, and soul-condition. Jesus did not teach severe asceticism and penitential practices, but that all self-giving should be done in Love; in the knowledge that detachment from [non-attachment to] the flesh [carnal ego-self] and materiality, is key to higher Life in the Spirit. See 'Concupiscence', 'Fasting', 'Flesh' and 'Penance'.

Sin: There are two classes of sin: original sin and actual sin. Original sin is that which we *inherit* from Adam, while actual sin is that which we ourselves *commit* in act [in thought* word, or deed]. **Sin is the three-fold act of: Doing evil; 2) Failing to do good; and 3) Failing to do better, as the opportunity arises, as inspired by the Holy Spirit.** The latter two sins of omission, are deficits in self-giving. **Every stain of sin, is an injurious and destructive act of the human will [heart's desire] operating apart from God.** It is a self-defeating decision [meaning] *"to divide" or "cut off"* [in Hebrew] against oneself in the indivisible Godhead, by looking at, or to oneself, and others as individuals apart from God, rather than in the One and Only reality of Him. Every sin is a failure in Charity, which breaks trust [Love-union] with God, and with everyone and everything in Him. Sin is an act of self-exaltation or self-appropriation says St. Francis of Assisi; of preferring self-love to 'Poorness in Spirit', that agrees with [consents to] the law of God's Love [Charity]. Every sin mis-creates both a human and Cosmic ripple effect, that works against everyone and everything. When we speak of sin, we normally speak of actual sin.

[*Bad thoughts are not sinful in themselves, unless the human will consents to them, and the mind considers them, instead of immediately rejecting them. Unholy and afflictive thoughts are weakened and driven out by prayer and holy living. Our morning offering is the best time to unite all acts (thoughts, words, and deeds) of the day, to the divinely creative acts (works, joys, and sufferings) of Jesus Christ, and to claim His Precious Blood on the entirety of our being, for our protection and good of our neighbour. This weakens and constrains the works of evil to do good. This offering, together with the sign of the Cross, and an invocation for afflictive thoughts to depart in Jesus Name, can be repeated in the immediacy of any attack. See 'Praying God's Word - The Sword of the Spirit', in Chapter on 'Prayer'].

> **Original sin** - the sin committed by Adam in eating the forbidden fruit of The Tree of Knowledge of Good and Evil. A fateful act, which because of his position as head of the human family, became the sin of all his descendants. In eating of the apple [or *"tappuach"*, meaning *"breath of self"* in Aramaic], Adam and all his descendants lost the gift of sanctifying grace, and the primordial state of original innocence and justice [Eternal Beatitude], which contains Paradise. **Where originally every act [of thought, word, and deed] was a divinely creative act saturated with the Light of God-being [John 10:34] and Good-being, man became a being divided against himself, as thought of God was replaced with thought of self. Original sin, means inclination to sin [particularly carnal concupiscence], suffering, and mortal death.** Heaven was closed until Jesus Christ, the Heavenly new Adam [1 Corinthians 15:45-48], re-opened the avenues of grace. The right to the Life of grace is conferred in the sacrament of Baptism, by which we become adopted children of God, and members of His Church. *"Original sin is not only the violation of a positive command ...but...attempts...to abolish Fatherhood... placing in doubt the Truth about God who is Love, and leaving man with only a sense of a master-slave relationship"* Pope John Paul II.
>
> **Actual sin** - Two kinds of sin can be committed by the human person: mortal sin and venial sin. Mortal sin is the more serious of the two, because it is a grave violation of Truth and deprives the soul of

sanctifying grace, which means it is without, and cannot receive God. Examples of mortal sin include blasphemy against the Holy Spirit [wilful rejection of Truth], fornication, and murder. Venial sin unlike mortal sin, does not completely deprive the soul of sanctifying grace, but nonetheless deprives it of many actual graces which assist its ability to overcome further and greater sin, and grow in sanctifying grace. Examples of venial sin are impatience and slight fault-finding. The Church teaches us that if we die with but one unrepented mortal sin on our soul, we cannot enter Purgatory or Heaven because we are without God - regardless of what 'good' we appear to do, apart from Him. If we die with venial sins on our soul, we must expiate these in the purifying flames of Purgatory. **Church saints tell us that all but very few of the souls who avoid Hell, will also avoid Purgatory; the intensity and duration of which depends upon our soul-condition, relative to the height of sanctity [spirit-bearing union] to which we were called [invited to and capable of attaining].** *"It is definite that only a few chosen ones do not go to Purgatory"* says St. John Vianney [The Curé D'Ars]. Acts are not sinful when we *truly* do not know they are sinful; when committed through no fault of our own; or when we do not consent to, or co-operate with the evil done.

Soul: is the tripartite memory, will and intellect, given life by the Spirit of God. The soul is the principle of life in man, and lives on after mortal death [1 Corinthians 5:3]. **Interchangeably referred to in this book as 'it' [in the general sense], or as 'her' [in the specific sense], representing the primacy of the divine feminine in man's positive and active abandonment back [consent] to God, to first allow and receive Divine Life from Him, in order to operate in the divine masculine, in Him.**

Soul economy: the reaping [conceiving and birthing] of perpetual Light, which transfigures the life of man into the complete *Livingness* of Jesus Christ. The soul's investiture of Light [Light-consciousness or Light-relationship], is its divine currency [Spiritual wealth] that is its willingness and capacity for walking upright in Jesus Christ on earth, and therefore for being consumed in the Kingdom of Heaven. **God is Spirit and action, and man's re-union with him depends upon *living* words and actions.** Sacred Scripture advises us that man cannot presume to serve both God and mammon [money and materiality] [Matthew 6:19-24 and 1 John

2:15-16], because he becomes *only* that which he [freely] joins himself to [1 Corinthians 6:17; 15:50]. And so, the more the soul is authentically free from worldly and fleshy [carnal-ego] interests, investments, and gatherings, in favour of interior union with Jesus Christ, the more it is capable of being raised up and invested [by degrees] with the Light-riches and glory of the Kingdom [Matthew 20:16]. Everything the soul truly sacrifices for this purpose, is returned back to God in Jesus Christ, and gives Him back His reign within the soul, as He heals its desire for Light-union with Him. The fruit of this *action* is also balm for Jesus Christ's Mystical Sufferings, and dynamically assists with the abolition of evil [kingdom of Satan] and the reinstatement of the Fatherland. This is because the Light-presence of Jesus Christ within the self-empty soul, divinizes and justifies its upright acts, and amplifies and multiplies their worth in the Spiritual realm, while embellishing it with the imperishable riches of the Kingdom. Conversely, apparent good works, and acts of 'Charity' carried out while the soul conducts itself in violation of Truth [the Truth of its being in God], or with a motive of earthly attention, esteem or advantage are without value or power in the Spiritual realm. See 'Detachment', 'Poor in Spirit' and Self-sacrifice', and p. 289-293 in Chapter on 'Gifts'.

Spiritual intellect: infused divine knowledge in a purified heart. *"God's presence within the soul by grace, brings in more Light than any [natural] intellect. And all the light that the [natural] intellect can give, is but a drop in the ocean beside this Light"* says Meister Eckhart. See 'Grace'.

Spiritual poverty: The state of dis-order, affliction, and immaturity of the Light-deprived *"old man"* who 'sees' and 'walks' in the ways of the flesh [carnal ego-self] and the old world. Spiritual poverty, is the opposite of 'Poor in Spirit', which is the condition of the Eucharistic *"new man"*, who consents to being healed and re-created [re-birthed] anew, to the power and privilege of *real Life and purpose* in Jesus Christ. See 'Man'.

Suffering: see 'Passion' and pp. 237-238 in Chapter on 'Agape'.

Truth: correspondence with hallowed reality. From the Hebrew word *"emeth"*, conferring testimony and judgement; stability, firmness, and faithfulness. It also stands for fidelity, constancy, peace, and grace. Figuratively, Truth stands for Light. **Jesus Christ is the fullness of Truth.**

He is the fullness of Light-being, and the infinite, unfathomable treasures of Eternal Life. Truth is direct [interior] experience of God, because Jesus Christ is the direct Light-consciousness [Light-relationship] of our being.

The World: when we speak of the world, we tend to think of the terrestrial earth [as the fallen shadow of Paradise]; its geography and politics, or other social and cultural contexts. However, what we really speak of, is the order and patterns of relationships between all created things, which was broken by the fall, and which is brought to restoration in Jesus Christ. The empire of the world is divided into two orders or Kingdoms: the Kingdom of God [Life] and the kingdom of Satan [death].

> **Old world** - the kingdom of Satan. This is the pattern of fleshy [carnal-ego] desires and relationships, mis-created by fallen man. It is the 'spirit' of the relation, but has no reality other than witnessing to man's illusions, and afflictions caused by his wayward human will [heart's desire], and the works of evil. The conceptual old world testifies to man's inability to overcome his inherited fleshy nature, and the works of Satan by his own efforts, to reconcile himself with God, and Eternal Life in Him.

> **New world** - the Kingdom of God. This is the primordial way of knowing [illumination] and being in the Love and Divine Will of God, and is restored to man by way of his healing and re-creation [re-birth] in the Perfect [Whole and All-Perfecting] Cosmic Personhood of Jesus Christ. When one person meets another, and each has a *living* relationship with Jesus Christ [and with all things in Him], the Kingdom of God [hallowed reality] is within their midst. See 'Culture'.

Will [Divine]: the Divine Will is the Whole and All-Perfecting Cosmic Will or Heart's Desire of God, by which He continuously creates and holds all things in being. Otherwise explained as the primordial Divine Thought, it is an emanation that is immanent and all-embracing, and which contains within itself the Blueprint of the Universe, in its infinity of possibilities and potentialities, while transcending all of its acts. Rooted in God's boundless creative energies, it is the original perfect [whole and all-perfect] Edenic state of Adam and Eve in Loving union with Him, in the Light-freedom of Paradise. **When the human will [illuminated by grace],**

whole-heartedly co-operates with the Divine Will [*which is what we pray in the Our Father*], the Kingdom of God is within the soul. Living in the Divine Will, for and in the Love of God, is the means by which man and all creation are recovered from evil and death, and restored to the safety and splendour of the Homeland. See 'self-forgetting' and 'Spiritual Intellect'.

Will [Human]: the faculty or power of the soul, by which man desires, deliberates, and make judgements, tending towards value judgements of personal and temporal good and provisional reality at the natural level, and which is susceptible to existence-ignorance, sin [particularly carnal concupiscence] and evil, or towards absolute good and Spiritual reality [The Light of Truth] in Jesus Christ. Otherwise known as the heart's desire or delight, or the rational appetite of man; the human will is bound by man's natural intelligence, perceptions, prejudices, and circumstances, and shifting societal and cultural norms; ultimately his finite struggle for existence. By virtue of his *free* human will, man [unlike animals] is master of his acts, and is responsible for them. Distinct from wilfulness or will power, which are associated with force.

Work: God made man to work [Genesis 2:15]. A great part of Jesus Life on earth was spent working as a carpenter, while the twelve apostles worked before being called [invited] into divine service. Work is vital to man's perfection [wholeness and all-perfection], and only the fall made it toilsome and unpleasant. All honest work that serves man's vital needs on earth, and which assists his neighbour, and does not hinder or derail his true purpose [Genesis 4:9; Leviticus 19:17; Matthew 16:23, 25:40], is honourable and enriching, regardless of how menial or insignificant the task may appear to be. This is because **meaning, value and fulfilment is primarily realized [made real] in man's interior state of being; in drawing the Light of Jesus Christ into every act [of thought, word, and deed], rather than any particular type of work. This work of learning and action[ing] learning, by conceiving and birthing Jesus Christ within the soul is what really *'makes a difference'* in the absolute sense. It is the one way to be *'well-connected'* and *'influential'*** [from the Latin *"influere"* meaning *"to flow into"*], because the continual practice of the presence of God, dynamically uniting every act with the divine acts of Jesus Christ glorifies God by transfiguring the work and the soul, while sharing His Light with all. It is man's dynamic participation in the undoing of the ways and works of the old world, the flesh [carnal ego-self], and the devil [Satan], and the re-instatement of the Kingdom of Heaven. In utilizing his natural gifts and talents [Matthew 25:14-30; 1 Corinthians 12:5-11; 1 Peter 4:9-11], man's highest and most important qualification and occupation, is then the creative realization of higher Life in Jesus Christ. *"The most important work, is not that which you do; it is that which you allow Me to do among you"* Jesus speaks to Sr. Mary of the Holy Trinity. See 'Neighbour', 'Religion' and 'Soul economy'.

Additional notes:

Some words have been capitalized through this book, for the purpose of highlighting the distinction between God as uncreated source, and man as a created person held in being by God. Others words are highlighted to distinguish the singular privilege of the Blessed Virgin Mary's being in God; and the Angels as pure Spirit beings.

The Church teaches that Light-union with God operates **through, with, and in** Jesus Christ. This tripart common reference is shortened and used interchangeably throughout this book, for the sake of readability.

God knows and expresses Himself as relationship, unity, and community. In the same way, man discovers his true personhood through mutual life with others operating through, with, and in God, in Jesus Christ. Words which express the sharing and reciprocity of God, are also used interchangeably throughout this book.

In understanding God as man, it is important to remember that the One uncreated God became man, not *a* man. He assumed the nature of created man, but without sin, and while remaining One in Substance [Essence] and in Energies [Actions] with the Godhead. Created man becomes as God, by co-operating with Him to allow the Perfect [Whole and All-Perfect] Divine-Humanity of Jesus Christ to be born within and through the human soul.

Emmanuel with an *"E"* is used throughout this book, and substituted in public domain bible quotations. This version is a transliteration of the Greek

"Emmanouel" while Immanuel with an *"I"* is a transliteration of the original Hebrew word composed of *"Immanu"* [with us] and *"El"* [God].

References to bible 'sister' languages of Aramaic and Hebrew are included throughout this book, together with Greek and Latin. It is understood that Jesus first language was Aramaic, as befitting His time and place on earth, while He was also familiar with Hebrew. Unlike modern and western languages, Aramaic and Hebrew words are rich in sound, and resonate with many layers of meaning. While the beautifully poetic Aramaic language - like the teachings of Jesus, maintains continuity between inner qualities and outer actions [between inner and outer life], and the co-presence of means and end [fulfilment].

Introduction

*"Therefore, the Lord himself will give you a sign.
Behold, the Virgin will conceive, and bear a Son,
and shall call His name Emmanuel
[which means God-with-us]."*

Isaiah 7:14 and Matthew 1:23.

The word Advent, derived from the Latin *"Adventus"*, meaning *"Coming"* or *"to Come"*, is a comprehensive name that embraces the Incarnation, and all that the outpouring of the Love and Divine Will of the Most Holy Trinity accomplishes in *"Emmanuel: God-with-us"* Old Testament: Isaiah 7:14; 8:8 and New Testament: Matthew 1:23; John 1:14; 14:8-11; Colossians 2:9. In these three words, is the most sublime mystery of Jesus Christ's Coming to Live on earth as a God-man among men; to die and rise again, and gift His Divine-Humanity to human souls. We recognize His Life pouring out abundantly upon us every day, in the sacraments and provisions of His appointed Church on earth.

*"I AM the root [the source of Life],
and the offspring of David,
the Bright Morning Star."*

Revelation 22:16.
[Numbers 24:17; Isaiah 11:1,10].

Foreseen from Eternity, the Incarnation of the entirety and Perfection [Wholeness and All-Perfection] of God in Jesus Christ, confirms our Father's intention of restoring and raising human nature to the highest point of glory [blissful magnificence], by re-uniting it with the divine nature. The Greek translation of the Latin word *"incarnatio"*, defines the Incarnation of Jesus as the *"enhumanment"* of God, capturing beautifully the astonishing reality that Jesus is God-made-man; fully Human and fully Divine, in Substance [Essence] and in Energies [Action]. Yet, as to what *"Emmanuel: God-with-us"* means by way of our creative co-operation with the divine Plan, it is only in bringing this mystery together with an early interpretation of the word *"Coming"* in Aramaic, that we can conceive of what is involved. **For *"Coming"* in this beautiful ancient language of biblical times, speaks of Lovers - the soul and God, Coming together in the nuptial chamber; a place deep within the human soul, where mutual Cosmic desire is fulfilled, and where re-birthing [re-creation] takes place. Jesus became man, so that man could become God; raised up again to higher Life in the Spiritual dimension, by conceiving and birthing the perpetual Light-consciousness of Jesus Christ [the Spiritual state of the Kingdom], within the holy land of his soul.**

Beginning on the fourth Sunday that precedes Christmas Day, Advent marks the start of the Church's liturgical year. It is a sacred and glorious time of expectant waiting and preparation, for the feast of Light and joy, which is the Nativity of Jesus Christ. In story and in parable, the season of Advent links together all the divine mysteries and Revelation of the Old and New Covenants of Love [legal agreements or sacred partnerships between God and man]; carrying us on a voyage of re-discovery, contemplation, and dynamic realization of the Father's deep and hallowed designs upon our lives, and His longing to gather each of us Home.

The announcement of the Old Testament Prophet Isaiah, and New Testament Apostle Matthew, that a Virgin would conceive and bear a Son, confirms that Jesus is the long-awaited Messiah, and the fulfilment of all the Old Testament predictions, concerning the One who would come to rescue God's people Israel from the bondage of Egypt [the land of idolatry].

In the spectacular culmination of the season, which is God's descent from Heaven to earth in Jesus Christ, is the unified triple-fold mystery of His First, Second and Third Advent, or *"Coming"*:

1. **In person, as our Saviour in His Divine-Humanity**, in *"the fullness of time"* Galatians 4:4, walking on the earth amidst human flesh [carnal-ego selves] and weakness, in order to divinize and redeem us. The birth of Jesus Christ initiates the Kingdom of God on earth, and inaugurates *"the last days"* Acts 2:17; 1 Corinthians 10:11.

2. **In Spirit and in power in His Mystical Body**, at *"the end of the [present] times"* [Revelation 16], abolishing all wickedness [evil and ungodliness], renewing the earth, and setting up the fullness of His Spiritual Kingdom [His reign] in divinely wise and faithful [prepared] souls. In these *"times of the [earthly] Kingdom"* says St. Irenaeus of Lyons, walking in the flesh [carnal ego-self] will be replaced with the peace and consolation of walking upright in the Spirit, in the Life of grace and favour as the beloved.

3. **In person again, in the fullness of His glory [blissful magnificence] and majesty as our Supreme Judge**, at *"the [final] end of time"* [Revelation 20:7-15; 21], which is the end of the world, when time will be no more. On this great day of the liberation of faithful souls, Jesus Christ will pronounce the ultimate word on all history, banishing all evil to Hell forever, and bringing forth the new Genesis [creative beginning] of the transfigured Kingdom of Heaven. Faithful souls will receive [according to the degree of Light reaped during their time on earth] the investiture of a glorified and incorruptible new body and soul. They will rest from all struggle with and in God, and with everyone and everything in Him, in the Ever-alive tranquillity and contentment of the New Jerusalem [Paradise].

God too will rest from all His labours across the ages, in His Loving quest to bring His lost children Home. No longer will sun and moon be needed for light, because the Light of Jesus Christ, who will sustain the new Heaven and earth will eclipse them [Isaiah 60:19-20 and Revelation 21:23-24].

Descriptions of the three Advents include the famous excerpt from a sermon on the three Comings of Christ, by St. Bernard of Clairvaux.

> *"In the First Coming, He comes in the flesh [body] and in weakness;*
> *in the Second, He comes in Spirit and in power;*
> *in the Third, He comes in glory and in majesty.*
> *And the Second Coming is the means,*
> *whereby we pass from the First to the Third."*
>
> St. Bernard of Clairvaux.

In the ending of each appointed time of *"Coming"* or Advent, is creative beginning [Genesis] and continuation. Each new beginning in time speaks of cycles of correction, renewal, and transformation, while in the Spiritual realm of the Eternal Now, the means and the end are always present. In the First Advent, Jesus Christ came in time, never to depart again. He is both present, and He is Coming [again]. Therefore, the word Advent in the complete sense, unites past, present, and future, in newness [Ever-newness] of Life, which is Eternal Life in Jesus Christ.

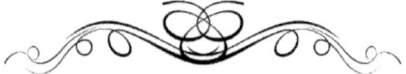

The glory [blissful magnificence] of Jesus Christ's First Coming [or arrival], marks the beginning of salvation [from the Latin word *"salvus"*, meaning *"time of healing"*] history. It calls [invites], but never forces each one of us to *"come"* **to holiness [whole-hearted fullness of being] Now in Jesus Christ,** who is the living Light of God present in time, to redeem man in time. Therefore, to understand

God's Plan of restoration, is to understand that every moment [in the Life-breath of the Holy Spirit] is a new beginning, in which creation is renewed in Jesus Christ, whose birth suffuses time and Eternity. And while we are to be vigilant of the *'signs of the times'*, and the divine schedule, we are not to sink into fearful and distracting projections about the future. For as every yesterday dissolves like mist, and we have no assurance of tomorrow [Matthew 6:33-34], which means *"things depart"* or *"pass away"* [in Aramaic]; creative healing, and holiness [whole-hearted fullness of being] is here and Now, by way of our dynamic co-operation with and participation in the Life of sanctifying grace. **Now is the right time and the only time, for receiving and re-connecting with hallowed reality and All-unity, by realizing [making real] the Spiritual state of the Kingdom, within and through our souls.**

*"...be perfect [whole and all-perfect]
as your Father in Heaven is Perfect [Whole and All-Perfect]."*

Matthew 5:48.

Let us then invite grace to really know the gift of God [John 4:10], and meet Him in our heart's desire [human will], by asking of ourselves these questions:

- Who am I, rather than What have I, at the natural level?
- What am I being, and to what do I draw attention to?
- From where have I come, and to where am I driving and pointing others, in the gift of every day?

If we regard God, and ourselves, and others as children of God, these questions are sincerely within us. So too are the answers, which we will receive by illumination from the Holy Spirit, who takes us as far as we are disposed into the depths of Truth, and enables us not only to re-hear [understand], but re-see [conceive, with the interior eye of the Spirit] the astonishing gift, responsibility, and purpose of life [Sirach 17:7]. As far as we 'go out of ourselves' to meet Him; **to learn**

and to action what we have learned, with a spirit of transparency and willingness for Truth, will He realize [make real] within us, the most prodigious and beautiful gift of immortal and Divine Life.

> *" ...that you may be filled with all the fullness of God."*
> Ephesians 3:19.

The Nuptial Light-ring of the Homeland

The Ever-abundant, Never-ceasing, and Never-ending Light-ring of Eternity; the difference between 'lust for life' and 'fullness of Life'; deep healing and transfiguration by conceiving and birthing Jesus Christ [the Spiritual state of the Kingdom] within the human soul; the true heroism of Spiritual athletics and fitness testing; reaping what you sow; symbolism of candles, and the purple, pink and white candles of the Advent wreath.

The Advent wreath with its four coloured candles, is a central tradition of the season which marks the beginning of the new liturgical year.

Originally adopted by Christians in the Middle Ages, it has grown rich in Spiritual meaning and symbolism, and has much to reveal to us about the splendour of hallowed reality, and the work of our Redemption and Sanctification in Jesus Christ.

In the circular ring-form of the wreath is represented the Never-ceasing, and Ever-expanding Eternity of the Triune God, who is without beginning or end. The circle betokens wholeness [holiness and all-perfection], unity and continuity; the unbroken Love and fidelity that is sought in the **nuptial Light-bond** between the Father and His faithful child in Jesus Christ. Prepared with a mix of evergreens to symbolise the immortality [Ever-aliveness] of our soul, and the continuation of Life which we find in Jesus Christ, our attention is drawn to the spectacular reward of Eternal Life. Holly with its thorns and red berries, symbolise the Divine-Human sufferings and Blood shed by Jesus Christ, on behalf of all mankind. We are reminded that He came into this world to be ransomed for us, that we may be redeemed and recovered to the *'fullness of Life'* [Eternal Life] in Him. A free invitation to re-enter Paradise, which comes by way of co-operating with and participating in His Love operating in His Divine Will, through the tests and trials of everyday life. Laurel represents the crown of victory [Spiritual wealth] gifted to faithful souls who honour fidelity, and thus *truly* Love Him.

The entire form and decoration of the wreath, symbolises the infinite variety and richness of God's creation. It reminds us that the only actual goal [future] is the Eternal goal [future], and the only worthwhile and lasting reward is Eternal Life. Our task and purpose during our appointed time on earth is to awaken and remain awake; to conceive, and birth Jesus Christ within and through our souls. It is to *"all attain to the unity of the faith and of the knowledge of the Son of God, to a full-grown man, to the measure of the stature of the fullness of Christ"* Ephesians 4:11. **This recovery of our lost God-being [John 10:34], which is our Good-being**, requires that we outgrow all that is not God, by giving up the illusory pursuit of a 'perfect' earthly life ['good life'], for a revelation of sanctifying grace. For it is by grace alone that we are led and drawn into a living, dynamic relationship with God, and with **the One All-Good Life of the Kingdom.**

This transformation is set in motion by an intentional act of the human will [heart's desire] to recognize the great mystery of our being, as two-dimensional created [and finite] beings in time, who experience death, and as immortal [and infinite] beings in Eternity. It is to acknowledge a continuous Spiritual conflict between good and evil; Truth and falsehood; and Light and darkness both within [interiorly] and without [exteriorly]. It is to adjust our lives to Jesus Christ-consciousness, the Perfect [Whole and All-Perfect] God-Man who not only did not pursue [old] worldly ways, validation, rewards, and titles during His earthly Life, but refused all such ways and esteem, going as far as to adopt the anti-title *"Son of Man"* [recorded in the Gospels of Matthew, Mark, Luke, and John].

> *"Don't you know that those who run in a race all run,*
> *but one receives the prize? Run like that,*
> *so that you may win. Every man who strives in the games*
> *exercises self-control in all things. Now they do it to receive a*
> *corruptible crown, but we an incorruptible [crown]."*
>
> 1 Corinthians 9:24-25.

In fidelity to Jesus Christ's Perfect example, St. Paul amidst the noise and commotion of the personal and business enterprises of his time, offers the analogy of athletes in training, to urge us as children of God, to **expend our life energy in training as Spiritual athletes, for the only real glory, which is Ever-lasting Life in the Kingdom of Heaven.** To otherwise mis-govern and dissipate our life energy in the imitations of Life; in initiatives, noise, and activities, and in pursuit of rewards and titles that ultimately lead nowhere, is to mistake good feeling in the flesh for Good-being [God-being, John 10:34]. It is to **mistake *'lust for life'* for the *'fullness of Life'*,** which is realized in Jesus Christ. It is to remain asleep, as the apostles, in the Garden of Gethsemane, while the Spiritual treasures of the Kingdom lie buried deep within our souls. For while many such pursuits require us to compete and 'give our all', or prove something; generating and ingraining association with, reliance on, and pride in the works of the flesh [carnal ego-self], and the unreliable relationships and fragmentations of the old world; Spiritual reality moves in the opposite direction. It is the true discipline and heroism of positively abandoning the ways of the flesh [carnal ego-self], and the old world, to the sanctifying work of the Cross. A **perennial Lenten Springtime in the soul**, that allows it to reap [conceive and birth] the One true glory of Eternal Life in Jesus Christ. Only as far as we have [by a free act of our human will], directed our life energy upon knowing and Loving God with His own highest Love, operating in His Divine Will, will we have reaped His Light [Life] within our soul. While the measure of Light reaped, will be the measure of our strength and capability [fitness] for penetrating the immensity and magnificence [glory] of the Kingdom of Heaven. See Chapter on 'Fiat'.

> *"Hence the teaching of certain holy commentators of Scripture:*
> *'In Ever-lasting Life, so deep a Love shall the elect have for one*
> *another, that is one sees another gifted with greater joy and higher*
> *contemplation than himself, this will be to him as much happiness*
> *as if he himself had merited it, and were now enjoying it.'"*

John Tauler [The Illuminated Doctor].

As we seek to make use of the natural gifts and talents given to us, let us then keep before our minds [in our hearts] the higher gifts of the Spirit, which serve the noble purpose, privilege, and responsibility of our being in the blessed Light of Truth. Let us moderate and safeguard the investment of our life energy, approaching our appointed time on earth, as divinely wise and confident children of the inheritance [Romans 8 - Letter of our Inheritance]; children of a paternal, Heavenly Father, and brothers and sisters of a King. Citizens of Heaven, and temporary pilgrims on earth, with an unknown gift of days to become who we really are, and can be, in Jesus Christ.

> *"The Lenten Springtime is here!*
> *In these all-hallowing days, let us purify the temple*
> *of our body and soul, stripped bare and wounded by enfeebling*
> *passions and sensual appetites. With hearts illuminated*
> *and quickened grace, let us perform the works of God in the Light.*
> *Victors striding forth in gladsome radiance,*
> *as Children of the Resurrection!"*

Anon.

With the gradual lighting of the candles on each of the Sundays of the season, we remember the four stages of our salvation [healing] history, prior to the Coming of Jesus Christ, as man. Each candle represents 1,000 years, commemorating the 4,000 years that God's people waited in exile from the time of Adam [*"Adamos"* in Greek, meaning *"earth"* or *"rich clay"*] to the birth of the Messiah. It symbolises the long night of darkness [the Spiritual blindness and evil of the kingdom of Satan] giving way to the Light of Jesus Christ, who in His Self-disclosure as the prophetic, redeeming Light, illuminates and dispels the darkness, and gives rise to the One Ever-lasting Day. The first three weeks of the season are three full weeks, while the fourth week ends the day before Christmas. The length of the fourth week depends upon when Christmas occurs.

Once used primarily for the purpose of giving light, all candles used in the Church stand for Jesus Christ *"the Light of the world"* John 8:12 and 9:5. While the three symbolic [liturgical] colours of the Advent candles are richly symbolic of the specific elements of Spiritual preparation required to receive Jesus Christ; in His First Coming at Christmas, and in His Second Coming Now, within and through our souls. Three purple candles and one rose [pink] candle, for each of the four weeks, are evenly arranged around the wreath, while a white candle is placed in the centre.

- **Purple** symbolises the divine royalty and Universal sovereignty of Jesus Christ, the *"King of kings and Lord of lords"* 1 Timothy 6:15; Revelation 17:14 and 19:16, and anticipates His reception in and among us. Purple also symbolises the prayer, penance, and other good works [such as fasting and all self-sacrifice, and acts of Charity] undertaken by the faithful at this time.

- The **rose [pink]** coloured third candle signifies joy as we reach half-way, and rejoice in the nearness of Christmas. It marks a lessening of the penitential practices* [which were more widely practiced in Medieval times], in expectation of Christmas joy.

- The fifth **white** [or gold] pillar candle is placed in the middle of the wreath for Christmas Eve, or Christmas Day. This candle is called 'The Christ Candle' and speaks of the sublime purity and Divinity [as superior to the Humanity] of the Perfect [Whole and All-Perfect] Cosmic Personhood of Jesus Christ. White also signifies the re-creation [re-birth] and victory of our souls [in God], which was won by Him, and is gifted to us in Him.

A blue bowl may be placed at the base of each candle, to honour the Blessed Virgin Mary, who called God from Heaven to earth; carrying Him in her most pure heart and womb, and delivering Him into the world, that He might deliver us back to our place of origin in the Homeland.

[*During thanksgiving after Holy Communion close to the feast of Christmas, Blessed Dina Belanger (a 20th Century Church religious and mystic) receives the following words from Jesus: *"How many Catholics concern themselves little or not at all with penance during the season of Advent! How many, neglect to prepare for My Coming at Christmas!"*].

Sunday **liturgical readings and teachings** during the three-year cycles of Advent, both commemorate the ancient expectancy of the First Coming of Jesus Christ the Redeemer at Christmas, and anticipate and prepare us for realizing [making real] His Second Coming within our souls on earth. Old Testament readings are the Messianic prophesies, normally from the Prophet Isaiah, telling of the Coming of the Messiah, who will ennoble, perfect, and replace the old law by becoming its *Living* and real, permanent foundation in Himself. New Testament Gospel readings, usually from Matthew and Luke, serve more immediately to encourage us to realize [make real] Jesus Christ's Light-presence within our being, bringing the Kingdom to earth. In the Gospel readings of weeks two and three, we hear the compelling and urgent messages of John the Baptist, the last and greatest Prophet of the Old Testament Covenant of Love, who came to prepare the way for Jesus. Gospels closer to Christmas, relate the events that preceded and prepared for the feast of the Nativity.

Throughout Sacred Scripture, which is the perfect journal of God's actions, we are strongly advised and encouraged to stay awake, and be vigilant and attentive; to recognize God's presence and sovereignty, and the triumph of His Justice. We are called [invited] to understand that there is no other wisdom, goal [future], or glory, except the Kingdom of God; and to be confident and joyful, as we commemorate His birth in time, and realize [make real] His Spiritual return within and through our souls.

> *"Whoever has the Son, has Life.*
> *Whoever does not have the Son, does not have Life."*
>
> 1 John 5:12.

Thankfulness, Gratitude & Relationship

The Prophesy Candle/Candle of Hope

The actual and mystical properties of Light; Jesus Christ - the fullness of Light and Life; Children of Light; our predicament and privilege of being; only God knows and Loves us absolutely; rights are relational; our neighbour's keeper; the gift of thanksgiving; false lights vs. living Light.

"I AM the Light of the world."
John 8:12 and 9:5.

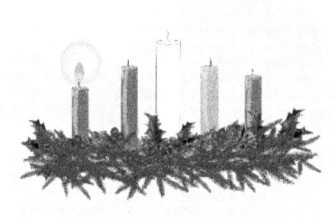

The First Sunday of Advent is a time of new beginning, as we celebrate not only a new liturgical season, but the beginning of a new liturgical year. The **first candle** is lit in grateful remembrance of the great prophets, who foretold the Coming of Jesus Christ; the Messianic Saviour [healer] of the world. Its light extols the **super-abundant hope and promise** of the inextinguishable Light of Eternal Life.

Generous and life-giving, the vigour and movement of the first flame of the wreath, symbolises the primordial unfolding of Light, which began and which sustains the Universe [Genesis 1:3]. Light is God in operation. Wave and particle, it is that radiating and pulsating Life-force, that lives in and ignites every person and living creature, and which precipitates in all inert matter. This figurative Light, is the Light of the star of Bethlehem; the All-knowing illumination of the divine [Spiritual] intellect. It is the radiance of Love and Lovingness; the living Light-fire of God, that warms and illuminates; that burns, purifies, refines, and re-creates [re-births]; and Spiritualizes all that would be bathed and consumed in it.

Throughout his Gospel and Epistle, St. John uses the word Light to characterize Jesus Christ as *"the true Light, that enlightens everyone"* John 1:9. **Both God and man, Jesus Christ is the full measure of God. He is the fullness of perpetual Light, which is the Life of God; the Truth of His Love operating in His All-perfect [and All-perfecting] Divine Will.** He is the One through whom, and for whom, *all things* were created and hold together [Colossians 1:16-17]. In Him, is the illumination of the sacred and mysterious I AM, and our re-union with the Father in the Light-union of the Most Holy Trinity. As the totality of the infinite God, we look to Him as the Life of all life; the *real Life and purpose* of our life, and **our One absolute standard of Good-being [God-being, John 10:34].**

> *"In Him was Life, and the Life was the Light of men."*
> John 1:4.

St. Paul speaks of those who walk [awake and sober] in Jesus Christ, as *"Children of Light" Luke 16:18; John 12:36; Ephesians 5:8; 1 Thessalonians 5:5;* as divinely creative vessels, and channels of Jesus Christ-consciousness. They are those whose way of knowing, thinking and being are One, with and in Jesus Christ.

Today's readings look beyond Jesus Christ's imminent First Coming in His Divine-Humanity at Christmas, to His Second Coming in His Mystical Body, at *"the end of the [present] times"* [Revelation 16]. These readings call [invite] us to double preparation; to realize [make real] His Second Coming within and through our souls Now, as we prepare to celebrate His First Coming at Christmas.

Thankfulness, gratitude, and right relationship with hallowed reality.

Man cannot *really* Love what he does not *really* know. He cannot Love God unless he consents to know Him, while to know Him is to Love Him, and all His people, living creatures and creation in Him. The most sure way of preparing for Christmas, and for conceiving newness

[Ever-newness] of being in Jesus Christ, is then to become ever-more alive to who God is; who we are in God; and everything that has been *freely* done for us. Only when we come into this conscious awareness, can we conceive of our predicament and privilege, as estranged and beloved children of a paternal Father God, and brothers and sisters of a King. Only then, can we be inspired to cultivate a spirit of holy fear [awe-filled reverence] and thankfulness, and come into right relationship with hallowed reality.

The first step to thankfulness, is to realize that God created man out of Love [Charity] and for Love [Charity]. He was created to be blessed and to be a blessing; to be glorified in God, and to be the glory of God. **He was made *by* God and *for* God [Hebrews 2:10], and lavished with all His free gifts of creation.** From the gift of our being, to the great gifts and mysteries of the Church, which offer the fullness of Eternal Life; all are pure gifts from the hands of our Loving Creator God and Father. God has Loved us and remained with us from all Eternity, while foreseeing our betrayal and falling away from Him, to live entombed in the flesh [carnal ego-self], and caught up in the old world [kingdom of Satan], as sinners and enemies [Romans 5:8].

> *"There is Only One reality.*
> *I Love you. You are Mine."*
>
> Jesus speaks to Sr. Mary of the Holy Trinity.

The Plan of the restoration of man [and through him, all creation] to higher Life, is the ultimate gift from God. Jesus tells a gathering: *"No-one can come to Me, unless the Father who sent Me draws him; and I will raise him up on the last day"* John 6:44 [Matthew 20:23]. He repeats this message [John 6:64] and affirms a third time, when says to His disciples: *"without Me, you can do nothing"* John 15:5. These profound quotes from Sacred Scripture, put the plain realities of our life before us. **Any true good that is in us comes from God, and is of God. He is the source of all power; all Love, hope, and promise.** Man is free to use and misuse God's creative power, but only God can create a soul, and only He can absolutely heal and restore a soul. While some souls are issued with greater propensity to know and Love Him, and ascend to holiness [whole-hearted fullness of being] in Him, it is only God's work within the consenting soul, that can heal its desire for re-union with Him. This is because the fall has altered man's condition. His mind [the seat of knowledge and wisdom] and heart [the seat of emotions] have become dis-integrated [divided]; his mind is darkened, and his heart is hard towards God and hallowed reality. Despite the best of intentions, he has at the natural level, and by degree of estrangement, neither the ability nor the desire to return to Him. He is naturally an enemy of God [Romans 5:10] and a lover of the self-centred flesh [carnal ego-self], and does not accept the things that come from the Spirit of God [1 Corinthians 2:14].

> *"Everyone who has listened and learned
> from the Father comes to Me."*
>
> John 6:45.

When we begin to come to terms with our state of being, we realize that our salvation [healing] and re-union with God, and our original glory in Him, is not so much about straining towards Him, but whole-heartedly abandoning back [giving the consent of] our human will [heart's desire], to *His work* of sanctifying our soul. For despite the best of human intentions, only God Loves us, and can Love us, absolutely. Only He knows the full glory [blissful magnificence] for which we were created. He is the Only One who fully takes [can take] our part in His Son-God, and He is the Only One who knows all that we are capable of being restored to. God is the Only One who can be wholly interested in our restoration and ascent to the fullness of Eternal Life.

As the fullness of God, Jesus Christ teaches us that thanksgiving is the gift which God manifests within the soul that turns back to Him [John 14:16]. Thanksgiving was the living expression of His own Life on earth, culminating in His complete Self-offering as the atonement [at-

One-ment], to become our Ever-Living Food in the Eucharist. Indeed, Eucharist with its origin in the Greek word *"eucharistia"* meaning *"thanksgiving",* expresses the reality that **a Eucharistic life is the *real Life and purpose* of perfect [whole and all-perfect] man.** That it is in the 'breaking the bread' of his being, in union with Jesus Christ that man fulfils his divinely creative role as *mediator* between God and creation, transfiguring and hallowing it, and offering it back to Him in a spirit of thanksgiving. This Life, made possible as pure gift by way of the Life of Jesus Christ, is the All-Good Life of gratitude [thanksgiving in action], because the complete nourishment of Jesus Christ in the Eucharist, gives the desirous soul the strength for consenting to the Life-creating work of the Cross, while inspiring it to gratitude for His Life-Food, and the opportunity to re-enter Paradise. Joy-filled gratitude, is then the [only] basis of right relationship with God, and with hallowed reality. It is the proper response to the infinite debt freely repaid for us, and without which we would be lost forever.

"Give thanks in everything.
For this is the [Divine] Will of God in Christ Jesus."

1 Thessalonians 5:18.

To be truly grateful, is to transform the way we look at our purpose of being, as immortal similitudes of God, by the renewing of our mind [re-united] in our heart. It is to both re-hear [understand]and re-see [conceive with our interior Spiritual eye], the astonishingly privileged and noble purpose of our being in God. It is to realize that all rights are in relation to [are relational and belong to] Him. And it is to **be vigilant over and take responsibility for all that we think, say, and do, and all that we dispose, tempt, and draw others to**; taking the part of their keeper [shield and salvation], rather than their tempter and enemy [Genesis 4:9; Leviticus 19:17; Matthew 16:23, 25:40]. For as baptised *"Children of Light"* Luke 16:18; John 12:36; Ephesians 5:8; 1 Thessalonians 5:5, we are our brother and sister's salvation [healing], in union with God.

Authentic gratitude is ordered in God in two ways:

- By preferring nothing to Him; turning to Him, and receiving His *real Life and purpose* within us. "*Prefer nothing to Christ, for He preferred nothing to you*" extols St. Cyprian.
- By receiving and sharing His Light-being; doing for others [free of self-interest] what has first been first done for us.

Joy filled gratitude ordered in God, is the secret to Good-being [God-being, John 10:34], bringing healthfulness of soul [memory, will and intellect] and body; mind, heart, and spirit. It is authentic [Spiritual] worship, and the worship God wants from us, because man was created to be a joy-filled worshipping being; the powers of his soul soaked with the blissful Light-presence and action of God. It is only man's wilful forgetfulness and desertion of God, and readiness to accept Satan's appealing and deceitful answers about the dark, that has led to his disregard for God, and his disconnection from the brightness, vigour, and healthfulness of Eternal Life.

> *"Everyone who has this hope set on Him purifies himself, even as He is pure."*
>
> 1 John 3:3.

As we look to the first flame of Advent that reaches upwards and moves freely in the air, our attention is drawn to the infinite difference between the staid and ineffectual false lights of the flesh [carnal ego-self] and the old world [kingdom of Satan], in all its guises, and the power, vigour, warmth, and effects of the *living* Light of Heaven. This blessed Light is the same Light burning within our soul since Baptism, and which longs to rise up in its all-cleansing purity, to lift us back up to the celestial heights for which we were created. We thank our Heavenly Father for the astonishing free gift of our being, and for calling us back to His Light-Womb; our place of origin in the Heavenly Homeland. We thank Him for the supreme gift of His Beloved Son, the Heavenly New Adam [1 Corinthians 15:45-48], who is the Ever-living and timeless Light [Life], and Head of the new and transfigured creation [Colossians 1:18 and Ephesians 13-22]. For the sublime purity and radiance, we lost in Adam, we Now find superabundantly in Jesus Christ, in whom we cross the infinite abyss between God and man.

Faithfulness, Courage & Compassion

The Bethlehem Candle/ Candle of Preparation

By royal appointment; the meaning of living faith; lessons of John the Baptist - true kindness, compassion and kinship, and shattering duplicity, superficiality, and counterfeit peace; intoxication and addiction vs authentic satisfaction; characteristics of a masterful Life.

"But you, Bethlehem Ephrathah, being small among the clans of Judah, out of you One will come out to Me who is to be ruler in Israel; whose goings out are from of old, from ancient times."

Micah 5:2.

The **second candle** of Advent remembers Mary and Joseph's journey from Nazareth to Bethlehem of Judah, and symbolises **faith or faithful waiting.** We ponder upon their preparations for this long, dangerous, and arduous journey across mountainous and unsure terrain, to the beautiful situation of the little town of Bethlehem of Judah; the hidden and tranquil place of their ancestors, near Jerusalem. Here in Bethlehem, meaning *"House of Bread"* in Hebrew, prophecy would be fulfilled, when Jesus Christ *"The Bread of Life"* John 6:35,48, would come into the world.

Bethlehem's smallness in size and worldly significance, evidenced by its original omission from the list of cities in Judah, named in Joshua 15, illuminates the marvellous ways in which the greatness of God works. For it is here in this margin place amidst the innocence of the shepherds and the stars, that God our Father planned from all

Eternity, that His Son-God, the long-awaited Messiah would arise; to be unknown and unmerited during the days of His Life on earth.

Bethlehem's divine appointment from all Eternity is called out in Genesis 35:19, at a time when it was called Ephrathah. It is clearly called out again by the Prophet Micah, who linked Bethlehem Ephrathah with his foretelling of a new King, who would come to re-unite the people of Israel, and reign over all nations. His adding the word Ephrathah to the word Bethlehem confirms that Ephrathah is exactly equivalent to Bethlehem in the book of Genesis. This more ancient Hebrew name for Bethlehem of Judah, derived from a verb meaning *"to be fruitful"*, signifies this town's most blessed appointment as the source of divine fruitfulness for all the earth. In ancient times, Bethlehem is the place of momentous happenings in the royal lineage from which Jesus came. Boaz, the great grandfather of David, the earthly Old Testament king of Israel, was from Bethlehem of Judah [Ruth 2:4] and David himself was born and anointed king here [1 Samuel 16:1-13]. See Chapter on 'King of kings'.

Mary and Joseph's mid-winter journey to Bethlehem by day and by night, reminds us of our pilgrimage as beings of Light and darkness, towards the One Eternal Day of the Heavenly New Jerusalem. And as the earth orbits around the sun, our days are characterized by movement away from and towards Light, in a state of continual conflict and renewal; of departures from, or passing away of, what does not belong to higher Life in the Spirit.

The symbolism of faith or faithful waiting on the second Sunday of Advent, presents to us the reality that to conceive and re-birth the Spiritual state of the Kingdom in our being, we must grow in **living faith and divine wisdom. An upward ascent, which means conscious awareness of Jesus Christ, as the *true centre* [Light-consciousness and Light-relationship] of our being.** This vital interpretation can be made, by looking to the meaning of the word *"faith"* in Aramaic, which speaks of Divine Life birthing within and through us, when we abandon back [give consent] to God. As far as we consent to knowing and Loving God [in His Love and Divine Will], as the direct Light-consciousness of our being, the Light-fire of faith becomes ever more alive and active within us. And we grow capable of moving into a state of continual [stable] becoming and maturing into the fullness of character and stature in Jesus Christ.

> *"When the Divine Light penetrates the soul,*
> *it is united with God as Light with Light. This is the Light of faith.*
> *Faith bears the soul to heights unreachable,*
> *by her natural senses and faculties."*
>
> Meister Eckhart.

Among the three-year cycle of readings, our attention is directed to the preaching and ministry of the strong and austere figure of John the Baptist. The last and greatest of all the Old Testament prophets, he is the one raised apart to *"prepare the way of the Lord"* Isaiah 40:3 and Mark 1:3. His, is the work of announcing Jesus Christ's First Coming in His Divine-Humanity on earth, and of teaching man what he must do to receive His Second Coming within and through our souls, during our earthly lifetime. It is the work of bringing to completion the mission of the great Old Testament Prophet Elijah, another solitary figure, with the same powerful and fiery spirit, symbolising Divine Justice. Set alight with the Spirit, and speaking fearlessly and powerfully of time, sin, repentance [meaning to *"turn back"* or *"come back"* to God in Aramaic and Hebrew] and deliverance, he leaves his listeners in no doubt, as to the predicament of man, and what is required to win Eternal Life. For without recognizing the deceitful lights of the world, and the serpent's [Satan's] cup of honeyed poison, which tastes much better to the unrefined worldly palate; man cannot become disposed to repent, and receive the Life of sanctifying grace. And **if he is not growing inwardly by divine illumination through grace, he is regressing in a de-generate flow of energy**, becoming more lost and busy with empty and evil works, attachments, and illusions, even under the guise of 'good', but apart from God.

> *"Blessed is he, who has found no offense in Me."*
> Matthew 11:6.

And so, it is with a motive of deep kindness and compassion [from the Greek word *"splagna"* meaning guts], and in the spirit of utter wisdom and *true* kinship [involving birth or begetting in Greek], that John the Baptist makes very clear that there is no assurance of salvation [healing] through presumption, or any way other than transformation of being and relationship on God's terms. A seismic shift in reality, which means re-birth [re-creation] in the Love and Divine Will of God, for the sake of the One absolute family and community of the Heavenly realm.

> *"Don't think to yourselves "We have Abraham for our father", for I tell you that God is able to raise up children to Abraham from these stones."*
> Matthew 3:9 and Luke 3:8.

Holding perfect balance between God's Mercy and Justice, and shattering the counterfeit peace offered up to the flesh [carnal ego-self], by the old world, and Satan, he offers his sincere listeners great words of encouragement, while also shocking the Sadducees and Pharisees with the reality of their superficial piety and ungodly ways, proceeding from estranged and dis-integrated minds and hearts. Calling them *"offspring of vipers"* Matthew 3:7, he warns them and all of us, that ***"even now, the axe [symbolising work and battle] has been placed at the root of the trees,*** *and every tree [soul] that does not produce good fruit shall be cut down, and cast into the fire [of Hell]"* Matthew 3:10; Luke 3:9. With uncompromising firmness, he calls us all out of complacency, to sobriety and preparation; reminding us that we are nothing, and have nothing, apart from what is granted to us from Heaven [John 3:27]. He asserts the need for the renunciation of the flesh [carnal ego-self], which contains all the hopes, desires, and ambitions of the ego-mask [ego-persona], to allow the *Living* God to well up and rise within the Home-ground [ground-centre] of our being. For the degree to which He is permitted to conquer us, is the degree to which we are absorbed in Him, and in the *Livingness* of Eternal Life.

We can learn much from looking more deeply at the life of this extraordinarily devout spirit-soaked man, who Jesus declares greatest among the children of men [Matthew 11:11; Luke 7:28]. Called to high office before the dawn of his days, he leaps for joy in his mother's womb at the approach of his unborn 'cousin' Jesus [Luke 1:41]. Sacred Scripture tells us that because of his high purpose, he would abstain from alcohol and be filled with the Holy Spirit [Luke 1:15]. Graced with pure thirst, and drinking only of the unadulterated wine of the Spirit, the life of John the Baptist, was one of intoxication [infusion] of the Spirit. He was the one who could be entrusted to carry this cup into the old world [kingdom of Satan] and not spill it, because those who have tasted this cup - encrusted with all manner of priceless jewels of redemptive suffering and release, know it to be the only one that *truly* satisfies. Avoiding the impairing effects of substances* which weaken and cripple the soul [memory, will and intellect] and body; the mind and heart, John the Baptist found **authentic satisfaction in "the fertile embrace of God"** [the Aramaic meaning of the word *"satisfaction"*], which alone can satisfy the human heart.

[*Abstinence from intoxicating substances can be understood in the complete sense, to include everything which renders man unprepared for Judgement, and unfit for the company of Heaven. For all false highs, addictions, pursuits, and investments in life are nothing other than desperate attempts to fill the dark voids within the soul, and keep fear, uncertainty, and discontentment at bay. All are shackles, that drug and dull the soul, and present problems to the Spiritual Life, even if natural life appears to continue normally. The short-lived highs, that turn to emptiness, boredom and sadness, and result in eventual lower lows, are evidence of the growing dark voids of negativity, falsity, and evil within the soul, which drive it to seek more of the same, or similar, to fill these clinging voids, which can only be satisfied (filled) by living in dynamic relationship with God, and all things in Him. Unless the soul repents (*"turns back"* or *"comes back"* to God), it risks sinking further into ever deeper and darker voids of illusion, existence-ignorance, and desperation, marked by soul slumber and dis-ease, from which it finds it ever more difficult and painful to escape].

Hidden and hardly known, there is little sign of external good works in the life of John the Baptist. He is a solitary, bedraggled figure, surviving on a diet of locust beans and wild honey [Mark 1:6; Matthew 3:4]. Seen in public only for a brief time, not a single public miracle is credited to him, and there is no story told. Yet, labouring in higher Life in the Spirit and waiting, His zeal for God was such, that when he leaves his desert abode to preach on the *"Coming"* of the Messiah, and to baptise, his messages are fiery and frank, and very different to anything that had been heard before. He teaches people that authentic outward actions, pleasing and acceptable to God, must proceed from one's interior state of being, or they are empty and vain. Practicing what he preached, he joyfully yields to God in all things, including baptising Jesus while recognizing Him as the Messiah, and the One who he 'felt' should baptise him.

"He must increase, while I must decrease."

John 3:30.

Yet, while the crowds swell around John the Baptist and his messages spread like wildfire, they produce little actual effect among the Pharisees and worldlings. For **eagerly listening to the messages of the Kingdom, and talking [even enthusiastically] about them, are worlds apart from putting them into practice, as an entire way of being and living.** When he speaks out to judge king Herod [the reigning earthly king of the Jews] for committing adultery with his brother's former wife, Herodias [divorcing his wife, and marrying Herodias], he is thrown into prison to appease Herodias, and loses his earthly life. This is the lot of the greatest among men, and the mark of Jesus own Life, in particular [Hebrews 2:10-11].

Indeed, the lives of the blessed; most particularly the Blessed Virgin Mary, as well as the apostles, the disciples, and the saints of the ages, teach us that the ways of those marked for the highest heights of sanctity, conform least to the ways of the flesh [carnal ego-self] and the old world. Theirs is an unearthly earthly life, that moves in the opposite direction. It is a quietly masterful life; a life of higher discipline and resolve, lived in fidelity to higher meaning and ways. It is a hidden life of interior suffering, solitude and thought of God in all things. If involved or distinguished in the world by obligation to public office, it is no less a life marked by all manner of difficulties, contradictions, and hidden Crosses, that craft upon the soul the sufferings, and therefore the glory of Jesus Christ. These are the most zealous souls of all time, who carry Jesus Christ within their being in differing degrees on earth. They are the fearless ones, whose way of being in the full depth and power of the *"Fiat"*, goes far beyond words, and outward gestures of kindness and community. Willingly sharing in His bitter-sweet chalice, and walking upright with and in Him, along the way of His Passion, they are the souls who die to themselves and stand at the foot of the Cross, when all His fair-weather friends have deserted Him [Mark 14:46,50]. Shielding Him with His own Love, and giving Him the strength to bear His most torturous execution, they are **a living revelation of Charity** whose ***'fullness of Life'*** and purpose on earth, is known only to God and the Angels. They are the ones whom God entrusts Himself to, and who will stand at the head of the Blessed in Heaven, in and for all Eternity.

> *"When the temple [of the soul] is thus free of obstructions [attachments and ignorance], then it glistens with beauty, shining out bright and fair above the whole of God's creation, and through all of God's creation, so that none can equal its brilliance, but the uncreated God alone."*
>
> Meister Eckhart.

Joy Like No Other

Gaudete Sunday/Shepherds Sunday

A *new and exalted Edenic state; the glory of the graciously [grace-filled] simple way; celestial joy, and the joys of Jesus Christ; His joy in the soul who turns back to Him; the perennial rejoicing of the Blessed Virgin Mary.*

"And there were shepherds in the same region, being vigilant and keeping watch in the night over their flock. And behold, an Angel of the Lord stood near them, and the brightness of God shone around them... And the Angel said to them: "Do not be afraid. For behold, I proclaim to you a great joy, which will be for all the people.""

Luke 2:8-11.

As the **third candle** of the season is set alight; the rose-pink candle of joy; we celebrate *"Gaudete"* Sunday, meaning **"Rejoice!"** in Latin. Taken from St. Paul's command to the Philippians *"Rejoice in the Lord always; again, I say rejoice!"* Philippians 4:4, rejoicing always was man's original way of being within the Ever-new and infinite Beatitude of the Heavenly realm. This rejoicing is restored in Jesus Christ, our Ever-lasting Joy, who has come to redeem and restore us, not only to the original Edenic state, but to a more exalted state, in the new and transfigured Kingdom of Heaven.

"...and I will give you even greater gifts than those you had from the start. And you shall know that I AM the Lord."

Ezekiel 36:11.

Our co-operation with God, by way of participation in the sacraments and provisions of His Church on earth, is central to our personal and collective healing [salvation] and re-creation [re-birth], as redeemed and joy-filled *Children of Light"* Luke 16:18; John 12:36; Ephesians 5:8; 1 Thessalonians 5:5. **Jesus confirms this when He says:** *"that My joy may be in you, and your joy may be made full and complete"* John 15:11.

The mix of purple and white, making the rose-pink colour of the candle, symbolises the [white] Light-presence of God, seeded within our soul since Baptism, and strengthened in Confirmation, rushing forth to connect with the royal [purple] sovereignty of Jesus Christ, by our Loving fidelity to His Divine Will. We partake in the joy of the Heavenly-minded shepherds, who represent the first faithful to be called [invited] to rejoice in the Ever-lasting Good News, in the mystery of Christmas.

Joy and rejoicing are prominent in today's readings, which continue to focus on the preaching of John the Baptist. Despite his many difficult words, like Jesus, John the Baptist's only intent was to shake man out of His cruel existence-ignorance, indifferentism, and self-destruction, for *"It is worse still, to be ignorant of your ignorance"* says St. Jerome.

The simple and humble shepherds fulfil the most fortunate office of the first chosen sheep whom Jesus Christ knows, and who are known to Him. Removed from the swell of cares, curiosities, and influences of the old world and upright, vigilant, and sincere [whole-hearted] in their longing for Christ's Coming, they represent the pure [clean and clear] of heart who will see God. For more deeply established in Him, and exalted above all things, they knew a freedom and promise in humble watchfulness [rooted in Truth] and graceful [grace-filled] simplicity of life, which guarded and preserved their integrity, and co-operation with higher meaning and ways. In no need of [without desire for] other earthly talents or possessions, it is right that they were first among those whom the Divine Child wished to be seen and adored by, for they were fit for the company of Heaven. We can imagine their amazement as the white brilliance of a heavenly cloud of joyous faces and harmonious voices, manifested around them bringing News of the birth of the Divine Child. Yet, pure in heart [Matthew 5:8] and ready in Spirit, Sacred Scripture tells us that they immediately accepted this astonishing message, and went with haste to the cave to worship Him [Luke 2:16]. Alive with and in God's own Light, that eclipses the 'worldly wise and clever' [Matthew 11:25], we can expect that they saw no strangeness in His swaddling clothes, and the humble abode of the cave. Gifted with steadfast confidence in His promise, the shepherds represent the faithful remnant of Israel, and the first true *"Children of Light"* Luke 16:18; John 12:36; Ephesians 5:8; 1 Thessalonians 5:5. They are the ones who walked as saints and flew with the angels; living and dying materially simple and Spiritually rich, in the lustrous Light of sanctifying grace.

> *"Who will ascend to the mountain of the Lord?*
> *And who will stand in His holy place?*
> *The innocent of hands and the clean of heart."*
>
> Psalm 24:3-4.

Together with the shepherds, celestial joy is our Father's divine purpose for us all. This joy is not the fleeting merriment of the flesh [carnal ego-self] or the old world which comes and goes, but the primordial Ever-freshness in our being, in union with God. It is supernatural rejoicing in the Ever-lasting Good News, brought about by, and in, Jesus Christ. **Contrasting with the gravity and instability of the *"old man"*; it is a deep, creative, and stable joy that transcends all time and circumstances. It is a Eucharistic joy that comes, and comes only, through a radical and extraordinary reversal of worldly values and temporal goals.**

Pope Paul VI draws our attention to the unfathomable celestial joys that dwell in Jesus Christ. Jesus knows that His Father Loves Him infinitely, and He wants us to come into the same realization [reality] by way of a *living* relationship with Him. Throughout His earthly life, He expresses joyful affirmation in all kinds of matters. From the joy of the sower and the harvester, and the shepherd who rediscovers His sheep; to the return of the prodigal son. From the joy of a marriage celebration; to the joy of the woman who has brought her child into the world. From the man who finds a hidden treasure in a field; to His joy in the little ones being given the revelation of the Kingdom, that remains hidden from the worldly 'wise and clever'; Jesus exults with joy in all things which point to higher Spiritual reality, and the restoration of Paradise.

Yet, Jesus greatest joy is to see us turn to Him with the trust and abandonment of children; accepting His Word and joyfully repenting [meaning *"turning back"* or *"coming back"* to God in Aramaic and Hebrew] to receive the healing [salvation], and deliverance promised. This celestial joy is conceived in thanksgiving and gratitude for all that God has done for us in Jesus Christ. It is a joy that lies in 'Poorness of Spirit'; in purity [cleanliness and clarity] of desire, that longs for the restoration of His Kingdom above all else.

> *"I delight to work in a soul.*
> *You see, I Love to do everything Myself,*
> *And from this soul, I ask only that she Loves Me."*
>
> Jesus speaks to Sr. Consolata Betrone.

The rejoicing of those who walk upright in the Light of the Spirit, is One with the rejoicing of the shepherds, for like them we know that because of the seal and pledge of our Baptism, we are Children of God [1 John 3:2] and Citizens of Heaven [Philippians 3:20]; Lights in the world [Matthew 5:14]; Servants of God [2 Corinthians 6:4] and Soldiers of Christ [2 Timothy 2:3]; empowered by God [Ephesians [6:10-11] as instruments for noble purposes [2 Timothy 2:20-21]. We are Children of Promise [Galatians 4:28]; beloved children of a paternal Father, who is in control of everything in the immutable Light of Eternity, regardless of circumstances and appearances on earth.

This rejoicing is nowhere better echoed than in the perennial rejoicing of the Blessed Virgin Mary, because she is full of God's own sanctifying grace, and divine purpose [Charity]. Raised above ordinary speech in her utter delight at being chosen for the supreme office of Mother of the Incarnate God, her song of Love, the Magnificat [Luke 1:46-55], extols her ecstatic joy, while also issues a most powerful battle cry for the glory of God. For in her perfect [whole and all-perfect] being, she realizes that through her Son-God, the kingdom of Satan [old world] will be overturned and destroyed, and the Kingdom of God re-established, within faithful and upright souls.

Joy and rejoicing, is man's only rational response to the Ever-lasting Good News of our Redemption and Sanctification. It is the character and radiance of a life lived in the bright increase of Heaven's Light. For the delight of God is the delight of man glorified in God, by the reinstatement of the fullness of His Light-presence [Kingdom] flowing within and through our souls.

> *"Rejoice always, pray without ceasing, give thanks in all things; for this is the [Divine] Will of God in Christ Jesus for you. Extinguish not the Spirit."*
>
> 1 Thessalonians 5:16-19.

Eternity is Ever-Now

The Angel Candle/ Candle of Love

Our working time is Now; i-dentity in the divine-human personhood of Jesus Christ; as salt and Light; individuality and personhood; daily vigilance and replenishment; in the care and friendship of the Angels.

"You are the Light of the world." aren't in darkness, that the day should overtake you like a thief. You are all Children of Light and children of the day...So then let's not sleep, as the rest do, but let's watch and be sober."

1 Thessalonians 5:4-6.

The **fourth candle** of Advent invites us to join in the melodious song of the Angelic hosts, in **Love and adoration** of our All-Good Creator and Father God. Uniting with these most pure and radiant beings of Light, we partake in a foretaste of the liturgy of the splendorous and Perfect City of Light; the New Jerusalem, towards which we journey [ascend] as temporary pilgrims on earth.

The wreath is now a complete ring of living Light, reminding us that our soul is created to be a beautiful orb of Light, connected by avenues of sanctifying grace to the Light-union of the Most Holy Trinity, in a continuous circle of giving and receiving. We realize that **to be full of Light, is to be *'full of Life'* in Jesus Christ, by way of His living within and through our souls.** This Life, bright within the flow of God's Light, is the Life of original glory [blissful magnificence] which came before original sin, and is to share in with God, the Life of holy [whole and all-perfect] Love in His Divine Will. It is the Life which fulfils the mystery of Christmas: *"Emmanuel: God-with-us"* Old Testament: Isaiah 7:14; 8:8-10 and New Testament: Matthew 1:21-23; John 1:14; 14:8-11; Colossians 2:9.

In beholding the flaming ring-fire of the Advent Wreath, we are stirred up to know the time. It is no longer the time of ignorance and of waiting in the Old Testament, but the time of knowing and of full provision. It is the acceptable time and it is working time, and everything is expected of us. It is high time to be awake and responsible, because Jesus Christ, the [Three-in-One] Mystical Sun has long since risen, and is shining directly upon us. During His earthly Lifetime, Jesus referred to the Kingdom more than one hundred times [particularly in the Gospels of Matthew and Luke]; the passionate urgency of His messages about its immediacy, bearing striking similarity to John the Baptist. *"Repent, for the Kingdom of Heaven is at hand!"* Matthew 3:2, urged John the Baptist, while Jesus warns us to *"Repent and believe in the Good News"* Mark 1:15" for *"unless you repent, you will all perish…"* Luke 13:5.

Our requirement to **recognize our time of golden harvest**, is echoed again in John 4:35-36, where Jesus advises His disciples to open their eyes and see that the fields are *already* shining for the harvest. By setting to work Now, the reward, which is the fruit of Eternal Life, is [only] available Now. Any idea of time between sowing and reward has disappeared, because as baptised children of God, the Light-seed of Eternal Life is planted within our being [Ecclesiastes 3:11]. This seed, just like a tiny human embryo, holds the fullness of being, and longing to grow and flourish towards fullness of Life [Love, Truth] and belonging. **The sowing; the free giving of our consent [our authentic "Fiat"], to conceive and birth Jesus Christ within and through our being while on earth, is the reaping of the victory of Eternal Life in Him.** This is *"so that both he who sows, and he who reaps may rejoice together"* John 4:36. In every moment of every day, we are called [invited] to come to terms with our own sacredness, as children of the Kingdom; to live as seed and leaven; as *"the salt of the earth…[and]…the Light of the world"* Matthew 5:13,14; ever-preserved in Truth, and exposing and overcoming the deeds of darkness by contrast [Ephesians 5:11-14] in a world that *"groans and travails in pain"* Romans 8:22 and *"waits with eager expectation, for the children of God to be revealed"* Romans 8:19.

> *"Salt is good: but if the salt has become bland,*
> *with what will you season it? Have salt in yourselves,*
> *and have peace among yourselves."*
>
> Mark 9:50.

This return to the Life of the Kingdom, can come in no other way than man's realization that **who we truly are, is not something we own or manifest individually, but is our authentic divine-human personhood, received from God in Jesus Christ, through the Life of sanctifying grace.** This means knowledge *and* Love of our Spiritualized person [i-dentity] in the Divine-Human Person [I-dentity] of God, in Jesus Christ, who reveals Truth to us, by birthing in and through us. This maturation into Life-giving wholeness [holiness and all-perfection] in Jesus Christ [Ephesians 2:4-5] in earthly time, is our co-operation with and participation in the Ever-present relationship of Love in the Divine Will, that is the One Light-community and family of the Kingdom of Heaven. It is the Eternal Now, which is and ever will be, the One [remaining] reality, when every transitory self-love and evil is obliterated, and space, time, and seasons converge together, in the Heavenly realm. See 'I-dentity' in Useful Terms.

> *"...whatever a man sows, that he will also reap.*
> *For he who sows to his own flesh will from the flesh*
> *reap corruption. But he who sows to the Spirit,*
> *will from the Spirit reap Eternal Life."*
>
> Galatians 6:8.

Sincere and desirous souls who rush to collect the harvest; who courageously take up their death-defying Cross, and submit to the All-purging and transfiguring fire of the Spirit [Matthew 19:12], will be rewarded [according to their strength of fidelity], with the All-healing blessedness of Eternal Life. Moreover, as the soul dies to itself and is re-created [re-birthed] in Jesus Christ's Mystical Body, the Cross will become its joy, safeguard, and release [freedom]. For the interior eye of the Spirit [Spiritual intellect] will become brightened, and each step will be lifted and quickened by grace, as it penetrates the Heart [Cosmic Heart's Desire] of God, and is soaked in the riches of His Light-bearing and boundless ways. *"For to me, to live is Christ and to die is gain"* says St. Paul [Philippians 1:21]. Grace sought for daily needs [daily bread] will keep the inner lamp of the spirit alight for today, and placed appropriately in the window of the soul, will glorify God's work [Matthew 5:16], while comforting and guiding others along the pilgrim way. And because tomorrow means *"things depart" or "pass away"* [in Aramaic], daily vigilance and commitment to the replenishment [renewal] of grace must continue in a circle of giving and receiving [Matthew 25:1-13]. *"For [we] do not know the day nor the hour"* Matthew 25:13 when we will be required to resist evil, or be called out of this world.

> *"Each day that goes by quietly and swiftly, our soul is being drawn towards Eternity."*
>
> Fr. Frederick Faber.

This Sunday's 'Angel Candle' reminds us that the Angels assist us greatly in our endeavour to come back to *real Life and purpose* in Jesus Christ. Perfectly filled with the Light-fire of God's own Love, they are ever employed in Loving divine service towards us, during our pilgrim days on earth. They eagerly assist and defend us, and ever encourage us to turn assuredly towards the purifying, warming, and illuminating effects of the Cosmic [Divine] Sun [Jesus Christ], whose radiance brightens the whole world. For [only] in sharing in these Life-giving rays, we too are rendered celestial; growing, rising, and rejoicing in our absorption in God, as candlelight is absorbed in the natural sun, while still existing of itself. We thank God for the providential care of His ministering Angels throughout our earthly life.

Let us then endeavour to follow the example of the great saints and mystics of the Church, who benefitted greatly from their familiarity with the Angels. Let us confidently call upon them [most particularly our Guardian Angels], in grateful awareness that they desire nothing more, than to offer us their most powerful and divinely wise, maternal friendship, guidance and protection.

> *"Call to mind his presence very often.*
> *We need to fix our Spiritual gaze upon him.*
> *Thank him and pray to him… Respect him.*
> *You must always be afraid to offend the purity of his gaze!"*
>
> St. Padre Pio speaking of our Guardian Angels.

Readings prepare us more immediately for the feast of the Nativity, by telling of the preceding events; including the dreams of Joseph [Year A], the Annunciation [Year B], and the Visitation of Mary to her cousin Elizabeth [Year C]. We see Mary and Joseph's faith and unflinching co-operation with and participation in God as *"Children of Light"* Luke 16:18; John 12:36; Ephesians 5:8; 1 Thessalonians 5:5, in the most humanly inexplicable, yet divinely arranged circumstances.

Light-fire & Victory in Jesus Christ

End of Advent & Beginning of Christmas - The Christ Candle

The glory-circle of the Kingdom; God dwells in Light-fire; the human soul – an arena of Spiritual fire and battle; the circling sword of Truth; consumed in Light or in darkness; infinite degrees of glory, freedom, and bliss.

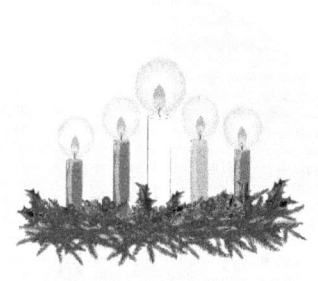

"For it was fitting that we should have such a High Priest: holy, innocent, undefiled, set apart from sinners, and exalted higher than the Heavens."

Hebrews 7:26.

The **fifth and final crowning candle** of Advent is placed in the middle of the wreath, and is lit on Christmas Day. This larger white candle is 'The Christ Candle', and represents **pure Light and victory.**

In the energised fullness of now all-blazing Light-circle, is represented the vigour and magnetism of the Universe, which turns around its rooted centre; the exalted Light of Jesus Christ, in the Light-union of the Most Holy Trinity. In it, is represented the ardour and superabundance of their dynamic relationship of Love in the Divine Will, at the heart of creation. An inexhaustible fount of energies, from which issues an Ever-verdant and endless bounty of potentialities and possibilities [Luke 1:37] to delight the heart of man.

We rejoice that this once incomprehensible and inaccessible Light, infinitely brighter than the flaming fire of the natural sun, has become accessible to us through the astonishing free gift of *real Life and purpose* in Jesus Christ. We rejoice because we know that in its consummate glory-circle, there will be no need of candlelight or of sunlight, nor will Heaven's gates ever be closed, in fear of evil

[Revelation 21:25; Isaiah 60:11]. For the inextinguishable Light of the One Eternal Day [the New Jerusalem], will be the majestic and brilliant Ever-living Light of Jesus Christ; the radiant Three-in-One Divine Sun [Revelation 21:23; Isaiah 24:23; 60:19,20], and the immutable centre of being of all the redeemed *"Children of Light"* Luke 16:18; John 12:36; Ephesians 5:8; 1 Thessalonians 5:5.

> *"He is the image of the invisible God, the Firstborn of all creation. All things have been created through Him, and for Him. He is before all things, and in Him all things are held together."*
>
> Colossians 1:15-17.

As we behold the burning ring of living Light, we are reminded that the Light of God is a consuming fire [Hebrews 12:29]. That in the Spiritual realm and the material [earthly] realm, fire burns on all sides.

- In the Spiritual Realm, Light is the living fire of Love-union between our soul and God. It is the intense primordial Passion of God in Jesus Christ, consumed for our sins, in the Light-fire of His own highest Love, operating in His Divine Will. This unearthly fire tests, proves and purifies; it judges and separates Light [good] and darkness [evil] in the earthly realm. Sacred Scripture tells us that God's throne is ablaze with fire, and fire flows out from it [Daniel 7:9-10], while with *"eyes like flaming fire"* Revelations 2:18 [19:12], Jesus Christ will return as our Just Judge. Sacred Scripture also associates fire with the Holy Spirit, and refers not infrequently to the fire of Hell.

- In the material [earthly] realm, fire is both above us and beneath us, both serving and destroying life on earth. The earth's molten core is about as hot as the surface of the natural sun, both fuelled by the burning up of radioactive particles of rock matter. More energy falls from the natural sun [the figure for the Three-in-One Divine Sun] in one hour, than is used by the entire world in one year.

Yet, it is in the human being that the primordial energizing fire of the Universe is centred. **For the human soul is an arena of Spiritual fire and battle, to be consummated in God [in Eternal Life] by the living Light-fire of the Holy Spirit, or by Satan [in Eternal death] in the dark fire of evil; of ungodly passions and appetites.** Church saints and mystics of the Church explain that the Light part of this Spiritual fire is that which burns, purifies, and illuminates the *"old man"*, and translates into the *unburning* fire of Heaven [Catechism 1023-1029], and the dark part is the *burning* Spiritual fire of Hell [Catechism 1033-1037]. All man's works on earth will be tested and revealed by fire to determine what kind it is, and therefore the fate of the soul [1 Corinthians 3:13-17]. Souls who are not completely self-damned, but who are yet unfit for Heaven, must be purified [by degrees] in the Spiritual fire of Purgatory [Catechism 1030-1032]. We are advised that **this purgatorial fire is not as sanctifying as the fire of Love offered to us on earth,** but is experienced in its Spiritual intensity, according to the condition of the soul, and the height of sanctity [spirit-bearing union] to which it was called [invited]. Such is the intensity of these unearthly Spiritual fires, that earthly fire may be considered painted fire by comparison. And so, in whatever state we find ourselves, Spiritual fire is unavoidable because God dwells in Light-fire, and nothing unclean will find its way in [Revelation 21:27]. When our appointed time on earth is over, and the earthen jar of our body returns to the ground, our souls standing in its white heat will be revealed. Presenting naked, alone and in silence, every last thing inside our soul, right down to the darkest hollows of hidden thoughts and desires will be called out, as our innermost allegiance to God [in Jesus Christ] or to Satan, is revealed [Luke 8:17 and 1 Corinthians 4:5].

> *"There is no creature that is hidden from His sight, but all things are naked and laid open before the eyes of Him to whom we must give an account."*
>
> Hebrews 4:13.

And while the bliss of Heaven's Light may be first experienced when the soul separates from the body, this is no assurance of its final destination. Rather, upon confirmation of its standing in this Light [of Truth], the spirits of Light or of darkness who have been the soul's companions during life, come to lead it away to its final sentence. Faithful souls who whole-heartedly abandoned back [consented] to the cleansing, proving, and illuminating Light-fire of God's Spirit while on earth, will find this fire manifesting to them as an *unburning* energy, which is the dazzling Light of Heaven. Those found capable of further cleansing will pass through the purifying Spiritual fire of Purgatory [in varying degrees] according to the height of Spiritual union [sanctity] to which they were called [invited]. While rebellious and remorseless souls, who refused to co-operate with and participate in God [Truth, Life and Love] in any measure, being led instead by the spirit of Satan, will collapse into the [Light-vacant] dark Hell-fire of their own insatiable, ungodly desires. This *burning* fire, will manifest as an unyielding and all-pervading tormenting power in the lost soul, where it will remain consumed but unconsumed, in the godless abode of evil spirits and lost souls, in and for all Eternity.

> "...the eyes of the Lord are much brighter than the sun, keeping watch over all the ways of men...and gazing into the hearts of men, even to the most hidden parts."
>
> Sirach 23:19.

We can be certain that the circling sword of Truth, which protects Love's Paradise, will admit no-one directly, but the purest and most refined Spirit brides and Spirit brides-men; the most faithful sons and daughters of the Father; brothers and sisters of the Lamb; and spouses of the Holy Spirit, who in prayer and penance, and in thanksgiving and gratitude, zealously reaped the Light of God's burning Love in their being, in the waiting and vigils of their earthly lifetime. Courageously taking up their Cross and walking upright in Jesus Christ on earth, there can be no condemnation for them [Romans 8:1-4], for they are the holy [whole and all-perfect] souls, arrayed in iridescent purity and simplicity, from whom mortal death cannot steal.

Such is the difference in degrees of glory which admits the soul to the treasury of Heaven, that several Church saints [such as St. Teresa of Avila, St. Francis of Borgia, and St. Faustina] declared their willingness to bear any earthly suffering, or burn in the purifying Spiritual flames of Purgatory until the Day of Judgement [Catechism 1038-1040], but to gain one more degree of Light-union. For in speaking of the many rooms in His Father's house [John 14:2], Jesus spoke of higher dimensions of Light-consciousness [Light-freedom and bliss], in the infinite hierarchy of fields, that is the Kingdom of Heaven.

The fully alight Advent wreath represents the reality, that life on earth is a continuous consummation of our soul in Light or in darkness; arising in our every act [of thought, word, and deed] in fidelity to, or in opposition to Truth [Life and Love]. And as the candles are consumed [sacrificed] quietly and gently in the light, as Jesus Christ was consumed [sacrificed] in the Light, so too, those who would be called *"Children of Light"* Luke 16:18; John 12:36; Ephesians 5:8; 1 Thessalonians 5:5, must be calmly consumed as *living* flames, in the Light of Love's own fire. For to be absorbed in the nuptial Light-ring of the Homeland, is to become the living Light on earth, in Oneness with Jesus Christ who is our true centre, and the axis on whom the Universe turns.

> *"The soul's only true purpose,*
> *is to realize the Divine Ideal within;*
> *as far as it is capable."*
>
> Blessed Dina Belanger.

The Alpha and the Omega

The Almightiness of our Creator and Father God; no-thing apart from Him, but the realm of perpetual death [Hell]; the primacy of divine wisdom; faith, holy fear, and wisdom; Person, Personal, Personhood - the Ever-dynamic relational Being of God; religion personified in Jesus Christ; knowing "Abba, Father"; Lion-Lamb - the seemingly paradoxical Personhood of Jesus Christ.

"It is done! I am the Alpha and the Omega, the Beginning, and the End. To those who thirst, I will give freely from the fountain of the Water of Life."

Revelation 21:6.

There is only God, and there is only *real Life and purpose* [Eternal Life] in Him. Appearing in both the Old [Isaiah] and New Testaments, these hallowed phrases announce God's Self-existence; His sovereign majesty and His free invitation to [Eternal] Life. A metaphor for God's Almightiness and Ever-livingness, the first and last letters of the Greek alphabet [Revelation 1:8; 21:6; 22:13], confirm the All-ness of His Being, and His presence for all time. God is the First and Last; the First Cause, and the Cause of Causes. He is the Author and Finisher [Hebrews 2:10; 12:2] of all created things; the cause and source of His existence in Himself, while all created things have their cause and source in Him. Ever-old and Ever-new, and without beginning or end, everything exists together in Him, with Perfect [Whole and All-Perfect] continuity of meaning [Truth]. Forever awake and forever vital, in both time and in Eternity, He is the Supreme and Ever-lasting *"I AM WHO I AM"* **Exodus 3:14**; the owner and conserver, and the ultimate measure and purpose of all creation, especially of our human person.

God's Self-revealed Names for Himself, disclose that all power and glory [blissful magnificence] belong to Him alone. He is the Ever-creative divine Artist and Architect, who created the Universe out of His own divine fecundity, and who keeps it in motion. We exist, because His omnipotence brought us into existence, and sustains our every life-breath in His Love and Divine Will. He is the core of our being, without whom we would cease to exist. Outside the fields of His Light-Being, there is nothing but darkness and chaos; the destructive voids of the soul's own unquenchable passions and ungodly desires, and the dark-fire of the demonic realm [of Hell], that exists in perpetual death.

Sacred Scripture tells us that God is Spirit and action; that He creates out of chaos [Genesis 1] with infinite wisdom, and according to the Blueprint of His own divine order [Job 38:4-11]. **Wisdom is the first of God's prerogatives,** *"the artisan of all things"* **Wisdom 7:21, and is hidden and present in all His creation**. So vital and precious is His wisdom to the prudent operation of human beings, that it was personified in the Old Testament, promising Eternal Life, and prosperity to those who embrace her [Proverbs 3:13-20]. *"She is a Tree of Life to those who lay hold of her"* says Proverbs 3:18. Those who conceive divine wisdom [are open to] discover divine knowledge and understanding, which are the same attributes that characterize how God created the triune Universe [of space, time, and matter]. *"The fear of the Lord is the beginning of wisdom"* says Psalm 110 (111):10. **Faith draws divine wisdom and divine wisdom draws faith**, co-essentially guiding and instructing the [willing] soul in godly ways. Unpolluted, subtle, and invulnerable; penetrating all things and passing into holy souls; evil does not prevail against divine wisdom [Wisdom 7:22,24,27,30].

> *"For God loves nothing as much as one who dwells with wisdom."*
>
> Wisdom 7:28.

Sacred Scripture tells us that holy fear and humility [Proverbs 11:2] equip the soul to listen to, and co-operate with God in his power and activity; discerning His Divine Will, and ways which are not our will and ways [Isaiah 55:8]. In this work, in Jesus Christ who is *"the power and the wisdom of God"* 1 Corinthians 1:24, **God selects what is considered foolish and weak by human standards, to shame the** *'worldly wise and clever'* [the seemingly knowing, cunning, and superior]; the unwise and the unteachable, whose ways of thinking, perceiving, and measuring are empty and foolish before Him [1 Corinthians 3:19-20].

"When the wise is instructed, he receives knowledge."
Proverbs 21:11.

God's unearthly ways, confirm that the ideas, ideals, wisdom and works of the flesh [carnal ego-self], and the old world, have nothing to boast of in His presence [1 Corinthians 27- 30]. Our fear of Him is holy [wholesome] fear. It is heightened awareness and awe of Him, and alertness to Him, borne out of the utmost reverence for who He is as a Father, and also as the supreme Eternal Being who abides in Truth. It is awareness of our obligation to be in right relationship with Him, on His terms [in His Love and Divine Will], for the sake of our Good-being [and God-being, John 10:34]; for the abolition of the old world, and the works of evil, and the re-instatement of His royal Kingdom.

*"For the foolishness of God is wiser than men,
and the weakness of God is stronger than men."*
1 Corinthians 1:25.

God is not something, but He is someone. He is the unchallengeable *"Father of Lights, with whom there is no change, nor any shadow of alteration"* James 1:17 [Malachi 3:6]. **This Name, and two of the most recognizable Names for Him in the Old Testament;** *"The Living God"* 1 Samuel 17:26 **and** *"The Most High"* Daniel 4:34, **speak of the primacy,** authority, and vitalness of His Eternal Personhood. Yet, while every Name, attribute and designation attributed to Him, point to His immensity, immeasurability and transcendent nature, no Name can adequately express the pure Substance-Essence and actuality of All that God is.

In the mystery of His Being, God is alone, but He is not alone. He is a Triune [Three-Part] Personhood, living in the Light-community [Light-relationship] of the distinct, and yet Perfectly [Wholly and All-Perfectly] united, Divine Persons of the Father, the Son, and the Holy Spirit. In an analogy of the sun, St. Cyril describes our Creator Father as the Generator [Source]; the Son Redeemer as the Light [of Truth, Love, and Life]; and the Holy Spirit Sanctifier as the burning Heat [Purifier and Illuminator], operating as distinct Persons, and yet One indivisible Divine Sun, in a dynamic relationship of Love in the Divine Will. **The Ever-dynamic, relational Personhood of God, confirms that *human personhood is not an experience of individual selfhood*, but an experience of relationship [community] in Love-union with the Most Holy Trinity, and with all that is absorbed in its Light-circle.**

God is our true and Loving Parent. He created us out of Love [Charity], because He is Love [Charity], and because He wants to be Loved by us [with His own purest Love] in return [Hebrews 2:10]. **"*God is Charity*" says 1 John 4:8,16.** In and above all His creation, He continuously dispenses Himself into the tripartite human person [of body, soul, and spirit], originally made in His own similitude [Genesis 1:26-27]. As a Father, who in the beginning personally approaches Adam calling out: *"where are you?"* Genesis 3:9, He is intimately personal and involved in every aspect of our being, which continuously issues from His hand. **No other person or thing, is capable of Loving us as God does, or deserves the Love and trust that we should place in Him.** For while we call Him our Father, His Whole-Hearted maternal care and tenderness towards His children, is immeasurably greater than that of a nursing or expectant mother [Isaiah 49:15]. Even the exact number of hairs on our head are known to Him [Matthew 10:30; Luke 12:7]. Despite the wickedness [evil and ungodliness] of man that *grieved*

Him in His Heart" Genesis 6:6, His One Cosmic Heart's Desire [Divine Will], is for the return of His estranged child's heart's desire [human will], that He may exchange our nothing-ness for the Paradise that moves within us.

> *"How can I give you up, Ephraim?*
> *How can I hand you over, Israel?...*
> *My heart is turned within Me."*
>
> Hosea 11:8.

God is also beyond personal. He is absolute and transcendent Truth and those known to Him on the Day of Judgement, will be those who abide in immutable Truth, which is the Wholeness [Holiness and All-Perfection] of His Supreme Being. Man's freedom to Love God in His own [unsentimental] Love and Divine Will, allows him in the absolute sense, to become that which he gives himself to.

Sacred Scripture tells us that Jesus alone knows God intimately as His Father. *"…no one knows the Son except the Father, nor does anyone know the Father except the Son, and those to whom the Son is willing to reveal Him."* Matthew 11:27. In three passages of Sacred Scripture, Jesus uses the familiar and affectionate Aramaic word *"Abba"*, meaning *"Beloved"*, followed with the word Father, emphasizing the complete Love, trust, abandonment, and reverence, that characterizes intimacy of relationship with His, and our Father God. He addresses the Father as *"Abba, Father"* Mark 14:36, in His intensely lonely and terrifying vigil in the garden of Gethsemane, while *"Abba, Father"* is also mentioned in Romans 8:15 and in Galatians 4:6, in relation to the Holy Spirit's work of our adoption through suffering and glorification. A mysterious paradox that alone makes us children and heirs, with and in Jesus Christ. For it is by way of Jesus Christ, in unchangeable Oneness with the Father [Hebrews 13:8], that we too are called to the privilege of entering into an intimate and liberating experience of God as *"Abba, Father"*. This is directly apparent in Sacred Scripture, where Jesus says: *"I AM the*

Way and the Truth and the Life. No-one comes to the Father, except through Me" John 14:6. In the book of Revelation, reference to God as the Alpha and the Omega points especially to the Son, as the One who came, and who is to come again, to pronounce Final Judgement on the living [Eternally alive], and on the dead [Eternally dead].

> *"Don't be afraid. I AM the First and the Last,*
> *and the Living One. I was dead, and behold,*
> *I AM alive forever and ever. Amen.*
> *I have the keys of Death and of Hades [Hell]."*
>
> Revelation 1:17-18.

In Jesus Christ, God our Father approaches us, and expresses His relationship with us, as a Person, embodied in the fullness of the Cosmic Personhood of Jesus Christ. Jesus confirms this when He says to His disciples *"whoever sees Me, also sees the Father"* John 14:9. Jesus always speaks to us personally, confirming the Father's zealous interest in every aspect of our lives, and His One Heart's Desire that we too come to experience him as *"Abba, Father"*; not as dutiful or reluctant slaves, but as divinely wise and Loving children who trust in Him. His upward call [invitation], to us to return to the Life of the Kingdom, is a personal call to enter into a living, joyous relationship with Him, and with all His people, living creatures and creation in Him.

> *"In the beginning was the Word,*
> *and the Word was with God, and the Word was God."*
>
> John 1:1.

In all that is written in Sacred Scripture about who God is, the above opening lines of the Gospel of John, are perhaps among most powerful and illuminating lines about His I-dentity, as revealed in

Jesus Christ. The Greek term that has been translated as *"Word"* in this verse is *"Logos"*, which carries the sense of the fullness of the Ever-living Light-Being of God. **An ancient Greek translation of the word *"Logos"* [Word], adds further luminosity, by identifying Jesus Christ as *relationship personified*; the unbroken continuity between God and man, and man and God.** Originating in the two Greek words *"dia"* meaning *"through"* or *"by way of"* and *"logos"* meaning *"relationship"*, we recognize that our restoration and re-admittance to Paradise, is *"through relationship"* with the Father, manifested in the Son, Jesus Christ. **Jesus Christ, in His Perfect [Whole and All-Perfecting] Divine-Human Personhood, is the *living* embodiment of religion. From the Latin word *"religio"* meaning *"bind back"*, He is our *living* relationship with, and way back to the Father, and the Spiritual state of the Kingdom [John 14:6], in the Life-breath of the Holy Spirit.** Going out from the Father and returning to Him in the Holy Spirit as in a circle, while enclosing the entire Universe within Himself, Jesus Christ is the re-integration [re-centring] and re-creation [re-birth] of our uniqueness of being, in the Life [Love and Divine Will] of the Most Holy Trinity. See 'Religion' in Useful Terms.

> *"The life of the body, is the soul;*
> *the Life of the soul, is Christ."*
>
> St. Anthony of Padua.

To know and Love Jesus Christ as He is, is to know and Love God our Father as He is, and as He wants to be known. It is to know ourselves as we really are [and can ever be known] in Him. It is the restoration of our relationship with all God's faithful people, and His living creatures and creation, which can only be known and understood in relationship with [within and through] Him. For to God belongs the absolute right of defining and determining the relationship that must subsist between man and God; between man and other persons; and all His living creatures and creation. **His Kingdom cannot be received gratis; nor can it be taken by force, or by stealth.** It can only be about honouring fidelity [from the Latin word *"fides"*, meaning *"faith"*] to Jesus Christ, as the complete manifestation of God [God-being, John 10:34] and relationship. Our personal call [invitation] to come follow Him [Matthew 4:19], is a call to drink our portion from the same cup of bitterness and suffering from which He first drank, and drank to the very dregs. This is the only prepared and acceptable way to the authentic Light-freedom of Eternal Life, in the primordial power of the Holy Spirit.

> *"Are you able to drink the cup that I am about to drink,*
> *and be baptised with the baptism [of fire],*
> *that I am baptised with?"*
>
> Matthew 20:22 [and Mark 10:38].

Sacred Scripture tells us much about the seemingly paradoxical Personhood of Jesus Christ, perhaps best portrayed in two primary aspects of His omnipotent nature; the Lion-Lamb of the tribe of Judah [Revelation 5]. For while a Lamb is innocent, gentle, playful, and beguiling, and has no form of defence; a Lion is mighty and majestic, fiery, fearless, and fearsome, and is equipped with powerful physical features, and exceptional night vision. **As a Lamb, Jesus was slain [sacrificed], and as a Lion, He conquered [was Resurrected]. As a Lamb, He symbolises Divine Mercy and as a Lion, He symbolises Divine Justice.** Throughout the Gospels, the fullness of His enigmatic Personhood is revealed. Primarily, He is a God-man on a divine mission; always intentional and always Whole-Hearted. Absolutely free of self-love, and Perfectly [Wholly and All-Perfectly] united to the Father in Substance [Essence] and in Energies [Action], He is the fullness of Light-Being, which is Eternal Life. In His Sunlight-Presence, He is brilliant and magnetic, most filial, and approachable, and humble and kind. He is supremely wise, divinely patient, and good-humoured and playful. He is also disruptively honest, and startlingly direct. He heals, He consoles, and He rebukes, sometimes severely. He makes much use of questions and intrigue. There is no relativism, nor is there any people-pleasing, ego-flattery or attempts to ingratiate

Himself for the sake of social acceptability and 'friendship' that rails against Truth, because *He is Truth*. He does not seek out frivolity, nor indulge in gross humour that mocks and diverts attention from the Life and death predicament of man. There is no self-referencing, but **He refers everything [All glory and honour] to the Eternal Father, with whom He is Ever-Now One.**

Continually on the receiving end of the most gross insults, abuses, and mockeries from His enemies [e.g., Matthew 9:24; Mark 5:40; Luke 8:53], He remains steadfast and unmoved in His mission of Love and Redemption. Reproving the works of self-love, existence-ignorance and evil, under the guise of 'good', He rebukes outward piety and charitable practices, for the sake of earthly esteem and reward. He calls out the outward pious culture of the Pharisees, with their conceited knowledge arrogance, teachings, clothing, and long prayers and solemnities, that mask hollow hearts which are far from Him, and their neighbour. Yet, He also encourages those who are yet to believe in Him; for example, commending the wisdom of God in the religious leader [Mark 12:32-34], who realized that Love [*"Agape"*] matters more to God than all Love-empty sacrifices and offerings.

> *"I AM more simple than you.*
> *Yes, I the Eternal wisdom."*
>
> Jesus speaks to Sr. Mary of the Holy Trinity.

Working as a carpenter, and living in a little house in Nazareth with Mary and Joseph, He is of innocent appetites [desires] and simple ways. He has no interest in material gains, honours, or rewards; or cultural cues, trends, fashions, or influences, which degrade and mock man, and expire in time. Warm and inviting, He is always generous in giving of His time to people, because He Loves them in the fullness of *"Agape"* [Charity]. Leaning his most pure and piercing gaze within them, and instructing them with the most enigmatic voice and ways, the worst of sinners ran to Him with genuine humility, and a confidence in something much greater than they had dared dream of.

Speaking simply the way of higher Life in the Spirit, there is no worldly cleverness that visits confounding human words, concepts and debates on others, and casts essential Truth into obscurity. When He speaks in parable and metaphor, it is so that those who have sufficient dominion over themselves, and desire and strength for Truth, can penetrate the profound mysteries of Divine Life by way of the infused Spiritual intellect [Matthew 13:10-17]. Always positive and purposeful [reversing the Old Testament golden rule *"do not onto others"* Tobit 4:15 to *"do onto others"* Matthew 7:12, Luke 6:31], **He neither manipulates nor forces anyone to believe in Him or to do anything; rather, He asks:** *"What do you want Me to do for you"* **Matthew 20:32;** *"Do you want to be healed?"* **John 5:6.** People can come or go in the freedom of their own human will [heart's desire] which flows from the Father's omnipotence. Never is He found campaigning or fighting at the level of the flesh [carnal ego-self] and the old world, to win a battle for the soul that is primarily Spiritual. Sacred Scripture tells us that He walked along dirt roads, and often went off to pray and preach in wild and open places; rather than in perfectly staged and manicured gardens, or grandiose buildings of His time. Involvement in the world was balanced with periods of solitude and recollection to invigorate His Spirit. Close to the end of His earthly Life, His Love and pain for the predicament of man, overflows into tears at the death of Lazarus [John 11:35; Luke 19:41; Hebrews 5:7-9].

> *"It was to the wildest part of the Garden of Olives that Jesus went to pray."*
>
> Blessed Anne Catherine Emmerich.

After His Resurrection, He is to be seen walking casually along the lapping waters of the shoreline, by the sea of Tiberias, embodying a Plan of *real Life and purpose* infinitely deeper than the life yet known to the fishermen [His apostles], of whom He enquires about their day's catch *"Children, have you any fish?"* John 21:5. For while the apostles fishing represents their work of bringing souls into His

Church, it also represents the infinite difference between natural life on earth, and the glory [blissful magnificence] of hallowed reality. It symbolises man's life, which is largely lived at, or close to the shoreline, dipping his toes into the infinite ocean of God's Love and Divine Will, that would bathe and flood his soul with the fullness of supernatural Light and Life. There is no grandiosity nor solemnity; no self-righteousness nor cloying sweetness, as Jesus makes His enquiry about the day's catch. Rather, there is complete ordinariness, intrigue, and playfulness, as He who is the Fountainhead of Life and Wellspring of *"Living Water"* John 4:10; 7:38, tells them where to cast their nets to improve their catch. In taking His advice, they find their nets so full of large fish, that all their strength is needed to pull them back in. We can only be astonished that this man walking casually along the shoreline is Almighty God as man; the same God-man who conquered all evil and mortal death, by ransoming Himself for all mankind in the greatest, and most unimaginable battle of the entire Cosmos. Yet, this *is* the second person of the Most Holy Trinity, who sits at the right hand of the Father, and who *"reflects the glory of God, and bears the fullness of His Being, upholding all creation by the word of His power"* Hebrews 1:3. **This *is* God as man; the Cosmic Divine-Human Personhood in its fullest and most authentically freest form.**

> *"The Godhead is a source from which all things do rush.*
> *And then return to it. An ocean it is thus."*
>
> Angelus Silesius.

In His All-giving Self-sacrifice, Jesus demonstrates to us that All-unity with our Life-source, is our One true and honest i-dentity. It is the only and ultimate purpose of our being, and the original and deepest longing of our soul, whether we consciously realize it or not. This return to relationship with the Father in Him, in the Life-breath of the Holy Spirit, is not an experience of the individual ego-self, but of God living in us, as us, and us living in Him, as unique expressions of ourselves in Him. It is our participation in, and relationship with, the shared glory [blissful magnificence] of Eternal Life.

"This is My beloved Son... listen to Him."

Matthew 17:5 and Luke 9:35.

The opening lines in this Chapter, which are Jesus last words on the Cross, *"It is done* [complete, consummated or finished]*"* appear three times in Sacred Scripture [John 19:30; Revelation 16:17 and Revelation 21:6]. The first statement of *"finishing"* was on the Cross, where He identified Himself as the Pascal Lamb; the second, at *"the end of the [present] times"* [Revelation 16], at the fulfilment of God's Holy and Just anger; and the third at *"the [final] end of time"* [Revelation 20:7-15; 21], when He creates the new [Ever-new] and transfigured Heaven and earth. For in Jesus Christ's Life, Passion, Death, and Resurrection, the scales of Divine Mercy and Divine Justice have been satisfied [equalized] and the Godhead has been 'freed' for all Eternity. The work of Redemption is done, and the work of Sanctification has begun. There is nothing for man to do, but wake up, give thanks, and co-operate with and participate in God, whose power working in and through us, can do infinitely more than we can dare ask for or imagine [Ephesians 3:21].

"I AM the Light of Lights: Where it penetrates there will be Life, bread, and happiness."

'God the Father speaks to His children.'
[Mother Eugenia Elisabetta Ravasio].

The Blessed Virgin Mary

Full of Light and Life - the unparalleled exemplar of the created human person; operating from a place of presence; calling Heaven to earth; the Mother of all created life; higher beauty; the paradox of barrenness and fertility; Light-purity and Eternal youthfulness; the soul's wedding garment; blessed life states and the virgin in the soul; *"chosen"* - only God knows the heart; God's ways are not our ways.

"The Angel said to her, "Rejoice, you highly favoured one! The Lord is with you. Blessed are you among women!""

Luke 1:28.

In the season of Advent, the Blessed Virgin Mary is celebrated in an exemplary way, on the feast of her Immaculate Conception. On this first beautiful and important feast day, and Holyday of obligation of the ecclesiastical year, we honour Mary as the most favoured human person ever created by God; the marvellous flower that sprung out from the desert of Israel.

Conceived **pure, noble, and free from original sin** to St. Anne and St. Joachim, Mary is full of sanctifying grace and hallowed reality. Uniquely and perfectly preserved from original sin by the merits of her Son-God, she is full of divine purpose, luminous intelligence, and celestial refinement. She is the living embodiment of the fundamental themes in the Old and the New Testaments; the daughter of Zion and the New Ark of the Covenant. Living in the fullness [and fulfilment] of desire for God [alone], in a state of perfect [whole and all-perfect] synergy with the Holy Spirit, she is the radiant and transfigured New Eve, who in the excellence of her humility [the mother of all virtues], meekness [positive consent or assent, gentleness and balance in

Aramaic and Hebrew], and self-emptying, infinitely surpassed the original Eve, to make possible the most amazing revelation of God's own humility, and Oneness with fallen man.

In the feast of the Immaculate Conception, we celebrate the absolute and prodigious work of God in raising the Blessed Virgin Mary to the highest heights of divinely creative service and glory [blissful magnificence] possible for a created human being. Conceived in the most immense outpouring of the Most Holy Trinity, and living in the complete [spirit-bearing] sanctity in union with and in them, Mary inherently recognized God as the source of her being, and the One who Loved her absolutely. Knowing no why, but operating always from the unimpeded fullness of His Light-presence [the I AM] living within and through her most singular being, she presents her spirit, soul, and body to God, in a state of utter undividedness, constancy and unstained purity [Romans 12:1-2]; worshipping Him as He can only be worshipped, *"in Spirit and in Truth"* John 4:24. Looking always and only to Him, she is the one found capable of setting about rebuilding the Kingdom of God on earth [as it is in Heaven], which the original Adam and Eve, in their prideful presumption and self-interest, had set about destroying. For in the Ever-fresh and verdant purity of her being, her womb is fit to be the safe and secure dwelling place for God's descent to earth, with the Virginal seed of His own Eternal fruitfulness. As silent and gentle; and as powerful, present, and contained as living candle light, she is the perfect *living* prayer, who offers warmth and luminosity to all. She is the blissful peace, repose, and refuge of perfect [whole and all-perfect] God-consciousness, and the resting point of all divine potentiality and prosperity. She is the woman of immaculate wisdom, prudence, and modesty; of invincible strength and serenity, who, unmoved by the insatiable hatred, provocation, and plots of Satan, overcame all the tests and trials of earthly life, that had defeated Israel for centuries. By virtue of her co-operation, God was 'given back' His Godhead, and all of Heaven hung on her every motion and act.

In every feast of the Blessed Virgin Mary, we celebrate a feast about the One to whom she gave birth. Infinitely more than the original created Adam, Jesus Christ is *"Emmanuel: God-with-us"* Old Testament: Isaiah 7:14; 8:8-10 and New Testament: Matthew 1:21-23; John 1:14; 14:8-11; Colossians 2:9, and the Cause of His Mother's election as the first redeemed among man. We rejoice in Mary's most singular privilege of being the daughter of the Father, mother of the Son and spouse of the Holy Spirit. We rejoice in her elevation to the throne and counsel of the Most Holy Trinity, as royal Queen-Mother of all creation. For by virtue of her participation in the mediation of her Son-God, all things are given new Life in and through her. She is Mediatrix and Co-redemptrix; the custodian and dispenser of all of God's healing graces and divine treasures. Together with her offspring in Jesus Christ; the *"Children of Light"* Luke 16:18; John 12:36; Ephesians 5:8; 1 Thessalonians 5:5, she will, in time, and in the final act of Divine Justice, effect a most radical and complete victory over the infernal serpent [Satan], and all the forces of Hell [Genesis 3:15].

> *"Joachim had accomplished a third part of the way when Anne met him in the centre of the passage directly under the Golden Gate, where stood a pillar like a palm tree with hanging leaves and fruit…. She was also accompanied by some women, among them the Prophetess Anna. I saw Joachim and Anne embrace each other in ecstasy. They were surrounded by hosts of Angels, some floating over them carrying a luminous tower like that which we see in the pictures of the Litany of Loretto. The tower vanished between Joachim and Anne, both of whom were encompassed by brilliant Light and glory. At the same moment the Heavens above them opened, and I saw the joy of the Most Holy Trinity, and of the Angels over the Conception of Mary. Both Joachim and Anne were in a supernatural state. I learned that, at the moment in which they embraced and the Light shone around them, the Immaculate Conception of Mary was accomplished… After this, Joachim, and Anne, praising God, turned toward the outer gate of the passage."*
>
> From the visions of Blessed Anne Catherine Emmerich.

And so, from her Immaculate Conception; to Gabriel's salutation, naming her as the one who is *"full of grace"* Luke 1:28; from her interior divine martyrdom, to receiving the divine Motherhood of all of mankind; to her Assumption into Heaven in both body and soul; we give thanks to God for the marvellous gift of our celestial Queen-Mother. For on account of her immaculate purity and fidelity to God, she is both the exemplary pilgrim on earth, and citizen of Heaven. **Above all, she is our Mother, who's singular whole-hearted Love for us, surpasses the best of all human loves put together. She is the one perfect [whole and all-perfect] model and exemplar of created human life; an unparalleled infinity of higher beauties, and the continuous enchantment of the Most Holy Trinity.**

The Immaculate Conception of our Blessed Mother, carries important Truths about the paradox of barrenness and fertility, in the sub-natural [old] and supernatural [new] world orders. The human births of the holiest of men and women, born of barren couples, is a miracle seen several times in Sacred Scripture. As St. Anne was the barren mother of the Blessed Virgin Mary, who gave birth to the Messiah; Isaac the son of Abraham was conceived by Sarah, who became the mother of many nations; while the Prophet Samuel was conceived by Hannah; and John the Baptist was conceived by Elizabeth, when long past natural child-bearing years. It is however the unequalled mystery of the Immaculate Conception, that elevates and expands the meaning of fertility, virginity, and motherhood, in an unparalleled way, and sets the standard for the relationship between nature and grace.

> "Mary's womb is the temple of God, and His sweet place of repose as a Bridegroom in His bride chamber, rejoicing with joy in the virginal body of His Mother, as in a sweet garden full of fragrant flowers, namely every kind of virtues and graces."
>
> Fr. Johannes Tauler [The Illuminated Doctor].

In the unique privilege of her divine Motherhood, Mary reconciles virginity with the fullness of motherhood, because in her absolute virginity, she alone was the suitable ground for bearing the All-pure and All-powerful Virginal Light-seed of God. And because Almighty God is her Child, she is the Mother of all re-created life in Him. This great mystery of virginity and pregnancy teaches us that while the self-giving nature of different life-states ordained and blessed by God affirm one another, the purer and more virgin the soul [in its Love and desire for God alone, and for all things in Him], the greater its capacity for the divine initiative [spirit-bearing God-being, John 10:34]. This is because the virgin element of the soul, is the inviolate and expectant [no-thing] space that is the pure substance-essence and likeness of God Himself. It is in this space, given over to inner stillness and listening [*living* silence]; more to Heaven than to earth, that **the mighty and majestic All-ness of God unites Himself with the no-thing-ness of created man**. This creative union of grace and [divine] freedom, is that which awakens in man, the Eternal youthfulness, beauty, power, and fruitfulness of his primordial being in God. It is his thirty-, sixty- or one-hundred-fold participation in God's Plan of salvation [healing], and in the higher Life of Heaven [Matthew 13:23; Mark 4:20].

In the depths and spaciousness of hallowed reality, God's upward call [invitation] is then not only as a select call [invitation] to the extraordinary offices of the priesthood and professed religious life, but a Universal call. **For as His adopted children in Baptism, every soul is tasked with the challenge of overcoming its own Spiritual barrenness, to become a bearer of [the Light of] Jesus Christ, and a**

builder of the Kingdom of Heaven. This state of being, which St. Paul refers to some eighty times as being re-created *"in Christ"* is available to everyone, according to their willingness and capacity for Light-union. The unequalled perfection of this state in the Blessed Virgin Mary, who lived on earth as virgin, wife, and mother, confirms the dignity and fruitfulness of the married, professed, and celibate vocations. And as a widow and solitary in the final years of her life on earth, also confirms the fruitfulness of widowhood, and the more rare eremitical [solitary] life, fully espoused to the Holy Spirit.

While some are called [invited] to a more exterior life, and others to a more interior life, we are given to understand that there is no condition of life which the all-surrounding Mercy and grace of God does not Will to sanctify. This is because the Assumption into glory of the whole *living* Church, is God's Plan for *everyone who truly desires* to be justified in Jesus Christ [Romans 8:28]. And so, from the chaste single, married, or widowed person, to the recovered sin addict [symbolised by Mary Magdalene], and the blind Truth seeker [symbolised by Nicodemus], **everyone is included in the 'All to nothing' call [invitation] to divine service,** corresponding with the potential degree of Light-union, written in his soul from all Eternity. All blessed states of life, nonetheless necessitate some degree of virgin purity, or the recovery of this state, which is Jesus Christ-consciousness, without which there can be no ascent to the company of the Heavenly realm of the pure [1 John 1:9], and the holy [1 Peter 1:15-16]. For this is the souls wedding garment [Light-garment of God-being, John 10:34], in which God awaits it, and without which, it is unable to stand in [withstand] the potency and fecundity of His Light-presence, in and for all Eternity [Mathew 22:11-13]. See 'Holy/Holiness' and 'Perfection' in Useful terms.

In this supernatural transformation of the soul in God, Desert Father St. John Cassian assures us that the Holy Spirit's work within the soul will not surpass that which it is called to, and capable of in the ordering of Divine Providence. For as a tree only bears fruit in the right soil and season, and according to its type and capacity, the sincere soul who is yet overkeen for things above itself [to strain in self-sacrifice, or contemplate what is incomprehensible at the natural level], will return to its proper equilibrium, according to the weakness of its flesh [carnal ego-self], learning to co-operate with the Holy Spirit, and proceed with moderation, and perseverance [commitment] along a suitable path. In this work says Meister Eckhart, man is [also] advised *"not [to] imagine his life too clever; so fresh and original, that [he] ends up throwing what God wants out the back door, like rotten eggs and brown apples."* For *"To Love God, is to consider that what God wants as good, and godly."*

In understanding our upward call [invitation] to the new [Ever-new] Life in the Spirit, it is then vital to recognize that God does not operate according to man's limited interpretation of states of being. While Mary, in her Immaculate Conception, is the unparalleled exemplar of the created human person, living perfectly [wholly and all-perfectly] in the Love and Divine Will of God, Sacred Scripture demonstrates that in selecting persons for office, **God is no discriminator of age, character, or of person, according to standards and perceptions at the natural level. He calls [invites] who He Wills, when He Wills, and how He Wills, and rewards them as He Wills [John 3:8],** because all exterior good, draws its value from the interior life of the soul. God alone sees the substance and texture of a soul, and its actual or potential relationship of Light, while He operates in right timing [Ecclesiastes 3:11], and in accordance with His Perfect [Whole and All-Perfect] divine Plan. The word *"chosen"* then, can in aspect refer to those who are foreknown by God, to be sufficiently humble, meek [positively consenting or assenting, gentle, and balanced in Aramaic and Hebrew], and open to instruction, as to turn back and be regathered in Him. In choosing David, the son of Jesse of Bethlehem to be king of Israel, in favour of his brother Eliab, God declares to Samuel *"God does not see as man sees; man looks at appearances, but God looks at the heart"* **1 Samuel 16:7.** God chose the aged temple priest Zechariah and his wife Elizabeth to bear John the Baptist, when Elizabeth was long past child-bearing years [at least sixty years old]. He chose Moses at forty years of age, and Abraham at the age of seventy years. He called simple apostles with neither credentials nor social esteem, and with great outwardly observable character flaws. Saul, who was persecuting the disciples was converted on the road to Damascus, to become the zealous Apostle Paul, while Mary Magdalene became one of Jesus most ardent disciples; standing at the foot of the Cross, and being first chosen to witness His Resurrection. God thus overturns all mistaken earthly [carnal] standards and criteria that would measure or compare a soul's suitability for His calling [invitation] to higher fruitfulness; to the substance, vigour, and freshness of the Eucharistic *"new man"*.

Jesus personal call [invitation] to authentic virginity for the sake of the Kingdom [Matthew 19:12]; *"Let him accept it who can"* Matthew 19:1, is a call to *"a Spiritual kind of marrying"* says St. Optatus, for the purpose of participating most fully in the divine Plan. The exception rather than the norm in this earthly life, those who respond to this call [invitation] to absolute self-giving, for Love of God and the sake of the Kingdom [Matthew 19:12] point to the *'age to come'* [Luke 20:33-36], when there will be no earthly marriages, nor family structures [Matthew 22:30-32; Mark 12:25-27 and Luke 20:34-38], and where everyone [who co-operates with and participates in God] will be Blood brothers and sisters, in the Ever-lasting community of Heaven. Courageously and trustingly sacrificing all that is seen [and desirable at the natural and material level], for all that is unseen [and desirable at the Spiritual and immaterial level] to live the Life of Heaven on earth, these souls will be distinctly rewarded in and for all Eternity, and will sing a special song with Jesus Christ, before the throne of the Eternal Father [Revelation 14:3-4 and Isaiah 56:4-5]. See 'Perfection' in Useful Terms.

> *"Suppose the sun to shine brightly on the violet,*
> *while the rose was under a thick mist; it [the violet]*
> *might perchance seem the brightest flower."*
>
> St. Francis de Sales.

In whatever life-state and office we inhabit, our perfect [whole and all-perfect] healing and sanctity involves co-operating with and participating in God, rather than comparing one another according to deceptive outward appearances. Church saints and mystics advise us, that while the relatively unstained soul, that lives in dynamic fidelity to God, is more pleasing to, and glorious in Him than the relatively recovered soul; the more zealous recovered soul, may yet be more pleasing to, and glorious in God than the seemingly less fleshy [carnal-egoic] soul, who yet does not co-operate with and participate in Him so zealously, as befits the height of sanctity to which it is called [invited]. While the work that God is free to do in one humble, meek, and repentant soul in a short period of time, many surpass what is possible in an inwardly resisting or proud soul in many years, if at all. In Sacred Scripture, Jesus speaks of tax collectors and prostitutes entering the Kingdom of Heaven ahead of the chief priests and elders of the community, because they are humble enough to recognize their weaknesses and waywardness, and turn back to God [Matthew 21:31].

And so, as the prodigal son who squanders his inheritance, before having a change of heart and returning home [Luke 15:11-32], there is no reason for any soul to be led by appearances, or to give up on, or despair of, the quest for their own healing and restoration to holiness [whole-hearted fullness of being]; at any point in time, or in any life-state, office, or soul-condition. For as a rainbow rises on a droplet of dew, man can reverse the ruination of his immortal soul in any moment. He need only turn his tearful gaze towards God, who looks continuously upon him with merciful eyes.

> *"The bruised reed he will not break,*
> *and the smouldering wick he will not extinguish."*
>
> Isaiah 42:3.

Furthermore, in sending His Son-God to Live and Die, and swallow up death for man, our Beloved Creator God and Father has confirmed that the fall has not lessened His Love for his estranged children, but has intensified it. While in the Ever-creative power of His own omnipotence and omniscience, He harnesses all the forces in play, to bring about His Plan of destroying evil and re-establishing His Kingdom, in desirous and faithful souls. The desires and evils of mortal flesh [the carnal-ego], with all its perceptions of emotions, circumstances, and fulfilment according to time, space, history, and culture that limit the vision of man and dishearten him, are no impediment to God who works all things together for good, for those that truly Love Him [Romans 8:28]. All are burned up and transfigured in the blessed flames of His Love operating in His Divine Will, which draws the faithful soul upwards and out of itself, and into the primordial Passion of the Spirit. In this creative re-orientation of the human person to *real Life and purpose* in Jesus Christ, the old [world] continuously gives way to the new [world], in an Ever-new state of being, that taps into the Life Substance-Energies of God. In this dynamic purification, re-ordering, re-integration [re-centring], and re-creation [re-birth] of the human person in Jesus Christ, those growing oldest in this world, may be those growing youngest - more virgin and Eternally youthful [2 Corinthians 4:16], in the Ever-real vigour of Divine Life, which has no evening. For time itself, is the moment-to-moment test and Truth of Eternal youthfulness, beauty, power, and fruitfulness, which grows more alive, bright, and graceful, in the souls reaping [conceiving and birthing] of perpetual Light, lighting the way for other souls.

On this glorious feast of the Immaculate Conception, let us thank Almighty God for the astonishing gift of our celestial Queen-Mother, and for all that He has accomplished within and through her singularly most pure being. Let us too be inspired to conceive of the magnitude of our responsibility and privileged purpose of being; renewing our zealous co-operation with and participation in Him, asking that the resplendent Light-purity and refinement of our celestial Mother rise and flow within and through us, as to draw His gaze, and blind the works of the enemy. For the healing and Sanctification of our souls, is the healing and hallowing of all God's suffering people and creation. It is the triumph of our Mothers Immaculate Heart [initiated in Fatima in 1917], and the New Advent of the Kingdom, on earth as it is in Heaven. See Chapter on 'Fiat'.

"For with God, nothing will be impossible."

Luke 1:37

The Tree of Life

The all-giving purpose of trees; three trees with powerful mystical meaning; the "apple" and the test of faithfulness; man created free and co-responsible; "choice"- deceived man divides against himself; Jesus Christ, the New Tree of Life.

> "The Lord God planted a garden eastward in Eden, and there He put the man, whom He had formed. And out of the ground, He made every tree grow, that is pleasant to the sight, and good for food; including the Tree of Life in the middle of the garden, and the Tree of Knowledge of Good and Evil."
>
> Genesis 2: 8-9.

From the acacia and almond tree to the olive, pine, oak and willow tree, many varieties of trees are mentioned in Sacred Scripture. Trees are vital living structures, that perform many functions to maintain life on earth. They replenish the oxygen supplies of the earth, without which man could not breathe. They provide fruits, nuts, and sap, and flowers and leaves for food and medicinal purposes, while nourishing and protecting the soil, and providing microclimates and habitats. Trees conserve water, purify waterways, and rebalance the water cycle. They offer shade and shelter, and homes and corridors for birds and animal life, and are a renewable material for buildings, paper, and fuel. Trees release phytoncides ['essential oils'] that help the immune system; they improve cognition and lower stress levels. In sum, trees give themselves in every way to assist man, and all life on earth.

The importance of trees, as the oldest of the earth's living structures [some can live for 10,000 years], is highlighted by the fact that every major character in Sacred Scripture appears in conjunction with a tree. Abraham sat beneath the oak trees of Mamre [Genesis 18:1] and

Moses stood barefoot before the burning bush [Exodus 3:2–5], while Zacchaeus climbed the sycamore tree, to catch sight of Jesus among a crowd [Luke 19:1-4]. God specifically instructed the Israelites to take special care of fruit trees [Deuteronomy 20:19-20]. Trees are cited frequently in parables, where they symbolise hope, strength, and longevity. While understood more broadly [in the Aramaic sense], they can refer to any vegetation and its instinctive growth. The only physical description of Jesus in Sacred Scripture, refers to Him growing up like a tender plant or tree; as a root, out of thirsty ground [Isaiah 53:2]. This prophetic description symbolises His divine lushness as the figure of the new Tree of Life arising out of the desert of Israel. It points to our absolute need of Him, as the oxygen of our soul. Jesus grew up in a carpenter's home and worked as a carpenter. He talked about seeds of faith, and said that the Kingdom of God was like a tree.

> *"A tree has hope... If its roots grow old in the earth, and its trunk passes into dust, at the scent of water, it will sprout and bring forth leaves, as when it had first been planted."*
>
> Job 14:7-9.

In all this pointing to trees, and the role of trees, three trees carry powerful mystical significance:

1. The Tree of Life;
2. The Tree of Knowledge of Good and Evil; and
3. The Tree of the Cross.

When God creates all good things for man, a specific tree is mentioned; the Tree of Life [Genesis 2:9]. God planted this tree in the middle of the Garden of Eden [Genesis 2:8], right next to The Tree of Knowledge of Good and Evil [Genesis 2:9]. Adam and Eve, the first man and woman created by God, lived in Eden. This garden - meaning *"place of pleasure and delight"* in Hebrew, was a place of God's blessing and prosperity; an ecological Paradise teeming with all the original, fully Spiritualized divine goods and fruitfulness of God's perfect creation. Above all, it was a garden of perfect [whole and all-perfect] intimacy with God, who walked along with Adam and Eve in the cool of the day, because there was no dividing wall of sin [darkness and estrangement] to separate them. Adam and Eve could feed and nourish themselves on the divine fruits given by the trees in the garden, most particularly the Tree of Life, which represented Eternal Life. In eating* of the succulent, Life-giving fruits of this tree, they would be immortal and untouched by the flow of time, old age, suffering, struggle, dis-ease, and death. Ever healthy, vigorous, and strong, they would forever grow in the knowledge and Love of God in His Divine Will [and all things in God]. This was man's participation in the glorious infinity of divine goods, joys, beauties, harmonies, and contentment's of Paradise. All fascinations, surprises, and possibilities in form, colour, and sound beyond human conception. This most splendid tree from which they would eat, was the original type of the Holy Eucharist, mentioned in the book of Revelation 2:7 and 22:2.

[*In man's original state of innocence and justice (Eternal Beatitude), to look at was to eat in the sense of Spiritual enjoyment in the entirety of ones being, ordered perfectly in union with (and in) God].

God's only instruction [test of Love] to Adam and Eve, was to avoid the fruits of the tree next to The Tree of Life, which was the Tree of Knowledge of Good and Evil. An association which unbeknown to them, would spell Spiritual and therefore physical death. With these two trees God represents the two ways open to man. One leads to Life; to all healthfulness, peace, joy, and blessedness; and the other leads to trouble, misery, and death.

> "The Lord God commanded the man saying:
> "You may freely eat of every tree of the garden, but you shall not eat of the Tree of Knowledge of Good and Evil, for in the day, you eat of it, you shall surely die.""
>
> Genesis 2:16-17.

Sacred Scripture tells us that the forbidden Tree of Knowledge of Good and Evil was among many trees in the garden that had an appealing ornamental beauty. Eve is described as seeing this tree as *"good for food, and... a delight to the eyes"* Genesis 3:6, **confirming that the problem was not in the tree, but in breaking the relationship of trust [Love-union] with God the Father. For in the [destructive] act of disobeying God and eating of the *"apple"* [*"tappuach"* meaning *"breath of self"* in Aramaic], Adam and Eve would fall into the trap of eating and digesting into their being, knowledge of both good [Light] and evil [darkness].** Sowing division within them, this human fruit [knowledge] would destroy their primordial state of innocence and justice [Eternal Beatitude]. It would sever them from the splendid and blissful state of Love-union with their Father, with each other, and with all living creation in Him. It would cause continuous internal conflict, changeability, and turmoil within their divided being. Ultimately, it would give double-death to their soul and body, rather than Eternal Life. Adam and Eve and all future generations would be subject to the germ of sin [see Pope Pius XII, 'Humani Generis'], experiencing de-generation and decay, and ultimately mortal death, as the soul would withdraw from the body, at the end of earthly life.

In this dilemma, God the Father confirms man as **free and responsible** for his own life and destiny, **as well as co-responsible** for other people, living creatures and creation. While His instruction was a call [invitation] to man to Love in His Divine Will, and therefore for the *Ever-livingness* of the Kingdom of Heaven. Man's created intelligence was to think of, comprehend, and Love His Creator God and Father, forming a crown of Spiritual wealth around all of his acts [thoughts, words, and deeds], thus sharing in the Priesthood of God. **God did not, and does not, ask man to *'choose'* between good and evil, any more than He asks him to *'choose'* between Life and death, for *'choosing'* in this aspect, disregards the reality that there is no counter position to Love; that evil is the negation and absence of Love [Truth and Life]; and that to God alone belongs the right to determine what Love [Truth and Life] is.** Adam and Eve's 'choice' was in reality a *'decision'* [meaning *"to divide"* or *"cut off"* in Hebrew] to sever themselves from the indivisible Godhead, in favour of their own human will acting in darkness, apart from God. A decision made in the knowledge of the glory and splendour of this perfect union of wills. This test was the validation that God the Father needed from free man, to confirm Him as His freely faithful child.

The olive branch [symbolising peace], which Adam and Eve took with them from Paradise into exile, and which Noah received by way of a dove, representing the Holy Spirit, to let him know that God's first creative act of correction and renewal by Flood had finished [Genesis 8:11], point to the third tree, which is the Tree of the Cross.

"In the centre of the glittering garden, I saw a sheet of water in which lay an island connected with the opposite land by a pier."

"Both island and pier were covered with beautiful trees, but in the middle of the former stood one more magnificent than the others. It towered high over them, as if guarding them. Its roots extended over the whole island, as did also its branches, which were broad below, and tapering to a point above. The leaves were fine, the fruit yellow and sessile in a leafy calyx like a budding rose. It was something like a cedar. I do not remember ever having seen Adam, Eve, or any animal near that tree on the island. But I saw beautiful noble-looking white birds, and heard them singing in its branches. That Tree, was the Tree of Life."

"[All in this garden] was transparent, as if formed of Light. I saw enclosed in Adam and Eve, the corporal and Spiritual Life of mankind."

"By the reception of the fruit [of the Tree of Knowledge of Good and Evil] Adam and Eve, became as it were, intoxicated, and their consent to sin wrought in them, a great change. It was a serpent in them. Its nature pervaded theirs..."

"I saw Adam and Eve reach the earth, their place of penance. Oh, what a touching sight; those two creatures expiating their fault upon the naked earth! Adam had been allowed to bring an olive branch from Paradise, and now he planted it. Later on, the Cross was made from its wood."

From the visions of Blessed Anne Catherine Emmerich.

This third tree would be richly symbolic in the mission of Jesus Christ; in the abolishment of existence-ignorance, evil and death, and the reinstatement of the Kingdom of the Fatherland. Jesus favoured place to pray was the Garden of Olives [Gethsemane], while His Cross was primarily a Cross of olive wood. His glorious Ascension into Heaven by His own power, took place on the Mount of Olives in full daylight; representing the restoration of the One Ever-lasting Day. Ultimately, the All-powerful Tree of the Cross represents the ransom of all human souls borne by the figurative new Tree of Life; the Perfect [Whole and All-Perfecting] Cosmic Divine-Humanity of Jesus Christ. For in His double-death of soul and body, He paid the debt of every man, and reversed the violation of our divinity, which caused the division and double-death of body and soul, in the Garden of Eden.

As long as freedom in Love is viewed as the other side of 'choice', there is no Love or freedom. Each time the soul chooses in self-interest, it ceases to be free".

Anon.

We rejoice in Christ's Coming! We rejoice that in remaining united with Him and in Him, on the Tree of the Cross, we partake in both His sufferings and glory [blissful magnificence]. And we rejoice that the privilege to eat again has been given to us, but of the sacrificial Food of Jesus Christ. For Jesus Christ is the Ever-alive New Tree of Life, who brings about our re-union with God our Father, and the primordial glory [blissful magnificence] of the Homeland. See Chapter on 'The Eucharist'.

"Blessed are those who wash their robes, so that they may have the right to the Tree of Life; and may enter in by the gates into the [Eternal] City."

Revelation 22:14.

Adam and Eve

The original glory before original sin; i-dentity theft - the gentle malice of Satan; breaking the Father's Heart; the devastating impacts of the fall; the strangeness of the insular "old man"; the Father's zealous Love and Plan of salvation; the Kingdom is within you.

> " They heard the Lord God's voice walking in the garden in the cool of the day, and the man and his wife hid themselves from the presence of the Lord God among the trees of the garden. The Lord God called to the man, and said to him, "Where are you?"
>
> Genesis 3:8-9.

In the beginning was relationship; Ever-Living, Loving, and dynamic relationship, between God the Father, and His beloved children. In the beginning, and in ecstasy of His own [Whole and All-Perfect] Love, God the Father formed Adam as His first-born son, to live in His company as head of the human family [Genesis 1:26-27; 2:19]. He created Eve from his side, as his other side, to be his companion [Genesis 2:18-24].

Living **pure, noble, and free** in the perfect [whole and all-perfect] union of wills [the human will with the Cosmic Divine Will], Adam and Eve's mind and heart were one in whole-hearted Love and desire for God. In a state of original holiness [whole-hearted fullness of being]; of innocence and justice [Eternal Beatitude]; and invested with the fullness of indivisible Light [right relationship with hallowed reality]; they went about without a why, looking at, and rejoicing in, the endless panorama of beauties, wonders, and delights of Paradise. Clothed in refulgent Light [the clean, dazzling robes of innocence and justice], their bodies were outshined by the all-pure radiance of their being, in complete union with and in their Father, and with all living creatures and creation in Him. Receiving and reflecting only Light, and thus perfect [whole and all-perfect] in both image and likeness [similitude] to God, the fullness of Divine Life was at their disposal. Faith as *"Children of Light"* Luke 16:18; John 12:36; Ephesians 5:8; 1 Thessalonians 5:5, and belief [from the word *"hayman"* meaning *"hymn"* in Aramaic] were as One, as they joined in the divine harmonies of the living Spirit of God, that infused all creation.

> *"He gave them counsel, tongue, eyes, ears, and heart to have understanding. He filled them with the knowledge of wisdom…Their eyes saw the majesty of His glory. Their ears heard the glory of His voice."*
>
> Sirach 17:6,7,13.

As the head of the human family, Adam was a pure channel of the divine. The supernatural Light, warmth, power, and effects of the living Light of the Most Holy Trinity, which contains all divine knowledge, enrichment, and blessedness; all possibilities and potentialities; streamed directly from the Godhead into Adam's forehead [mind], mouth, breast [heart], hands, and feet. These five avenues of grace, governed his soul [memory, will and intellect] and directed his five senses to celestial things. His five senses, in turn, reported to his mind in his heart, directing his unique creativity and personality, within the infinite Cosmic Personhood of God. Consumed in a brightness and vigour of a continuous relationship of Love in the Ever-Now, and free of [carnal-ego] self-reflection, Adam lived in a state of full Light-being. Living not only for God, but in God, and knowing and remembering God only, there was no division [of Light and darkness], nor discontinuity in his being, and therefore between Heaven and earth. Adam wisely wanted only what God wanted. His senses were engaged only in seeing, speaking, and hearing about God; Loving, desiring, and enjoying Him, and therefore himself, and all creation in Him. In this blissful state of interior, and face-to-face Light-union, in the ordered harmonies of Divine Life, he understood and experienced perfectly [wholly and all-perfectly], the Ever-creative and amplified divine purpose for which he was created. While as head of the human family, and custodian of all living creatures and creation, he knew that his noble purpose was to share fully in this Ever-revealing Light with Eve, and with all future generations, born out of a pure and holy multiplying out of God, in God.

> "They [Adam and Eve] were like two unspeakably noble and beautiful children, perfectly luminous, and clothed with beams of Light as with a veil...The glittering beams on Adam's head denoted his abundant fruitfulness; his glory; his connection with other radiations. And all this shining beauty is restored to glorified souls and bodies. Our hair is the ruined, the extinct glory; and as is this hair of ours to rays of Light, so is our present flesh [body] to that of Adam before the fall. The sunbeams around Adam's mouth bore reference to a holy posterity from God, which, had it not been for the fall, would have been effectuated by the spoken word."
>
> From the visions of Blessed Anne Catherine Emmerich.

Preserved in an Ever-new, multi-dimensional and multi-sensory state of being, each moment was supernaturally alive with Ever-fresh and endless possibilities and surprises; of innocent playfulness, joys, and enjoyments; in form, colour, and sound beyond human comprehension. Adam had no need to ask God for anything, because all divine goods [as far as God Willed for a created human person], were given to him in his absolute state of Light-freedom in Him. This dynamic and Ever-creative Life, was a Life of deep peace and rest; a state which knew no restlessness; no toil, struggle, nor discontentment; no sub-natural human need, passions, appetites, and inconveniences. For without the germ of sin, man could know no disease, pain, decay, or death. In this state of perfect [whole and all-perfect] understanding and communication, Adam found great ease and joy in his care and stewardship of all living creatures and creation, because all were fully Spiritualized and Light-bearing, streaming forth from the Cosmic source of all Life. He Loved and enjoyed communion [living in community] with all of God's creatures, who Loved and co-operated with him in God. The elements of earth, fire, air, and water, of which his own and Eve's body were formed, also obeyed him. This **All-Good Life of bliss**, was the privilege and power of man's *real Life and purpose*; of returning Love for Love in a continuous, Ever-expanding circle of giving and receiving, within the infinite Light-community of God.

Yet, all was not entirely well in this garden of delights. Evil was lurking in their midst, and Life for Adam and Eve was due to take a dramatic turn. This unseen peril, was in the form of the mighty Angel Lucifer; the *"shining one [day star], son of the dawn"* Isaiah 14:12, once dazzlingly beautiful and powerful beyond compare, but now hiding among the trees disguised as a serpent, and waiting for the opportunity to take revenge on God, and on man. For in a previous act of Cosmic anarchy, this once chief and commander of the Armies [Choirs] of God, and guardian of His glory [blissful magnificence], had turned against his Creator [Revelation 12:4,7], in an act of covetousness of the splendid gifts bestowed upon him by God. And of jealousy over God's Plan to raise human nature above his own mighty Angelic nature. Full of aspiration to climb to the zenith of the Heavens, and grasp Universal and Eternal dominion [Isaiah 14:13-14; Ezekiel 28:14-15], Lucifer instead found himself [and his fallen Angels] stricken down and banished *forever* from the presence of God [Isaiah 14:15; Ezekiel 28:16-17; Revelation 12:13]. Yet still, with the most excellent knowledge of both good and evil, because of his previous exceptional closeness to God, while consumed with insatiable hatred for Him, and for this human person, created in His image and likeness, he watched and listened for his chance to avenge, which was soon to arrive. Hearing God the Father personally tell Adam and Eve not eat of the fruit of The Tree of Knowledge of Good and Evil in the midst of the garden, lest they die, and believing that should they disobey God, they, like him, and the fallen Angels, would forever lose the sublime glory [blissful magnificence] for which they were destined, he found his opportunity to approach Eve.

We learn much from the way in which this minister of death approaches Eve, before she and Adam had the opportunity to eat of the Tree of Life, which contained immortality and all Divine Life. A creature *"more crafty than any of the creatures of the earth that the Lord God had made"* Genesis 3:1, he directs Eve's attention away from the Tree of Life, before they had the chance to eat of it, and onto the forbidden Tree of Knowledge of Good and Evil. And as confirmation of his cunning, instead of telling her what he so desperately wanted to tell her, he first asks her to clarify and sense-check what God had said about not eating of every tree in the garden. *"Has God really said, "You shall not eat of any tree of the garden?""* Genesis 3:1. In this way, he presents to her as **an interested befriender and flatterer, twisting God's words** and inspiring her to question God within herself, as he engages her in *'dialogue'* [meaning *"relationship"* in early Greek]. Then, when he has succeeded in casting a shadow of doubt across her thought of God, and kindled in her, prideful vanity towards herself, he whispers to her. Not with strong words, but with gentle malice, carried upon accursed breath, he executes his lying, murderous intent, to kill forever the endless power, beauty, and expansiveness of God [God-being, John 10:34] within her human soul. To Eve, and to Adam and to every human generation after them, he proposes the same most vain [from the Latin word *"vanus"* meaning empty] and avaricious presumption, which brought the human family into his death-grip: *"You won't really die, for God knows that in the day you eat it [the fruit of The Tree of Knowledge of Good and Evil], your eyes will be opened, and you will be like God, knowing good and evil"* Genesis 3:4–5.

Satan in an act of pure evil, offered Adam and Eve, what they already had, *as if it was something more* **than what they had, apart from God. His wicked [evil and ungodly] suggestion, was that humans could be like God but self-sufficient [*"I am who I am"* apart from God], because He was limiting their knowledge and freedom,**

and ultimately could not be trusted. If they ate of the forbidden tree, the power of the Kingdom would be given over to them *without Love of God in His Divine Will*. Rather then, than operating *in and along with* that power [as far as created man is permitted] they could be in control – as Gods in themselves, knowing good and evil. In this test of faithfulness and trust, which all *free* human beings must therefore face, came Adam and Eve's devastating failure of strength and heroism. Momentarily inspired by the foul pride of Lucifer, they forgot the Love-union of the powers of their soul [memory, will and intellect] with God their Father; most particularly their human will, which was the operation of their heart's desire.

Eating of the *"apple"* [*"tappuach"* meaning *"breath of self"* in Aramaic], Adam and Eve violently sank from the highest heights of sanctifying grace and blessedness, into the Ever-debasing circles of self-love, and self-idolatry. In this most dreadful conquering deception, which echoed Satan's own rebellious battle cry *"I will be like the Most High!"* Isaiah 14:14, Adam and Eve forgot their soul for their body. The currents of Light streaming from the Godhead into Adam's forehead [mind], mouth, breast [heart], hands, and feet, to govern his soul and direct his senses, were now significantly dimmed and dis-integrated. No longer able to participate in the full Life of God, and with his mind separated from his heart, **abandoning [consenting] to, and allowing God, was replaced with the staidness, and strangeness of safeguarding the illusory carnal ego-self.** Rather than resting in the single voice of the Father's Cosmic Divine Will, his soul [memory, will and intellect] became a confused [and ever-changing and restless] community of voices, apart from God, and given over more to [mis-directed towards] dis-ordered and unstable reasoning, feelings, and emotions in the flesh [carnal ego-self], than to hearing and seeing in the Light-purity of the Spirit. The avenues of grace became avenues of sin, which overwhelmed him and Eve, and became the Universal human condition [Romans 3:9-23].

In this violent fall through the thickness of space and time, [from God-consciousness to egoic self-consciousness], all living creatures and creation lost citizenship of the Kingdom of Heaven. And where before, man was endowed with the kingship of nature, now all in him became nature. In the immediacy of Spiritual death [dis-integration from God] and in progressive physical death in a lowly body, he found himself fettered and struggling against his own person, and all [fallen] creation around him. Driven by concupiscence [the rebellion of his lower nature against his higher nature], he found himself faced with all manner of temptations, toil, and suffering, on an earth that was cursed, and from which he and Eve [and therefore all living creatures] were fated to derive sustenance and shelter, through effort and struggle. Missing the fullness of divine knowledge, wisdom and presence, and projecting forwards and backwards in an afflicted state of pride, fear, and avarice [from the Latin word meaning to *"crave"* more than is needed in terms of money, materiality, and all self-satisfaction], in all curiosity and restlessness; profound peace of being and stability were painfully absent from the life of man.

> *"Isn't a man consigned to labour on earth?*
> *Aren't his days like the days of a hired hand?"*
>
> Job 7:1.

Having lived in the Paradise for One day, Adam and Eve immediately understood the devastating deception of the serpent [Satan], which had killed the seed of immortality within their souls. They understood the unutterable difference between the splendour and beauty of the fully Spiritualized Life, and the dreadful de-generation and misery of their new-found condition, as well as the corresponding effects on all living creatures and creation. Keenly aware of the deep division between their minds and hearts [desire], and feeling burning shame at their own nakedness [disgrace, indignity, and vulnerability], they ran and hid among the bushes. Their nakedness, they understood to be the magnitude of their dislocation from their full depth of being [God-being, John 10:34 and Good-being], in the Light-union of Paradise. For stripped of the beauty and radiance of blissful innocence and justice [Eternal Beatitude], and sunken inward in new found self-love, the endless Spiritual panorama outstretched before their eyes had vanished, and in its place was the shallow husk, and narrow circumference of the flesh [carnal ego-self]. The heat of their shame, was the mark of the serpent of fire; the inner worm [Mark 9:48 and Isaiah 66:24], which is the dark heat of inner Spiritual turmoil, born of self-love, and which Now must be burned off, in order to re-connect with their Divine Life-source and re-enter Paradise. It was yet also, a vital mark of remembrance of the original glory of their being in God, protecting them from shamelessness, sinfulness, and all downward transcendence, while signifying what needs to be burned off [purified] to re-enter the Homeland. God the Father seeing, and having foreseen, what had happened, came personally to look for them, calling out to Adam in Broken-Heartedness: *"Where are you?"* Genesis 3:9. And so began the long and painful story of God our Father's pursuit of His beloved, lost children.

> *"And the eyes of them both were opened.*
> *And when they realized themselves to be naked, they joined*
> *together fig leaves and made coverings for themselves."*
>
> Genesis 3:7.

The mark of the fall, is immediately apparent in Adam and Eve's initial attempts to **evade responsibility** for eating of the forbidden fruit, when confronted by God the Father. Yet, it is confirmation of the Father's own Perfect [Whole and All-Perfect] and immutable Justice, that saw them cast down to the earth, while placed at the gates of Paradise, was *"a flaming sword which turned every way, to guard the way to the Tree of Life"* Genesis 3:24, lest they unjustly *"reach out [their] hand, and also take of the Tree of Life, and eat, and live forever"* Genesis 3:22, after disobeying God. For it was as a result of their own uncooperative will, that God sent them to till the earth from which their bodies were taken, and to lead lives characterized by toil, hardship, and mortal death [Genesis 3:14-19], whereby their bodies would return to the earth. And since Adam was not only the first man, but appointed head of the human family, his sin [and not

Eve's] had grave consequences for all his descendants. All are born without the gift of sanctifying grace, and all other celestial gifts, first freely offered to him and Eve in Eden.

> "On reaching it, they became humble, and for the first time, rightly understood their miserable condition. I saw them praying when left there alone. They separated, fell on their knees, and raised up their hands with tears and cries."
>
> From the visions of Blessed Anne Catherine Emmerich.

Yet still, in the immediacy of their new-found state, and not essentially corrupted, Adam and Eve saw that God had not condemned them to Eternal death [as willed by Satan], nor did He curse them, but the serpent [Satan], together with the third of rebellious Angels that fell with him [Revelation 12:4,70]; and the earth as their place of exile. While having first truly Loved God with His own purest Love in His Divine Will, and knowing that they had been created for overwhelmingly generous Divine Life, the Light-fire of *living* faith, was still burning in their hearts [desire]. Still trusting in the Father's zealous Love for them, they did not despair of their dreadful limitations, but fell upon their knees and prayed. Recognizing their self-condemnation, they understood this land of thorns and thistles [Genesis 3:18] to be a place of penance, and mortal death as a consequence permitted, but not willed by God in His Loving Divine Providence, to recover man from the fallen realm. There was no impulse of pride in them, nor inclination to blame God for their great misfortune or to rebel against [seek apart from] Him again. For as the similitude of their Father, they were utterly devastated by the effects of their decision to divide against themselves in Him, and call death, rather than Life. And knowing that everything in living creation was not only the gift of God, but the responsibility of man, they were likewise devastated at the fear, suffering, struggle, and death brought to bear on all innocent living creatures, because of their dis-location from the safety and harmony of All-union.

*"He who knows himself, knows God.
In the knowledge of God, he can only Love as God Loves."*

Anon.

Adam and Eve wanted to be rescued. They wanted nothing more than to be restored to the blissful state of Love-union with and in God, by way of their co-operation with and participation in Him, in His All-Perfect Love and Divine Will. **Knowing that the Kingdom is entered** *from within*, **they were keenly aware of their responsibility for Spiritualizing all of creation, by first Spiritualizing their own body and soul in God, and offering it back to Him, on behalf of everyone and everything.** And so, in fidelity to the inviolable dignity of their being [and of all living creation] in God, Adam and Eve offered back lives of vigilant, sincere, and Loving divine service, characterized by readiness for perseverance [commitment]; by prayer, fasting and self-sacrifice [self-giving]; and by supplication and labour to liberate their soul from the fleshy [carnal-ego] desires, excesses, and complacency, driven by dis-ordered [and unstable] mortal senses. They made clothing and generated children, co-operating with and participating in God, in the use of His creative power, on His terms. They worked the soil to produce food, taking heart in God's Providential care in this land of thorns and thistles; where the thorn protects the rose, and where the thistle, from stem to seed, offers itself to wildlife. They Loved and cared for God's living creatures and creation, recognizing all as One with the beating Heart of the Divine Spirit. They learned very difficult lessons; witnessing the devastating effects of their fall in the tragedy that befell their first two sons, when the corrupt seed of selfhood in Cain, led to him murdering his more innocent and righteous brother Abel [whose just blood offering was affirmed by Jesus in Matthew 23:35, and is included in every sacrificial feast of the Mass]. Yet, they also witnessed the super-abundance of God's Mercy and forgiveness in His relenting upon Cain's sincere remorse. Haunted by the memory of Eden, and with their whole-hearted efforts to make reparation, and have their heart's desire [human will] healed and restored to the Fatherland, Adam and Eve are excellent examples of humility and holy fear [awe-filled reverence] of God, and of dedication to the restoration of lost Love-union with and in Him.

Information on the creation and fall of man, primarily sourced from the writings of Blessed Anne Catherine Emmerich.

The Lamb of God

Jesus Christ the at-One-ment; One Perfect Plan; the primordial suffering Love of God; the royal road to Calvary; consumed in Love's own fire, and converted to Living Food; replacing sin and death with Love, Truth, and Life; re-uniting and writing His law in human minds and hearts.

"I looked, and I heard something like a voice of many Angels around the throne, and the living creatures, and elders... saying with a loud voice, "Worthy is the Lamb who has been slain to receive the power, wealth, wisdom, strength, honour, glory, and blessing!""

Revelation 5:11-12.

The theme of the *"Lamb of God"* John 1:29, is present right through Sacred Scripture. Even before the foundation of the world was laid, and creation was made, our All-Seeing, All-Knowing, and All-Loving Father God, recognizing that created man would fail in a test of faithfulness in Love, and break His Heart, made provision for His Plan of salvation [healing]. *"He [Jesus Christ] was foreknown indeed before the foundation of the world"* 1 Peter 1:20 to be the incorrupt Blood offering; the unspotted sacrificial God-man [Lamb] ransomed for created man, to recover him from death. This All-encompassing offering has been *"revealed in this last age for your sake... that your faith and hope might be in God"* 1 Peter 1:20-21.

God requires atonement for all wrong-doing. And because blood represents life, and God is the giver of all Life, it is blood that makes atonement for one's life. *"For the life of the flesh is in the blood. I have given it to you on the altar to make atonement for your souls"* Leviticus 17:11. As created and fallen creatures, there is nothing of ourselves that we can do to destroy death and recover our relationship with God, and true purpose and power of being in Him. And so, God Himself, in the unfathomable excesses of His Love for us, has set One Perfect [Whole and All-Perfect] Plan in place for our **atonement [at-One-ment], in the All-pure and sinless Blood offering of His Son-God, Jesus Christ.**

In the establishment of the Old Mosaic Covenant of Love, through revelation to Moses, God first wrote His law [commandments] on tablets of stone, says St. Hildegard of Bingen, because man's encrusted heart had no softness for divine reason. Eventually, the Blood sacrifice of Jesus Christ, in the New and Ever-lasting Covenant of Love would be required, to makes possible the writing of His law, in the power of the Holy Spirit, upon man's fleshy [carnal-egoic] and divided, heart and mind. In the great day of the New Covenant of Love, Jesus Christ is identified as the Pascal [Passover] Lamb; the God-man manifestation, who includes and concludes the Old Covenant; both Perfecting [fulfilling] and transforming it [Ephesians 2:14-15].

As the pre-Eternal spotless Lamb, and Blood atonement [at-One-ment], Jesus Christ is the exalted and Heavenly New Adam [1 Corinthians 15:45-48], who in His All-encompassing Self-sacrifice, fully represented the evils of all humankind to Divine Justice, as only God could. In this work, He fulfils [reconciles] every legal issue separating man from reconciliation with his Father God. In the five times shedding of His most Precious Blood, and in His five wounds, the five original avenues of grace [Light], and the rights to healing and re-creation [re-birth] to the [transfigured] primordial Edenic state, have been re-opened.

> *"Do not think that I came to destroy the law or the prophets. I did not come to destroy, but to fulfil."*
>
> Matthew 5:17.

It is most chastening to reflect upon the figure of an innocent and harmless Lamb, being led away in silence to be crushed by the incalculable weight of the sin and evil of all time. Sinless and without guile [Isaiah 53:9]; yet numbered among sinners [Isaiah 53:12]; He was led as a Lamb to the slaughter [Isaiah 53:7]; bearing our griefs and carrying our sorrows [Isaiah 53:4-5]. Mistreated and hardly recognized [Isaiah 52:14]; He was wounded for our transgressions [Isaiah 53:5]; being made into a sin offering [Isaiah 53:10,11]; surrendering and forever swallowing up corruption and death in victory [Isaiah 25:8]; that by His bruises, we may be healed [Isaiah 53:5]. He is the Ever-living *"Bread of Life" John 6:35,48,* who gifts Himself to willing and co-operative human souls.

Jesus foresaw the full spectacle of the road that led to Calvary and not only did He take it, but He embraced it; for in His Passion, Death, and Resurrection, He remained the Ever-living God and Master of All. *"I have power to lay [My Life] down. And I have power to take it up again. This is the commandment that I have received from my Father"* John 10:18. No-one on earth but His Mother [in Spirit], shared the horrific cost of this Bloody sacrifice; the lonely and terrifying vigil in the peace-making olive press of Gethsemane, where He sank into the rottenness and revolting abyss of all sin and wickedness [evil and ungodliness]; calling it out in all its forms and guises, and loading it upon Himself, to become the sin-offering for all mankind. No human eyes, but those of His Mother, saw the turmoil and tyranny of evils gathering all around Him, and pressing down upon Him, as He prayed to the Father with crushed breath. No-one saw the nameless agony in His soul, which caused His most pure and innocent Blood to break through the skin of His sacred Body, and flow and pool upon the ground. An inexpressible agony of loneliness, neglect, and ingratitude, intensified by the terror of ever-lost souls, who would refuse to be incorporated in Him. **Jesus foreknew that almost everyone would desert Him, yet fearless and All-powerful; innocent and broken apart by human hands, He was consumed in Love's own fire, as He swallowed up and forgave the fatal darkness, in His own Life-giving death.**

> *"Before the Cross, the world was a quagmire,*
> *on which the Father could not fix His Holy gaze,*
> *nor could the Holy Spirit alight."*

Jesus speaks to Venerable Conchita.
[María Concepción Cabrera de Armida].

As the figurative sacrificial lamb offerings of the Old Testament lost all their vital fluids, so Jesus Christ lost every drop of His most Precious Blood in the unseen holocaust of Spiritual fire that tore through His Being, culminating in His finishing after three hours on the Cross. In the immensity of this Cosmic act, we understand the Passion of Christ as the absolute expression of the intense primordial suffering Love of God for at-One-ment with human souls. For **His very Life was converted into *Living* Food for man [in the Eucharist], so that with the substance of His own being, He could reach into the unplumbed [unconscious] depths of human darkness, and imbue it with His own Divine Life.** The Old Covenant of Love written on stone, has been transformed into a New *Living* Covenant of Love in Jesus Christ, penetrating, brightening and re-uniting man's mind and heart; and re-ordering and governing his every action and entire being, according to the standard of holiness [whole-hearted fullness of being]. No longer only Israel, but all nations [as ordered in Divine Providence] can Now share in these blessings, and become His Covenant people. See 'Man' in Useful Terms.

> *"Who then O God, is to take up the defence*
> *of this most meek Lamb, who never opens His mouth*
> *to defend himself, but speaks on our behalf alone?"*

St. Padre Pio.

In light of what Jesus Christ has freely done for us, let us be inspired to deepest gratitude, as we welcome His Second Coming within and through our souls, most particularly by receiving the sacred Food of the Eucharist, with sincere and virtuous acts of Holy Communion. And as our heart's desire [human will] is purified and healed, we too can become food for Him; offering back the food of all of our acts [of thought, word, and deed] in His Ever-creative, Life-giving acts, on behalf of everyone and everything that would be regathered in Him.

In living on earth to realize [make real] Jesus Christ's Second Coming, let us then also look forward to His Third Coming as the victorious and triumphant Lion-Lamb of the tribe of Judah; the Lion who has triumphed because He became a Lamb [Revelation 5; John 1:29]. For on this greatest of days, He will be openly revealed as the true power of the *"King of kings and Lord of lords"* 1 Timothy 6:15; Revelation 17:14 and 19:16, because He is the One, and only One, found worthy to open the seven-seal scroll, and the seals of our inner being, where nothing - not even a shadow of thought, will remain hidden. We give thanks that in His Life, Passion, Death, and Resurrection, new [Ever-new] Life has been won back for all those who would gladly be His people. A Love-crowned Kingdom that will joyfully honour and worship God in the Light-union of the Most Holy Trinity. Ruling this Kingdom, will be the One true King Jesus Christ; the All-conquering Lion-Lamb of the tribe of Judah.

> *"Behold, the Lion from the tribe of Judah,*
> *the root of David, has prevailed."*
>
> Revelation 5:5.

The Scales of Justice

Divine Justice – the ruling principle of the Cosmos; all equality and equilibrium found on the Cross; Jesus Christ - the One for whom the Father looks within our souls; all rights belong to God; our time of Mercy on earth; wise to the serpent; the Courts of Heaven and Satan's just claims against us; no cheap grace; the impacts of sin; the two sides of Confession; God's silence before human freedom; judgement as purely Spiritual; our neighbour's keeper; retribution belongs to God.

"The Father does not judge anyone. But He has given all judgment to the Son, so that all may honour the Son, just as they honour the Father." John 5:22-23. "Christ Jesus who has died, and who has also risen again, is at the right hand of God, and… intercedes for us."

Romans 8:34.

In God, all things are in equilibrium. Just balances and scales serve to balance His supreme rights as Creator and conserver of All that is. They are the base upon which His Perfect [Whole and All-Perfect] order and stability rests [Leviticus 19:35-37]. Mentioned some five hundred times in Sacred Scripture, Divine Justice is revealed as the ruling principle of the Cosmos. It is the levelling of the scales brought to balance in the New Covenant of Love made in Jesus Christ, whose utter consummation on the Cross [the figurative scales] has fulfilled the rights of Divine Justice, and rebalanced the scales.

"A false balance is an abomination to the Lord, but accurate weights are his delight."

Proverbs 11:1.

The Cross on which Jesus Christ hung between the good [repentant] thief, and the bad [unrepentant] thief, demonstrates to us that God our Father's Love is revealed in Perfect balance [equilibrium] between Justice and Mercy. On the Cross, every legal issue that separated us from Light-union with Him, has been reconciled in His Son-God, Jesus Christ. While by way of the Cross, our Father has given us everything we need to return to right relationship; to equality and equilibrium with Him, and with everyone and everything in Him, in His Son.

> *"...more darkness and division have come into the world ... through the lack of the Light of [Divine] Justice, and the advent of the darkness of injustice, than from any other causes."*
> God the Father speaks to St. Catherine of Siena.

The Scales of Justice call our attention to who Jesus Christ is. Jesus is our brother, teacher and advocate, and our most faithful friend. He is also God. Forever sitting at the right hand of the Father, He is the *Fathers Only Begotten Son"* John 1:14,18; *"the true vine"* John 15:1; who *"is in the bosom of the Father"* John 1:18. Partaking fully in the Three-in-One Life of the Godhead, He is the One acceptable and All-sufficient Blood atonement [at-One-ment], vindicating the supreme rights of Divine Justice, for all human sin and evil. He is our righteousness and Sanctification, and the Loving, All-powerful interface between our soul and the Father. He is our absolute authority; our wise and inscrutable Judge, and Justice is His way. While earthly authorities perish, Jesus Christ is the *"King of kings and Lord of lords"* 1 Timothy 6:15; Revelation 17:14 and 19:16; the ruler of the Davidic Kingdom, which will last forever. **He is the only One who fully can, and does, take our part, because outside of Him, we have and we are nothing [John 15:5]. Jesus is the One *on* whom the Father looks [Isaiah 66:2], and the One whom the Father looks *for* within our souls, because He can only Love, and therefore must find Himself [Jesus Christ] within us.**

> *"You have no other merits than through My merits, but My merits are infinite, inexhaustible."*
>
> Jesus speaks to Blessed Dina Belanger.

During our gift of days on earth [our appointed time of Mercy and healing], Jesus gazes upon us, not as what we are [fallen], but as who we are called [invited] to be in Him. He continuously calls forth the original glory [blissful magnificence], which wants to be conceived and birthed within and through us; that state of original innocence and justice [Eternal Beatitude], which is His own Life potential seeded within us since Baptism. He gives us the way and the confidence to abandon back [give consent] to Him. To journey with and in Him to Calvary, dying to the *"old man"* and rising again in Him, to the true vigour, power, and purpose of the *"new man"*.

> *"What you are looking for is looking."*
>
> St. Francis of Assisi.

Our primary task and purpose as temporary pilgrims on earth, is nothing other than to become the mirror eye; to become Light upon Light, the eye through which we see God, as One with the Eye through which God sees us [in Jesus Christ], in a state of mutual receiving and giving Eternal Life. For it is the way of Perfect and immutable Justice, that how we live is how we die [1 Corinthians 13:12]. The way we have treated [welcomed and shielded, or abused and rejected] Jesus Christ within and through our soul, and in the souls of others in mortal life, is the way we will be received in Eternity. In mortal death, Jesus will [and can only] look upon us the way we looked upon Him while on earth. With *"eyes like a flame of fire"* Revelations 2:18 [19:12], and as our Just Judge**, He will penetrate and scrutinize the very depths of our being for realized or unrealized potential within Himself.** Only deep fidelity, lived out in faithfulness, can render us recognizable and acceptable because when we come to stand before Him, we will stand responsible. His judgment will be final, and no plea will be entered to alter His verdict, because our working time on earth will be over. We will know then, if not before, that all rights belong to Him, and that it never was our prerogative, to question His inscrutable and Perfect [Whole and All-Perfect] ways [Truth] and Judgements.

> *"You shall not add to the word which I command you, neither shall you take away from it, that you may keep the commandments of the Lord your God which I command you."*
>
> Deuteronomy 4:2, Revelation 22:18-19.

Man's Life on earth is the time of Divine Mercy. God's Mercy is the All-powerful radiation of His Love for us, which makes provision for our weaknesses, releases us from our debt of sins, and shields us from the works of evil. Yet, because of sin, man's sense of the balance between Justice and Mercy tends to be one-sided and subjective, giving the impression that it is sentimental and lax, and negates man's responsibility to be in right relationship with Him. In reality, **while God's super-abundant Mercy is His greatest attribute [St. Faustina], and is offered to one and all, it is neither sentimental nor lax, but righteous, and puts the unassailable Truth about attaining Eternal Life before us.** We need only think of Jesus iron constancy during His Passion, and the purification of the souls in Purgatory, to realize that God's Mercy flows from, and with, His Justice. This incalculable work of swallowing up and forgiving, the ruthlessness and blind agony of sin and evil, in Love's own fire, has set the legal precedent that allows Him to be merciful. We are forgiven [meaning *"have our debt cancelled"* in Aramaic], because of God's Covenant keeping nature, and His immutable Justice, which operates in Oneness with His unfathomable Mercy.

Justice must temper God's Mercy, to maintain His Perfect stability, otherwise endless dis-order and chaos would ensue. All gains and victories are therefore found in the soul's positive abandonment [consent] to the Cross, on which Jesus was recognised as God, and on which alone, man can be recognizable to God [in Jesus Christ]. The Cross is the means by which our lives are transformed [in Charity], so that those who will refuse God's window of Divine Mercy while on earth, will justly suffer Divine Justice in the Spiritual realm of the All and the Only. For **there can be no** *"second death"* **Revelation 2:11, 20:6,14 and 21:8 for Jesus Christ, but only for the souls who would crucify Him twice, within their own, and others divided [meaning "severed" or** *"cut off"* **in Hebrew] being.** God's final work of grading and forever separating the good [wheat] from the evil [chaff], at *"the [final] end of time"* [Revelation 20:7-15; 21], demonstrates His Perfect stability between Mercy and Justice. For in the Wholeness [All-Perfection] of His divinity and goodness, He cannot, and will not permit, endless division within Himself, which is the pure and the good, living forever in company with the sinful and the wicked [the evil and ungodly]. God's royal Mercy should then never be mistaken as a sign of weakness and concession to the flesh [carnal ego-self] and the old world; to be taken for granted or misused. For without the power of repentance [meaning *"turning back"* or *"coming back"* to God in Aramaic and Hebrew] and forgiveness, Satan the accuser is justly empowered against us, and there is no legal right to Mercy.

> *"Every little sin merits infinite pain,*
> *because it is against Me, whom am Infinite Good."*
>
> God the Father speaks to St. Catherine of Siena.

Sacred Scripture warns us we must be remain vigilant, and make what Jesus did in His Life, Passion, Death, and Resurrection our own, to be reconciled with God our Father. The Prophet Ezekiel says that Satan, when he was the mighty Angel Lucifer in Heaven, walked upon fiery stones [Ezekiel 28:14]. This means that he was part of the Courts of Heaven and God's throne. And while he is no longer there, he is now crawling back and forth upon the earth, together with his legions of demons, for the purpose of searching our ways and gathering evidence against us, to present before God [Revelation 12:10 and Job 1:6-12]. **His right to operate against us, comes from his just** accusations against us. **Jesus therefore cautions His disciples that it is not enough to be as innocent [harmless] as a dove, but man must be as wise as [wise to] the serpent [Matthew 10:16].** While we are not to focus on evil or demons, we must *"Be sober and vigilant"* 1 Peter 5:8, and alive to the reality that evil spirits continuously prowl around, seeking to strike at *"an opportune time"* Luke 4:13, with the purpose of destroying our Eternal souls, and the souls of others through us. And as this legal right to operate against us can be found not only in our own lives, but in our ancestral bloodline, all manner of afflictions that plague families; from depression, to sicknesses and addictions, perversions, debts, and even death by fire, water, or suicide, may be evidence of this diabolical work. Cleansing our bloodlines of curses and demonic interaction is achieved by repenting of our own sins, as well as the sins of our ancestors*. An example of this prayer is found in Nehemiah 1:5-11.

[*Healing from generational curses and afflictions may also require fasting, Masses, and the intercession of a priest, or authentic Church healer].

Examples of Satan's **silent accusations** in the Courts of Heaven are found in the lives of Job [Old Testament] and Peter [New Testament]. Accusations of impure motives for serving God [only because he is materially wealthy] were brought against Job, who lost everything, including his health. Job however, did not lose his *faith as* a child of God - which was Satan's plan for him. Abandoning himself to God's Mercy, he forgave [released] and prayed for those who had persecuted him, qualifying [justifying] himself for God's restitution. In the end, God rewarded him with twice what he had before. Satan also brought accusations against Peter, but was saved by the intervention of Jesus, as a God-man, living on earth filled with the Holy Spirit.

In His Life, Passion, Death, and Resurrection, Jesus Christ has since won the Cosmic victory for us. As the *"Eternal High Priest"* Hebrews 4:14; 8:1, and by the testimony [voice] of His Precious Blood, He is our personal intermediary in the Courts of Heaven. Everything we need to co-operate with and participate in Jesus Christ, which is to say, to come into agreement with the voice of His Blood [His Spiritual

Passion within us], and overcome evil, is put at our disposal in His Church on earth. For when Jesus won back the Kingdom for us on the Cross, the enemy was brought into subjection to Him. He nevertheless fights untiringly against us, but is only permitted to do so in correspondence with our allowing him to bring accusations against us in the Heavenly realm. The primordial authority of God's Word, Ever-alive in the Name; the Cross, and the Precious Blood of Jesus Christ, has provided us with full power over his earthly kingdom of ruin. There is nothing that the merits of Jesus Christ in His Church cannot heal and make new, by means of grace. Even sin caused by natural faults and frailty [rather than a deliberate act of the will or voluntary infidelity], although never a means of grace, can be constrained to do the work of grace in an overcoming soul, who demonstrates conscious awareness and acceptance of what sin and degradation is, and makes a sincere appeal to His Mercy. They are both justified [restored to right relationship with Him], and receive more graces than they ask for, because God's transformation of the soul in Himself, is the expression and satisfaction of His infinite Mercy, which gives Him glory [and the soul glory in Him]. Satan and his demons thus become confounded and reluctant convicts, adorning the Eternal glory of vigilant and repentant souls, with the very enticements and plan of destruction they have devised to destroy them. **And so, as children of God, while we believe Satan exists, we do not believe *in* him [or demons], or focus upon him, because he is a created being [Ezekiel 28:13-15], and we have been given full power over his earthly kingdom in Jesus Christ.** As a created creature, he can no more explain Almighty God as his life-source, than he can explain the miracle of human thought. He has no creative power of his own, but can only delude, deceive, seduce, and destroy, by usurping the power of the human will [heart's desire], operating apart from [against] the Love and Divine Will [Cosmic Hearts Desire] of God.

"Satan vainly spends his rage against My power and My goodness. He cannot reach you hidden in Me. He can do nothing."

Jesus speaks to Blessed Dina Belanger.

In all temptations and assaults, we can look to Jesus strength of overcoming in the desert, when as a God-man in a state of Self-permitted weakness, He was tempted three times by Satan but overcame [Matthew 4:1-11; Luke 4:1-13]. We know He understands our every temptation, while in securing the once and for all Cosmic victory on Calvary, He remains forever the *merciful and faithful High Priest"* Hebrews 2:17, in whom All is done, and All is given. It is then our personal task and responsibility to co-operate with and participate in Him, to answer and silence the accusations made against us, and secure our divine destiny [degree of glory], while assisting others. In this life's work of battle and conquest, it is encouraging to keep before our minds, that God and His Angels behold us as we work to win victory over evil, and re-claim the primordial dignity, purpose, and power of our being [God-being, John 10:34], in Jesus Christ.

When an injustice [sin] happens, we can legally avail of God's Mercy by our participation in the sacrament of Confession [Reconciliation]. **Sacramental Confession is both the gift of sacred washing, and the power and authority granted us in Jesus Christ in the Courts of Heaven, to take authority for [confess] who we are in Him.** It is the privilege of being acquitted of and released from our sins [failures and debts], and of acquitting and releasing others from their sins against us, because **it is only this complete circle of Reconciliation with our neighbour [in God], that we attain to sanctity.** Sacramental confession involves the three-fold confession of actual sins of thought, word, and deed, as well as omitting doing good, or doing better, as the opportunity arises. While venial sins are relatively less grievous than mortal sins [which deprive the sinner of sanctifying grace], every act of sin involves taking the role of, and being laid claim to by the adversary [Satan]. Each act of sin:

- Breaks our relationship of trust with God, and with everyone and everything in Him];
- Inflicts injury; crucifies Jesus Christ anew within our soul, and in the souls of others;

- Soils our soul, and strikes blind our interior Spiritual eye;
- Carries the odour of uncleanliness;
- Cripples our human will, and movement towards [or in] God;
- Blocks our receptivity to the delicate operation of the Spirit;
- Empowers Satan against us, and those we have sinned against; and
- Propels a downward trajectory of chaos and destruction.

"I Love God so much, but He is so sad because of all the sins. We mustn't commit even the tiniest sin!"

St. Francisco Marto - Child Visionary, Fatima.

Each sincere sacramental Confession is most pleasing to God, because it is awareness, and agreement with Him that all rights belong to Him. It is recognition of what even the slightest act of sin is, and the damage it does. In agreeing with God about what sin is, and what needs to be washed clean, we agree with who we really are [and ever can be] in Him. We demonstrate sorrow for our movement away [ex-communication] from Him, and confirm our heart's desire [will] to return to Him. The bath of Confession not only cleanses us of sin, and releases us from the death-grip of the serpent [Satan], but allows the Holy Spirit to work [more powerfully] within us. **Confession allows us to receive with facility, the very Life of Jesus Christ, in the extraordinary act of Holy Communion.** Confession and Holy Communion together with prayer, fasting, and all self-sacrifice and good works, is the divinely creative work of burning off the mask of the false self, which separates Heaven and earth within our soul. In this essential work, the Holy Spirit moves us towards God. He heightens our awareness of what sin is, and strengthens and protects us against future assaults of the enemy, and [injurious and destructive] acts of sin. He inspires in us Life as Charity [Love in action], enabling us to Love our neighbour as ourselves, and He continues to make forgiveness and healing possible.

Sacred Scripture frequently tells us we must Love our neighbour as ourself in order to be in right relationship with hallowed reality. This second commandment, together with the first and greatest commandment, to Love God supremely and above all else, are those on which Truth [centred and personified in Jesus Christ] stand [Matthew 22:37,40]. In terms of the human person, **this means that we are required to both speak and live [confess] Truth [the Truth of our being in God].** To do otherwise, is to both embody within ourselves, wrong-thinking, wrong-doing and wrong-being, and concur with another's wrong-thinking, wrong-doing and wrong-being. It is to fail in Charity [Love in action], and be guilty of alliance against Truth [Ezekiel 3:17-21, 33:7-9; 2 Corinthians 6:14-18 and Ephesians 5:11-12], in which alone man can be sanctified [John 17:17]. *"You shall not hate your brother in your heart. You shall surely rebuke your neighbour, and not bear sin because of him"* Leviticus 19:17. In the same way, if our neighbour justly has something against us, we must leave our gifts at the altar, and first be reconciled with them, before coming to God [Leviticus 19:17, Matthew 5:23-24 and 1 John 4:20-21]. For only *"if you will forgive men their sins, your heavenly Father also will forgive you your offenses."* Matthew 6:14 [John 20:23]. **Only in this complete circle of receiving and offering forgivingness, can we learn to walk upright in Jesus Christ.** Only in this way, can we stand [in Truth] empowered as executers of God's Mercy, who faithfully steps in, in the All-conquering power of the Holy Spirit, supernaturally gifting pardon to all, because [the Love and Divine Will of] Jesus Christ is in us, and we are in Him. Recognizing sin, and seeking and offering heart-felt forgiveness, allows God's Light to flow and manifest higher Life in and among us. We receive healing for our own soul, and we take part in the privileged work of healing the grievously wounded Mystical Body of Christ. For in every creative act of forgiveness [release], is the divine embrace, which releases and embraces everyone and everything. It is the essential means by which we are set free from the deceit and bondage of sin and evil, and return to our original state of glory [blissful magnificence] in God [John 10:34].

When we avail of God's Mercy, to re-unite our human will [heart's desire] with His Cosmic Divine Will [Heart's Desire] in Jesus Christ, we win victory over Divine Justice. We no longer remember or reflect upon our own or others past sins, because they are gone [forgiven]. No further punishment is necessary because Jesus Christ has already made All-sufficient payment to redeem us. While to believe or do otherwise is to offend God's righteousness, and to withhold healing and restoration from ourselves and from others. The just soul [being in justice] that works to maintain this balance also has the effect of placating Divine Justice, and even converting Justice into Mercy.

The Life of Jesus Christ confirms how God avails of His Mercy, more than His Justice. His earthly Life was all Mercy, from His conception and birth, to His words and works, and ultimately the outpouring of Divine Mercy in His final agony on the Cross. Only once, in holy anger, did He draw upon His divine authority to drive profaners out of the temple. In this act, He drives out the wayward human will [heart's desire] that desecrates and makes into a marketplace the temple [or holy land] of our souls. St. Paul draws our attention to God's perfect balance between Mercy and Justice urging us to *"notice the goodness and the severity of God. Certainly, toward those who have fallen, there is severity; but toward you, there is the goodness of God, if you remain in goodness"* Romans 11:22-23.

No life is without sin, and no state of human sinfulness is greater than God's super-abundant Mercy. Sacred Scripture tells us that *"If we say that we have no sin, we deceive ourselves, and the Truth is not in us"* 1 John 1:8. We also deceive ourselves if we think we can cure ourselves from sin, by being our 'own priest' rather than availing of sacramental Confession [St. Hildegard of Bingen]. While the sin that is neither pardoned in this world or the next, is that of judging one's misery to be greater than God's Mercy [St. Catherine of Siena, and St. Faustina]. All three states of wrong-thinking depreciate His unfathomable Mercy. Therefore, regardless of how shameful or difficult our sins may be, when we return to God with genuine remorse, for Love of Him, they are thrown as drops of water into the furnace of His Womb-Heart. It is only man's violent rebellion against God, and failure to avail of His Mercy, that forces Him to make use of His Justice, in order to restore equilibrium. Jesus suffers this violence in Himself, for the enormous weight of sin bears down upon Him, while He forms a continuous shield for the Father.

> *"This is that sin which is neither pardoned here nor there, because the soul would not be pardoned, depreciating My Mercy."*
>
> Jesus speaks to St. Faustina [Divine Mercy].

In understanding the operation of God's Mercy and Justice, it is vital to recognize that every unrepented sin, [both venal and mortal], weighs on the scales of Divine Justice, and must be accounted for. Sins such as the taking of human life; the corruption of innocent children; disregard for the Eucharist; the failings of professed souls; and ultimately blasphemy against the Holy Spirit [resistance to Truth], weigh so heavily, that man gives course to the full force [re-balancing rights] of Divine Justice. For when Jesus Christ is rejected, we have nothing other than a demonic and chaotic world that sinks to the very depths of darkness. Many calamities; from personal, to social and environmental degradation and disaster, are a sign of this breakdown. Creation itself, deprived of God's Spirit in human souls, which infuses and orders all things, becomes the instrument of chastisement.

If we lose the brightness and vigour of Eternal Life, or if we cannot rise to the degree of glory [blissful magnificence] of which we were capable, it is not because God desired this, or has not provided the remedies required. For although Jesus Christ is the ultimate and final Judge, it is really we who first pronounce judgement upon ourselves. **The divine action, says Meister Eckhart, corresponds with, or is adjusted to, our human condition; it does not reflect God's 'choice', but our particular state.** No shadow of impurity can enter the Light of Heaven, and so if we live to borrow God's Spirit, *which is every breath* *we take*, to stand in reproach of Him; or walk in lukewarmness, with heavy feet and dull hearts, we will be spewed out like tepid water.

> *"As you have believed, so, it shall be done unto you."*
> Matthew 8:13.

We need only look to the spectacle of the Passion, to understand Satan's vehement loathing of God [Truth] and man, and his devastating works by way of those caught in his death-grip. We can also see what God in His Perfect Justice thinks of sin and evil, and therefore the self-elected fate awaiting the unrepentant sinner, and those who charm themselves with ideas of **cheap grace**, despite clinging to fleshy [egoic], worldly and evil ways; despite Spiritual slothfulness, lukewarmness and waywardness. As our spent breath freezes upon blue lips, says the poet O'Shaughnessy, and the doors close upon the things that our spirit *truly* sought in *"the half-light of the wandering world"*, we will have nothing more to say or do, but come face-to-face with the opportunity and blindness, we had on earth. Set before us, will be the measure of our deadness or aliveness to Truth; and the Spiritual destination that befits our state of being.

> *"Whatever is in a man or woman's mind,*
> *apart from consent to know and Love God,*
> *and Jesus Christ, cannot justify a man or woman."*
> St. Anthony of Padua.

While natural justice [human laws or ordinances] must prevail in cases of crimes and abuses, to bring natural order and avoid uncontrollable anarchy and violence on earth; and while we are not to be complicit with wrong-thinking, wrong-doing, and wrong-being, that violates Truth, and makes us complicit in sin [Leviticus 19:17, 2 Corinthians 6:14-18 and Ephesians 5:11-12]; we must realize that there are very many degrees of crime, and that all misconduct is committed by a soul held in bondage by the serpent [Satan]. Further, because good and evil are so deeply enmeshed in the fallen realm, while pure good and pure evil operate at the Spiritual level, we cannot be certain of what led a soul to crime. Nor can we be certain of their degree of responsibility, capability, and culpability, or their purity of motivation or intention in all matters. Jesus also warns us that the children of Satan [chaff], can be so *"skilful in doing evil, but they don't know how to do good"* Jeremiah 4:22 [and Luke 16:8], and therefore similar in appearance to the Children of the Kingdom [wheat], they will only be known and separated at Final Judgement [Matthew 13:25-28]. We then avoid self-deception and hypocrisy, and abide in Truth by:

- First attending to the plank [blindness] in our own Spiritual eye [Matthew 7:3-5]; all sin and deficiency in self-giving;
- Teaching and admonishing one another in all wisdom [Romans 15:14; Colossians 3:16], and in Love [Ephesians 4:15], as inspired by the Holy Spirit;
- Correcting one another in a discrete manner [Matthew 18:15-17], and without insistence, while knowing when to step away [Matthew 8:22 and Matthew 10:14];
- Forgiving one another, just as God in Jesus Christ has generously forgiven us [Colossians 3:13; Ephesians 4:32]; and
- Judging one another, not in the fire of the flesh [the carnal ego-self], but in the Spirit [1 Corinthians 2:15], because this alone glorifies God [and the soul, and all things in God], by knowing oneself, and others *only* in the Light of Truth.

"Do not judge, and you will not be judged; do not condemn, and you will not be condemned."

Luke 6:37.

St. Paul explains **judgement as purely Spiritual**, by way of identifying four kinds of people: natural man [1 Corinthians 2:14]; Spiritual man [1 Corinthians 2:15); infants in Christ [1 Corinthians 3:1]; and fleshly [carnal-ego] man [1 Corinthians 3:3]. Of these four groups [which are not mutually exclusive, but which demonstrate the teaching], only the [repentant] Spiritual man judges all things, and is not subject to anyone's judgement [1 Corinthians 2:15], because he is in Jesus Christ, who is Truth. Only the Holy Spirit knows the work that needs to be done, or that can be done in any soul. Only He can do the work, in the right way, and in right timing. Natural man cannot judge because he refuses to receive or accept the things of God, considering them foolish [1 Corinthians 2:14]; while the fleshy man [1 Corinthians 3:3] and the infant Christian [1 Corinthians 3:1] may not categorically refuse Truth, but yet do not have the Spiritual mind [and discernment] of Christ. **When the unspiritual man attempts to judge or define another, he serves no good purpose**, but rather exposes to everyone, including Satan and his demons, the voids of existence- ignorance, ungodliness, and self-distain within his soul, while [further] soiling and crippling it, and deepening the dark prison of the ego self.

> *"...make it your ambition to lead a quiet life,*
> *and to do your own business,*
> *and to work with your own hands..."*
>
> 1 Thessalonians 4:11

The maturing soul, who is sufficiently purified and re-ordered in higher Life in the Spirit, recognises sin and all ego-projection as the derailed action of an afflicted and suffering soul, in bitter bondage to the flesh [carnal ego-self], the old world, and fallen spirits. While they do not condone or encourage what is wrong, and speak only Truth [as inspired by the Holy Spirit], they recognise the adversary is ultimately not the other person, but the spirit of Satan preying upon the voids of darkness in human souls, and perhaps unrepented ancestral sins. In the knowledge that Jesus Christ, our absolute authority, and Just Judge, is suffering [by degrees] in every person [Romans 15:3], and that we all must face the sober Day of Judgement, they take the part of their keeper [shield and salvation], rather than their tempter and enemy [Genesis 4:9; Leviticus 19:17; Matthew 16:23, 25:40]. They do not avenge those crippled and afflicted self-destructors, who insist upon wrong-thinking, wrong-doing and wrong-being, that would also afflict and destroy them, and others around them. Operating as salt and Light [Matthew 5:13–14], and abiding in innocence and justice, their work of overcoming evil with good, is the work of mirroring the primordial Light-splendour of all that God is in all things, which is One with His Cosmic Heart's Desire [Divine Will] for their restoration in Him. It is also the work of heaping coals of fire upon the heads of the enemies of God [Romans 19:20; Proverbs 25:22], because God Himself will rebalance the scales of Justice. *"Vengeance belongs to Me, I will repay, says the Lord"* Romans 12:19. [Deuteronomy 32:35].

And so, **keeping before our mind the operation of Divine Mercy and Divine Justice, and the reality that Jesus Christ Himself could do nothing for so many of His hearers [St Augustine]**, we offer everyone to God in forgiveness and in a prayerful embrace, as to weaken and destroy the works of evil, which would draw all of us into the terrible abyss of Hell. Remaining at peace in this work [allowing Jesus Christ to remain at peace within our soul], because no-one can be forced to abandon back [give the consent of] their human will to God, we thus give our hearts to others in Jesus Christ, but we do not give them our soul, which belongs to, and rests in God. Only with this conception of Truth can we fulfil our task and responsibility of bearing Jesus Christ, and destroying the kingdom of Satan [old world], for the sake of everyone and everything that would be regathered in Him.

> *"(My daughter) Speak to the world about My Mercy; let all mankind recognize My unfathomable Mercy. It is a sign for the end times; after it will come the Day of Justice. While there is still time, let them have recourse to the fount of My Mercy; let them profit from the Blood and Water which gushed forth for them."* **Diary, 848** [John 19:34].
>
> *"Write: before I come as a Just Judge, I first open wide the door of My Mercy. He who refuses to pass through the door of My Mercy, must pass through the door of My Justice."* **Diary, 1146** [John 10:7].
>
> *"Secretary of My Mercy... tell souls about this great Mercy of Mine, because the awful day; the day of My Justice, is near."* **Diary, 965.**

Fiat

The All-conquering power of the *"Fiat"*; modesty, manners, gentleness, chastity, and all wisdom, graceful [grace-filled] simplicity and glad sharing - Mary teaches authentic interior and exterior fidelity to the Life of the *"Fiat"*; the full substance and depth of chastity; wise to the everyday work of demons; the Brown Scapular - the Garment of Salvation; God is waiting for you.

"Thy Kingdom come,
Thy Will be done,
On earth, as it is in Heaven."

Matthew 6:10.

The words of the Our Father prayer, express God our Father's One Heart's Desire from all Eternity, which is to receive His child's breath of consent; their *"Fiat"*, in His All-powerful, All-healing and All-fulfilling Love and Divine Will.

It is with this most beautiful and prolific Latin word meaning *'" let there be"*, in the power of the Holy Spirit, that God began, and pronounces all His works. He *needs and waits for* His child's sincere *"Fiat"* to begin the most prodigious work of re-creating within them, the infinite expanses of His Divine Being. For it is only the free act of abandoning back [giving the consent of] the human will [heart's desire] to the operation of the Divine Will [the Father's Cosmic Heart's Desire], that returns back to Him, His right to restore and re-create [re-birth] anew within the soul, the glorious meaning and purpose of our being. All Heaven celebrates and joyfully participates in establishing the dominion of the Kingdom within the desirous child who gladly gives their *"Fiat"*, amidst life on earth. For they know that the All-conquering *"Fiat"* is Life [and Light] itself; all lives proceed from, and exist upon it; and all lives find their fulfilment and completion [operating] in it alone. In it, is contained the infinity of all divine goods, joys, beauties, harmonies, and contentment's, which is the child and Father's delight.

The Blessed Virgin Mary, is the unparalleled exemplar of the *"Fiat"*, because it was her breath of consent [her *"Yes"*] in the power of the Holy Spirit, that allowed God to descend into time, and carry out His works of Redemption, and Sanctification. Free from original sin, and living perfectly and whole-heartedly in the Love and Divine Will of God, the primordial *"Fiat"* was the cause of her fullness of grace; her ripeness, stability, and readiness for the supreme privilege of being the Mother of her Creator. It was the cause of all the sublime prerogatives for which she is honoured; her Immaculate Conception, her perfect [whole and all-perfect] sanctity, sovereignty, and divine maternity.

Enveloped in an atmosphere of mildness and modesty; of discretion and composure; the Blessed Virgin Mary demonstrates exemplary faithfulness to higher Life in the Spirit. Her purity [Matthew 1:23 and Luke 1:26-38]; generous obedience to God [Luke 1:38]; authentic modesty and humility [Luke 1:48]; solicitous Charity [Luke 1: 39-45,56]; profound wisdom [Luke 1:29,34]; worship of God [Luke 2:21-44]; her attitude of gratitude towards Him [Luke 1:46-55]; fortitude in exile [Matthew 2:13-14] and in suffering [Luke 2:34-35 and John 19,25]; her 'Poorness in Spirit', and material simplicity that trusts in God [Luke 1:48], confirm that always and in every way, she is the handmaid of the Lord, and the perfect [whole and all-perfect] replica of the Life of her Son-God.

Invested with the full depth and power of God-being [John 10:34], Mary is truly beautiful, because in the all-purity of her being, she is full of God's own original and radiant beauty. **In her knowledge of God, and of herself in Him, and taking to heart nothing but His Love and Divine Will [Romans 12:1-2], her every exterior action flowed from the interior action of God within her most pure soul.** From her refined manners, contemplative gaze, and prudent use of her five senses and tongue; to her modest and simple clothing, and absence of vain indulgence and staging; her immaculate interior holiness [wholehearted fullness of being] was mirrored outwardly in her unstrained and gracious presence, which attested to her perfectly chaste being. Operating always and only in **pure Charity**, Mary honoured and respected the inviolable dignity of the being of others in God, taking the role of keeper [shield and salvation] rather than tempter and enemy [Genesis 4:9; Leviticus 19:17; Matthew 16:23, 25:40]. Ever-preserved and Ever-new in God, she could know neither dis-ease nor normal decay, while her death at sixty-four years, was a gentle passing from life on earth to the Life of Heaven [Blessed Anne Catherine Emmerich].

> *"Oh, if you know how gentle the Blessed Virgin is and how happy I am among the gentle; they delight Me."*
>
> Jesus speaks to Sr. Mary of the Holy Trinity.

With the primordial seal and power of the *"Fiat"*, Mary's feet were already upon the head of the serpent [Satan], as she set in motion God's Plan for man's liberation from mortal death. For as one woman [Eve] had once been devastatingly deceived by the serpent [Satan], it was God's Heart's Desire [Divine Will] that another woman*, who **worshipped Him as He can only be worshipped,** *"in Spirit and in Truth"* John 4:24, would be the vessel through whom Satan and all evil, would come to a most crushing defeat. St. John gives witness to Mary's primacy in God, in his most splendid vision of a woman clothed with the sun, with the moon under her feet, and a crown of twelve stars around her head [Revelation 12:1], who Pope John Paul II explains is pre-eminently Mary, *"the woman of glory"*.

[*Together with her faithful offspring; the *"Children of Light"* Luke 16:18; John 12:36; Ephesians 5:8; 1 Thessalonians 5:5, **united in Jesus Christ**].

In raising Mary to the most privileged office of Queen-Mother, God raises every man and woman again to their true personal dignity, and rightful place as a divinely-human person, in the divine order. Their value is no longer limited to the privileged office of wife, mother, husband, or father etc., at the natural level, but every person is called [invited] to be a Spirit bride or Spirit brides-man of Jesus Christ, and a fecund Spiritual mother or father in the Spiritual order. The liberation of women in particular, is demonstrated many times in Sacred Scripture, where we see Jesus [appear to] risk His reputation and personal safety for the sake of a woman. As God, He did not subordinate women or measure their purpose and worth by earthly standards. Mary Magdalene was one notably sinful woman who recognized Jesus as her true liberator, signified in her smashing a jar of expensive ointment over His feet, and wiping them with her hair. Women follow Jesus along the way of His Passion and stand at the foot of the Cross, while Mary Magdalene was chosen to first witness the Resurrection.

We look to our most Blessed Queen-Mother, as the most exalted, grace-filled instrument of God's Plan of the Redemption and Sanctification of our souls, as to befit us for the Kingdom of Heaven. The fully co-operative and participative divine complement; she is Prophetess, Mediatrix, and Co-redemptrix, encasing the treasury of all divine graces. We cannot attain to Sanctification without a *living* relationship with her in Jesus Christ, who will reign as King through and with her; His own and our own celestial Mother.

> *"Let not your heart be disturbed.*
> *Am I not here who is your Mother?"*
>
> Our Blessed Mother speaks to St. Juan Diego.

As our celestial Mother, Mary has made many appeals to us, to turn back to God in fidelity to our *faith as* children of God. She has pleaded many times with us to amend our lives; to pray much, do penance and make reparation for our own sins, *and* for the sins of the world. Calling out the Father's Cosmic Heart's Desire [Divine Will] for our zealous *"Fiat"*, she appeared as Our Lady of Mount Carmel, and held out the Brown Scapular, and the Rosary to us over one hundred years ago at Fatima, and more recently, accompanying her stark **last warnings** through four children of Garabandal, Spain. For as Noah was instructed to build the Ark and enter it to be saved [preserved] from the Flood, we are asked [but never forced] to enter the Ark of Our Lady's Sorrowful and Immaculate Heart [intimately united with the Sacred Heart of her Son], within which a safe place has been prepared for each person, who would willingly co-operate with and participate in Divine Life. **We have every reason to gratefully receive this most high gift, not least because she is our Mother; the unequalled exemplar of the Love and Divine Will of God in a human person, but because she desires it, God our Father also desires it.**

"Before the cup was filling up. Now it is flowing over...
Less and less importance is being given to the Eucharist.
You should turn the wrath of God away from yourselves by your efforts.
If you ask for forgiveness with sincere hearts, He will pardon you.
I, your Mother, through the intercession of St. Michael the Archangel, ask you to amend your lives.
You are now receiving the last warnings.
I Love you very much and I do not want your condemnation.
Pray to us with sincerity and we will grant your requests.
You should make more sacrifices. Think about the Passion of Jesus."

Message spoken by St. Michael the Archangel, on behalf of our Blessed Mother, at Garabandal, October 18, 1961.

[Although the Church is yet to officially approve the apparitions of Garabandal, Spain in the early 1960's, that spoke of the imminency of a personal Illumination of Conscience, Great Miracle, and Great Chastisement;

among the many who confirmed their belief, were Pope Paul VI, Pope John Paul II, St. Padre Pio, and St. Teresa of Calcutta].

The appearance of our Mother as Our Lady of Mount Carmel, is not without vital biblical and prophetic significance. For this fertile green and dominating mountain in Israel, which name means *"vineyard of God"* or *"garden of God"* in Hebrew, is directly associated with:

- The Old Testament Prophet Elijah, who brought idolatrous Israel back to God;
- The Blessed Virgin Mary's primacy in the order of Carmelites, and her role as Prophetess; and
- The primacy of the interior Spiritual Life, and zeal for re-union with God, as taught and exemplified by the Carmelite Order.

The actions proposed in our Blessed Mother's messages, emphasize prayer, penance, self-sacrifice [self-giving], and devotion to the Eucharist. Lived out in fidelity to the three Evangelical Counsels [virtuous dispositions and practices] which are Poverty ['Poorness of Spirit'], Chastity [holy purity] and Obedience [co-operation with God in His Love and Divine Will], it is that Eucharistic state of being, which *alone* allows us to be drawn upwards and into mystical union with Jesus Christ. In gathering under her little *'garment of grace'*, which is the Brown Scapular of Mount Carmel, and living a life of fidelity to the guiding practices of the Confraternity of the Brown Scapular [which are the teachings and standards of the Church], we adopt the sign and pledge of Eternal Life. While to be enrolled by a priest in the Confraternity, is to be consecrated to our Blessed Mother, and the Life of the *"Fiat"* that she herself lived; while in her Light-presence, and **under her maternal care and protection**. This way of life, requires the whole-hearted dedication of our being; our spirit, soul [memory, will and intellect] and body [namely our five senses, mind, heart, and tongue] to divine service, taking Mary as the consummate exemplar of created holiness [whole-hearted fullness of being]. Our consecration to her is complete, when Jesus Christ is birthed within us, and is continuously present in our lives.

To this end [fulfilment], the Confraternity sets out three essential practices for authentically living our *"Fiat"*:

1. A life of chastity [holy purity] as an entire way of being, according to our state in life [single, married, or widowed]. The full spirit of a life of chastity, is best understood by looking to the original meaning of the word. For the original meaning of **chastity, captures two concepts joined together, which are wholeness and wisdom.** Chastity, in its absolute sense, is the return in divine wisdom, to a life of wholeness [holiness and all-perfection] in God. It brings refinement, temperance [continence], and prudence to bear in all matters, including our appearance*. The seal of purity upon the soul, it is closely related to the virtues of humility and meekness [positive consent or assent, gentleness and balance in Aramaic and Hebrew], which incline us to refrain from thoughts, words, or deeds, that lead or expose oneself or others to curiosity or excitement of the carnal passions and appetites. For we are not only responsible for our own integrity, but are required to take the part of our brother's and sister's keeper and salvation [Genesis 4:9; Leviticus 19:17; Matthew 16:23, 25:40], *if* we are to be in Jesus Christ. True chastity requires self-sacrifice, and the curbing of one's lower tendencies in the operation of the five senses, most particularly the eyes, ears, and tongue. It is reflected in all aspects of being, including Mary-like modest and simple clothing, and the absence of vain adornments, and enhancements. In sum, all showiness, or efforts to draw attention and esteem, even in respect of holy things.

   [* Our Blessed Mother warned at Fatima of immodest 'fashions' that would offend God very much.]

"Either we must speak as we dress, or dress as we speak. Why do we profess one thing and display another? The tongue talks of chastity, but the whole body reveals impurity."

St. Jerome.

Chaste and Mary-like [godly] ways of being, are fundamental to true and authentic worship, that expresses respect for, and friendship with, Jesus Christ and our Blessed Mother. It is essential to keep in our awareness, that we were bought at an incalculable price, and it is only right that like Mary, we glorify God in our body, which is intended to be a *living* temple of the Holy Spirit [Romans 12:1; 1 Corinthians 3:16; 6:19] *"The sins which cause most souls to go to Hell are the sins of the flesh [against chastity]"* warned Our Lady of Fatima, in 1917. We must also never forget, that the business of Satan and his demons, is to look for accusations to bring against us in the Courts of Heaven, and thus gain a [stronger] foothold within our soul, and the souls of others, through us. Their everyday business is the work of reading the hunger [wantonness] in every man's eyes; watching his words; his interests, curiosities, and pursuits; his clothing, and adornments; and even the expression on his face. In everything, they look for overt and subtle cues that the soul is weak, naïve, duplicitous, or rebellious, and not Spiritually sighted or capable; not prudent, strong, or committed to higher Life in the Spirit. Chastity is then essential to honouring and glorifying God with the entirety of our being [John 4:24]. It is the key to celestial peace and harmony, which is the foundation of Good-being [God-being, John 10:34], and right relationship with hallowed reality. It is the state of a God-bearing soul, who, like Mary, realizes and honours the presence of God in their own, and in every other soul. See 'Appendix 1: Paradise Lost.'

2. To live up to the teachings and standards of the Church - as set out in the Catechism.

3. The daily recitation of the Rosary*. The Rosary is inseparable from the Brown Scapular, and is our Blessed Mother's most beloved and powerful weapon of choice, for winning victory over the forces of evil. *"The Rosary and the Scapular are inseparable"* says Sr. Lucy of Fatima. *"One day through the Rosary and the Scapular, I will save the world"* were reported

words from our Blessed Mother to St. Dominic. **The Rosary was the favourite prayer of Pope John Paul II, and has been extolled by many other Pontiffs across the ages.** Pope Pius X calls the Rosary *"The most evangelical prayer, and the prayer richest in graces."* **We should therefore entreat all of our needs through the Rosary, most particularly of all, the grace and inspiration to live up to the Life of the** *"Fiat"*.

[*Or recitation of the Little Office of the Blessed Virgin Mary, if not bound to say the Divine Office].

The inexpensive brown woollen cloth of the Brown Scapular, serves as a great lesson as to the 'Poorness of Spirit' of the Blessed Virgin Mary, as the unparalleled exemplar of the **All-Good Life of the** *"Fiat."* Spiritually rich and materially simple, her life with Jesus and Joseph was a very plain and frugal life, of modest material means [money and possessions] and desires, in a little house in Nazareth. While what they did have, was selflessly shared with others [See the Revelation of Blessed Anne Catherine Emmerich, and Venerable Mary of Agreda].

Extraordinary graces, favours, and blessings are offered in return for continually wearing our Blessed Mother's *"Garment of Salvation"* [Pope Gregory XIII], **and committing to live our authentic** *"Fiat"*, **in fidelity to the practices of the Confraternity:**

- The pledge of Mary's unceasing maternal care and protection from evils spirits, and from all dangers to our body and soul;
- The right to participate in all the good works [prayers, fasting, penances, and self-sacrifice], and merits of the members of the Carmelite Order, and the entire Church;
- Protection from the loss of Eternal Life; and
- Quick release from Purgatory.

*"For the height of the Godhead,
seeks nothing but the depths of humility."*

Meister Eckhart.

The authentic Life of the *"Fiat"*, is intimately linked with the Eucharist, and the liberated Eucharistic life, expressed as Charity. Selling everything [Matthew 19:21 and Luke 18:22] of the dark night of the human will, in exchange for the Light, power, and sanctity of the Divine Will, we are numbered amongst Mary's seed. Living in deep fidelity to Jesus Christ, and sheltered under her mantle, we become through her the true *"Light of the world"* Matthew 5:14; the Spirit brides and Spirit brides-men of the Lamb, who fearlessly disarm and destroy the relentless forces of evil with one hand, and rebuild the Kingdom of God with the other. For the Life of the *"Fiat"*, is the means to fulfilling the Our Father prayer. It is the means to rendering ourselves fit for the company [Light-community] of Heaven, because **the Kingdom of God is the Kingdom of the *"Fiat"*.**

[Among the many popes and saints (other than Carmelites) who flocked under the sure refuge of the original Brown Scapular, and testified to its power and miracles, were: Pope John Paul II, Pope Pius XII, Pope Pius X, Pope Benedict XV, Pope Leo XIII, and Pope Gregory I; St. Alphonsus Liguori, St. John Bosco, St. John Vianney [the Curé D' Ars], St. Claude de la Colombiere, St. Maximilian Kolbe, and St. Robert Bellarmine].

> *"Because all the forms of our Love for the Blessed Virgin, all its various modes of expression cannot be equally pleasing to Her, and therefore do not assist us in the same degree to Heaven, I say without a moment's hesitation that* **the Brown Scapular is the most favoured of all....**
>
> *No devotion has been confirmed by more numerous authentic miracles."*
>
> St. Claude de la Colombiere ['Perfect Friend of Christ'].

Should our celestial Mother appear personally to us today, holding out her Brown Scapular, and inviting us to take the pledge of the *"Fiat"*, would we not immediately say *"Yes"* in a spirit of humility and gratitude, knowing that she will mother our re-birth in God? God waited for Mary's free answer, and He is waiting for each one of us.

The Holy Spirit

Free and indefinable; our Breath of Life and Sanctifier; the scent and effects of a clean and unclean soul; the sharp sword of Sanctification – purifying, re-ordering, and re-creating [re-birthing] the soul in Jesus Christ; sincere fidelity essential to His work; His gifts and those we forget to ask for; His fruits in the soul.

"You will send forth your Spirit… and renew the face of the earth."

Psalm 104:30.

The Holy Spirit, from the Latin word *"spiritus"* meaning *"breath"*, is the Spirit of Truth [John 14:17; 15:26], and the Giver of Life [John 6:64; 2 Corinthians 3:6]. The Third Person of the Most Holy Trinity, He is the radiant and magnetic All-embracing Breath of Life [Genesis 2:7], who breathes though every stirring of life, and translates energy into life.

With a secret and elusive quality, we find it hard to define the Holy Spirit in human terms, but we know that He is a Person. Normally invisible, He has on occasion appeared in visible forms, which are symbolic of His free and dynamic actions. When Jesus was baptised in the river Jordan, He descended in the form of a **dove**, symbolising the gentleness, simplicity, and sincerity, with which He works within and through our souls. On Pentecost, He came as a mighty rushing **wind**, symbolising the strengthening of the human will [heart's desire], and rested over the apostles in the form of tongues of **fire**, signifying purification, zeal, and the illumination of the Spiritual intellect.

"He [Jesus] breathed on them [His apostles], and said to them; receive the Holy Spirit!"

John 20:22.

When Jesus speaks of sending us the Holy Spirit, He refers to the *"Paraclete"* John 14:16,26;15:26 [from the Greek word *"Parakletos"*] meaning *"Advocate"*, *"Counsellor"*, *"Helper"* or *"Guide"*. The Holy Spirit is the executor of everything that Jesus Christ purchased* for us. He is God's personal care for us in action. **His work, in the Oneness of the Love of the Father and the Son, is the divinely creative work of healing and sanctifying our souls, through the gift of grace, because He is the One who will** *"renew the face of the earth"* **Psalm 104:30.**

[*Sacred Scripture tells us that *"full of the Holy Spirit"* Luke 4:1, Jesus while living on earth as a God-man, was led into the wilderness, to fast and to pray. When He returned, He came *"in the power of the Spirit"* Luke 4:14. At this higher level, the full power of the Holy Spirit was freely at His disposal for use in His appointed mission on earth. All grace is ultimately derived from Jesus Christ, and belongs in its fullness to Him, by His All-sufficient Self-sacrifice on Calvary. Only because of Him, and in Him, we can experience the fullest effects of yielding to the creative work of the Holy Spirit.]

All three Persons of the Most Holy Trinity enter a soul which truly Loves God, and lives in right disposition to grace. The Second and Third Persons are sent; the Son by the Father, and the Holy Spirit by the Father and the Son. In this great mystery of One singular and tripartite Light-union, the Holy Spirit is the Three-in-One Life-breath of our soul [Genesis 2:7], and therefore our closest, and most faithful friend. Cleansing, illuminating, and delivering; comforting, consoling, and warming; He purifies, strengthens, and matures us, and heals and restores us to *living* temples of God. **With His Light and warm touch, He animates our souls and teaches us Truth, bestowing His celestial gifts upon us, and granting us their fruits, making us capable of discerning how to act [in thought, word, and deed] in each moment, as to direct ourselves and others towards God.** He seals the entrances of our souls, forbidding Satan and his demons from approaching and entering with all kinds of temptations, deceptions, and afflictions. He is the Spiritual 'Oil of Gladness', and author of Spiritual joy. He is our inspiration, when we reach out to help others. In His three-fold All-ness, He is the source and giver of all power and reality to the Mystical Body of Christ [the *living* Church], while His presence and operation is integral to, and cannot be separated from, the sacraments and provisions of the Church. Authentic unity with God, is the gift of the Holy Spirit.

> *"For as many as are led by the Spirit of God, these are children of God….and if children, then heirs - heirs of God and joint heirs with Christ, if indeed we suffer with Him, that we may also be glorified with Him."*
>
> Romans 8:14,17.

The operation of the Holy Spirit as our Breath of Life [Genesis 2:7], is confirmed in the several verses in Sacred Scripture, which speak of the nostrils of God. The book of Genesis tells us that **by the sheer force of His Love, God breathed into the nostrils of man, raising him from the dust of the ground, to give him the Breath of Life [Genesis 2:7].** This divine privilege confirms man as a created being, issued from, and existing upon, the pure Life-breath of God's Spirit of Love. **Our life-breath is then not our 'own', but the gift of the Life-breath of God breathing within and through us.** During our lifetime, we continuously receive and return the gift of our life-breath to Him, in a relative state of purity [Light], or impurity [darkness], depending upon our soul-condition, and therefore His creative freedom to act within and through us. When this Divine Life energy breathing in us is withdrawn, our body expires, and is separated from our soul.

The lives of the saints attest to the reality that our life-breath [the breath of our soul] carries a supernatural odour, that corresponds with our soul-condition [2 Corinthians 2:15-16]. The odour acquired by the saints, and those who co-operate with and participate in God, and persevere in [commit to] pure and holy living, is the beautifully fresh and fragrant air, that is known as the *"odour of sanctity"*. This clean celestial air, signifies a life lived in the Light and vigour of sanctifying grace. Breathed through the Holy Spirit, it continues to work to purify the faithful soul, and dispose it to continue to offer

God the *"odour of sweetness"*; of holy thoughts, desires and living [Ephesians 5:1-2], through a life of self-sacrifice [self-giving] and mortification, for Love of Him and all things in Him. The faithful soul, is the soul that is **truly present [in faith] to one and all**. While learning to walk ever stronger in the purity of God's Spirit, it becomes in Him, the all-cleansing, and all-integrating life of all, and a place for the Holy Spirit to rest. The delight of God, and all of Heaven, this is the soul who upon mortal death, is ready to take flight in fragrant odour to the perfumed land of promise; the Paradisaic New Jerusalem.

> *"Behold, the smell of My son, is like the smell of a plentiful field, which the Lord has blessed."*
> Genesis 27:27.

Yet, while the crystal air of a pure soul is beneficial to everyone, the breath of a soul who borrows God's Spirit and lives according to its own way, emits foul and sickly air, that intoxicates God, and everyone around it. For the soul who does not drink from the Life-giving spring of *"Living Water"* John 4:10; 7:38, which is Jesus Christ, but drinks instead, from the tepid and stagnant pools of ungodly thinking, reason, and desire, exposes itself [and others] to corruption and death. The divested and dis-ordered operation of the five senses act as the doorways through which the desires of the flesh [carnal ego-self] and the old world [kingdom of Satan] continue to enter, and soil the breath of the soul. Without repentance [meaning *"turning back"* or *"coming back"* to God in Aramaic] this unclean air disposes it to further sin and evil [of thought, word, and deed], because Satan and his demons have been justly granted a [stronger] foothold, while the Holy Spirit cannot endure to abide in an unclean soul.

> *"The devil invites men to the water of death."*
> God the Father speaks to St. Catherine of Siena.

St. Philip Neri who was granted the gift of smelling the souls of the living, was known to hold his handkerchief to his nose in passing those whose soiled soul emanated the odour of impurity. And so, while natural and chemical scents may temporarily mask impure odours, the purest 'nostrils' detect the true [supernatural] scent of the soul.

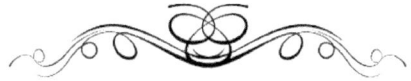

The Holy Spirit is key to fulfilling our primary mission on earth, which is the recovery of the lost depth and deep blessedness within our soul. Only the Holy Spirit, from the heights of the Spiritual realm, can interrogate the mysterious depths of our soul, to uncover our deepest and most hidden fears, longings, and needs. Only He knows our personal ability to Love God in His All-Perfect Divine Will; which is our willingness and strength for self-renunciation; for re-hearing [understanding] and re-seeing [conceiving] Truth. Only He can discern our readiness for co-operation, and purify our inner darkness to create the space that allows us to receive more expansively than we can ever dare to imagine [Romans 8:26-27]. In whatever state of readiness, we find ourselves, He must however, be granted the freedom to act, if we are to grow in the Spiritual Life. *"He is so wise, gentle and discrete"* says St. Padre Pio, He makes no effort to usurp, or take from us our freedom. He judges the motives and intentions of our heart [Hebrews 12:7-11], and works according to the good will and strength of our soul, as well as right timing. He will never pour Himself into a resisting soul, or take anyone beyond where they can go. For in His ineffable Mercy, He will not add to our debt of insensibility, defiance, and ingratitude towards Him.

> *"The Holy Spirit breathes where He Will.*
> *When you think to detain or bind Him, by the*
> *limits of your [human] understanding, He escapes."*
>
> Jesus speaks to Sr. Mary of the Holy Trinity.

The soul-condition for all Spiritual and bodily healing, must then be that of *living faith as* that which we are in God, and a pure and repentant heart. **Repentance [meaning *"turning back"* or *"coming back"* to God in Aramaic] means a sincere change of heart. It is a primordial longing for God, and for becoming real without any fleshy [egoic] and worldly expectation of what this means.** The repentant soul must be prepared for *"even now, the axe [symbolising work and battle] ...[being] placed unto the root of the trees"* Matthew 3:10; Luke 3:9, because **the sharp sword of Sanctification, which pierces the divide between soul and spirit, and judges the thoughts and attitudes of the heart [Hebrews 4:12], is the only way to be tried, tested, and found fit for the Kingdom of Heaven.** It is the only way to separate what is nice and pleasing at the natural level, from what is *truly* good and just on God's terms. This divinely creative work, is the work of shattering the hard ego-mask [ego-persona], and strengthening, focussing, and re-ordering the human person to allow the Light-fire of the Spirit to flow. It is the work of stirring up immature infant souls, including comfortable slaves and pretenders of the flesh and the old world; those who oppose transformation and completeness of their own being, and the being of others, in Jesus Christ. For natural man tends to operate according to outward earthiness; his five senses and speech, mis-directing his soul, while the weak and scattered powers of his spirit are oppressed by the flesh [carnal ego-self] and the old world. His predicament is further complicated by the fact that he can only perceive good or evil relative to his soul-condition, when in Truth **all good is relative to Jesus Christ.** His predicament is complicated by the fact that good and evil are deeply enmeshed on earth, while he cannot of his own accord [at the natural level], perceive the inertness of pure evil, or the dynamism of pure good, both of which operate at the Spiritual level.

> *"Behold, I have refined you, but not as silver.*
> *I have chosen you in the furnace of affliction."*
>
> Isaiah 48:10.

Only the Holy Spirit can unravel good and evil in both Spiritual and material matters, and safely and assuredly restore man's relationship with God [and with all things in Him]. In this work of the purification, re-ordering, and re-integration [re-centring] of his being in Jesus Christ, man's soul must withdraw from the flesh [carnal ego-self] as it re-integrates in the Spirit. In this work of healing and re-creation [re-birth], his spirit is focussed and strengthened; the five avenues of grace unblocked; and his mind re-united with his heart. His spirit can then begin to govern his soul, and in turn the operation of his five senses, which report back to his mind, bowed in his heart.

Repentance necessitates self-discipline and remedial pain for man [according to the state of his soul], because it is the death of the *"old man"*, and the only one he 'knows'. It is however, is the essential means of breakthrough to sorrowful recognition of the gravity of one's own self-centredness, insensibility, waywardness, and ingratitude, towards his Loving Father God. In this work of reconciliation with higher meaning and ways, Sacred Scripture points out the vital importance of the **gifts of divine wisdom, knowledge, and discernment, which we should ask for** *with right motive* **in prayer** [Philippians 1:9; Matthew 21:22; James 1:5, 4:3]. While our Blessed Mother tells St. Catherine Labouré, that **humility, gentleness, and mercy** are the graces which souls forget to ask from her, and which greatly assist Spiritual growth. An insincere, overzealous, or resisting soul on the other hand, exposes itself to all manner of deceptions and afflictions at the hands of the enemy, whose business it is to gather evidence against him. God in His goodness does not give Himself to such a soul on a higher level, knowing that not only would it fail to benefit, but would fall into a worsened state. Therefore, only according to the degree to which the soul consents [by an act of the human will] to the primordial operation of the Holy Spirit, can it be healed from all obvious and subtle carnality and divisiveness, that would derail its own and others Spiritual growth, and Light-reaping work [1 Corinthians 2:14-15; Jude 16,19; James 3:13-15].

> *"God assigns Spiritual food,*
> *as befits the state of the soul."*
>
> Anon.

As the sincerely humble, meek [positively consenting or assenting, gentle, and balanced in Aramaic and Hebrew], and repentant soul reaps the Light of grace, the efforts of Satan and his demons are confused and confounded, because they are unable to experience remorse for sin, and rebellion against God [St. Hildegard of Bingen]. In this soul, pain gradually turns to celestial joy, because re-integrating [re-centring] in the Light of Jesus Christ, it begins to uncover the endless hidden treasures within its inner being. Awakening to its primordial longing for the embrace of the Homeland, it learns to co-operate with and participate in God out of a pure motive of Love, rather than self-reflection, self-pity, fear, or guilt. Ever-more alive to the present moment as God's presence and its One reality, it becomes more **attentive and stable** in the act of being, and of growing fit for the incorruptible and Ever-lasting Kingdom of Heaven.

> *"For I know the thoughts that I think toward you",*
> *says the Lord, "thoughts of peace, and not of evil,*
> *to give you hope and a future.""*
>
> Jeremiah 29:11.

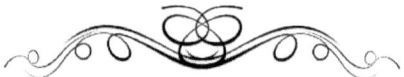

The Two Kinds of Grace - Sanctifying Grace and Actual Grace

Sanctifying grace: is the actual Life of *"Emmanuel: God-with-us"* Old Testament: Isaiah 7:14; 8:8-10 and New Testament: Matthew 1:21-23;

John 1:14; 14:8-11; Colossians 2:9. It is an abiding or permanent supernatural grace [Light], that is first conferred upon our soul by the Holy Spirit [the Sanctifier] in a very special way in the sacrament of Baptism. It is further strengthened and perfected, in the sacrament of Confirmation, and sustained and increased through the ongoing life of the *"Fiat"*. This involves attending Mass, and receiving the Eucharist; receiving the other sacraments [particularly Confession, which restores our disposition to receive graces, favours, and blessings], and maintaining a life of *living* prayer and Charity. It is lost by mortal sin. By sharing in the Divine Life of God Himself, the soul is said to be a partaker of the divine nature [1 Peter 1:4], and is [relatively] holy [whole and all-perfect] and pleasing to Him. The degree to which the soul has renounced itself during its earthly lifetime, for the sake of reaping [conceiving and birthing] the Light of sanctifying grace, will determine its strength and capability for penetrating, and sharing in, the communal bliss, joys, and goods of Heaven. Insufficient sanctifying grace [Light] within the soul upon mortal death, necessitates short or prolonged purification in the Spiritual fire of Purgatory [1 Corinthians 3:12-15], while the absence of sanctifying grace [Light] upon mortal death, is a state of Spiritual death [absence of Light]. In this state, the soul cannot enter either Purgatory or Heaven [Galatians 5:19-21].

Actual Grace: is the supernatural, transient grace which enlightens our mind, and strengthens our human will [heart's desire] to do a good act [in thought, word, or deed], and to avoid or overcome temptation, deception, and all manner of evil. While not an abiding gift like supernatural grace, it is a divine impulse, helping the soul to perform [divine] acts above its lower nature. Actual grace can be obtained by the same means as sanctifying grace, as well as using sacramentals, such as Holy Water, scapulars, and blessed medals. It is obtained by all manner of good works motivated and enabled by Love of God [and all things in Him], including prayer, fasting and all self-sacrifice, participation in the sacraments, and pure acts of Charity.

The aim and purpose of all actual graces, are to sustain and increase sanctifying grace, which depends upon the disposition of the soul.

The Gifts of the Holy Spirit

The variety and abundance of gifts and graces of the Holy Spirit are generally identified in Sacred Scripture as personal gifts and ministry gifts, for those who would be appointed to minister to the faithful. Personal gifts are dispositions of the soul, giving it the ability to respond quickly and with ease, to the inspirations of the Holy Spirit. Among these gifts, the prophet Isaiah [11:2] names six of the seven gifts received in the sacrament of Confirmation, and which are reinforced by fidelity to higher Life in the Spirit:

1. Wisdom;
2. Understanding;
3. Council;
4. Fortitude [Strength];
5. Knowledge;
6. Piety [Faithfulness]; and
7. Fear [Awe-filled reverence] of God.

St. Thomas compares these personal gifts of the Holy Spirit to the sails of our boat, which is moved and directed by the gentle breeze of the Holy Spirit. Ministry gifts meanwhile include special charisms, such as healing of the sick, prophesy, celibacy, or the gift of tongues, to make manifest the power of grace, and to heal and draw souls upwards and out of themselves, and into the Life of the *"Fiat"*.

Discernment is an essential aspect of all gifts of the Holy Spirit, as well as a particular gift in itself, for the purpose of discerning good and evil spirits, and human spirits.

The Nine Fruits of the Holy Spirit

These are virtuous acts performed under the influence of grace. St. Paul [Galatians 5:22] numbers nine symbolic fruits:

1. Love* [*"Agape"*];
2. Joy;
3. Peace;
4. Patience;
5. Kindness;
6. Goodness;
7. Faithfulness;
8. Gentleness, and
9. Self-control [Continence].

[*lived as Charity - Love in action].

These fruits are the perfections that the Holy Spirit forms within the purging soul, as the first-fruits of the glory [blissful magnificence] of new [Ever-new] *Life and purpose* in Jesus Christ.

The Mass

The greatest 'show' on earth; three-fold purpose and three-act sacrifice; co-sacrificial and co-creative - authentic participation in the Mass; the astonishing effects and benefits of the Mass; Satan's relentless efforts to turn souls away; the Church – a Spiritual organism; the true living Church on earth.

"Blessed are those, who have been called to the wedding feast of the Lamb."

Revelation 19:9.

Church bells ring out to call us to sanctity, for the Mass is our inheritance and the [Mystical] Sun of our existence. Illuminating and reconciling Heaven and earth in its every celebration, the Mass is at the heart of a direct relationship between the Father and His child, pouring out the super-abundance of His Love, and carrying the promise of the One Eternal Day.

Prefigured in the Old Testament, in the Israelites offering of the Passover Lamb in celebration and memorial of their delivery out of Egypt [the land of idolatry], the Mass is Jesus Christ's supreme gift and legacy to His Church on earth. With its origin in the Latin word *"missa"* meaning *"mission"* or *"sending"*, the Mass [and the Church], exists for One sole purpose, which is God our Father's divine mission on earth. Christmas, finding its origin in the middle English word *"Cristenmasse"*, [from old English *"Cristes-messe"*], is a literal contraction for *"Christ's Mass"*, or *"Mass of Christ."*

There is nothing greater on earth than the Church, and in her, there is nothing greater than the co-sacrificial feast of the Mass. **For the Mass, is the unbloody renewal and continuation of the Holy [Whole and All-Perfect] and Eucharistic sacrifice of Jesus Christ on Calvary.** Each celebration of the Mass, makes real the absolute power and authority of God, in the Passion, Death, and Resurrection of Jesus Christ, for the three-fold purpose of:

1. Atonement [at-One-ment] for our sins;
2. Victory over Satan and his demons, and all evil;
3. The restoration and re-creation [re-birth] of man to the transfigured Edenic state, for which he was created.

Jesus Christ instituted the Mass to satisfy the constant need of man for self-sacrifice [self-giving], and as a means by which the divine riches [graces, favours, and blessings] He merited by His Passion, Death, and Resurrection, would be applied [gifted] to our souls.

To this end, the Mass includes a three-act sacrifice:

1. **Offertory:** we offer [return] back the gift of our being, and the fruits of our earthly labour [bread and wine, which will become Jesus Christ] to the Father, who first gifted them to us in the power of His Love operating in His Divine Will, which creates and sustains all things;
2. **Consecration:** our offering is united with Jesus Christ's complete Self-giving on Calvary, making our gifts acceptable to the Father [satisfying His Perfect Justice], as He transforms them, in the power of the Holy Spirit, into Jesus Christ;
3. **Holy Communion:** we receive within our being, the return of the now transformed gift we have given [back to] the Father, which has become the *living person* of Jesus Christ. Jesus Christ is mystically incarnated [birthed] in each Host for the purpose of being incarnated [re-birthed] in human souls.

Every Mass contains the complete works of our personal and collective salvation [healing], accomplished *by and in* Jesus Christ. It is His Incarnation and Nativity; His Passion and Death on Calvary; and it is His glorious Resurrection. It tells us everything about the sublime and profound mysteries of *living in faith as* beloved children of a paternal Father, and brothers and sisters of a King. The Mass, is the ritual sacramental action of memorial and presence; of birth, sacrifice, and thanksgiving. In every celebration of the Mass, Jesus Christ is the sacrificial [All-giving] Lamb of God, the priest, and the altar.

Participation in the Mass, is the greatest act of worship, because our worship is transformed by Jesus Christ, who makes it His own to offer to the Eternal Father. No other worship gives more glory to God, and so by no other means are all manner of sanctifying graces, favours and blessings offered so generously to our souls.

> *"It is easier for the earth to exist without the sun, than without the Holy Sacrifice of the Mass."*
>
> St. Padre Pio.

The Catechism of the Catholic Church applies the obligation of participating in the Mass, to all Sundays and Holy Days of Obligation. All Catholics who have reached their 7th birthday, and have the use of reason are considered responsible [unless by exception of health, or other extenuating circumstances], and obliged to attend Mass on these occasions. Sunday, a day set apart from the rest of the week, is man's opportunity to return from outward motion [all unnecessary work and commerce] and multiplicity [of thought, word, and deed] to interior motion [luminosity] and solitude [*living* silence], that moves him to [greater] unity with his Life-source; the [Three-in-One] Divine Sun, seeded within his being.

Satisfying our divine calling as active participators requires:

- Bodily presence at the whole Mass*;
- Appropriate attention to the Mass; and
- Right intention or disposition to participate, which determines the measure in which the extensive treasury of gifts offered, can be applied to our souls.

[*Unless a dispensation has been granted by the Church, or ill health, or other circumstances make it impossible to attend].

The deepest and most reverential *living* silence [consciousness of the unspoken primordial voice of God, as the rooted Light-centre of our being] **is fitting during our presence in the Church building, and our participation in the Mass. We should leave all thoughts of the world [of past, present, and future], and all natural sense curiosities at the door, entering and departing with a recollected mind and heart, focussed on God alone. For the Mass is Calvary. It is the withdrawal from the flesh [carnal ego-self] and the old world, and its interests and activities, and the re-entering into the inner sanctuary of our being, to actively participate in the astonishing mystery of our co-sacrificial offering with the Son-of-God made man.** St. John Chrysostom testifies that early Christians went into the Church building, as into the Palace of a great King, where the Angels are servants, and Heaven is open; where Jesus Christ sits upon a throne, and where the whole edifice is filled with invisible spirits. Many took off their footwear before entering, imitating Moses whom God commanded to take off his shoes, for the place where he was standing was holy ground [Exodus 3:5].

Every Mass is the birth of Jesus Christ, because in each divine act of consecration of the bread and wine, the Holy Spirit overshadows the priest, and acts upon him in the same way as He acted upon the Blessed Virgin Mary, mystically transforming these simple gifts into the Body and Blood; Soul and Divinity of Jesus Christ. The prayer of the Communion Rite: *"Behold the Lamb of God. Behold Him, who takes away the sins of the world",* echo the words of John the Baptist [John 1:29] and of Pontius Pilate: *"Behold, the man!"* John 19:5, as Jesus was presented to the people and condemned to Death. These repeated calls [invitations] to behold the Lamb of God, are an upward call [invitation] to conceive of the mystery, and to behold with ever-greater reverence and gratitude, what has been freely done [and is being done] for us. In this act of beholding, which is an act of Love, we cross the infinite distance between God and natural man. Jesus comes to enter under our roof, which is to say, into our souls, to rebuild His temple, and make of us His clean, stable, and safe dwelling place on earth. The repetition of the word *"Lamb"* again in the words *"Blessed are those called to the Supper of the Lamb",* resonate with joyful expectation of the place prepared for the blessed at the wedding feast of the Lamb, in the Kingdom of Heaven [Revelation 19:9].

With the consecration of the host, and the *"breaking of the bread"* Luke 24:35, the full co-sacrificial [self-giving] purpose of the Mass is achieved. The Eucharist 'makes' the Church [the Mystical Body of faithful souls] because the *"Host"*, from the Latin word *"Hostia",* is the *"Victim"* Jesus Christ. In being united with Him, in offering to the Father, we are active partakers in the mystical and prophetic action that fulfils God's mission, which is the Coming of the Kingdom on earth [within and through our souls] as it is in Heaven. **The co-sacrificial offering of the Mass confers upon us, the privilege of not only receiving the *living* reality of Jesus Christ, but of entering into a mutual giving and receiving as co-Victim *and* co-Creator with Him. We consume Him, and are consumed and re-created [re-birthed] by Him, and in Him, absorbing His Light [Life] into our being.** In this continual creative act of consecration, communion and self-giving, beyond the natural intellect and sense perception, is the purification of our motivations and intentions, and the ennoblement of our souls. **In this divine exchange, we learn that the receiving is in the giving [back],** without the expectation or perception of material or Spiritual consolations and satisfactions at the natural level. For to receive, we must first learn to give back our human will, purified of earthly motives of self-satisfaction and reward, because our souls healing and embellishment with its Eternal reward, requires passing by the way of the Cross. Only in this way, our soul is *truly freed* to rise and expand towards God; towards becoming Love [and Life] itself.

It is fitting that whole-hearted praise and thanksgiving is emphasized throughout the liturgical prayers of the Mass. Indeed, the Mass is termed the sacrifice of thanksgiving, because the celebration of the Eucharist, originating in the Greek word *"eucharistia"*, meaning *"thanksgiving"* provides man with the means of offering back, in union with Jesus Christ, the greatest and most pleasing act of gratitude and worship towards his Creator God and Father. **The words**

of the Mass, express the reality that it is both right and just, and necessary for our salvation [healing], as creatively Eucharistic beings, to give thanks to God everywhere, and in all things. Thanksgiving, expressed as gratitude, is the only possible response to the divine calling [invitation], to live to receive and return back to God, the abundance of *real Life and purpose* in Jesus Christ. Uniting our human will [heart's desire] to the Divine Will [the Father's Cosmic Heart's Desire] in Jesus Christ, as an act of Love and gratitude on behalf of everyone and everything, is right relationship with hallowed reality. It is the foundation of our integrity and healthfulness; to celestial joy, harmony, and peace, which is our Good-being [God-being, John 10:34], and recovery to the blissful state of the Kingdom.

The concluding rite of the Mass, sums up our real and active participation in the Church's mission, which is to go out into the world transformed into pure, holy [whole and all-perfect], and strong, Eucharistic bearers of Jesus Christ. Walking upright in Him, and carrying His Light-presence into the streets, and to all points of the world, that He may reach and embrace all souls, including those who do not look for Him.

> *"When attending Holy Mass, renew your faith and meditate on the Victim who is being immolated for you, in order to placate Divine Justice."*
>
> St. Padre Pio.

In every celebration of the Mass, our Blessed Mother, and the Angels, and saints descend into our midst to assist; standing in astonishment and exhilaration at the excesses of God's Love for man, as Jesus Christ is sacrificed anew and the newness [Ever-newness] of His *real Life and purpose* is offered to us in the sacramental species of the Eucharist.

Many saints attest to the infinite value and rapturous spectacle of the Mass, and to the reality that there is no greater feast, gift or blessing on earth.

Every Mass that we attend *well**:

- Delivers us from the dangers and evils of this world;
- Comforts and consoles us at the hour of our death;
- Goes with our soul to judgement; and
- Raises our glory in Heaven, in and for all Eternity.

[*In a state of right disposition to grace; regularly availing of sacramental Confession, while sincerely undertaking to *live the Mass* as an entire (inner and outer) way of being. This means *offering ourselves back to the Father as a co-sacrificial and co-creative offering in Jesus Christ*, who transfigures our lives into the complete *Livingness* of His own.]

It benefits not only us, but all souls, while diminishing and blinding the works of Satan and his demons. Every Mass, offers a cooling bath of relief and atonement for the purging souls in Purgatory, who cannot assist themselves, but who can help us abundantly in return for our prayers and assistance. Every living Mass is of considerably greater benefit to our soul, than those heard for us after our mortal death.

> "In Mass, I come with such humility that there is no sinner, no matter how depraved he be, that I am not ready to receive, if only he desires it. I come with such sweetness and Mercy, that I will pardon My greatest enemies, if they ask for pardon. I come with such generosity that there is no-one so poor that I will not fill him with the riches of My Love. I come with such Heavenly Food as will strengthen the weakest; with such Light as will illuminate the blindest; with such plenitude of graces as will remove all miseries, overcome all obstinacy, and dissipate all fears."
>
> Jesus speaks to St. Mechtilde.
>
> "One day when I was assisting at the Holy Sacrifice, I saw an immense number of holy Angels descend and gather around the altar, contemplating the priest. They sang Heavenly canticles that ravished my heart; Heaven itself seemed to be contemplating the great sacrifice."
>
> St. Bridget of Sweden.

It is of no great surprise then, that Satan vehemently despises the Mass, working every possible diabolical means of turning souls - weak and strong alike - away from it, and from receiving the *living reality* of Jesus Christ [the Eucharist] within our being. For he knows only too well, that by the power of the Mass, the Eucharist, and the work of the Cross, he and his demons are defeated.

> *"What we do not obtain in the Mass, we may scarcely hope to receive by all other prayers, penances, or pilgrimages."*
>
> St. John Chrysostom.

In understanding the primacy of the Mass, in the work of re-uniting Heaven and earth within and through our souls, it is important to make the distinction between the Church as an institution and physical structure in which we attend Mass, her congregation, and the *living* Church as the Mystical Body of the risen Christ.

The Church institution with her divine teachings, sacraments, and provisions; and her hierarchy of ministers, religious and lay persons; is the Spiritual Body and Bride of Jesus Christ, formed by Him, and from His own side, as from the side of Adam, He formed Eve. Arising in the Blood of the Lamb, and breathing in the Life-breath of the Holy Spirit, she is in her fullest expression, the bearer and living organism of the immutable Divine Spirit; the earthly figure of the Homeland, which is the New Jerusalem of Heaven. All of Paradise is veiled in her, and her One sublime mission on earth, is to gift it to those who would open themselves to receive it.

As a Spiritual organism, defining man from above [from a Divine Life conception], the Church institution is not and never can be, a social organisation that re-defines [identifies] man from the ground up [the carnal ego-self], or which mirrors the egotisms and shifting values of sub-cultures and popular culture. Representing God's order and authority on earth, while living Eternally in the Light-Womb of the Father, **her One mission, is the creative realization [making real] of the synthesis of God and man, in the Mystical Body of Jesus Christ.** She has a duty to uphold and preserve her divine mission, because to God alone belongs the right of defining the Truth of relation between God and man, man and God, and man and his fellow man, and all His living creatures and creation.

Over the centuries, the Church institution has battled the cruel and cunning works of Satan and his demons, as they have sought to destroy her One mission on earth. A most dedicated and masterful work, directed primarily at derailing and destroying priests and professed religious souls, preventing them from living the Life of Jesus Christ, as an entire [inner and outer] way of being. The far-reaching consequences of this most heinous work, is that the infidelities of these souls wound the Heart of Jesus as grievously as their Love delights Him, while they suffer much greater punishment, because being gifted with more, much more is expected of them [Luke 12:47]. Their failure, together with that of the laity, also has the consequence of scandalizing, discouraging, and disuniting others, preventing souls [the Spiritually strong excepting] from knowing God as He is, and as He wants to be known. The insincere and Spiritually unsighted attack or desert the grievously wounded Mystical Body of Christ. While among those who remain, Spiritual literacy and dedication to dynamically co-operating with Jesus Christ, in the transformation of the entire human person, is replaced with all manner of 'soulish spirituality' and 'spiritualism'; of acquiescence with the crude norms, trends, biases self-satisfactions, and ways of sub-culture and popular culture [e.g., youth fixation, materialism, commercialism, in-group self-interest, and 'pop' Christianity]. In sum, all shades of insincerity and duplicity that turns attention to, and gives false witness to, the flesh [carnal ego-self], the old world and the works of evil, rather than higher Life in the Spirit. See Chapters on 'Agape' and 'Fiat'.

> *"To turn away in disgust at the wounds of the Church,
> is to turn away from [deny] the wounds of Christ."*
>
> Blessed Anne Catherine Emmerich.

Those divinely wise and faithful souls who Love Jesus Christ, and His Church on earth, and who are alive to their own failings and need of the Father's Mercy, as well as *the real battle* with *"the spirits of wickedness"* Ephesians 6:12, bear with, and intercede for the struggles and failings of His Mystical Body on earth. Recognizing that natural justice must prevail in cases of crimes and abuses, they pray and repair for all, thus serving to crush the works of the enemy, while healing the deepest, most putrid, and agonizing wounds of Jesus Christ's Mystical Body. For they know that Jesus foresaw these most horrific wounds and carried them to the Father on Calvary, where He pleaded forgiveness on behalf of all.

The physical Church in which we attend Mass, is the House of God and the most sacred built edifice on earth. Jesus Christ, the *"King of kings and Lord of lords"* 1 Timothy 6:15; Revelation 17:14 and 19:16, is truly Ever-present in our Churches, burning in the Tabernacles day and night, for the purpose of giving Himself to us for our salvation [healing]. Implementing the mysteries and sacraments of the faith, the purpose of the physical Church is to draw and gather the *"Children of Light"* Luke 16:18; John 12:36; Ephesians 5:8; 1 Thessalonians 5:5, into the Eucharistic Kingdom of Heaven. Every Church building is a most hallowed space. It is served and protected by multitudes of Angels, and attended by Heaven, as well throngs of invisible and purging souls, in its every celebration of the Mass.

In recognizing the Church as the living and breathing Spiritual organism [Body] of the Divine Spirit, we understand that **the faithful and true *living* Church**, is not everyone in the parish or Church congregation, or even everyone formally professed in religious life. Rather, **it is expressed personally and collectively, as *faith [lived] as* who we really are in Jesus Christ. It is those who are vigilant and**

active in striving to *live the co-sacrificial offering of the Mass in their entire way of being*, by willingly and gladly giving themselves fully to co-operate with and participate in what has been taught by, and fulfilled in Jesus Christ. For the place where God the Father desires to be restored to glory, is in the *living* temple [or holy land] of our souls, re-created [re-birthed] anew, and gathered in Jesus Christ. See Chapter on 'Eucharist',' Fiat' and 'St. Nicholas'.

> *" Not everyone who says to Me, 'Lord, Lord,' will enter the Kingdom of Heaven, but he who does the [Divine] Will of My Father, who is in Heaven."*
>
> Matthew 7:21.

Entrance to the Kingdom of Heaven, is by way of personal desire to cultivate a *living* personal relationship with God our Father in Jesus Christ. Every soul who has consented [abandoned back] to being purified, re-ordered, re-integrated [re-centred] and re-created [re-birthed] in the Mystical Body of Jesus Christ, by way of sanctifying grace, are sanctified as members of one another. Casting off the flesh [carnal ego-self], the old world [kingdom of Satan], and the works of evil, to realize [make real] the dynamic fruitfulness of their being in His, these souls are *living* pages in the Book of the Church, which is the Book of Life. **Defenders of the faith, they are the sacrament of Jesus Christ's presence and action in the world; Loving and shielding Him with His own Love, while annihilating Satan's plan, and bearing authentic witness to the Kingdom.** They are the *living* pillar of Light-fire that holds up the embattled Church on earth, while forming the One Eternal Blood family and community of the Kingdom of Heaven.

We have Jesus Christ's own word, that His Ever-crucified Church will stand preserved forever in the wholeness [holiness and all-perfection] and radiance of Truth, because she is *"the pillar and the foundation of Truth"* 1 Timothy 3:15, and the final arbitrator of Truth [Matthew 18:17]. Despite the relentless assailment to redefine, derail and destroy her divine mission, both from without and from within, *"the gates of Hell will not prevail against her"* Matthew 16:18. **For** from the beginnings of the Old Testament, we are given to understand that God resolves to do great things on account of a few *truly* faithful and courageously Loving souls [Genesis 18:22-33], while His greatest prodigies are worked by way of singular privileged souls, most particularly the Blessed Virgin Mary.

And so, as Jesus Christ resolves to continue to come to us, and give His Life to us through His Church, we lower our eyes and raise our hearts, standing steadfast on Calvary with our Blessed Mother and the Mystical Body of the risen Christ. For as the Christmas star shone out most brightly in the deep night of the sinful world, Jesus Christ, Ever-crucified and Ever-sacrificed in the *living* members of His Church on earth, will bestow healing and peace, not on this old world, but on a new world regathered in Him. Out of deepest darkness, will arise the most astonishing triumph.

> *"The Church edifice is a miniature Heaven.*
> *Whoever takes no delight in entering this little Heaven*
> *on earth, will not be admitted into the great Heaven above."*
>
> St. Ambrose.

The Eucharist

The All-giving and Ever-Living Food of Charity; the incalculable price of this gift; the act of Holy Communion; to receive is to first give freely; eating and living the Eucharist as a divinely-human Eucharistic being; preparing to receive; a Life that cannot be stolen.

"I AM The Living Bread who came down out of Heaven. If anyone eats of this bread, he will live forever. And the bread that I will give for the Life of the world is my flesh."

John 6:51-52.

Containing the complete Spiritual good of the Church, which is Jesus Christ, the Blood-White Lamb of God, the sacramental species of the Eucharist, is the full, complete, and actual Life-nourishment of Jesus Christ. It is the *Living* Food of His Being; awakening, resurrecting, and preserving His Life within the human soul, with every virtuous act of Holy Communion.

Made real in the words of consecration of the Mass, **the Eucharist is nothing less than *"the source and summit"* [Catechism, No. 1324] of Church life,** because it is the real and living reality of *"Emmanuel: God-with-us"* Old Testament: Isaiah 7:14; 8:8-10 and New Testament: Matthew 1:21-23; John 1:14; 14:8-11; Colossians 2:9. It is the fullness of the primordial Love [*"Agape"*] and Life of the Most Holy Trinity, personified in Jesus Christ; the Perfect [Whole and All-Perfect] Eucharistic Being, who is offered to us in the entirety of His Body and Blood; Soul and Divinity, under the veil of bread and wine [transubstantiation]. The Eucharist is the Ever-creative act of the Son giving Himself to the Father as our atonement [at-One-ment], and the Father giving His Son to us in Love, through the dynamic action of the

Holy Spirit, as The Living Bread [John 6:51-52] who restores us to fullness of being [personhood] in Himself.

The sacrament of the Eucharist is prefigured in the manna of the Old Testament; the miraculous food with which God nourished the Israelites during their forty-year exile in the desert. Jesus explicitly referred to manna as a figure of the Eucharist [John 6:31-35; 48-59], while St. John calls the Eucharist hidden manna [Revelation 2:17]. In the New Testament, it is prefigured in the miracle of the feeding of the five thousand [as recorded in all four Gospels], where the smallest amount of food is multiplied to provide full and equal sustenance to many. This miracle, confirms that the Eucharist is the complete richness of pure and Heavenly Food, that gives full and equal Spiritual Life to all who *truly* desire it. It restores to man, his lost God-being [John 10:34], which is his Good-being, realized only in Jesus Christ. The moment of consecration of the Eucharist during the Mass, is always the supernatural manifestation of the end [fulfilment] and ultimate reality for which man and all of creation was created, which is to be re-consummated in the Paradisaic Kingdom of the Fatherland.

> *"I thirst; I thirst for souls; I thirst for Love!*
> *I beg for hearts and I am not heeded...I am rebuffed,*
> *insulted, repulsed. O how I thirst! How I suffer!"*
>
> Jesus speaks to Blessed Dina Belanger.

The Eucharist invites our utmost respect, because we are given newness [Ever-newness] of *real Life and purpose,* at the cost of the annihilation of the Life of another, without whom we would perish. It is most humbling to recognize that in Jesus Christ's absolute Self-giving, is made possible the unfathomable divine exchange of our nothing-ness with His All-ness, in the Light-union of the Most Holy Trinity. That, **while we must eat dead food energy removed from its life-source, to survive in the body; it is the complete sustenance of this Ever-Living Food [Eternal Life] of another, that heals and re-creates [re-births] us to new [Ever-new] Life in the Spirit.** For as in the beginning, our first parents ate of the forbidden fruit of the Tree of Knowledge of Good and Evil, bringing about all mankind's separation and estrangement from God, **we have been given the privileged opportunity to eat again, but of the All-giving Food of Jesus Christ, who is the type of new sacrificial fruit of the Tree of Life.** The Eucharist is our justification in the One acceptable and All-sufficient sin offering of Jesus Christ. It is the fruit of the Cross, and God's supreme gift of His total Self-giving to our souls. It is His abiding presence with us in His Mystical Bride, the *living* Church, until *"the [final] end of time"* [Revelation 20:7-15; 21]. See Chapter on 'The Tree of Life'.

> *"Amen, Amen I say to you, unless you eat the Flesh [Body] of the Son of Man and drink His Blood, you will not have Life in you."*
>
> John 6:54.

The icon reminds us, that the price of this Ever-Living Food, which the Church calls the *'Food of Charity'*, is unfathomable and immeasurable in human terms. It is the fruit of the fullness of Love and agony, which saw Jesus Christ oppressed and trampled as a grape in a wine press, and implied and bleeding upon a Cross, as He was burned up in Loves own fire, for the sake of mankind. We can only stand in amazement at the spectacle of His innocent Blood pouring profusely from His tortured and forsaken Body, to pool upon the ground, and mix with the tumult and dry dust of the earth, and earth man; confirming His resolve as the Incarnate Word of the Father, to stay with us, and never withdraw from us again.

> *"He Loves, He hopes, He waits… His Love never knows rest."*
>
> St. Julian Peter Eymard.

The act of Holy Communion; of physically *and* mystically receiving the species of the Eucharist; **asking that our soul shall be healed**, is the act of coming to Jesus saying *"You are my real Life"*, for the purpose of uniting and sharing together. It is the act of consuming, and being consumed in *living* relationship [community] with God, and with all things in Him, in the All-pure and Ever-living freshness of Jesus Christ. In Holy Communion, Jesus Christ and our soul are intimately united in Charity, extinguishing the flesh [carnal ego-self] and all evils, and conferring upon us torrents of transformational graces, favours, and blessings, which [as far as we are disposed, willing and capable] restore our dynamic wholeness [holiness and all-perfection] of divine-human being, in His Perfect [Whole and All-Perfecting] Cosmic Personhood, and gift us back our place in the Light-community of the Heavenly realm.

Eucharist expresses the reality of man's *real Life and purpose* in Jesus Christ. **Originating in the Greek word "*eucharistia*", meaning "*thanksgiving*", it i-dentifies man's original creative purpose as a divinely-human Eucharistic being, with an unencumbered Eucharistic attitude to life.** Co-operating with and participating in the boundless creative energies of God, he was to recognize and draw upon himself, upon others, and all living creation, all good gifts, which are God's free gift to him [James 1:17].

And so, while we can never equalise the debt that was atoned for us, by being willing to *live the Eucharist* in union with Jesus Christ, the One Perfect [Whole and All-Perfect] Eucharistic Being, **we allow God to do within us, what Jesus Christ has already done for us.** For when Jesus asks us to *"Do this in memory of Me"* Luke 22:19, He is also saying that we are called [invited] to be co-Victim and co-Creator with Him. We should offer our bodies and souls as a living sacrifice as He has first done, because we are His Body and His Members [1 Corinthians 12:12; Romans 12:1]. This means that the Eucharist is both the bread of Eternal Life, but also the bread of redemptive suffering and release, because while the absolute Light-nourishment of Jesus Christ in the sacramental species feeds and consumes our soul, the Cross serves as the disbursement that expands it. Together, they make the barren soul fruitful, allowing *real Life and purpose* to blossom forth, while conferring upon it the brightness and vigour of Eternal Life.

In this privilege of co-operating with and participating in the primordial Passion of God, we take responsibility and authority for who we really are in Him. For in being willing to be consumed in Loves blessed fire by suffering corporally and Spiritually for Him, and in Him, in our daily lives, we are given His Life, and can give His Life to all that would receive it; returning all back to Him in a spirit of reparation, thanksgiving, and joy.

> *"To His Bread, I myself the bread am,*
> *the stream and tide of glad new wine,*
> *of endless rise and flow."*
>
> Anon.

In this divinely creative work, God does not ask us to bring anything, but only to abandon back [give the consent of] our estranged human will [heart's desire], to the operation of His Cosmic Love and Divine Will, because *"without [Jesus Christ], [we] can do nothing"* John 15:5. Awareness of our estrangement and brokenness in the Light of Truth, allows us to freely abandon back to Him, that He may do the work of restoration for us, and in us, as far as we are willing and capable of Light-union. In this **continuous circle of returning and receiving**, His increasing Light-presence within us, increases our good will and gratitude, and draws us ever deeper into the healing circle of receiving and giving Life to all things in Him.

> *"Every soul, that with pure intention, continues to feed*
> *on My Eucharistic Food, will be awakened to new Life...*
> *Be assured, I give to souls, if they know how to follow Me."*
>
> Jesus speaks to Vera Grita - Third Order Salesian and Mystic.

The Eucharist and the Eucharistic life - expressed as Charity, confirms that Eternal Life is not something that starts when we pass from this mortal life. Our personal passage through the thickness of space and time, to creative realization of who we are [or ever can be] in God, is *right Now*. Jesus Christ therefore made receiving His actual Life in Holy Communion, a necessary pre-condition to winning back the crown [Spiritual wealth] of Eternal Life.

It is then of little surprise, that Satan and his demons work furiously to turn souls away from this sacrament of sacraments, just as He turned Adam and Eve away from the Tree of Life. For they know very well, that our failure to eat of the Eucharist species*, is the key to the failure of our souls [Luke 8:11-15]. *"By the Eucharist, Satan is defeated by His own words 'You shall be like God' because by feeding on the Body and Blood; Soul and Divinity of Jesus Christ, the soul is transformed, divinized, and changes its state, assimilating into Him"* says Venerable Conchita [María Concepción Cabrera de Armida]. **Church saints and mystics assure us that Satan and his demons, flee from faithful and desirous souls, who wash in the bath of Confession, and feed with facility on the Eucharist and on the Cross.**

[*An act of Spiritual Communion is not an alternative equivalent to the sacramental species of the Eucharist, but a prayerful expression of desire to receive Jesus Christ *fully and substantially* in the Eucharist, when we are genuinely not able to do so].

> *"If people would understand the Treasury of the Blessed Sacrament, they would be trampling over one another, to get in front of it; Churches would be bursting with worshippers!"*
>
> Blessed Dina Belanger.

Our at least hour long fast, and other preparations before receiving the ultimate gift of the Eucharist, gives honour to God. It focuses our continual work of vigilance, repentance, and readiness for receiving Jesus Christ; recognizing Him, not only as the source of our earthly supply, but as the beginning and end [fulfilment] of our longing for completion in Him. It represents our humility and gratitude to Him, and our joyful anticipation of the transfigured reality of the Kingdom of Heaven, where there will no longer be any need for bodily ingested food and drink [Romans 14:17]. **In every preparation for Holy Communion, it is therefore appropriate to ask ourselves how we would answer Jesus questions:** *"What do you want Me to do for you?"* Matthew 20:32; *"Do you want to be healed?"* John 5:6.

In His sermon on the Bread of Life, Jesus said that we must eat [chew] His Flesh [His Body in this context] in order to live Eternally. As to the full translation and meaning of these words, St. Augustine speaks of the *"teeth of the communicant"*, while St. John Chrysostom speaks of us *"planting our teeth in the Flesh [Body] of Christ."* We are therefore asked to **respectfully *chew* the Eucharist,** as we would chew ordinary bread, although this Bread is the living reality of Jesus Christ. St. Hildegard of Bingen sheds light on this request, which is to say, that we are to imitate Jesus Christ's work in both our spirit [inner being] and our body [outer being], as the Holy Spirit inspires us. It expresses the necessity that man's interior [Spiritual] and exterior [bodily and material] life authentically mirror one another, according to the Life of Jesus Christ. It is summed up and expressed in the Life of the *"Fiat"*, as one with Charity [Love in action]. See Chapters on 'Fiat' and 'St Nicholas'.

We can only be awe-struck at the invincible patience of Jesus Christ in the sacrament of the Eucharist, in which He continually burns with Love and desire to give Himself to us. Our soul's requital in this exchange of Love [Charity], is His greatest joy, while our refusal to receive Him, or our receiving Him without best disposition, is His greatest agony, because this is the deprivation of our soul [Revelation to St. Gertrude]. In Truth, few souls truly consent [desire] to know and Love God in Jesus Christ, and receive of the treasury of Spiritual riches, present in this sacrament of sacraments. Souls may appear to receive the Eucharist [commune with God], but fail to benefit from the Light, warmth, vigour, and effects of Divine Life, because of the lack of right disposition [co-operation]. Yet, despite the sacrileges and offences committed against Him; His nausea at the uncleanliness, insensibility, and ingratitude of souls, and lack of right disposition to the effects of His Divine Life within them; He continues to offer Himself to us, until the end [fulfilment] of time.

While we cannot ever be truly worthy to consume Jesus Christ's Body and Blood; Soul and Divinity, by living a faithful and upright life according to the teachings, sacraments, and provisions of the Church [including frequenting the sacrament of Confession, accompanied with true purpose of amendment], and consciously preparing for each act of Holy Communion, we demonstrate our genuine motivations and best intentions. This suffices before God, who in the excesses of His Charity, longs for nothing more than to heal us and realize His full Life potential within and through us. Understanding our unworthiness and absolute need of Jesus Christ, in light of His absolute Love for us, is a vital part of right disposition to commune with Him, and to receive the abundance of sanctifying fruits offered. See 'Sin' in Useful Terms.

> *"...whoever eats this Bread [Body], or drinks the Lord's cup [Blood] in a way unworthy of the Lord, will be guilty of [sinning against] the Body and Blood of the Lord."*
>
> 1 Corinthians 11:27.

To otherwise presume to receive Jesus Christ in the act of Holy Communion, without sincere self-examination, in respect of the three-fold nature of sin, regular sacramental Confession, and the will to be transformed into the *Livingness* of Jesus Christ by way of the Cross, can be to no avail for the soul. For as a flaming sword was placed to guard the way to the Tree of Life after Adam and Eve ate of the forbidden fruit [Genesis 3:24], lest they unjustly attempt to reach out and eat of it [Genesis 3:22]; and as twelve basketfuls of extra bread were picked up after the feeding of the five thousand; **God's real Life in the Eucharist, cannot be stolen. It cannot be taken by force or by stealth; misappropriated, or wasted, by those who would**

steal it, without Loving abandonment [consent] to Him. Indeed, to come before Him, asking that *"my soul shall be healed"*, while failing to mean, and act upon what we are saying, is in reality the act of betraying Him anew, like Judas Iscariot. It is the act of eating judgement upon ourselves, while causing Him to agonise more, because it is the act of despising Him and His Mystical Body; demonstrating lack of interest in, discernment about, or respect for, the ineffable gift of His Life. Sacred Scripture carries strong warning against such ill-judgement which scandalizes others, while resulting in the soul's failure to benefit, as it [further] **withers and hardens** in its own being. For contrary and corrupt energy, cannot mix with higher Spiritual energy; *"neither will corruption possess [share in the Life of] incorruption"* 1 Corinthians 15:50. See Chapter on 'Fiat'.

On every occasion on which we come to the table of the Heavenly banquet, to receive the *Ever-Living* Food of the Eucharist [in the act of Holy Communion], let us approach with the utmost reverence and awe; alive to the astonishing reality that we have been given the opportunity to eat again of the figurative Tree of Life, who is Jesus Christ. Let there arise within us, ever livelier preparation, and deeper desire to feast gladly on the wealth of extraordinary gifts veiled in this most sacred Food. Let us always yield to Love, and the vastness of transformation and re-birth [re-creation] in the All-hallowing celestial Perfection [Wholeness and All-Perfection] of Jesus Christ, in the Light-community of the Most Holy Trinity.

> *"But He who is joined to the Lord,*
> *is One Spirit with Him."*
>
> 1 Corinthians 6:17.

Holy Hour

Getting away from it all; face to face with self; interior battle and revolution; as living Tabernacles – bearing Jesus Christ for the sake of all.

"Couldn't you watch with Me for one hour?"
Matthew 26:40 and Mark 14:37.

The Church Tabernacle, is God's crib, tomb, and dwelling place on earth. It is a burning furnace of His Charity, and the earths one true treasury, harbouring an infinity of Spiritual riches which He longs to give to our souls. Jesus deeply aggrieving words to His so-called friends - the sleeping apostles, in the Garden of Gethsemane, who could not stay awake for one hour, echo down through the ages. They are the words of our Blessed Mother, in her last apparition to little Conchita at Garabandal, in the 1960's: *"Conchita, why don't you go more often to visit my Son in the Tabernacle? He waits for you there, day and night."* Had the apostles stayed awake for one hour, they would have witnessed the tremendous Cosmic drama and battle that was being played out, as the final confrontation and victory over evil was being won. Were we awake, we would understand the essential task and purpose of our life on earth, as the immense Spiritual battle for our Eternal soul. That God longs for nothing more than to take our part in this battle, by consuming our human will [heart's desire] in the blessed fire of His Love and Divine Will. For His purpose is to make living Tabernacles of our souls; that He may live and act in and through us, as He is carried always and everywhere.

> *"Our present life is given only to gain the Eternal One, and if we don't think about it, we build our affections on what belongs to this world, where our life is transitory."*
>
> St. Padre Pio.

To take the time to step away from the world, and come willingly and gratefully in person* to keep company with Jesus in Holy Hour, is to take a vital step on the way to recovery. For as in the beginning, God first breathed the Breath of Life [Genesis 2:7] into man's nostrils by the sheer force of His Love, He breathes in and absorbs man in the sacrament of His own Life; the Eucharist.

[* As man's full participation in the Mass requires his bodily presence, *unless* he is genuinely prohibited, participation in Holy Hour is best completed in the Church, where Jesus Christ remains continuously present in the Blessed Sacrament. St. Padre Pio and Pope Pius XII sounded strong warnings about living through the TV screen, while St. Elizabeth Seton, the first US-born canonized Saint, had a prophetic vision of a 'black box' in every home, through which evil would enter. It is ultimately not God's Plan for man's divine purpose of personal, embodied presence, to be subsumed to, and consumed in, a virtual world of screens, regardless of what is represented].

Man cannot *truly* Love what he does not know, and to *truly* receive Jesus Christ, he must first desire to know Him, and what He is offering. This requires coming to terms with the privilege and responsibility of his immortal being in God, and the no-thingness of his being apart from God. **It means recognizing the error of the** human condition, that tends to fixate upon, or look at, oneself and others as individuals, rather than in the One reality of God.

The practice of Holy Hour, taught by Jesus to 17th Century Visitation nun, St. Margaret Mary Alacoque, has a two-fold purpose of Love and Mercy. It has no particular formula of prayers, but requires the setting aside of one's daily life, to focus wholly on one's personal relationship with God in Jesus Christ. Sacred Scripture tells us, that even when the spirit is willing, the flesh [carnal ego-self] is weak [Matthew 26:41 and Mark 14:38], and that God speaks, not amidst noise, but in the profound silence of our hearts. It is therefore only when the mind comes to silence, and ceases to be distracted by everyday life, that the heart begins to operate. This is amply demonstrated in Sacred Scripture, where the wilderness [desert] is declared a place of prophesy and revelation - God leading the Israelites through the wilderness to the Promised Land. John the Baptist is described as *"the voice of one crying in the wilderness."* Isaiah 40:3 and John 1:23, while Jesus too often withdrew from the crowds to quiet wilderness places for periods of prayer and solitude, to revive His Spirit.

> *"The word of God came to John [the Baptist], the son of Zechariah in the wilderness."*
>
> Luke 3:2.

Holy Hour is then first and foremost, a wilderness experience. It is the befriending of *interior and exterior* silence, to allow the dualistic division [between Light and dark] in our being, to be identified and faced up to. This coming to terms with our moment-to-moment mode of operation which tends more to Light [of faith] or to darkness, is the means of creating the essential interior silence and spaciousness, in which God can operate; in which Jesus Christ can be conceived and birthed through. It is also the work of the Cross [powered by the Eucharist], because **to receive, the soul must first learn to give [back] its human will [heart's desire] to God, purified of every selfish motive of self-interest and reward.** For God only *really* comes to know man, and man know God [and all things in Him] on the Cross; when challenged to renounce himself, and abandon back to Him, with perfect [whole and all-perfect] Charity. The wilderness experience also allows man to come to terms with the vital reality that **every soul has its own free will, capacity for God-being [John 10:34], and Eternal destiny** [Matthew 23:14-30 and Matthew 25:1-13]. While we participate in mortal life according to our life-state and office, we do not know when we will be called out of this world, and when we are called, we will travel alone. And while we can benefit from the holiness [whole-hearted fullness of being] of others, we cannot live through them, because what goes with us, is nothing other than the Light-riches within our soul; which is our *living* personal relationship with God in Jesus Christ [See Parables of the Ten Virgins and the Talents - Matthew 25:1-13; Matthew 25:14-30].

> *"When worldly things occupy your thoughts...your memory... and your will, you are not Mine...When your heart is not void of earthly affections, you are not all Mine."*
>
> Jesus speaks to Venerable Conchita.
> [María Concepción Cabrera de Armida].

The beginner, who struggles to remain for any length of time, must first come face-to-face with himself; with the voids of Light, and illusions of selfhood, which manifest as restlessness and resentment in not seeking for oneself from moment to moment. For while in this age of instant gratification, experience, and worldly 'success', vast swathes of time and energy are expended on self-satisfactions, and curiosities, it is in the starkness of silence and solitude, before the All-powerful and gentle majesty of God, that the derailing veil of illusion, denial, fear, and treachery - even under the guise of 'good', is cast into the Light. For all obvious and subtle obstacles to recognizing God, and God-being [John 10:34] as the privilege and responsibility of life; and to trusting, and persevering abandonment to Him, for the good of everyone and everything, are the works of the flesh [carnal ego-self], the old world, and the spirit of darkness. It is the work of the dis-integrated [and ever-changing and restless] community of voices within the soul, that prevent it from relinquishing its own agenda and receiving with facility the substance-energies of Divine Life. This may include even seemingly pious or charitable pursuits, which tend to, or mask a motive of pride, self-gratification, attachment, or ease, rather than an authentically Eucharistic life, which alone pleases God. All such discovery is good, if the soul is sufficiently humble and willing to recognize its condition, because if truly desirous of healing and re-creation [re-birth], **Jesus promises to meet everyone where they are.**

> *"Beneath these rays [from the Eucharist] a heart will be warmed, even if it were like a block of ice; or hard as rock."*
>
> Jesus speaks to St. Faustina [Divine Mercy].

The well-known Old Testament encounter between the Prophet Elijah and God the Father prefigured what was to come, and what is given to us, by the Spirit of God, as He works silently within and through the soul who truly desires Him. Taking refuge in the silence of the wilderness, the word of God comes to him asking him [twice] *"What are you doing here, Elijah?"* 1 Kings 19:9,13], which is to say, what do you really want in the freedom of your human will [heart's desire]? In answer to this question, Elijah pours out his heart to God; bemoaning the Israelites forsaking Him, to live lives of idolatry and plunder. He is listened to by God, who first allows him the opportunity to freely vent and unburden himself. He is given fresh water and food, and the opportunity to rest. He is given Spiritual strength in powerful words of hope and encouragement, which fall gently upon the silence of his heart in *"the whistling of a gentle breeze"* 1 Kings 19:12. **He is given divine work to do for God, and the power and means to do it.**

> *"The Holy Hour became like an oxygen talk, to revive the breath of the Holy Spirit, in the midst of the foul and fetid atmosphere of the world."*
>
> Venerable Fulton Sheen.

Having come like Elijah to converse with God, souls who come before Jesus Christ in Holy Hour, receive nourishment and strength in the silent depths of their being. According to their sincerity and disposition to grace, they are drawn into His friendship, and are infused with innumerable graces, favours, and blessings for themselves, and for others. These gifts are primarily subtle, yet profound, because the Holy Spirit works in ways beyond human perception. Some apparent effects however, are a growing sense of interior peace, courage, and *living* silence [consciousness of the unspoken primordial voice of God, as the rooted Light-centre of our being], as **the Spirit ever moves the souls focus away from earthly outwardness, and inwards towards its original heart's desire for God-being [John 10:34] and Good-being in Jesus Christ**. And if willing to co-operate with the divine crafting in everyday life, it will come to discover that His yoke is easy and His burden light [Matthew 11:29-30], as it grows ever-more alive to the sober and magnificent reality of its life's work, as the blessed mission and battle for its immortal soul.

> "Into the silence oh soul, and there find the glowing pathway of the Spirit. In the silence, all perplexities shall vanish, all troubles shall cease, all sorrow assuaged. In the silence the clouds shall lift, and the Light that is ineffable encompass thy soul.
> From the silence, oh soul, thou shall return, seeking no longer far and wide thy mission in the world, for the message of thyself in glowing and burning eloquence, speaks in thine every act."
>
> George Fuller.

Those who can sit quietly and gratefully in *interior and exterior* silence, in Holy Hour - or at anytime, anywhere in prayer, are none other than those who are sufficiently invested with the Light of sanctifying grace, as to breathe in the Life-breath of the Spirit, and rest in the blessed resting point of the single voice of God, manifesting in and through their soul. Strengthened and equipped for Spiritual battle and triumph, they are inspired to become more vigilant and attentive to their Spiritual health and that of others;

eagerly watching, praying, and growing swift, stable, and strong in overcoming temptations and sin, while resting in interior *living* silence, which lies beyond human comprehension. The more alive the soul is with the Light-fire of the Spirit, the more desirable this practice becomes, because in Jesus Christ, who is the living dialogue between the soul and the Father, it is at once present [by degree] to the All-embracing Light-unity of the Kingdom, running invisibly and indivisibly everywhere and in all things. See 'Detachment' in Useful Terms.

> *"I desire that [Eucharistic] Adoration take place for the intention of imploring Mercy for the world."*
> Jesus speaks to St. Faustina [Divine Mercy].

Fervent souls led by inspirations of the Holy Spirit, also attend Holy Hour for the purpose of making reparation to Jesus Christ's most grievously wounded Mystical Body; for the deep coldness and sinfulness of mankind, especially ingratitude for, and neglect of, His sacramental Life in the Eucharist. Lifted up between Heaven and earth [on the Cross], they continually adore Him within their soul, and unite with Him in intercession for the undoing of evil, and the Coming of the Kingdom. As Living Tabernacles in the world, they maintain a state of interior self-emptiness, and *living* silence, invisibly and dynamically participating in the Light-circle of giving and receiving His *real Life and purpose* in them, for the sake of everyone and everything. Their Light-infused prayers and works appeal to the supreme rights of Divine Justice, drawing graces, favours, and blessings upon all, while warding off the divine wrath [Justice], and personal and worldly calamities and chaos, that result from man's relentless pride, defiance, insensibility, and ingratitude, towards his own Creator God and Father.

> *"Be My living Tabernacle, and let Me meet the souls of your brothers. Keep Me in you; present in all My Divine and Human reality."*
> Jesus speaks to Vera Grita - Third Order Salesian and Mystic.

Water

The remarkable actual and mystical gift of water; the passing point of the Cross; Jesus Christ - Love's Fountain-Heart; Sacramental Baptism; Sacramental Confession - a washbowl and harbour for our souls; the gift and power of Holy Water.

"In the beginning, God created the Heavens and the earth...and the Spirit of God moved upon the face of the waters."

Genesis 1:1,2.

Biblical revelation begins with this most simple and powerful affirmation; declaring and confirming that the existence of everything in the Universe, depends upon the Almighty Ever-creative power of God, who is the absolute owner and conserver of all that is.

Moving across the face of the waters, God sanctifies their purpose by filling them with Himself. This is His first act, because without water, there can be no life on earth. Water is the major covering of our planet [thanks to perfect earth-sun distance], and is the major composition of our bodies. It is as vital to our life on earth as the air that we breathe, the sun that shines, the microbes that support higher life, and the gravity that holds us down. Contained in everything, and giving life to everything, its beneficent properties for regulating the earth's temperature, sustaining life, and quenching thirst; and for washing and purifying, are particularly well acclaimed. Hidden and silent in some things, while filled with power and might in others, water reminds us of the omnipotence and continuous Eternal motion of our God's Love operating in His Divine Will, which flows and runs in everything, and sustains everything in existence. In walking across the water in time, as a shortcut to Capernaum [a distance of 25 miles on land], Jesus confirms that He is God; the source of, authority over, and conserver of water, and of all that is. For by the power of His Divine Will, He can go wherever He Wills.

Water, too, is associated with the womb and the female principle of generation. Man's life issues out of the womb, which figures the waters of the primordial Light-Womb of God; an atmosphere of radiant Light upon Light, in which his soul is first formed, and which is the place of all divine treasures and contentment's, for which he is created. Water therefore, has from earliest times, been a powerful religious symbol of life itself, as the element God uses to come to meet us in the mysteries of faith. **The icon reminds us that from his very beginning in the waters of the womb, man's purpose is to be washed clean, healed, and re-created [re-birthed] anew in time, by the Life of sanctifying grace. In this work of healing and re-generation [re-creation], he is carried along the royal way of the Cross; the crossing point between Heaven and earth, and the way back to his place of origin, in the Light-Womb of the Homeland.**

> *"Amen, Amen, I say to you, unless one*
> *has been reborn by water and the Holy Spirit,*
> *he is not able to enter into the Kingdom of God."*
>
> John 3:5.

As children of the New and Ever-lasting Covenant of Love, our understanding and gratitude for water takes on the most profound supernatural meaning. Jesus much uses the element in His witness to who He Himself is, and to the Kingdom of Heaven. He is baptised in water, and He calls [invites] those who are thirsty to come drink from the wellspring of *"Living Water"* John 4:10; 7:38 which is His Life [Eternal Life]. He walks on water; washes His apostles' feet in water; and approves of giving actual and Spiritual water as an act of Charity [Love in action]. Water symbolises God's desire to quench, reconcile, and re-create man in higher Life in the Spirit.

As to how water acts on man, the Apostle John tells of three things [signifying the Most Holy Trinity] which are as One, and which give testimony to God in Heaven, and which correspond with three things that give testimony to Him on earth. In Heaven, these are: the Father, the Word [Son], and the Holy Spirit; and on earth, these are: the Spirit, Water, and the Blood of Jesus Christ [1 John 5:7-8].

In the enormity of the opening of His Side and Heart on the Cross, from which gushed forth Blood and Water, Jesus Christ became Love's Fountain-Heart; the Triune re-generative spring of Eternal Life that surged through the gates of death to bestow upon all, new and Everlasting Life. By way of divine privilege, we are freely invited to come and drink with hallowed hands; to be warmed and enkindled to holy [wholeness and all-perfection of] living in His justifying Life-Blood, and to be washed dazzlingly clean, and re-created [re-birthed] anew in the purifying mystical Water [One with Eden's river of Life Genesis 2:10] gushing forth from His side. In this consummation, man is made pure and transparent, and capable of receiving with facility, the living reality of Divine Life. For his purpose is to become as fluid and yielding as water to the operation of God's Spirit, in the entirety of his being; to become refreshment, inspiration, and healing for all God's estranged and suffering people and creation.

> *"I will sprinkle clean water on you, and you will be clean...I will also give you a new heart, and I will put a new spirit within you."*
>
> Ezekiel 36:25-26.

Water has a strong actual and mystical presence in the sacraments, particularly Baptism and Confession, in which dramatic representations of God's power are manifested. Jesus therefore made the divinely cleansing and healing waters of sacramental Baptism and Confession, a condition necessary for salvation [healing].

The sacrament of Baptism was prefigured by the Crossing of the Red Sea, when there was no other way for the Israelites to escape Pharo, other than by passing through water. It was again prefigured in God's re-creative [re-generative] act of the forty-day Great Flood [Genesis 7-9] which destroyed wickedness [evil and ungodliness], and renewed the face of the earth. Baptism cleanses us of original sin and restores original blessing, by planting within us, the Light-seed of re-creation [re-birth] in Jesus Christ. Indeed, one of the early meanings of the word, was for a garment to be dyed right through, and it is in the same way that God must bathe and soak our entire being; healing, cleansing, and delivering us, by the power of Water and the Spirit. St. Paul calls the sacrament of Baptism *"the washing of re-generation and renewing by the Holy Spirit"* Titus 3:5.

As we celebrate the new and Divine Life that is bestowed through the sacrament of Baptism, we call to mind Jesus Baptism in the river Jordan. In this momentous event, the Holy Spirit, who in the beginning moved upon the face of the waters to fill them with His Spirit, descends upon them again, now polluted by the fall, to cleanse them once again. Jesus as God, is in no need of cleansing [and Sanctification], but in a Cosmic act of liberation, marking the beginning of re-creation and salvation [healing] history, carries us down with Him into the waters, with the mighty power and witness of the Holy Spirit. Once bitter to Moses and the Israelites, but now filled with gladness, these transfigured waters anticipate the mark of our re-birth [re-creation] at the baptismal font, while offering us an instrument of divine healing, protection, and grace. In this act of pure gift to us, Jesus confirms that all the riches of the Father belong to the Son, through the Holy Spirit. All flow throughout the *living* Mystical Body of the Church, offering communion [relationship] of Light and participation in the divine Sonship, by way of His Life manifesting within and through us. He verifies our Father's Cosmic Heart's Desire [Divine Will], to be One again with man, and through us, with all His suffering creatures and creation. For in the end [fulfilment of time], as in the beginning, all righteous things will be consummated in God, when He fills all things with Himself. This means that material things can too be renewed and made holy [Spirit bearing], to be used *wisely and sparingly* as a vital means of communion with God [most particularly bread and wine; and water and oil] while we are on earth. St. Hildegard of Bingen offers us a most inspiring glimpse of the magnitude of difference between the fallen material world, and the glory of restored creation in the Kingdom of Heaven, assuring us that in the Kingdom water be transparent and calm, and will no longer have the power to drown or to flood.

As Baptism is about i-dentity, the sacrament of Confession [Reconciliation] and absolution is about i-dentity mission for the faithful pilgrim soul. Instituted by Jesus Christ, through the power of the Holy Spirit [John 20:23], **sacramental Confession is a washbowl for our souls, as we work upon our wedding garment [nuptial clothing], that is a figure for sanctity and holiness,** making it clean, fragrant, and acceptable to God. Sacramental Confession confirms that we can only approach God in His Love and Divine Will, because it is the One means of becoming i-dentified with Him in Jesus Christ. As human and mortal souls, we are engaged in non-stop Spiritual warfare between good and evil; Truth and falsehood; and Light and darkness. While every sincere sacramental Confession, motivated by Love of God [Truth] and sorrow for sin - rather than crude guilt, or fear of punishment, accompanied by a firm purpose of amendment, washes, and preserves our wedding garment. It prepares us to receive with facility the Eucharist, in each *virtuous act* of Holy Communion, as to confer upon our soul all sanctifying gifts of the Holy Spirit, and ultimately the Light-garment and [Spiritual] crown of Eternal Life [Revelation 22:14]. See 'i-dentity' in Useful Terms.

Sacramental Confession is a harbour of rest for the soul tossed *"to and fro"* Ephesians 4:14 by inner divisiveness, which breaks trust with God, and crucifies Christ anew in every [injurious and destructive] act of sin. Confession releases our soul from the continued weakening and scattering of its powers, and from looking back at the *"old man"* or forward to the future, in as far as it is not relevant to the present moment. And so, as we take care to often wash our temporary earthen body clean, we must ever more diligently take care to often wash our immortal soul clean, to avoid its stagnation in fetid pools of sinfulness, which swell and intensify, while radiating unclean air and blocking the avenues of grace.

> *"If I do not wash you,*
> *you will have no place with Me."*
>
> John 13:8.

In its fullest sense, sacramental Confession renders our soul **free and responsible,** allowing the conception and birthing of Jesus Christ within, for the purpose of participating in the undoing of evil, and restoration of the Kingdom of Heaven. The greater perfection of the sacrament is best exemplified in the lives of the saints, who aided by the Light of grace experienced supernatural sorrow for even the slightest act of sin, together with a desire to suffer anything rather than offend God, and soil itself [and others] by a future act of sin.

To recover our perception and experience of water is to recover a faith filled Cosmic experience of hallowed reality. In the Eucharistic blessing of water, natural water is imbued with the invisible manifestation of the Holy Spirit, and restored to its true function. Holy Water offers us a powerful Spiritual weapon and aid for our Sanctification. Used for blessing the everyday works and events of our lives; for cleansing, and healing the human body and soul; for blessing and healing animals; for blessing homes and belongings; for driving away visible and invisible dangers and evils; and for every other beneficial purpose; in Holy Water, the entire Cosmos is revealed again as God's gift to man.

The prayers of the Roman ritual for the blessing of Holy Water, explains its power and widespread use. The water is exorcized in the Name of the Three Divine Persons of the Most Holy Trinity, removing from it the power of evil. The presence of the Holy Spirit invokes the power to uproot and drive away the presence and influence of evil, while blessed salt is added to signify preservation from evil. We are recommended to make the invincible sign of the Cross often with this venerable water, marking ourselves as *"Children of Light"* Luke 16:18;

John 12:36; Ephesians 5:8; 1 Thessalonians 5:5. **Many Church saints, such as St. Teresa of Avila, testified to the blessing and benediction of Holy Water, and to its power to immediately drive away evil spirits.**

We give thanks to our Heavenly Father, that in His Son's Coming to earth, divine power has been manifested, and man blessed and enlightened; and purified and sanctified; in the actual and mystical gifts of water. We thank Him, that in conceiving and birthing Jesus Christ within our being during our earthly lifetime, we become in Him, the pure waters of Justice and righteousness, running in all things like an Ever-flowing stream.

*"But Judgement will be revealed as water,
And Justice like a mighty torrent."*

Amos 5:24.

Prayer

Prayer is essential; what is prayer and who is praying; coming to prayer; everything depends upon our neighbour; discernment and keeping God's secrets; everything depends upon our neighbour; every word is an instrument; living words and living silence; growing in prayer; every prayer is new; a journey of but one [three-in-one] step; the Angels gather our prayers; the fullness of prayer; well-known prayers illuminated; the power of praying and singing God's word.

> "Call to Me, and I will answer you, and show you great and mighty things, which you do not know."
>
> Jeremiah: 33:3.

Jesus taught us that prayer is essential. Prayer was the Heart and Soul of His own Life on earth, and continues in His Resurrected Life. Entreating the Father with the Whole of His Being, and confessing, adoring, and praising His Divinity as superior to His Humanity, He demonstrated to us, that it is sincere and zealous prayer that releases [manifests] God's power, and realizes His One mission on earth. Prayer is our schooling in the Divine Life. It is the portal through which the Light of God enters the world through our souls.

The first mention of prayer in the Old Testament is made in Genesis, when Enos calls upon the Name of the Lord [Genesis 4:26]; then Abraham prays to God to spare the sinful city of Sodom [Genesis 18:22-33]. The letters of the apostles instruct us on the four-fold purpose of prayer, which is to thank God; praise and adore Him; to call for help and healing; and to intercede and atone for sins. In both the Old and New Testaments, God made promises to hear our prayers

[Deuteronomy 4:7; Luke 11:5-13]. Prayer in a state of right disposition to grace, is the most efficacious means of obtaining anything.

The Name of Jesus, meaning *"Yahweh saves"* or *"Yahweh is salvation"*, is the shortest, sweetest, most powerful prayer. His Name is benediction, and the divine seal upon our souls. It is through His Name, that we have Life [John 1:12]. St. Irenaeus says that by invoking the Name of Jesus Christ, Satan is driven out of men. On many occasions, when Jesus instructs on prayer, He uses a word akin to the Greek word *"euche"*, meaning *"vow" or "witness"*. In this frame, He identifies prayer in the most profound and complete sense as a sincere statement of ***living faith as* who we really are** in Him. Therefore, to understand prayer, is to first understand that faith is not an expression of something we believe [in] outside of ourselves, nor something we 'have', or call 'mine'. **Faith is the measure of the Light of sanctifying grace, that is the presence of Jesus Christ at [as] the core of our being.** It allows us to believe [not in our ego-selves, but] in God, being and living with us, within us, and through us, as the One absolute reality. Flesh [the carnal ego-self] comes to silence, as we participate and share in His Divine Life, flowing within and through our souls. *Living faith as* a child of God grows stronger and deeper in the reaping of His Light within our soul, in and by which, we operate with divine knowledge, wisdom, and purpose in Him. See 'Possess' and 'self-forgetting' in Useful Terms.

> *"Amen, Amen I say to you, if you ask the Father*
> *anything in My Name, He will give it to you.*
> *Until now, you have not requested anything in My Name.*
> *Ask, and you will receive, so that your joy may be full."*
>
> John 16:23-24 [Colossians 3:17]

Who is praying?

When we conceive what faith really is, we understand that **praying is first and foremost, not about *what* words we are praying, or what we are praying for, but is *who we are praying as*.** Prayer is *living*

faith in operation. It is the *living* declaration or witness of the bond of Love in the Divine Will between the soul and God, in Jesus Christ. It is the confession of His presence within us, and throughout the entire triune Universe. When Jesus said that we should pray in His Name, that we may receive, He was therefore telling us to pray in His Light-consciousness, to allow God to receive our prayers [as they can only be received] *"in Spirit and in Truth"* John 4:24. The word *"Amen"* sums up prayer as *living* faith expressed as belief in action. Common in several biblical languages, and meaning *"truly"*, *"assuredly"* or *"so be it"*; it is the seal of absolute trust and confidence, that gives power to what is said from the rooted Light-centre of our being, in God, from where all pure and upright acts [of thought, words, and deed] flow. St. John goes further than the other Evangelists to amplify the word *"Amen"* as to mean: **"I speak [as] Truth in both heart and mouth"**.

To understand prayer as faith's ability to operate, is to understand that God does not so much listen to our words, as to what He Himself utters through His own Light-presence flowing within us. **The correct dispositions must therefore be present within our soul, to allow prayer to be *living and effective* [bear fruit], because we cannot attempt to take by force, what God would give us by grace. Nor can we blame God when our words; that which we call 'prayers' are not answered. For *what we pray and receive is the entirety of our being*; the sum-total of our Christ [Light] or anti-Christ [dark] consciousness.**

In healing the blind beggar Bartimaeus [Mark 10:46-52], as well as a man who had been an invalid of thirty-eight years [John 5:5-9], Jesus first asks them what they want from Him, which is to say, what is their heart's desire? Do they *really* want the three-fold healing Love of God, in the entirety of their being [spirit, soul and body – including the mind and heart]. To Bartimaeus, Jesus then declares *"your faith has made you well [whole]"* Mark 10:52. Many times, Sacred Scripture points to calling things that are not as though they were, to confirm healing [salvation] by faith. In the Gospels, we see Jesus telling the apostles that even a little faith carries extraordinary supernatural power [Matthew 17:19]. He repeats much the same message about **operating in faith** in Matthew 21:21 and Luke 17:5-6. St. Paul speaks of a *"God who gives Life to the dead, and calls the things that are not, as though they were"* Romans 4:17. When the Prophet Elijah persevered in praying [calling forth] rain [1 Kings 18:41-45; James 5:18] in a state of right relationship with God, He had the inward assurance of an answer, before he had rain. Praying and receiving is then about giving in to conceiving and birthing through, the living Light-seed of the Kingdom within the inner temple of our being. Desire for and co-operation with and participation in God, complete trust, and confidence in Him, and yielding to grace, are inseparable from *living* prayer.

Prayer must be kindled in **holy fear of God**; in awe-filled reverence for who He is, and what He has done for us. The opposite of natural earthly fear and doubt, holy fear is positive, exhilarating awareness of the power, glory, and mystery of God, and of our being in God. It is to understand that all is done, and all is given in Jesus Christ.

> *"Now faith is assurance of things hoped for, proof of things not seen."*
>
> Hebrews 11:1.

During His ministry on earth, Jesus amply demonstrates that prayer is not a stand-alone activity. Simultaneously preaching the Word, praying, and delivering [healing] souls from dis-ease, oppression and bondage to Satan and his demons, He showed us that prayer is inseparable from the Word of God, and deliverance from the works of evil. To this end [fulfilment], we are given various avenues and gifts for release and healing that work together with faith-filled prayer, to draw and radiate Light, and cast out the darkness. Sacred Scripture speaks of the Word of God* [Isaiah 48:3; Matthew 16:19; Ephesians 6:17; Hebrews 4:12]; fasting [Isaiah 58:3-14; Mark 9:17-29]; deliverance from spirits [Matthew 8:16]; the anointing of oil - known as the blessing of the sick [Mark 6:13]; the breaking of generational curses [Exodus 20:5, 34:7; Deuteronomy 5:9; Galatians 3:13]; holy relics [2 Kings 13:20-21, Acts 19:11-12] Holy Water; and the gift of healing [1 Corinthians 12:9,28], which may involve the laying on of hands [Luke 4:40]. All work together to heal and strengthen us, and enable us to pray with the entirety of our being, as the full expression of the flowing together of our soul and God. And as God's providential Love and care includes His living creatures, animals can benefit from God's blessings, and receive healing from injury or sickness by way of prayers, and the use of sacramentals [such as Holy Water and relics].

[*See 'Praying God's Word - The Sword of the Spirit' later in this Chapter.']

Coming to Prayer

The beginning and root of *living* prayer, is nothing more than the return to a simple sense of awareness, of the miracle of our life-breath, and the presence of God in our breathing. It is to remember that **God is, and therefore I am**; to realize that the free gift of our life-breath is for the purpose of His breathing and living within and through us. Every breath is proof of the Father's absolute Love for our soul, as He upholds our being in His Divine Will. In every breath, He silently calls His beloved child back from wandering oblivion to the ***'fullness of Life'***, in the All-healing embrace of Jesus Christ.

One of the Aramaic words for prayer, *"shela"*, can mean *"to listen"*, and we first then learn to listen for [sense] God in the quietness of our life-breath, which is the ground of every cause and effect. This involves attention to the two sides of breathing - Spiritual and natural breathing, which are co-essential to the healthfulness of our spirit, soul, and body. Healthy Spiritual breathing means an abiding awareness of God as the source of our life-breath and breathing; and of His presence living in us and as us, in Jesus Christ-consciousness. The quality of our Spiritual being affects the quality of our natural breathing, and therefore our mental and physical health. Sound natural breathing, which is gentle and deep, nourishes our body and mind with vital oxygen, and optimizes our functioning on all levels.

To breathe in the Life-breath of the Holy Spirit, requires a simple movement of the human will [heart's desire], to allow a gentle and constant act of detachment from all outward earthiness [fears, hopes, desires, and sorrows of the flesh and the old world]. This silencing of the dis-ordered community of voices within the soul [memory, will and intellect] is essential to the re-centring [re-integration] of its scattered powers in Jesus Christ, who does not think apart from God, and who is our true centre. **And so, from the beginning, prayer first requires an act of giving; which is an act of giving back our conscious awareness to God, primarily through an act of our human will [heart's desire]. For it is not by first asking that we receive; it is by freely giving [abandoning back].** In freely returning our heart's desire to God, we ask to conceive that which is seeded within us, and wants to be born, which is Eternal Life. It is to offer our being as an empty cup, to be a channel in and through which the Light of *real Life and purpose* in Jesus Christ flows.

> *"Love breathes in two lands,*
> *as I flow in the vastness of God."*
>
> Anon.

We can only truly come to prayer free from unforgiveness [personal bondage and resistance to grace], so that the Holy Spirit is free to operate within and through us. This first requires our awareness and admission that we are all sinners, as confirmation that Truth is in us [1 John 1:8]. If we resist desiring forgiveness for ourselves and offering the same to others [by an act of the will, enabled by grace], we do not have a *living* relationship with God in Jesus Christ. In this state, regardless of what or how much we assume to pray, what we have is prayerful non-prayer, imbued with the poison of unforgiveness, and without power or effect. Frequent [Life-giving] acts of reconciliation [sacramental Confession] on the other hand, accompanied with a firm purpose of amendment, acquits us of wrong doing in the Courts of Heaven. It cleans the fetid pools of sinfulness within our being; and revives the Life-breath of the Holy Spirit, who alone can look into the depths of our soul. In this divinely creative work, He cleanses our unconscious mind; reveals our condition; intercedes for us in overcoming frailties [including difficulty forgiving others]; and enables us to **truly pray and worship God** *"in Spirit and in Truth"* **John 4:24.**

> *"...the Spirit also helps our weaknesses,*
> *for we don't know how to pray as we ought.*
> *But the Spirit Himself makes intercession for us with*
> *groanings which cannot be uttered."*
> Romans 8:26.

Prayer is the essential means of our dynamic healing and re-creation [re-birth] in Jesus Christ. In its All-embracing power in the Life-breath of the Holy Spirit, it is God's medicine for our soul and body. It is a cleanser of sin, a preventative of sin, and a creative and dynamic confession of Truth. Prayer prevents our soul from becoming [further] congested, because of the [naturally] dis-ordered and unstable operation of our being. Ultimately, prayer re-creates reality, healing our soul of dis-union with God, and with the Homeland. Every prayer well said in union with Jesus Christ, pours out Light; nourishing the one who prays with all manner of graces, favours, and blessings, as well as everyone and everything, that would draw into the glory-circle of Light-union. Prayer is the work of the undoing of original sin, which was forgetfulness of God and prideful thanklessness and ingratitude towards Him, as our beloved Creator and Father. Truth assure us, that even the most debased sinner, who is yet sincere and contrite of heart, and who prays with perseverance [commitment], will find their way back to purity of desire and healing [salvation], because **prayer is God's gift to those who pray.**

The Church was birthed in a spirit of prayer [Acts 2] and thrived despite fierce and unrelenting diabolical attack, both from without, and from within. This is because the spirit of continuous prayer is the shield of God; it is our safeguard and the key to perseverance [commitment] and victory, in the Sanctification of our souls

[Ephesians 6:18]. Every sincere prayer and reparation perfumed with Love of God, and of our neighbour as ourself, rises to the throne of the Eternal Father, and draws [further] Light. It forms the crown [Spiritual wealth] of a faithful soul, and adds to its blessedness in Heaven. The letters of St. Paul are mindful of praise and thanksgiving as the very heart of prayer, counselling us to *"sing psalms and hymns and Spiritual music, with thanksgiving in your hearts"* Colossians 3:16-17. Wedded together, prayer, praise, and thanksgiving drive our faith and Love; which in turn increase our [divine] knowledge and wisdom, and praise and thanksgiving.

The first prayer of the day is our morning offering. With this prayer, we offer God our Father all our works, joys, and sufferings of the day in union with and in Jesus Christ, in the power of the Holy Spirit, and through our Blessed Mother. In every temptation, or challenge that we face throughout the day, we can call upon Jesus for Mercy and Mary for help, placing all pains, struggles and fears in their hands. We also call blessing and protection, by making the invincible sign of the Cross, which marks us as *"Children of Light"* Luke 16:18; John 12:36; Ephesians 5:8; 1 Thessalonians 5:5. Grace before meals, reminds us that all provision is the gift of God, as we bless God, and ask for God's blessing on ourselves, on our material food and on all God's people, living creatures and creation. 'Prayer for Daily Neglects' at the end of each day, following examination of conscience, allows us to reflect on our soul-condition, and to ask God to expiate our sins, purify the good we have done, and supply for the good we should have done, or done better, between sacramental Confessions.

The Expediency of Prayer

Sacred Scripture tells us that prayer united with fasting is particularly efficacious [Exodus 34:28; Matthew 3:4; Luke 4:1-4], while by way of His own Life and words, Jesus confirms that self-sacrifice [self-giving], is the necessary way and means of our salvation [healing]. *"If anyone is willing to come after Me: let him deny himself, and take up his cross every day, and follow Me"* Luke

9:23. Prayer is then inseparable from fasting [from sin, and the carnal passions and appetites] and all self-sacrifice, with a motive of Love of God and the will [heart's desire] to be restored to our native purity, and radiance of being in Him. Self-renunciation and prayer is the two-fold penitent and creative work of grace that frees our soul from lower tendencies and outward earthiness, to allow us to give [more fully] of ourself to higher meaning and ways. Pope John Paul II encouraged prayer and fasting in order to *"break down the walls of lies and deceit…. [and instead build] resolutions and goals, inspired by the civilization of Life and Love."* Fasting and self-sacrifice, combined with prayer, improves our alertness to our utter dependence on God, and wakefulness to the inspirations of the Holy Spirit. It drives away evil spirits, and increase our hunger [desire] for God. Every act of self-sacrifice united with Jesus Christ serves the good of all, and relieves the suffering souls in Purgatory. Ultimately, **prayer, united with penance, fasting, and all self-sacrifice, together with participation in the sacraments and Church life, can be seen as Eucharistic good works [Charity], and the ground on which the Spiritual Life stands.** Together, they draw the Light of grace into our soul, to make possible our higher purpose of feasting on the Light-presence of God within and amongst us, while transforming us into dynamic participators in the abolition of evil and the re-instatement of the Kingdom. The divinely creative power and effects of prayer and fasting, is demonstrated in Jesus fast of forty days and nights in the desert; during which time He was tempted by Satan to the sins of greed, vainglory, and avarice [from the Latin word meaning to *"crave"* more than is needed in terms of money, materiality, and all self-satisfaction], but overcame in the power of the Holy Spirit, who manifested Wholly and All-Perfectly, in and through His Divine-Human being [Matthew 4:1-11; Luke 4:1-13]. The vital power of this work of overcoming and drawing the Holy Spirit [Luke 4:14], is revealed in His subsequent work of going around preaching the Gospel and healing the sick - which included casting out evil spirits. The necessity of this work is again confirmed, when Jesus counsels His disciples that only prayer and fasting can expel more difficult evil spirits.

> *"Fasting strengthens prayer and prayer strengthens fasting, and offers it to the Lord."*
>
> St. Bernard of Clairvaux.

As to how we should approach prayer, fasting and all self-sacrifice [self-giving], Jesus advises us to do these acts in secret [Matthew 6:1-8;16-18], so that our Father who sees what is done in secret [which is to say, not deliberately for human attention and reward, but for His glory alone] will reward us. From the Latin word *"intimius"*, the *"inner room"* Matthew 6:6, in which we are to pray, is the shrine of our hearts; the Holy of Holies, and the energy centre of our being. Here, we can pray in a way known only to us and to God, who always deals with us personally; tending, cultivating, and growing with Love and care, the One life of *living* prayer and *living* silence within our soul. Wherever or however, we are praying, authentic progress necessities prudence and gentleness. It should be humble and not purposively done for outward attention [Matthew 6:5-8; Luke 18:9-14], and should be accompanied with firm confidence and perseverance [Luke 18:1-8]. See 'Fasting' and 'self-sacrifice' in Useful Terms.

We can learn much about *living* prayer from the human heart that God trusted most. For although the heart of our Blessed Mother, held the greatest gifts within itself for the span of her earthly years, no sign came of them; no self-righteousness nor public zealotry about divine knowledge, privileges, signs, wonders, and ways. Rather, **in her faultless wisdom and prudence, all drawn about her was a serene and stable *living* silence** [consciousness of the unspoken primordial voice of God, as the rooted Light-centre of her being]; her perfect [whole and all-perfect] crown [of Spiritual wealth] was hidden [including from Satan and his demons], while God's omnipotence operated most powerfully and quietly within and through her.

> *"But Mary treasured up all these things, and pondered them in her heart."*
>
> Luke 2:19,51.

While some souls are called to a more exterior life, and others to a more interior life, those divinely wise and mature in faith [God-centred], honour their duty of care to protect and preserve God's work within their soul. Leading by *living* example, rather than many words and goings-on, they dynamically participate in the Evangelical mission of the Church on earth. Graced with silent lucidity, they know that their first priority is the work of their personal Sanctification, because **to bear the Spiritual state of the Kingdom in their being, is the vital means to proclaim it.** They know too, that the whispers of the unspeakable mysteries of the Kingdom are more pure and delicate than what can be spoken of by a human person. While to spill its secrets in their soul - unless inspired by God to speak, is a violation of their relationship with Him, and inspiration for Satan and his demons. Like Mary, these souls ponder upon, and pray about those things that they do not yet fully understand. In everything, they, like Mary, look to God for divine illumination. See Chapter on 'Fiat'.

> *"Ah, I shall drink of you, and you of Me.*
> *Happy is he who stands firm and does not let spill,*
> *what God has poured into him."*

Jesus speaks to Mechthild of Magdeburg.

While perhaps extraordinarily difficult at first, this new [Ever-new] way of being becomes a most sweet task for the soul growing and rising up above the flesh [carnal ego-self] and the old world, and into Loving union with God. It has come to understand that **everything it refuses itself [sacrifices] at the natural level is given back to God, and allows it to receive from the Light-treasury of Spiritual riches, for the good of everyone and everything.** And when it has reached the point of forgetting itself in everything [selling everything of the desires of the human will, in favour of the Divine Will], God will bestow upon it the priceless gift of nuptial Light-union. In this vital work of self-renunciation, for the purpose of healing and re-generation [re-birthing] in higher Life in the Spirit, 'The Golden Maxims of St. John of the Cross' [Appendix 3] are a most sure guide.

Everything depends upon our neighbour

To this end [fulfilment], the efficacy our prayer life is ever-revealed in our mirroring of the two beams of the Cross, which demonstrate that we must be both in right relationship with God [vertical] and with our neighbour [horizontal] in Jesus Christ, in order to be operating in right relationship with hallowed reality. For as the Kingdom of God is both within us and among us, as relationship and as community, the authenticity of prayer and inner Spiritual growth [purity of motive, and proof of progress], must have a corresponding way of being in community, which reflects the communal reality of the Kingdom of Heaven. The double length of the vertical beam demonstrates that our relationship with God, in the Cosmic Personhood of Jesus Christ, is primary, and regulates our relationship with our fellow man, and with all of God's living creatures and creation. Indeed, every aspect of our relationship with God is put to the test, and reflected in our relationship with other people, and with all living creatures and creation. The soul's movement in a necessary and inseparable state of ascending [retreat] from and descending [returning] into the old world [according to its calling], is thus the ultimate test of living in the old world, but not being of it, while allowing God to work within, and through us. It is the essential means by which the soul increases in knowledge, wisdom, and Love of itself and others, in its divinely-human soul-condition, for the purpose of learning, sharing, testing, and authentic growth. To this end [fulfilment] the soul must rest in abandoning back [consenting] to the work of the Holy Spirit, who in His All-knowingness, will provide what is needed, and what the co-operative soul is capable of receiving, in right timing and in accordance with its good will and strength. Offering Light and shade and guiding it in rhythms of growth and rest, His boundless goodness and Mercy will burn up all the darkness that it is susceptible to.

Your *Living* Word ~ *Living* Silence

To learn to pray with power and effect, is to realize that we are not passive victims waiting and hoping that a distant, abstract God will do something for us. For from the beginning of Genesis, God's Word and authority are confirmed with *action*. All creation came from the Father's spoken word, and in Coming to earth *as* 'The Living Word' [John 1:1; 1:14], Jesus gave human words His own power. He taught us that we exercise authority, and enforce the Kingdom of God or the kingdom of Satan, with our every spoken word. The power of blessing and curse are in the tongue [James 3:1-12]; which is to say, *"Death and Life are in the power of the tongue"* Proverbs 18:21.

Every word we speak is an instrument that carries fear [defeat] or faith [victory]; Life or death; a blessing or a curse. Every word announces our soul-condition as Light or as darkness; drawing or driving out the Holy Spirit. Every word sends out fragrant, Life-giving air that manifests the voice of God, or sickly air that manifests the voice of darkness. It focuses the direction of our own heart's desire [human will] and that of others, while awakening or deadening our own and others' consciousness. Indeed, the quality of our every thought, as well as those carried by our voice, has Eternal resonance; affecting, and becoming part of, not only ourselves and those who hear us, but the entire vibration and texture of the Cosmos, in continuous befriending of and consummation in Light or in darkness. **We need only think of Eve's wilful engaging in conversation with the serpent [Satan], to know the dangers of thinking and speaking apart from God, and to recognize that we have an immense duty of care to ensure that every word we speak is spoken under grace. It should honour and uphold the relationship of Love between God and the soul, and carry and spread the spirit of *living* prayer. For to learn to pray, is to learn to listen and to speak, not out of ourselves, but out of God in Jesus Christ** [2 Corinthians 2:17]. It is to honour God and who we all are in Him, and assist in the healing and restoration of all His people, living creatures, and creation.

> *"Amen, I say to you, whatever you will have bound on earth, shall be bound also in Heaven, and whatever you will have released on earth, shall be released also in Heaven."*
>
> Matthew 18:18.

True and awake speaking means being real. God operates not based on natural human reason, feelings, and emotions, but on Truth. In speaking in, and out of Him, we are mandated to express the genuine [hallowed] relationship between things, and have something of substance to give [from God] to others*. Mortal flesh [the carnal ego-self] becomes silent, and our words become like God's, which means *"alive and active "*Hebrews 4:12. Rooted in, and issuing from *living* silence [consciousness of the unspoken primordial voice of God, as the rooted Light-centre of our being], in Oneness with the Life-breath of the Holy Spirit, our speaking is chaste [pure] speaking, coupled with an outstretched hand, that consciously and selflessly builds up the Kingdom of God, rather than tears it down.

> *"I condemn and detest talking much with men; but we can never talk too much with God."*
>
> St. Bernard of Clairvaux.

As our soul is gradually purified and re-ordered in the Love and Divine Will of God, we learn to express ourselves more effectively; with a greater sense of perspective, vigilance, and balance, that reflects His growing Light-presence in our being. In His Light, we gladly abandon outer reflections characterized by self-centred speech that flatters or criticises at the level of the flesh [carnal ego-self] and the old world. We leave behind words [confessions and projections] of natural fear and negativity, which serve only to compound our problems, and oppress and afflict others, as well as all living creation. We leave behind wanton curiosities about the lives of others; and the gross gratification of gossip, speculation, and mocking laughter [the sin of detraction], that parades and mocks our own brokenness. We leave behind crude double-meaning and hilarity; comparisons and foolish arguments; and negative monologue about the darkness, that does nothing but drive further darkness. And we leave behind 'feel good' philosophical sound bites and phrases; *"the wisdom of human eloquence"* with its mundane values, that have nothing to do with the *living* Word of the Gospel, and by which the Cross of Jesus Christ, and its fruits are robbed of meaning and power [1 Corinthians 1:17]. For all [thinking and] speaking apart from God is Light-impoverished [thought and] speech that exposes our separation from God, while corrupting the creative purpose of language. It crowds and distorts our thoughts and silence; and misdirects and wastes our time and that of others; time that should be spent serving God, and our neighbour in Charity. Sacred Scripture tells us that Jesus found refuge in the home of siblings Lazarus, Martha, and Mary, because here He found peace and rest from the wearisome conversation and curiosities of worldly people.

> *"If anyone among you thinks himself to be religious, while he doesn't bridle his tongue, but deceives his heart: this man's religion is worthless."*
>
> James 1:26.

Genuine prayer must then first unravel, purify, and empty the soul of dis-ordered and unstable fleshy [egoic] and old worldly thinking, ways, and desires [everything external], and re-direct it [interiorly] to the One source of Truth, found in a *living* relationship with Jesus Christ. While the soul truly growing and maturing in its relationship with Him, finds itself moving into right rhythm of listening [*living* silence] and of speaking [*living* words]; of receiving God's Word and returning it to Him, in the Life-breath of the Holy Spirit. Acutely aware that *"the tongue of the wise heals"* Proverbs 12:18, while its misuse causes the loss of blessings, as well as the efficacy of grace, it is capable of actively listening, and of speaking appropriately; saying what needs to be said, while expressing the true [divine] relationship between things. Speaking only Truth in Love [Ephesians 4:15], it understands the words [and deeds] that the other person needs, giving healthy and healthful [Life-giving] words; the word of righteousness, knowledge, wisdom, courage, peace, lightness, and joy. This soul knows that to speak Truth of oneself, and of others, is the expression of *true* compassion and kinship. It is to i-dentify as One with them in Jesus Christ, who continuously calls forth Himself in all of us, until our working time on earth is over. *"When I delivered Myself up to the wicked, they bound My hands and did as they pleased with Me. They could not, however, bind My tongue, but I Myself fettered it, that I spoke only what was useful for them"* Jesus speaks to St. Mechtilde.

Every time we are about to speak, let us remember that **true speaking is full of grace and hallowed reality.** Let us bow inwardly before Christ's presence within ourselves, and in others [regardless of the situation or circumstances], and be mindful of the presence of our Guardian Angels. For on the day of Judgement [Matthew 12:36], we will be required to account for every ungodly word spoken. See 'Praying God's Word - The Sword of the Spirit' at Chapter end.

> *"Let any who wish to talk to you, learn your language. And if they will not, be careful never to learn theirs."*
>
> St. Teresa of Avila.

Growing in Prayer

Prayer is both in the *living* words that issue from the rooted Light-centre of our being, and in the *living* silence beyond words. Words are necessary because God creates with His spoken Word, and because evil and deception also flourish in silence and in darkness. However, to pray, it is not always necessarily to use words. God is Spirit and action, and prayer is not about piling up words and phrases [Matthew 6:7-8], or about ritual perfection, but about presence. The deepest and most powerful prayer in one moment may be to simply listen for God, while a particularly meritorious prayer is to reflect devoutly [with Love and humility] upon the Passion of Jesus Christ. All dryness, difficulty, and restlessness [wantonness], is food for thought; for humility and reality-checking; for we cannot take by force what God would give us by [right disposition to] grace. Neither can we perceive at the [dis-ordered] natural level the refined and delicate communications of pure Spirit. A good indicator of the quality of our interior life [our connectedness or disconnectedness from the All-unity of God within], is our willingness and capability for sitting alone in prayer. Those who struggle to remain for any length of time are faced with their own restlessness [inner Spiritual turmoil] brought about by the voids of Light, which is the absence of God's Light-presence and harmony within the soul. **While the more mature [and free] the soul, the fewer the words needed, as it finds aliveness in the *living* silence [and action] of the divine freedom.** See 'Holy Hour'.

In prayer, communing with God is the priority, because God does not so much give us what we want [at the natural level], but what we need. His gifts are first and foremost, not of the voids of the flesh [the carnal ego-self] and the material world, but the immaterial, subtle, and powerful gifts of the Spirit. **He is always pointing and moving us upwards, to the fullness of prayer.** Jesus expresses the meaning, purpose, and fulfilment of prayer, in His own most beautiful prayer of the Our Father [Luke 11:2-4 and Matthew 6:9-13], and in His moving High-Priestly prayer to the Father, that through Him, the Father may be glorified [John 17]. The saints of the ages, and those who live in Jesus Christ, have therefore returned to a sense of unknowing, and a willingness to be a beginner. Alive with *living* faith and divine wisdom, they have learned to ask for [desire] godly things, and receive from the divine treasury all that meets their essential earthly needs, as well as the ultimate Spiritual gift of the Kingdom. While those most perfect in prayer, ask for no-thing in particular, but rather await Jesus Christ.

> *"I give great graces to souls*
> *who meditate devoutly on My Passion."*
>
> Jesus speaks to St. Faustina [Divine Mercy].

Every Prayer is New

No two prayers are ever the same. The expression in words may be the same, but the effects are different, because a deepening Spiritual quality is impressed upon the [sincere] soul; kindling in it, the Light-fire of Love, and awakening and intensifying its desire for re-union with God. Inspiring testimonies of the saints confirm that the Angels gather around us when we pray, bearing witness, to and recording the disposition of our soul. They listen to us, pray with us, and gather our words and acts of worship, divinized in Jesus Christ, ascending with them to the throne of the Eternal Father. Prayers, well said, ascend like incense, while those of unfaithful soul cannot rise at all.

> *"Some Angels wrote in letters of gold, others in letters of silver, others in ink, others in water, and others held their pens but did not write anything. This shows that the Angels watch over our prayers, recording the disposition of our souls. Gold typifies Charity and fervour; silver denotes devotion, but little charity or fervour; ink writing careful attention to verbal recitation but little else; water means distraction and little attention to the meaning, or to the words. The Angels who wrote nothing, watched the insolence of those who were voluntarily distracted."*
>
> A vision of St. Bernard of Clairvaux.

The Fullness of Prayer: Life in Jesus Christ

Growing in the life of prayer, is growing towards the promise of a closer and higher state of Light-union with the Most Holy Trinity. This blissful state of being, to which St. Paul refers to some eighty times in Sacred Scripture as our re-creation [re-birth] *"in Christ"*, is mastered by following Jesus Christ into the Truth of His Being; to be joined with Him in spirit, soul, and body, and without outward or inward division, or instability. **Incalculably more than outward pious words and practices, and in faithfulness to the first two and greatest Commandments, it means to be a living revelation of Charity;**

worshipping God as He can only be worshipped, *"in Spirit and in Truth"* John 4:24. See 'Man' and 'New Man' in Useful Terms.

> *"If I were to speak in the language of men, or of Angels, yet not have Charity, I would be like a clanging bell or a crashing cymbal."*
> 1 Corinthians 13:1.

Living always in right relationship with hallowed reality, *living* prayer was the absolute expression of the Blessed Virgin Mary's soul-condition. Birthing every act [of thought, word, and deed] in the Love and Divine Will of God, *being* and *living faith as,* was One thing within her. Her instantaneous and sublime prayer *"let it be done to me, according to your Word"* Luke 1:38, was not a passive and dutiful acceptance of God's Cosmic Divine Will [Heart's Desire], but **a fully aware and alive, why-less embrace** of it. *"Not as I will, but as You Will"* Matthew 26:39, was the utterly magnificent immortal prayer of Jesus in the Garden of Gethsemane, as He faced into His horrific torture and execution, at the hands of us all. Where Adam and Eve had failed in the Garden of Eden, Jesus triumphed in the Garden of Gethsemane, and Mary triumphed by the merits of her Son-God. For in His One singular and tripartite, Self-offering [at-One-ment], Jesus witnesses to prayer in the absolute sense, perfecting forever all who would be sanctified in Him [Hebrews 10:14]. In Him, our prayers and worship of God receive their redemptive value, and attain their goal of sanctifying our souls. For He alone has re-opened the avenues of Light [sanctifying grace] that originally flowed from the Godhead into Adams's forehead [mind], mouth, breast [heart], hands, and feet, and united us with the Father [Fatherland].

> *"No action taken on your own, even though you put much effort into it, pleases Me."*
> Jesus speaks to St. Faustina [Divine Mercy].

To be re-created [re-birthed] in Jesus Christ, is to realize that while various types or modes of prayer are necessary and good*, **the fullness of *living* prayer is nothing more than a journey of one [three-in-one] step, and nothing less than a *flight of faith*,** the three powers of the soul [primarily the human will] rests in, and operates in harmony with the Divine Will, in Love of and desire for God [alone], and the good of his neighbour in all things. In this way of being and living in Jesus Christ, in fidelity to the first two and greatest commandments, the ordinary becomes extraordinary as our every act [of thought, word, and deed], including our breaths, steps, works, joys, and sufferings, fused with the Mystical Life [works, joys, and sufferings] of Jesus Christ are rendered divine. And as our inner reality and what we do, is transformed by knowledge of God and of ourself in God, intuition supersedes contemplation and we become a participation in the divine operation, and attain to the blissful state of the Eucharistic *"new man"*. In whatever blessed life-state or office we occupy, our purity [cleanliness and clarity] of heart and willingness for perseverance [commitment] are essential to this work, to allow the inflowing of the Holy Spirit, who enables the soul to **become *as* another Christ**. For God grows and flourishes only in the inviolate, or recovered, virgin element of the soul, which is the substance-essence and likeness of Himself. Therefore, according to the degree to which our heart's desire [human will] rests in Him, in a state of right disposition to grace, can the life of the soul, and the Life of Jesus Christ [although distinctly different in substance and in energies] flow into One, through the witness of the Holy Spirit. See Chapter on 'The Blessed Virgin Mary'.

[*The Church teaches that various types or modes of prayer are necessary and good, and operate concurrently, at all stages of Spiritual maturity].

> *"Raised above earthly dullness, to the likeness of the Spiritual and the Angelic, whatever they take in; whatever they reflect upon and whatever they do, will be the most sincere and pure prayer."*
>
> St. John Cassian.

In this unity and transformation of the human will [heart's desire] in the Father's Love and Divine Will, I AM of Jesus Christ living within and through the consenting soul is the prayer and the praying; and the giving and the receiving; as Jesus Christ recognizes His own voice within the soul, and it recognizes its voice in Him, in the Life-breath of the Holy Spirit. **God receives these *living* prayers and answers them as His own, because Jesus Christ, the Perfect [Whole and All-Perfect] centre and Light-consciousness of all creation does the work within the soul.** In Jesus Christ, this blessed soul becomes an oasis of Life, flowing and circulating in the Heavenly and earthly realms, fulfilling its responsibility to everyone and everything by drawing and sharing His Light, fragrance, and harmony, while also benefitting from all answered prayers. This dynamic circle of receiving and returning the Life of Jesus Christ [in the Light-union of the Most Holy Trinity] as pure gift, is the Sanctification of man and the Sanctification of time. For **Love is not an end in itself, but *real Life and purpose* in Jesus Christ, is the purpose and fulfilment of Love. Brief in words and abundant in actions [Life-giving acts], it is** *"the full-grown man...measure of the stature of the fullness of Christ"* **Ephesians 4:11 that works miracles and moves mountains [Mark 11:23].** It is the privileged work of participating in the atonement [at-One-ment], and bringing about the triumph of the Immaculate Heart of Mary, through the merits of her Son-God. Creation is placed in safety [from the works of evil], and transfigured and restored to sanctity; to a continuous relationship with God the Father in the present moment.

> *"The more perfect a soul is, the stronger and the more far-reaching is the Light shed by it.... its holiness is reflected in souls, even to the most distant extremities of the world."*
>
> Jesus speaks to St. Faustina [Divine Mercy].

While not perceived [at the natural level] or perfected in this earthly life, this is the beginning of man's creative realization of the *'fullness of Life',* that honours and glorifies God and his own being, together with all creation in God. For the heart united with the Heart of God is the music of *living* prayer and praise, that is its wedding to the divine harmonies and freedom songs in which all life began. Above all, it is the Life which returns to God, on behalf of all creation, all that belongs to Him, that He might be All in All again, as He originally planned. This higher Life remains in us, so long as we remain in the state of sanctifying grace, and is strengthened through the reception of the Eucharist, and other sacraments; through ongoing prayer, and the use of sacramentals, such as Holy Water, scapulars, and medals.

Overcoming souls, who are zealous for the Love and glory of God, and who commit to realizing [making real] the *'fullness of Life'* in Jesus Christ within their being on earth, are divinely empowered, guided, and protected during their life. For as fire renders all things impossible to touch, Satan and his demons dare not approach the Light-fire of Jesus Christ living within them. Raised above the limitations of human thinking; Love and holy [just] anger; silence and speech; involvement and withdrawal [holy disinterest]; and action and contemplation are as One. In touch with the Eternal Now, every day is a sacred day, because the gift of time is fulfilling its One true meaning and purpose within them. Time and space; and past, present, and future, all exist in the present moment, as the unfolding of their days, become one continuous prayer of their souls Ever-flowering, in the promise of Eternities Perpetual Light.

> *"They are virgins, martyrs, and all other kinds of worshippers of God, who in full knowledge tread worldly things underfoot, and desire the Heavenly; and they surround the devil and crush him... But they cannot be injured... for they are protected by God with such strength and constancy, that neither the open flame nor the hidden persuasion of the devil's wickedness can touch them."*
>
> St. Hildegard of Bingen. [1]

Many saints and mystics of the Church have been given to conceive the full expression of prayer as a state of Mystical [Spiritual] Marriage. More recent faithful souls [of the 20th Century] such as St. Elizabeth of the Trinity, Blessed

Dina Belanger, Venerable Conchita [Concepion Cabrera de Armida] and especially the 'Servant of God', Luisa Piccarreta [an Italian 19th-20th Century, Third Order Dominican, and Mystic], have described a state of Mystical [Spiritual] Incarnation in which the Life of Jesus Christ is reproduced within and through the soul. In this work, the co-operative soul is made of, a most munificent [suffering] victim and participator in union with Jesus Christ, sharing in and relieving His corporeal and interior sufferings, in order to accomplish His Plan of Love. St John Paul II wrote of a *"new and divine holiness"*, at the dawn of the third millennium, which would *"make Christ the heart of the world"* [John Paul II, 'Letter to the Centenary of the Rogation Fathers'.] Souls raised to the state of Mystical Incarnation, first traversed the high state of Mystical Marriage. While the complete gift of the Mystical Incarnation given to Luisa Piccarreta *followed* Mystical Marriage, at the age of twenty-three, *and* three further nuptials. Her private Revelations, are currently under review by the Church, and her cause of beatification and canonisation is progressing.

The Sign of the Cross

The sign of the Cross, is a Christian ceremony that represents the primordial Passion of God for human souls. It is a profession of our *faith as* children of God, and of our absolute belonging to Him. It is a blessing, and a means of invocating Jesus Christ, by way of whom all divine graces, favours and blessings draw their power and strength.

The sign of the Cross is ultimately a way of life. It is a reproof to Satan, and confirmation that we have no glory [blissful magnificence], other than the Eucharistic life, marked by our share in the Cross of Jesus Christ. We recognize that the Cross is not an end in itself, but is the death-destroying and life-giving means and mark of man's crossing point between Heaven and earth. It is our master key for passing away from the insular *"old man"*, to arise again to the exalted state of the Eucharistic *"new man"*; the divinely-human [Spiritualized-] self in Jesus Christ.

The all-conquering sign of the Cross reminds us of the primacy of the interior life. It reminds us of God's Perfect [Whole and All-Perfect] balance between Mercy and Justice [Romans 11:22-23], and our task and responsibility of passing from darkness into Light. As with all *living* prayer, it should be made carefully and meditatively, with the interior bearing the mark of the exterior sign.

Adapted from the writings of St. Francis de Sales.

"The Sign of the Cross, is the most terrible weapon against the devil [Satan]. For this reason, the Church displays images of the Cross, so that we have it continually in front of our minds, to recall to us just what our souls are worth, and what they cost Jesus Christ. For the same reason, the Church wants us to make the sign of the Cross ourselves at every juncture of the day... and above all, when we are tempted. Respect for the Cross will protect you against the devil, from the vengeance of Heaven, and from all danger" says St. John Vianney [The Curé D'Ars].

The Lord's Prayer – The Gateway to the Kingdom

The Our Father, is the one prayer that Jesus taught us to pray, and it teaches us what God our Father wants us to want. Each word contains immense Light, setting out the way of convalescence to right relationship with hallowed reality, which is the Kingdom of God within our soul. The complete and better-known form of the prayer is found in Matthew 6:9-13, while a shortened form is found in Luke 11:2-4.

To live the Our Father prayer, is to align our human will [heart's desire] with the Father's supreme Divine Will [Cosmic Heart's Desire], and receive *real Life and purpose* in Jesus Christ. It is both a *living* confession of, and surrender back to, who we truly are [and ever can be] in Him. We understand that God's One and only Plan on earth, is for the restoration of our souls, because the One thing He desires is to receive us in the Homeland, which He has prepared for faithful souls. The words of the Our Father confirm that there can be no conception or re-birth [re-creation], without abandoning our human will to the Divine Will [God's Cosmic Heart's Desire], to allow Jesus Christ [God] to be conceived and birthed within and through us. **The task and purpose of the Our Father prayer, is therefore that we live it, and carry it in our being.** It is the perfect *living* prayer that moves us into a state of intimacy with our paternal Father, and with all His creation in Him. It sets the standard for what we should ask for, and the order in which we should ask for it. A prayer of confession, praise, and contemplation, it is a perfect expression of faith, hope, and Charity as a child of God, and as lived, is the perfect act of worship.

"Our Father who art in Heaven"- we call out to the One, absolute, Eternal, and supreme Divine Being, in humble and adoring recognition that we can confidently call Him Father, because of our Brother and Saviour [Healer] Jesus Christ's sacrificial [All-giving] Life, Passion, Death, and Resurrection for our sake. We identify as His beloved child, knowing that we are immeasurably precious to His Heart. We recognize Heaven as the Spiritual realm of the All and the Only; the origin and destiny of our immortal soul, and the splendorous *'fullness*

of Life', prepared for on earth, and received - according to our soul-condition, beyond the temporary physical realm.

"Hallowed be thy Name" - We bow our heads [minds into our hearts] in recognition of the sublime purity and fullness of God's Name, which is the fullness of Life itself; our heritage, our authority, and our hope.

"Thy Kingdom Come, Thy Will be done" - We proclaim our sincere heart's desire [will] for the return of the Empire of our Father's Kingdom. With these words, we call for [confess] the Light of His Love and Divine Will to be realized [made real] within and through us, in return for our abandonment back [consent] to the authentic Life of the *"Fiat"*. We endeavour to be faithful members of the Mystical Body of the risen Christ; re-birthed [re-created] and living in Him, who is the full expression of the Father, and at peace with our neighbour, which includes all people, living creatures and creation.

"On earth [in me] as it is in Heaven" - To bring Heaven to earth, is to conceive and birth the Spiritual state of the Kingdom within and through our soul, encased in an earthen body. We again profess our heart's desire [will], that the Light of Jesus Christ manifests within and through us, in the way God originally planned; which is His Life of Love operating in His All-Perfect [Whole and All-Perfect] Divine Will.

"Give us this day our daily bread" - We confess our need for daily sustenance, and our grateful recognition of God as the Three-In-One source and conserver of All [good] supply:

- The Father Creator creates and sustains our being, and all that is, in His Love and Divine Will, in every moment of every day. He gives us corporal food, to sustain our mortal bodies;
- The Son gives Himself to us, in The Living Food of the Eucharist [John 6:51-52] in each virtuous act of Holy Communion*; and
- The Holy Spirit, our Comforter, Guide, and Sanctifier, gives us our life-breath in His Life-breath, and the bread of the Father's Cosmic Divine Will, in each moment.

[*An act of Spiritual Communion, is a prayerful expression of desire to receive Jesus Christ *fully and substantially* in the sacramental species of the Eucharist, when genuinely unable to receive Him].

We remain humble, meek, and constant in faith, knowing that God will provide what we need for temporal life, as well as Spiritual [supernatural] sustenance, if we abide in Him, by abandoning back [consenting] to His Love operating in His Divine Will.

"And forgive us our trespasses, as we forgive those who trespass against us" - In a reciprocal circle of healing, we entreat the Father's forgiveness and release from our sins [of thought, word, and deed], and in the same way, we forgive and release everyone who has sinned against us. In this act, we participate in **the two sides of confession,** as confessor of who we are in God, and as forgiver of sins [Matthew 6:14-15]. **We recognize trespassing in the complete sense, of all that is our neighbour**, which primarily includes ourselves, those people present to us, and those who we think of, as well as those who have passed from this world, and those who have yet to come. We also recognize the lives of God's living creatures who share the earth with us, and who are entrusted to our care and stewardship. For all belong to the One living Spirit and Heartbeat of God. All have life in Jesus Christ [John 1:1] albeit not in the same way as man, and all have a future in the new Heaven and new earth where *"no hurt shall be done; no life taken"* [Isaiah 11:6-9]. All play an essential part in the health and prosperity of the planet, and the healthfulness and prosperity of man. We therefore endeavour to live up to what we are calling [confessing] in the Our Father prayer, by taking personal responsibility for our neighbour, in every act [thought, word, and deed], living as dynamic participators in the restoration of the Kingdom.

And lead us not into temptation, but deliver us from evil [from the evil one]" - We ask that we may not lose ourselves in forgetfulness and desertion of God, thus falling prey to the [direct and indirect] temptations, deceptions, and afflictions of evil. We ask that we are led away from all evil and temptation that would derail us from living up to our privileged task and responsibility of co-operating with and participating in the abolition of evil, and restoration of the Kingdom.

Hail Mary – The Golden Arrow

The Hail Mary contains and renews the most beautiful praises, honours, and joys that Mary experienced in being made the Mother of the Incarnate God. Each word carries immense Light of understanding about who she is, and in honouring her in God, it Lovingly wounds the Divine Heart of her Son-God, Jesus Christ.

"Hail Mary's that you pray with faith and Love, are golden arrows that go straight to the Heart of Jesus. Pray much and recite the Rosary for the conversion of sinners, of unbelievers and of all Christians" The Blessed Virgin speaks to Italian convert Bruno Cornacchiola in 1947.

"Hail Mary, full of grace"- We honour our celestial Mother; the Sovereign Queen of Heaven and earth. Free from original sin, and all pure, beautiful, and holy [whole and all-perfect], she is full of the whole-hearted purpose, luminous intelligence, and refinement of God. Intimately united with her Son-God, she intercedes for us as our celestial Mother, and is the vessel of all graces, favours, and blessings.

"The Lord is with thee" - Mary's entire being is continuous *living* prayer, because she is inundated and invested with Light; with all divine prerogatives and riches. She operates always and only together with God, and for His glory in all things.

"Blessed art thou amongst woman" - She is uniquely and singularly favoured in all divine knowledge, wisdom, dignities, and glory [blissful magnificence]. Centralized in her, is all purity and nobility; all the glory [blissful magnificence] that is the infinity of divine goods, joys, beauties, harmonies, and contentment's, that everyone was to enjoy.

"And blessed, is the fruit of thy womb, Jesus" - Never wanting to know her own human will [heart's desire], she is all that she is because of what the divine majesty has operated within her, through the merits of her Son-God, Jesus Christ.

"Holy Mary, Mother of God" - in calling the Incarnate Word into her most pure womb, she fulfilled the most extraordinary office of

becoming Heaven on earth for God, and the celestial Queen-Mother of all mankind. She is thus Mediatrix and Co-redemptrix of our Redemption.

"Pray for us sinners, now and at the hour of our death" - **We find in her divine maternity, the endowment, support, and help for all our Spiritual and temporal needs, until the end of our earthly pilgrimage. Church saints assure us that the death of a truly faithful soul, is itself a revelation of Divine Mercy and consolations, as the world of the Spirit comes to meet the faithful pilgrim child of the Kingdom.**

Glory Be – Carrying Earth to Heaven

"Glory be, to the Father, and to the Son, and to the Holy Spirit" - **The 'Glory Be', is the ultimate declaration of hallowed reality. All glory [blissful magnificence], honour, and triumph belong to, and is owed to, the Three Divine Persons of the Most Holy Trinity.**

"As it was in the beginning, is Now and ever shall be, world without end" - **Eternal things, which are without beginning or end, can only be found here and Now, in God's Love and Divine Will. Everything else perishes. The co-operative soul who desires above all else, to live [participate] in the Father's Love and Divine Will while on earth, is as far as it is disposed, already in communion of relationship with the blessed in Heaven, and the faithful on earth; sharing in everything that they do for the good of all. This soul will, as far as it perseveres [commits], grow capable [by degree of Light-union], of enjoying the fullness of glorious being, and the endless Beatitude of Heaven.**

Prayer to the Holy Spirit

O, Holy Spirit, beloved of my soul. I adore You. Enlighten me, guide me, strengthen me, console me. Tell me what I should do. I promise to submit myself to all that You desire of me, and I accept all that You permit to happen to me. Let me know only Your [Divine] Will. Amen. Cardinal Mercier. **See Chapter on 'The Holy Spirit'.**

The Rosary - The Spiritual Weapon of Mary

Given to the Church in the year 1214 by St. Dominic [as received from the Blessed Virgin Mary], the Rosary, meaning *"garland or wreath of roses"*, is a most powerful divine weapon, conferring the richest of graces, favours, and blessings through Mary, the vessel of grace.

In saying the daily Rosary, we honour the Life of Jesus Christ [in the Most Holy Trinity], and call upon our Blessed Mother to assist us in entering into the mysteries of Divine Life. Over the centuries, incalculable miracles have testified to the power of the Rosary in freeing those held in the death-grip of evil; in healing and sanctifying souls; thwarting and dispelling temptation and evil; and placating the just anger [Divine Justice] of God. **The circular form of the Rosary, whereby we finish where we started, reminds us of the call to our ancient beginning. It reminds us, that our purpose is ultimately not about driving 'forward' for some worldly goal [future] that perishes, but is a return to the beginning, which is the original [and exalted] primordial state of innocence and justice [Eternal Beatitude].** Crowned with the Cross, the Rosary teaches us that the Cross is the authentic gold standard; the holy and desirable way Home, because God only *truly* comes to know man, and man only *truly* comes to know God, on the Cross.

"When you say your Rosary, the Angels rejoice, the Blessed Trinity delights in it; my Son finds joy in it too, and I myself am happier than you can possibly guess. After the Holy Sacrifice of the Mass, there is nothing in the Church that I Love as much as the Rosary" Our Blessed Mother speaks to Blessed Alan de la Roche.

"The Rosary is the most beautiful and the richest of all prayers to the Mediatrix of all grace. It is the prayer that touches most the heart of the Mother of God. Say it each day!" Pope Pius X.

"The Rosary is a powerful weapon to put the demons to flight, and to keep oneself from sin... if you desire peace in your hearts, in your homes, and in your country, assemble each evening to recite the Rosary!" Pope Pius XI.

Prayer to St. Michael – Angelic Battle Prayer

St. Michael the Archangel, defend us in battle. Be our safeguard against the wickedness and snares of the devil. O God restrain him we humbly pray. Do thou O Prince of the Heavenly Host, by the power of God, thrust into Hell, Satan, and all evil spirits, who wander through the world, seeking the ruin of souls. Amen.

This well-known prayer to St. Michael, captures perfectly the crucial importance of this pre-eminent Angel in the ferocious battle against evil, and the work of our salvation [healing]. Confronting and overthrowing Lucifer [Satan], when he raised his proud head against God before the creation of the world [Revelation 12:7-9], he is the leader and prince of the Armies of Almighty God, who passionately defends His honour. He is patron and protector of the *living* Church on earth, and guardian of the dying. If we Love God and His Church, we will call upon his daily assistance in the work of the undoing of evil, and restoration of the Kingdom. We will invoke him and the Heavenly Armies [Choirs], to come to the aid of the *living* Church, leading her through the swarms of enemies of God, that rage across the face of the earth, and on to the safety and splendour of the Homeland.

The Angelic Crown or Chaplet

Also known as the Chaplet of St. Michael the Archangel, this is another most powerful prayer that invokes the assistance of the nine Armies [Choirs] of God, under the stewardship of St. Michael. Given by St. Michael to Sr. Antonia d'Astonac, a Portuguese Carmelite nun in 1750, God promises to sincere and faithful souls who say the Chaplet, the daily assistance of the Angels during life, and an escort from each of the nine Armies [Choirs] in the act of Holy Communion. After death, is promised the faithful souls deliverance from Purgatory, and that of their relations, who have been committed to Purgatory.

Prayer to St. Joseph

As foster father of God on earth, St. Joseph holds highest honour among the saints, and his intercession is particularly powerful.

Healing Prayer at Bedtime

Lord Jesus, through the power of the Holy Spirit, go back into my memory as I sleep tonight. Every hurt that has ever been done to me, heal the hurt. Every hurt that I have ever caused another person, heal that hurt. All the relationships that have been damaged in my whole life that I am not aware of, heal those relationships. But, Lord, if there is anything that I need to do, If I need to go to a person because he or she is still suffering from my hand, please bring to my awareness that person. I choose to forgive, and I ask to be forgiven. Remove whatever bitterness may be in my heart, Lord, and fill the empty spaces with Your Love. Amen.

This is a most powerful night-time prayer for forgiveness and healing, in a state of positive abandonment [consent] to the All-sufficient power of God's grace. With it, we call [invite] Jesus Christ to enter into our souls, as the All-seeing and gentle Housekeeper, who shines His Light into all corners and hidden places within our being, and makes forgiveness, healing, and transformation possible.

Deliverance Prayers

As baptised children of God [while we don't have a priest's power of exorcism], we can, if in a state of sanctifying grace, call on the authority of the Name of Jesus Christ; His Cross and His Blood, to bind evil and forbid them to operate against us. This includes evil attached to, or oppressing, another person, or persons, as well as any evil spirits of the earth and the elements [earth, air, fire, and water]. See example prayer at Chapter end.

The Chaplet of Divine Mercy

This is one of the most efficacious gifts of prayer, given by Jesus to the Polish nun St. Faustina. In His words recorded in St. Faustina's diary, He offers mankind this daily prayer as a powerful tool in the fierce battle for souls, especially for obtaining Mercy for the dying, and for the conversion of hardened sinners. It is also a vital means of drawing special graces and favours to appease God's just anger [see Diary, 476]; to avert natural disasters; and to thwart and dispel the attacks of Satan [see Diary, 1798].

" While I was saying the Chaplet, I heard a voice which said: "Oh, what great graces I will grant to souls who say this Chaplet; the very depths of My tender Mercy are stirred for the sake of those who say the Chaplet"" Jesus speaks to St. Faustina.

Praying God's Word - *The Sword of the Spirit* [Ephesians 6:17]

The Word of God *"is living and active, and sharper than any two-edged sword"* Hebrews 4:12. Sacred Scripture tells us that God's way of operating is to first declare things, and then to do them. In the omnipotent power [I AM] of His own Word, He called all of creation out of nothing and into being. He also let Israel know ahead of time, that He was going to do great works in their lives. *"I have declared the former things from of old. Yes, they went out of My mouth, and I revealed them. I did them suddenly, and they happened [says the Lord]"* Isaiah 48:3. During His ministry on earth, Jesus manifests the *living* Word; as He simultaneously preaches, prays, and delivers souls from oppression, and bondage to demonic spirits; thus, drawing Light and expelling the darkness. While in allowing Himself to be tempted by Satan in the desert [Matthew 4:1-11; Luke 4:1-13], He demonstrates to us the power of God's written Word, as a sure means of binding and overthrowing evil; beginning His answer to every temptation of Satan with the phrase **"It is written…"**

Every word in Sacred Scripture is thus charged with God's Ever-creative power. Every word is alive Ever-more, and is supernatural medicine for our soul and body. It has a remedy for every difficulty and temptation in our task of overcoming the old world, the flesh [carnal ego-self], and the devil [Satan]. When the Holy Spirit is free to act within us [in a state of right disposition to grace], we can grow and live in the knowledge, wisdom, and power of God's Word. This creative authority in Jesus Christ, is created in our heart's desire [human will], and released out of our mouth. Direct quotations, even of a few [paraphrased] words from Sacred Scripture, can be both meditated upon, and spoken or sung aloud, as a means or weapon of [continual] prayer. **This act of speaking, singing, and praying God's Word, is the act of confessing - drawing and releasing, *faith and victory as* children of God, by way of praying the answer, with the answer that God our Father has already given [gifted] to us.** Some suggestions for healing confessions or declarations are as follows:

"I follow the Good Shepherd, and I know His voice, but the voice of strangers I will not follow" John 10:4,5.

"I speak [confess and live] the Truth in Love, and grow up into the Lord Jesus Christ in all things" Ephesians 4:15.

"I let the Word of Christ dwell in me richly and in all wisdom" Colossians 3:16.

"I take up the shield of faith, and quench all the fiery darts of the evil one" Ephesians 6:16.

"I present my body to God, holy and pleasing as a living sacrifice. For I am the temple of God, and the Spirit of God dwells within me" Romans 12:1 and 1 Corinthians 3:16; 6:19.

"I have put off the "old man" ...and put on the "new man" [Jesus Christ], who is being renewed in knowledge, after the image of his Creator" Colossians 3:10.

"I cast down reasonings and imaginations that exalt themselves against the knowledge of God, and I bring every thought into captivity to the obedience of Jesus Christ" 2 Corinthians 10:5.

"…the peace of God which passes all understanding, keeps my heart and my mind through Christ Jesus. And things which are true, honourable, pure, lovely and of good report, I think on these things" Philippians 4:7-8.

"I put on the whole armour of God, against the principalities, the powers, the world's rulers of the darkness of this age, and against the Spiritual forces of wickedness in the heavenly places" Ephesians 6:12-13.

"The Spirit of God who raised up Jesus from the dead dwells in me… and gives life and healing to my body" Romans 8:11.

[In declaring and confessing the Word of God, it is vital to remember that the life of grace is received as pure gift from God. We are cautioned to avoid presumption, turning back to God in all humility, prayerfulness, and repentance, in recognition that He does the work [Luke 11:13] on behalf of, and within the faithful soul, while of ourselves we can do nothing [John 15:5]. We do not address demonic powers in our *authorized work* of overcoming evil in the *terrestrial* realm, nor address them in the superterrestrial realm. Rather, we fix our attention upon God, and address our prayers to Him, placing ourselves under the protection of our Blessed Mother, who glorifies God, and mediates and intercedes for us in an unparallelled way.]

Agape

Highest Love; self-less, whole-hearted, and unsentimental suffering Love; abides in Truth; personified in Jesus Christ; 'well-connected' and 'upwardly mobile' - the Blood-bond of the One family and community of the Heavenly realm; obstacles and challenges to its realization in the soul; remedial suffering vs. redemptive suffering; resistance and release; the primordial power of redemptive suffering; little souls and strong souls; the less travelled way of overcoming souls who God gives Himself to.

"If you knew the gift of God, and who it is who says to you, "Give me a drink", you would have asked Him, and He would have given you Living Water."

John 4:10.

Man knows that Love is the answer. His heart has always been inspired by, and drawn to it, because in it he knows he finds fulfilment. *"The soul cannot live without love, but always wants to love something, because she was made out of [Spiritual] Love, and by [Spiritual] Love, I created her"* says God the Father, to St. Catherine of Siena.

All relationships ordained and blessed by God on earth have a Heavenly purpose and value. Natural man instinctively orientates to three well-known faces or names of love, which are [defined in Greek as]: *"Eros"* - romantic and physical love; *"Phileo"* - friendship or camaraderie love, and *"Storge"* - familial love, as well as community, empathy, and interest group bonds. His genuine hopes for love are good, because they originate in his primordial desire to re-create [re-birth] the wholeness [holiness and all-perfection] of his being. Yet, his hopes will only be completely fulfilled, if and when, he consciously desires to recognize All that is contained in the Divine Ideal of God's own highest Love.

This fourth type of Love, to which everything must ultimately defer, is defined in Sacred Scripture with the Greek word *"Agape"*, meaning *"Divine Love"*. Rooted and generated in the Godhead, and governed by the Holy Spirit, it is God's own All-pure, All-powerful, and super-abundant Love, that runs everywhere, and in all things, in His Divine Will. Creating and conserving, and supplying the prime movement in all activity, it is the absolutely Whole-Hearted, unsentimental, and free-flowing Love, that is the very Substance-Essence of God, and of our God-Being [John 10:34], and Good-being in Him. **In His own Life, Passion, Death, and Resurrection, Jesus Christ identifies Himself as the living embodiment of *"Agape"*; the Good News of Paradise re-opened, through new [Ever-new] and transfigured *real Life and purpose* in Him.** Jesus Christ is the beating Heart of the New Covenant of Love. He is the new and better *"wine"* [from the same Aramaic root word for *"Blood"*] of the wedding feast of Cana, and He is the Spiritual drink of *"Living Water"* John 4:10 and 7:38 that flows into and wells up inside every soul that consents to its purification, transfiguration, and assimilation in Him, into the Spiritual Love-marriage of Light-union, at the passing point of the Cross.

> *"When Jesus calls someone a friend,*
> *He speaks by way of reproach"*.
>
> St. Claude de la Colombiere [Perfect Friend of Christ].

In bringing News of this thoroughly different and highest Love-union, Jesus positions Himself outside the naturally understood and accepted order of earthly [mortal] things. Raising tough questions, and challenging all carnal-egoic self-interest; from the idolization of natural family, and all earthly bonds, alliances, allegiances, desires, and investments; to counterfeit peace and contentment; He embodies disruptive honesty and freedom, which natural man was not ready or willing to accept. This is because the three loves to which man orientates, are overtly or subtly in union with motives of selfish self-love, fear, and possession [meaning *"power"* in Latin]; with reason, feelings, and emotions in the flesh [carnal ego-self] and the [conceptual] old world. While His own highest Love replaces all inward-looking and superficial solidarity, with outward-looking solidarity of person-to-person relationships in Himself. Therefore, while He does not teach the complete renunciation or severance of the bonds of earthly relationships, they must not be preferred or allowed to be a stumbling-block to the creative realization of this most pure and excellent Love. He points out that those with any such favoured bonds are not equal to, or in equilibrium [in Justice] with Him, who is the fullness of *"Agape"*. This is abundantly demonstrated in His own Life on earth, most poignantly when, as a Child, He goes missing for three days in the Temple, telling his anguished parents that He must be about His Father's business [Luke 2:49].

> *"Whoever loves father or mother more than Me,*
> *is not worthy of Me, and whoever loves son or daughter*
> *more than Me, is not worthy of Me."*
>
> Matthew 10:37.

"Agape" births a seismic shift in old world reality, because it is the Love that abides in absolute Truth. It is the priestly Love that is foreign to every fear, limitation, self-interest, and bias, that stifles and derails one's own Spiritual growth and transfiguration, as well as that of others - even under the guise of 'good'. It is the perfectly holy [whole and all-perfect] Love that knows no shadow of insincerity, duplicity, objectification, pretence, deception, cruelty, betrayal, and corruption; in sum everything that tears the heart of man, and betrays the dignity, power, and purpose of his being in God. Moving in the opposite direction, and consummated only at the passing point of the Cross, **"Agape" is that which returns to man his God-being [John 10:34], and confers upon him the gift of Eternal Life [Matthew 5:46-48]. It is the substance-essence of the Blood-bond of the family and community of Heaven,** in which glory-circle, there will be no relations

of the earthly order, but only the Blood brothers and sisters of Jesus Christ [Luke 18:29, Revelation 22:14], gathered together in the care and company of our Eternal Father, Blessed Mother and the Angels.

> *"Your children are not your children. They are the sons and daughters of Life's longing for itself. They come through you, but not from you. And though they are with you, yet they belong not to you."*
>
> Kahil Gibran.

It is therefore not surprising, that while *"Phileo"* and *"Storge"* are mentioned in the New Testament, they are challenged to mature. This is perhaps most poignantly seen where Jesus challenges Peter three times with the question: *"Do you Love Me?"* John 21:15-17, because He is asking of him [asking him to confess], highest Love [*"Agape"*]. For while Peter enjoyed the consolations and pleasantness of his association with Jesus, he was not prepared to bear the burning and suffering that comes with Love's own fire. And so, although he professed Love for Him, he later denied Him three times [Matthew 26:69-75]. *"Eros"* meanwhile, is conspicuously absent from the New Testament, while the imagery of spousal love is notably strong. In offering us the analogy of Himself as the 'Bridegroom' in the Gospels [Matthew 9:15; Mark 2:19-20; Luke 5:34-35], **Jesus confirms that God Loves us with a supernatural Spousal Love, and that *"Agape"* is the suffering Love [Passion] of God, in pursuit of Oneness with His Bride, the *living* Church on earth.** See 'Passion' in Useful Terms.

In the quest to fulfil His One Cosmic Heart's Desire [Divine Will], God comes to earth to meet man where he is. Natural man, of his own volition, cannot separate earthly loves [in their best form] from Heavenly Love, any more than he can point to the separation between the positive and negative charge of a battery. For he perceives that there abides in them, something of a desire for Truth, goodness, and beauty, which calls him outside of, and beyond himself. In taking temporal marriage into the mystery of Christ and

His Church, earthly spousal love is redeemed, transfigured, and elevated by supernatural grace, to the noble sacrament of conjugal love. In this sacred union, the married couple are indissolubly united [unless by exception] as one body and one soul, walking in one united human will [heart's desire] through, with, and in God. **Distinct from the other faces or names of earthly love, marriage becomes a Covenant of Cosmic significance *looking outwards and beyond itself*, to Jesus Christ's ultimate nuptial Light-union with His Mystical Body, the *living* Church.** St. Paul confirms both the vital goodness and symbolism of marriage when he says *"husbands, Love your wives, just as Christ Loved the Church"* Ephesians 5:25. And as Jesus Christ is head of the Church, and the husband is head of the human family, wives are also called to submit to their husband, as the Church submits to Jesus Christ, who is its head [Ephesians 5:22-24; 1 Peter 3: 1-7]. Husband and wife being *"subject...to one another, in the fear of Christ"* Ephesians 5:21, and operating in a circle of mutual Love and respect; of giving and receiving in co-operation with God; both provide the vital societal structure of family life on earth, while representing the bridge between one-to-one fully earthly love, and One-to-All fully Spiritualized Love, for which man is destined.

Man must yet resist the great temptation to merge what he understands of earthly loves into the deathless marriage [Luke 20:34-36], which is the distinct [Spiritual] freedom of *"Agape"*, realized only at the passing point of the Cross. For while natural love wants to 'have' and to weigh and measure, and keep for itself [possess], fearing loss, *"Agape"* is not possession or objectification of, but whole-hearted and self-less participation in the absolute and highest good of the beloved [1 Corinthians 13] without thought of self. And while natural loves change; rising, fading, or growing contemptible with familiarity and time, *"Agape"* remains Ever-fresh and Ever-new, because it's Fountain-Heart flows into and rises up within the soul that is healed and re-created [re-birthed] anew in Jesus Christ. Truth then necessitates that all one-to-one, and one-to-select persons earthly loves be eventually re-dimensioned [in fidelity to one's life-state and office], and transformed into the All-dimensioned purity and stability of *"Agape"*, in which they find their highest and most fulfilling reality. The degree to which the soul is re-dimensioned in the One reality of Jesus Christ, is the extent to which it will be fit to penetrate the endless Light of Heaven, and One reality of Divine Life.

> *"I have given them Your word [Father]; and the world has hated them. For they are not of the world, just as I too, am not of the world."*
>
> John 17:14.

Jesus warns us that those who abandon [consent] to realizing the fullness of *real Life and purpose* in Him, will find themselves at odds with worldly people; including family members [Matthew 10:35-37; Luke 12:51-53]. For while the Light of Lucifer offers an intoxicating brand of unholy freedom; of counterfeit peace and all-unity, that serves the flesh [carnal ego-self] and the old world, by appeal or by passive force, **restoration to right relationship with God and with hallowed reality, must be rooted in the Whole-Heartedness of *"Agape",* as pure gift from Him.** To this end [fulfilment] Jesus tells us that we must *"sell everything"* Mark 8:34; 10:21, of the perceptions, hopes, desires and fears of the flesh [carnal ego-self] and the old world; with all hollow and unreliable appearances, distortions, illusions, and evils, to re-unite with God.

The challenging reality of walking upright in *"Agape"* while on earth, is demonstrated in Jesus own Life on earth. Whilst known to be filial and approachable, and a 'friend' of sinners, He did not seek out their company for the purpose of creating alliances and unity at their level. Jesus knew every weakness, evil and hideous betrayal to which man's heart was vulnerable, and did not need anyone to testify about the darkness and instability of human nature [John 2:24-25]. A state of being, which [by degree of estrangement], prefers darkness to Light [John 3:19]. **Knowing and experiencing the fullness of this agony of separation from Divine Life [Isaiah 53:5; Hebrews 4:15], He came to seek and to save the lost [Luke 19:10].**

> *"The heart is deceitful above all things...
> who can know it?"*
>
> Jeremiah 17:9.

Ever engaged in raising man's motivation higher, He undertook the task of exposing all superficiality, duplicity, hypocrisy, and evil; calling out what was expected of those who would propose to Love God by walking upright in His ways. Remaining in pure divine service to the Father, and keeping Perfect [Whole and All-Perfect] balance [equilibrium] between Justice and Mercy, He never once compromised His Holiness [Wholeness] or allowed Himself to be drawn into blending His Perfect Cosmic Divine Will with their impure and wayward human will, which would draw Him, and them [further] towards death. **Never did He encourage, condone, or have alliance with, wrong-thinking, wrong-doing and wrong-being, because to do so is no act of Love [Charity], but is alliance against Truth [Ezekiel 3:17-21, 33:7-9; 2 Corinthians 6:14-18 and Ephesians 5:11-12]**, in which the distance from Truth, and the danger to the soul grows greater. Indeed, Sacred Scripture warns us that God rebukes not only those who do evil, but those who agree or abide with them [Leviticus 19:17, 2 Corinthians 6:14-18 and Ephesians 5:11-12]. Yet, walking Perfectly [Wholly and All-Perfectly] upright in Truth, Jesus Loved all people, because in Him every person is a 'Loved one', while sojourning on earth. He put people enough at ease, so that they listened to His message, which dealt in hard facts and hallowed reality, rather than superficial flattery and falsity of Love that panders to the flesh [carnal ego-self] and the old world. Of those whom He called His friends, it was on condition that they do the things He commands them [John 15:13-15]. For **His *true* friends are those who abide with Him, by living in Him, in His Love and Divine Will**. And in life as in death, and at the onset of the Kingdom of God, it is [only] the recognizable friends of Truth who are members of the One Eternal Blood family, and community of Heaven.

> *"Are you able to drink from the chalice from which*
> *I drink, or be baptised with the baptism [of fire]*
> *with which I am to be baptised?"*

Mark 10:38.

"Agape" is realized [made real] as pure gift, in the measure of the souls' desire and capacity for healing and restoration to the lost Love-union of Paradise. The vigilant and desirous soul who withholds nothing [in ego-selfhood] from God, and who co-operates with and participates in Him, is consumed in the blessed fire of *"Agape"* until there is no-thing but it left. This is because **"Agape" is who we really are. It is the whole-heartedness of the 'i' living within the 'I AM'.** Everything else passes away, says Sacred Scripture; only Perfect Love [*"Agape"*] remains [1 Corinthians 13:8]. *"Agape"* is the One and only way to be *'well-connected' and 'upwardly mobile'*, because we belong to God, and we only belong to one another as far as we co-operate with and participate *in* God. It is only those who are *in* Jesus Christ, who are [by degree of Light-union] *in* one another here on earth, and continue so beyond the temporal realm. Everything must then move towards God's own highest Love, operating in His Divine Will.

> *"Jesus said to her, "give me a drink.""*

John 4:7.

Every man must overcome three primary obstacles in realizing *"Agape"*, as the source and summit of his being. Impediments, which as demonstrated by the parable of the Samaritan woman at the well [John 4: 4–26], arise out of his [inherited] natural *'What's in it for me?'* self-centredness, inclination to evade responsibility, and unwillingness to first return back his human will to God, in order to receive at the higher Spiritual level. The first obstacle, is that which attributes a sense of absolute significance to the transient ego-persona, and 'value' of the self, or another persona, or group by way of the three earthly loves, as to affirm or safeguard one's own ego-selfhood and earthly sense of meaning and 'value'. For with earthly loves and alliances - even in pious things, there is always an element of irrational idealization [idolization] of the object of love; of sentimentality, and of inclusion and exclusion [by earth appearance, views, age, 'social status', 'reputation', 'wealth' or 'success' etc], which casts a false light of earthy sensuous perception, emotional 'value' and attachment upon ourselves and other select persons. In all such dis-ordered worldviews and alliances, parts of dis-integrated [carnal] reality [in all its guises] swell out of proportion, and predominate over others, in an ugly distortion of Truth, that adversely impacts the collective unconsciousness of all. For the [self-absorbed] *"old man"* does not, and cannot, Love himself or the other, but only its illusory ego-persona reflected in another, who is the object of its self-interest and self-validation. It is the mis-representation of wholeness [holiness and all-perfection] of being that confuses the appearance of self, others, and reality with their actuality [Divine Ideal] in the immeasurable heights of the Godhead.

> *"If we do not Love the God above and within us, how can we Love the person beside us?"*
>
> Anon.

The second [related] obstacle is the fixation [and displacement] of new hope in, and therefore responsibility upon, new generations of people, instead of within one's own being. A problem exacerbated by popular culture, which reveres and attempts to cling to temporal youthfulness, and all its fleeting trends and ways, rather than [in the example of Jesus and His Mother] encourage man's dynamic growth and maturing in Light-bearing wisdom and ways. The tragedy of this derailment is clear set against the teachings of Sacred Scripture, where from the first book of Genesis [Genesis 10:21] the importance of elders as community leaders, as well as the importance of honouring and respecting one's elders is called out [Leviticus 19:32]. These first two problems result from an abstract attitude to faith and to life itself, that looks outwards and elsewhere through the eyes of the flesh [carnal ego-self], rather than inwards through the eye of the Spirit, for meaning, Truth, healing, and Life itself. Both point to mis-created and mis-guided self-love, that has yet to lay the axe at the root of the tree, and produce good fruit [Matthew 3:10; Luke 3:9]. Both result in a chaotic, immature, infantilized, and Spiritually degenerate society. The soul who would propose to come into right relationship with hallowed reality and assist others, must learn to walk upright in Jesus Christ, who *"increased in wisdom and stature"* Luke 2:52 throughout His earthly Life. They must detach from operating by way of outward earthiness, in favour of inward luminosity, and the relationship of Light that is the substance of the *"new man"* within the soul.

As a remedy to the problem of carnal fragmentation, and in the spirit of serving those who truly desire Spiritual growth and transfiguration, the Trappist monk, Thomas Merton offers the vision of a 'Republic of Athos'. Here, souls in different states of strength and weakness; levels of maturity and immaturity; in all life-states; at all ages; and with diversified observances; co-exist in informal networks, and assist one another with authentic growth and maturity, by giving witness to the free work of the Spirit.

> *"I want Love. I seek it, and I find so little.*
> *I am treated like an absent person, when*
> *in reality, I am present with, and in souls."*
>
> Jesus speaks to Blessed Dina Belanger.

The third obstacle is fear of suffering*. While suffering is not a good in itself, *"Agape"* is suffering Love, because it involves self-giving, which is the unavoidable labour before re-birth [re-creation]. It involves shifting one's centre from self-serving love to the Self-giving Love of God; which is the work of conquering the old world, the flesh [carnal ego-self] and the devil [Satan]. Sacred Scripture teaches us that there can be no ascension to glory [blissful magnificence] without the pearls of suffering Love, because it is the cup which Jesus drank to the very dregs [Matthew 20:22]. And if it is befitting the nobility and majesty of God that His Life be made perfect [crowned] through suffering [Hebrews 2:10], *"if children...and joint heirs with Christ... we suffer with Him, that we may also be glorified with Him.* Romans 8:17 [Hebrews 2:11]. Suffering and release are essential to the soul's expansion beyond its limited natural range of thought and desire, and into the spheres of supernatural freedom and Truth. **Without suffering and overcoming [release], we would be forever lost in the dark voids of the ego-selfhood - with all its perceptions and attachments, and the works of evil.** In His All-seeing goodness, God therefore allows into our lives the tests and trials that confront in us, the obstacles to the creative realization of His own highest Love within us, which is our Oneness with and in Him. And as *"everyone will be salted with fire"* Mark 9:48, it is divinely wise and profitable to bear patiently all *true* suffering in Love, because *"all things work together for good for those who Love God"* Romans 8:28. Suffering united with the acceptable Cosmic sufferings of Jesus Christ, not only test, guide, strengthen and release the soul; but offer relief for the sufferings of Jesus Christ, and His grievously wounded Mystical Body; while being a dynamic participation in the undoing of evil, and reinstatement of the Kingdom. Suffering is the essential means to mastery and ennoblement of our soul, restoring and embellishing its crown [of Spiritual wealth], in and for all Eternity.

> *"When you suffer, think only upon the suffering of Christ, the man of sorrows, and all your own griefs will be healed."*
>
> Blessed Angela of Foligno.

Desirous and persevering [committed] souls who courageously take up their Cross, knowing that God our Father, reconciling the world to Himself in Jesus Christ, is the work that He desires to do in each one of us, will never be taken beyond that which the grace of God will not support. For the Light-fire of *"Agape"* is safely ignited through the work of the Holy Spirit, who lays secure foundations. It is realized only in its growing and rising slowly and steadily to fit our proper dimension, which is our personal desire and capacity for growth, and strength for Truth, as ordered in Divine Providence. Ever-newer thoughts and ways of being must prevail amidst suffering, and continue as the soul is united with God, according to its willingness and capacity for ascension. All obstacles and erroneous temporal ideals, fears and desires should however manifest less, and less directly, as the faithful soul is healed and re-generated [re-birthed] in Jesus Christ, which furthers draw the omnipotent power of the Holy Spirit.

[*Although natural man cannot plumb the depths of every cause of suffering; Sacred Scripture demonstrating that any manifestation of suffering can be for God's glory, and for the edification of the soul (e.g., Jesus healing the blind beggar Bartimaeus in Mark 10:46-52, and His leaving the thorn in St. Paul's side in 2 Corinthians 12:6-10); a general distinction can be made between remedial suffering and redemptive suffering. For although suffering is unavoidable in this earthly life, Jesus never incited us to *seek* earthly suffering of our own human will, but rather demonstrated that **we should discern suffering**. We must then be very careful about how we interpret and respond to suffering, because although it is never superfluous, it is a vital tool of Satan and his demons, who can be the direct and indirect cause of interior and bodily sufferings. In Truth, much suffering is self-created, or may also be inherited. This is **remedial suffering**, which signifies that something is wrong in one's own sinful, blind, and wayward (self-willed) way of life, which may include failure to forgive or seek forgiveness for oneself, or to extend forgiveness to other weak and rebellious souls; or it may indicate that something is wrong in one's ancestral bloodline (Exodus 20:5, 34:7; Deuteronomy 5:9). While all such problems allow inroads to the malevolent operation of evil spirits, there is yet good in this suffering, because it points to the need for forgiveness (release) and healing for oneself or in the family tree, which would otherwise go undetected. Such soul-crushing suffering can manifest in all manner of mental and physical dis-eases, afflictions, and calamities; from depression, to addictions, perversions, debts, and even suicide. It may also manifest in suffering or death by fire, water, or natural tragedy, because evil forces also operate in the elements, and in nature. Healing from superficial suffering that man mis-creates in his own human will, requires the breaking of the hard shell of the ego-mould. For it is the dark voids of the flesh (carnal ego-self), which perceives effort and pain in sacrificing self-love, with all its expectation and sorrows, to rise above its fallen nature, and return to Divine Life. Healing from mental and physical dis-eases, and generational curses and afflictions may however require prayers of release, fasting, Masses, and the intercession of a priest, or authentic Church healer. Whatever the source of remedial suffering, the soul must not fall into the trap of claiming the suffering as its own. This is to confess alliance with the enemy (Satan), and allow a chasm to form between the soul and Jesus Christ. See 'Your Living Word' and 'Praying Gods Word - The Sword of the Spirit' at the end of the Chapter on 'Prayer'.

Redemptive suffering on the other hand, is that which involves fasting and all self-sacrifice (self-giving) to overcome self-love, with all natural carnal passions and appetites. Suffering, which united with the Cosmic sufferings (Passion) of Jesus Christ, is transformed into purest (purifying) redemptive suffering that carries infinite power and value, for the sake of everyone and everything. Hunger for this soul-uplifting suffering (the Cross) as expressed in the lives of Church saints and mystics, refers to positive abandonment to the redemptive trials, tests, and contradictions of life. Crosses which annihilate self-love, and draws the Light [Life] of Jesus Christ into the soul, empowering its capacity for further suffering, expansion, and release. Redemptive suffering is the three-fold battle for the salvation (healing) of one's soul, the abolition of evil, and the Coming of the Kingdom. Those most desirous souls, who are given to share in and relieve Jesus Christ's corporeal and interior sufferings (share in His Cross), also share more abundantly in His glory, according to their response to His Love and Divine Will, as ordered in the knowledge and wisdom of Divine Providence].

> *"Suffering is necessary for all, but how much more for my chosen souls!...It purifies them, and I am thus able to make use of them to snatch many from Hell's fire."*
>
> Jesus speaks to Sr. Josefa Menendez.

In our life's work of learning to overcome and walk upright in the whole-heartedness of *"Agape"*, it is both deeply chastening and inspiring to keep before our minds [in our hearts], the primordial power of this Love [rooted in the Divine Will], that enabled Jesus Christ to endure the Roman soldier's relentless assailment of His convulsing agony, as His innocent Life was claimed. Up-mounted between Heaven and earth, and outstretched between good [the repentant thief] and evil [the unrepentant thief], He concealed the most ferocious pains in His tortured and forsaken body, as the Light-fire of *"Agape"* tore through the entirety of His Being. We cannot begin to imagine the fullness of His Human, and moreover, Divine agony, as in this Cosmic act of *true* kinship [Charity], He was consumed in Love's own fire, while embracing and reconciling each one of us, and all things to the Father in Himself. Yet, **we can recognize, that there is and never will be, any place in the white heat of this highest Love, for the shadow fragments of the proud, duplicitous, and rebellious** *"old man"*, **driven by ego-selfhood.** For this is the insurmountable, free, and untouchable Love [Truth], that is greater than one's own life [John 15:13]. It is the Love next to which the best of human loves put together, is like comparing the heat and light of the natural sun, to the heat and light of a candle. It is the unchallengeable potency of our Creator God and Father, that forever broke the powers of Hell, and unleashed Light for the life of every person who would return to Him, in His Son-God. It is the Love that exposes Satan's diabolical plan and counterfeit love in the flesh [carnal ego-self] and the old world; and all unholy and impure alliances, and deceptions, through which he makes inroads to destroy human souls [Judges 2:16-20]. It is the inscrutable Light to which our souls will be delivered up alone and in silence, upon mortal death.

We ever look to the passing point of the Cross, as the One Eternal design for our Sanctification, and our final victory over the kingdom of Satan. Only with this vision of triumph, can begin to understand this most difficult paradox that leads to authentic freedom in Jesus Christ. We must proceed with great courage and humility, trusting that **we are created beings with a responsibility, mission, and privileged purpose, more utterly wonderful than we can ever dare to imagine at the natural level.**

> *"I prefer the little soul to console me and Love me...*
> *I yearn for the strong soul to die in Me, and be only Me."*
>
> Jesus speaks to Vera Grita - Third Order Salesian and Mystic.

Those courageously Loving souls who truly abandon back [consent] to the Life-bearing work of the Cross, grow more stable and strong in the purity and holiness [whole-hearted fullness of being] of the divine freedom. *"For God didn't give us a spirit of fear, but of power, Love, and self-control"* 2 Timothy 1:7. Knowing that the reproaches that fall on anyone have already fallen upon Jesus Christ [Romans 15:3], they are keenly aware that the battle and revolution is primarily Spiritual and interior. They know that we are ultimately contending, not with flesh and blood, but *"against principalities and powers, against the rulers of this world of darkness, against the spirits of wickedness in high [heavenly] places"* Ephesians 6:12, who prey upon, and operate through, weak, lost, and rebellious souls. These souls are alive to the hardness, insensibility, and pain of the flesh [carnal ego-self], and the violence of sin committed against ourselves, and others, as well as the immense silent agony in the entirety of living creation, because of man's estrangement from his true centre. Filled with holy fear [awe-filled reverence] of God, and with the call of divine freedom reverberating in their breast, they recognize their own need for deep healing and restoration, and the Father's Mercy in allowing them to rediscover their own true worth, for *"All have sinned and fallen short of the glory of God"* Romans 3:23.

Deeply alive to the sober reality of the Day of Justice, and the unutterable terror of Eternal self-damnation, these souls of Charity are faithful to the calls of Sacred Scripture to be children of salt and Light [Matthew 5:13–14]. То speak and act [and therefore be preserved] in Truth, to confess our sins and pray for one another, and to bless those who persecute you [Romans 12:14], for the sake of the Kingdom. Their *living* prayers are particularly powerful before God [James 5:16], because they know that in the flesh [carnal ego-self] nothing good dwells [Romans 7:18]. **They know that the best in anyone is the best in any one of us, while the worst in anyone is the**

worst in any one of us. While natural justice must be upheld to deal with, and prevent greater dis-order, anarchy and violence on earth, these souls understand that **the soul can only give what [Light] it has first received from God, while it cannot give what it does not have [partake of].** Centred in pure and zealous Love of Jesus Christ, and filled with true compassion [from the Greek word *"splagna"* meaning *"guts"*], they look beyond human misery to see others as He sees them while still on earth; calling forth their native magnificence [glory], as healed and re-created [re-birthed] members of His Mystical Body [1 Corinthians 12:27]. And in fidelity to the supreme rights of Divine Justice, they too know that this steadfast [divine] work of overcoming evil with good, is also the work of heaping coals of fire upon the heads of the enemies of God [Romans 19:20; Proverbs 25:22], because retribution belongs to God alone, who will rebalance the scales of Justice [Romans 12:19; Deuteronomy 32:35].

Keeping their inner lamp alight by merging with the All-embracing Divine-Humanity of Jesus Christ, all that is mortal is swallowed up in the Light-fire of God's own Love, burning within their being, as they form another humanity and shield for Him on earth. Replenished [renewed] daily in a circle of giving and receiving His Life [Matthew 25:1-13] through unblocked avenues of grace, they Love and desire as He does, to the point of taking His corporeal and interior sufferings for His estranged and lost children as their own; enclosing and offering recompense for everyone and everything in Him. Praying, suffering, and repairing, they relieve and shelter Him from the relentless rejection, bitterness, and violence of broken man, while their supernatural fruitfulness is realized as Spiritual mothers and fathers of countless multitudes of souls.

> *"God shelters me, as much as I shelter Him.*
> *His Being I sustain; sustained I am therein."*
>
> Angelus Silesius.

Growing ever more spacious in the power and peace of simple presence, they have found that to look upon the suffering God on Calvary and *truly* Love Him in His Divine Will, is Every-thing. Resting in Him as the One reality, they are neither impressible nor impressionable by the faulty and degrading standards [projections, judgements, and neediness] of the flesh [carnal ego-self] and the old world, because *"Holy Love puts to shame all the temptations of the devil and the flesh, and all natural fear."* St. Francis of Assisi.

Having given themselves up to the Father in Jesus Christ, they have no desire to be anything [of carnal-egoic meaning] to anyone, nor do they fear, or place their hope in others, regardless of how they may appear to be, for they know that **God alone knows purity of heart.** Raised by the Light of sanctifying grace, while faithful to their life-state; they neither flatter or criticize others; identify with the flattery or criticism of others; or agree or abide with [take upon themselves the guilt of] those whose ways violate Truth, and the Truth of their being in God [Ezekiel 3:17-21, 33:7-9; 2 Corinthians 6:14-18 and Ephesians 5:11-12]. For the one who walks and judges in the Light of Truth [1 Corinthians 2:15 is no friend or lover of the flesh [carnal-ego self] or wicked [evil and ungodly] ways, but looks only to the primordial nobility, power, and purpose of the soul in God.

"The value of your existence is not in what you have done, or said, or suffered. It is in the part of your being that you have given to your Saviour; in what you have allowed Me to do with you."

Jesus speaks to Sr. Mary of the Holy Trinity.

Ever-alive with the **'fullness of Life'** and immortality, they give no concern to earthly fears or sorrows; or to paradoxes and contradictions, but remain open to all of God's teachings and remedies. Whether bitter, or sweet, or surprising, they receive and return all to God in a spirit of Love and gratitude, knowing [by way of the infused Spiritual intellect] that His highest [celestial] gifts are those which purge and purify the soul from every self-love and attachment. Reproof in the Spirit, they receive as the Loving reproach of God [Proverbs 15:5], for their strongest roots in the Home-ground of Truth, are humility and chastity [holy purity; wholeness and wisdom]. Full of innocent, celestial joys, and pouring out the Light of God, their unencumbered spirit rises softly and quietly, as a feather on the breeze of the Spirit. The further they rise, their peace and detachment increase, because more freed from the web of old worldly relationships, with flesh-driven expectations and desires, the more closely they are united with God, and with all things in Him. Their unstrained and gracious presence represents the Spiritual richness of their soul, and the broadness of their interior Spiritual vision. Loving God above all things, while yet in all things, they reconcile all [apparent] opposites; Love and holy [just] anger; silence and speech; involvement and withdrawal [holy disinterest]; and time and Eternity. In everything, they turn to the fullness of Jesus Christ within, ensuring that nothing interferes with His presence and peace.

Scaling the heights of sanctity, and burning with Love's own fire, their time on earth is spent washing clean in the sanctifying Blood of Jesus Christ, and nourishing themselves with His Life; as they dress in their wedding garment [nuptial Light garment of God-being, John 10:34], and [Spiritual] crown of Eternal Life [Revelation 22:14]. Treading lightly like Him, and engaged in unknown service [by the standards of the flesh and the old world], these souls may seem to do little, *"for holiness dwells in life, the way that the Eternal dwells; secretly and hidden underneath the surface of things; sustaining but not intruding"* says St. Augustine. Their primary purpose is quiet presence; silently praying, suffering, and repairing; holding spaciousness [emptiness and wholeness] and radiating Light, while offering everyone and everything back to the Father in Jesus Christ. They do not readily speak of good works or supernatural things, nor do they attempt to guide or instruct those who are not open to, or capable of listening [Matthew 7:6]. Nor do they fight for rights or causes at the level of the flesh [carnal ego-self] and the old world, for those who fight in this way, do not embody peace, but fighting. They do not worry, for *"There is no fear in Love; but Perfect Love casts out fear"* 1 John 4:18.

Standing at the threshold of completeness on earth, until their bright soul is poured out into the nuptial Light-ring [deathless marriage] of Eternity, **these souls are the warriors and endurance athletes of the Spiritual Life.** They are the veiled brightness of the Heavenly bodies in waiting, whose Ever-lasting high beauty will be revealed in Paradise. For the fulfilment of Love in them, in a mutual exchange of Love [in the Divine Will] in Jesus Christ, is nothing less than the outpouring of God the Father's own paternal Heart in their being. This re-dimensioning of the soul [the i] in the whole-hearted Life [I AM] of Jesus Christ, is truly Loving and glorifying God, and all His people and creation in Him, blending time and Eternity, and bringing the reign of His Kingdom to earth. It is the return to knowing and being as One, in which is held the promise of the Beatific Vision, and the glorious infinity of divine treasures and contentment's of Paradise, promised to the faithful pilgrim soul of earth.

The Garden of the Soul

The celestial Gardener sets to work in the consenting soul; faithfulness in all weathers allows Him to continue with higher and greater works; re-birth [re-creation] in the dark, hot, and dry desert land of suffering Love; dying to self and cultivating divine freedom; the joys of God's own Heart; the flowers and fruits of higher Life flourish; Father and child are reunited in the transfigured holy land of the soul.

"He has made everything beautiful in its time; and He has planted Eternity in their hearts."

Ecclesiastes 3:11.

In the beginning, all things were green. The evergreen foliage of the traditional advent wreath, symbolises the Ever-fresh Eternal blessedness, innocence, and healthfulness, which contains all the joyfulness of Paradise, sown deep in the soil of man's soul. These celestial joys, are the whole-hearted, perennial joys drawn from the harmonies and delights of living in the Light-union of the Most Holy Trinity. Man's sublime task and purpose on earth, is to discover and reclaim anew, the fullness of these joys, which is the planned and planted purpose of his being.

In His Plan of restoration, God our Father is the celestial Gardener, and we are living earth in His hands. When the inspired soul who conceives of her* absolute purpose, gives her breath of consent [her *"Fiat"*] amidst life on earth, He sets to work in the field of her soul. As far He is permitted, He will work the poor soil of the soul, which contains the inexpressibly precious Light-seed of Divine Life, conferred in Baptism. This seed, as a human embryo, holds all the reality of Jesus Christ-being; which is God's image and likeness in His true child and heir. It is for the sake of tending to, grading, and gathering His seed [the wheat of faithful souls], and forever separating them from corrupt seed [the chaff of unfaithful souls] that He continues to sustain the world [Matthew 3:12; Hebrews 10:13-14 and 2 Peter 3:9-10].

[*The soul is referred to in the divine feminine, representing the primacy of man's positive abandonment back to God, to first allow and receive Divine Life from Him, in order to operate in the divine masculine in Him].

> *"In the heights all things are green; on the 'mountaintop' all things are green and new. When they descend into time, they grow pale and fade. In the new 'greenness' of all creatures our Lord will 'feed His sheep'. All creatures that are in that green and on that height, as they exist in the Angels, are more pleasing to the soul, than anything in this world. As the sun is different from night, so different is the least of creatures as it is there, from the whole world."*
>
> St. Augustine.

With the most immense Love and care, the celestial Gardener digs and unblocks channels closed to grace, and thins out the thickets of weeds [of fleshy and old worldly desires, and attachments], to make space for Light-fire and [Mystical] Water to flow. He ploughs the soil with the law of Divine Life, to break up the hard ground of the flesh [carnal ego-self], with all its perceptions, and to overturn and cool the heat of its passions and appetites [Sirach 23:16]. He irrigates and anoints the soil with the *"Living Water"* John 4:10; 7:38 and Precious Blood of His own Life; gently healing open sores, and nourishing her with the most blessed goods of chastity [holy purity; wholeness and wisdom], self-control, patience, and discernment of good and evil, to restore her to support higher Life. For the Light-seed of Divine Life must take root in a depth of good soil, that the [Three-in-One] Divine Sun may not scorch or wither it, or the winds of the Holy Spirit blow it away. The Mystical Divine Sun then begins His Heavenly work of lighting and warming with grace, the prepared, but still hard ground of the soul, that the Light-seed may begin to germinate. The celestial breeze of the Holy Spirit carries the dew of grace and ineffable peace, to dispel the cold dark mists and night frosts of human thinking; of emotions, feelings, and reasoning, that would descend and destroy the first fragile little plants, springing forth from the first delicate roots of *living* faith, hope, and Charity.

With divine patience, and the eyes of His understanding, which *"are ten thousand times more penetrating than the sun"* Sirach 23:19, the celestial Gardener watches and tends to the field of the soul, to clean and weed out man's lower and hidden tendencies. Every plant which He has not planted is rooted up [Matthew 15:13]. That is to say, everything that is sinful, useless, and evil; beautiful weeds and dead leaves; every knowledge, desire, or conduct, competing interest or human alliance, including those which appear 'good', but which arise out of, and serve the flesh [carnal ego-self], and the old world, are torn out *"because it thrives not on the dew of Heaven, but on the moisture of the flesh"* says St. Hildegard of Bingen.[2] In this divine action, that which draws Life away from, and chokes the Light-seed of Divine Life, is destroyed. The natural tendencies of the seed now unimpaired, direct their energies towards Heaven.

In the warmth and pristine air of the Divine Sun, the soil of the soul continues to bring forth the signs and scents of holy living, which calls the Loving hand of the celestial Gardener. In His goodness, He continues to offer the cooling dampness of the Waters of Life [John 4:10; 7:38], and the warmth and brilliance of His Light, to the emerging garden of the soul, while nourishing and nurturing her with many blessed and surprising gifts of the Spirit. As all manner of little plants [such as peace and humility] stretch upwards in the fresh sap, He trims and prunes anything that stands in danger of causing the garden to run wild, or become sour and unfruitful. With this delicate work, He preserves and manages her to better receive, and return Divine Life in Him.

In His divine jealousy, which speaks of His desire for personal union with the soul, the celestial Gardener may allow thorns and bitterness's to form around the plants, to protect them from harm, and to teach the soul to maintain holy indifference [detachment] towards all people, and in all things. For some time, nothing much seems to happen, as the soul lives in rhythms of Light and shade, but then something unexpected happens. The rain [of sensible graces, and the sweetness of Spiritual perceptions and attachments] stops falling, while the Divine Sun shines brighter, and the winds of the Spirit rise. The ground beneath the little plants become as dry desert sand, as the soul's efforts of prayer, self-sacrifice [self-giving] and holy living are dry, savourless, and unrewarding, at the natural level, while the contradictions and trials of life increase. This early garden of the soul has turned into a burning and arid desert place, in which she deems herself estranged from, and without taste for, both Heaven and earth; and faced with nothing but the knowledge of her own misery, and the grey shifting light-shades of earthly loves.

> *"The less there is of you, the more I shall be your Life,*
> *and you will be My Heaven of rest...*
> *on earth My Heaven is in souls."*
>
> Jesus speaks to Sr. Josefa Menendez.

Yet, this place is not as it seems, because the celestial Gardener in His ineffable Goodness and Mercy, is searching the heart and testing the mind [Jeremiah 17:10], as to verify the soul's willingness for greater abandonment, and readiness for perseverance [commitment]. This seemingly barren place [of interior and exterior desolation] is therefore nothing other than the field of inaccessible Light. It is the All-revealing Light-transcending, that would completely purge the soul, and consume her in her own nothing-ness, before setting her alight with Loves own fire. For while the sprouting of the seeds and roots, and early growth depend upon the moisture, it is in this dark and trackless desert, amidst the tempests of earthly temptations and desires, that the soul begins to truly comprehend the awfulness of all sinfulness and unbeautiful beauty, that moves towards decay and death. And she begins to recognize the depth of her own misery and estrangement from God [God-being John 10:34]. **This supposedly boundless desert place, is the crossing point [passing point] of the *"old man"*, and his re-integration [re-centring] and re-generation [re-birth] to the character and stature [Ephesians 4:11], and power and purpose of the *"new man"* in Jesus Christ.** Only here in the healing [paradoxical] emptiness of awareness and unknowing, is the safety of her conception of God [apart from all else], protected, and re-birth generated. Only in these conditions, can the *living* roots of faith, hope, and Charity grow deep and strong, and the plants grows lush. Only in this way, can the soul first learn to bear with, and then gradually learn to see, and live in, the Light-blaze of the Divine Sun.

> *"The more obscure the mystery is to us,*
> *the more Light it contains in itself; for its obscurity is*
> *due to a radiance, too intense for our feeble vision."*
>
> Jean-Pierre de Caussade.

And so, the increasing clarity and heat of the Sun-Light-presence of God within the soul, is felt as searing darkness, as the thick clouds of self-love [of fleshy and worldly self-interest]; of sin, existence-ignorance, and indifferentism; and of Spiritual imagination, self-satisfaction, romanticism, and legalism are being dispelled. For the soul's motive should be pure Love of God alone, rather than sense perceptions of reason, feelings, comfort, and reward. Refreshment offered by God is so delicate, that it remains unperceived by the still unrefined tastes of the infant soul, who has yet much to learn about the vast difference between the moonlight soul-kiss of earthly loves, and the Sunlight soul-kiss of God's own *"Agape"*.

> *"To whomever much is given,*
> *of him will much be required."*
>
> Luke 12:48.

At times, the celestial Gardener still seems to find much to improve; clearing and sweeping away, pruning heavily, and uprooting and burning up swathes of ground [the remaining dead weight of the flesh [the carnal-ego self, with its impurity and illusions, human affections, internal and external distractions, attachments, selfish motivations, duplicity, and dead works], on which the soul formerly stood. This arduous fault-finding with everything, is His way of inspiring immediate trust, and drawing the soul away from outward earthiness, and higher and closer to Himself, that an abundant crop of flowers and fruits may appear. Without the crutch of natural human reason, and even stripped of human supports, the soul is left in a state of pure redemptive suffering, to be proven, cleansed, and refined, in a test of faith, hope and Charity, and to create the field for God's new and even greater graces and works. For it is *"in the heights of dark faith"* says St. John of the Cross, lifted up above the realms of nature [on the Cross], that God raises the soul to Light-union, and manifests His own glory [blissful magnificence] within and through her.

> *"Those whom I Love, I rebuke and chastise.*
> *Therefore, be zealous and do penance."*
>
> Revelation 3:19.

This is a most challenging time in the life of the soul as its strength and capacity for greater abandonment and purification is tested. It is however the most transformational, for suffering is not for the sake of suffering itself, but for Love of Jesus Christ, as she shares the privilege of His bitter-sweet chalice, to be restored to her native glory [blissful magnificence] in Him. *"Because the wretchedness and corruption of the human heart is a bottomless pit, the deeper it is penetrated by God's Light and wisdom, the more melancholy and humiliating discovers are made in it...Yet these discoveries, ...by strengthening its inner humility, bring it the consolation it knows to be the firm foundation of every Spiritual edifice"* says Fr. Jean-Pierre de Caussade. And so, as the soul learns to trust God in humility, rather than herself, regardless of natural feelings, reasoning, emotions, and circumstances, she will gradually adjust to the yet unendurable Light-brilliance and effects of the Divine Sun. For in the centre point of this immense glory-fire, is a place of unburning coolness and rest, where *real Life and purpose* dwells unharmed. In this hidden place, where no enemy dare pass, the soul will reap even higher graces without withering away. Her roots in God will deepen further, to find the purest Waters of underlying unity [community] with Him, and with all things in Him, in the Home-ground of Truth. These deeper mystical Waters, are the primordial Waters of the pure Spirit of God, which communicate upon pure spirit, beyond the natural intellect and sense perception. Ever more purged of course tastes and appetites in material and Spiritual matters, the soul will rise again with greater [divine] strength, to proceed more safely in pure Love of God alone, because by allowing this space for sips of the divine purity to enter her, she can eventually conceive in the nakedness of suffering Love, that all sufficiency and contentment comes from God alone. She will learn to drink more deeply of these sweet Life-giving Waters, and breathe more deeply in the purest Life-breath of the Holy Spirit.

> *"The Godhead is my sap, what in me greens and flowers.*
> *It is the Holy Spirit, who all the growth empowers."*
>
> Angelus Silesius.

The celestial Gardener continues to watch and listen for authenticity and stable perseverance [commitment] in holy living, as well as peacefulness, patience, and confidence in Him in all weathers [temptations, passions, and appetites; and difficulties, consolations, and circumstances of life]. For the one who whole-heartedly yearns for God, will grow constant and stable in sacrificing [giving] itself, for Love of Him alone, while he who fears, cannot be made perfect [whole and all-perfect] in Love [1 John 4:18]. This contentment [fearlessness] is the custodian of purity, perseverance [commitment], and stability, and allows the celestial Gardener to continue His work. In finding these goods within the soul, He shines with greater brilliance directly upon her, and into her innermost depths. Acting, teaching, and Loving; He inundates her with the Light-fire of His Love, and Waters her with greater divine knowledge and wisdom; while showing up anything that is not of Himself. If weeds are still permitted to remain in the field of the soul for a time, it is only to serve as manure for the soil, fertilising the plants and making them grow.

> *"Love draws purity, and purity draws Love."*
> Anon.

Soon, things can begin to change again, but more rapidly this time. For as Love follows the Light of the Spiritual intellect, the more the soul knows God, the more she can Love Him, in whom she has her being, without any thought of reward. Growing in grace with primordial Life-force, beautiful green plants flourish and spread freely across the field of the soul, in which new lushness, is the promise of flowers and fruits, as she is re-created [re-birthed] within her Beloved. Feeding and resting on the rarest delights of Love operating in the Divine Will, she expands towards true and transcendent beauty, as the flower of her original desire [for re-union with God] is healed. The green leaves which cover the plants, are the soul's modesty, which preserve her outer dignity, as a *living* temple of God [Romans 12:1; 1 Corinthians 3:16; 6:19].

> *"And He will make her wilderness like Eden, and her desert, like the garden of the Lord."*
> Isaiah 51:3.

The fruits of holy [wholeness and all-perfection of] living are now filled with refined Spiritual sweetness, because the gift of celestial joy is infused in the soil of the faithful soul, who has relinquished earthly joys, in favour of sharing in the intense Passion of Spirit, that consumes the soul in Charity, bringing union with God, and with all things in Him. These vivid and substantial joys, which rise upon hope, and rest in interior solitude of being, inspire the soul to give yet more fully and generously of herself, to the sanctifying passing point of the Cross. **Issued from the Father's strength, these Eucharistic joys are Jesus Christ's own strength [Nehemiah 8:10], which nourish her with ever-deeper understanding of the unutterable mysteries of God; with distaste for the sour and perishable fruits of the flesh [carnal ego-self] and the old world; and with a burning of heart [as the disciples on the road to Emmaus, Luke 24:32] for nothing but the sweet and imperishable fruits of Heaven.** Found everywhere and even in dryness, anguish, and all suffering, these Spiritual joys form the soul's continuous sunrise, refuge, and safety, for the greater her purity of motivation and intensity of Love for God in His Divine Will [Cosmic Heart's Desire], the more perfectly [wholly and all-perfectly] she is united to the joy of His own Heart.

> *"Divine joy is a delicate thing,*
> *which is not given to one who seeks any other."*
>
> St. Bernard of Clairvaux.

Cultivating divine freedom [holy dis-interest] from self and from everyone and everything around her, allows the soul to take herself lightly; to disregard the ego-prison; relinquish fear and earthly lamentation, and be attentive to pleasing God alone. Her Love thus becomes more noble; driven by the joys of Eternal Life, rather than crude fear of earthly or Eternal loss. Sheltered and at peace in her nothing-ness, and quenched with her deepest longing, she takes no account of particular virtues or celestial gifts; nor does she take in the praises or criticisms of others. **For rather than reflecting upon herself [of herself, and in relation to others], she reflects herself [and others] in Jesus Christ alone, who has become the One true Life of her soul.** Full of the abundance of His Life within, no disturbance can shake her inner peace, and no earthly sorrow can claim her, because she has found that God comes to help her, so that she is untouched [Isaiah 50:6-9]. Her only lamentation, is the silent cry of her heart for the glory of God in souls, and for the Homeland. Ever-greening and maturing, and raised in *living* faith and divine wisdom beyond the edge of all known possibilities, she grows more grateful and less prone to the disturbances and destructive work of temptations [of fleshiness or worldliness] and exterior strife, that would pollute or rot the field of her soul. Whether the winds of the Holy Spirit blow from the south bringing warmth and consolation, or from the north bringing coldness and suffering, she is strong, stable, and enduring. As the mighty eagle soars highest, and turns its gaze towards the sun, yet sees more clearly, in **her flight in the self-forgetting freedom of Charity**, the soul knows and lives in God alone.

> *"When you Love Me, you purify yourself."*
> Jesus speaks to Gabrielle Bossis –
> Third Order Franciscan and Mystic.

Now gladly replacing unrefined human tastes, with refined and nourishing divine tastes [Romans 14:17], the pains of circumstances and sufferings become ever sweeter and lighter, because this replenishment is the [unseen] beginning of the Beatific Vision [direct and immediate sight of God]. Drawn ever higher in pure Love of God, corporeal, and Spiritual suffering give way to ever more unspeakable joys and strength, as beautiful and fragrant flowers of virtue, and ripe [good] and delicious fruits of Love and redemptive suffering begin to issue forth, in all colours, varieties and sweetness. These flowers and fruits are the good works and sufferings [Charity] of the Divine-Humanity of Jesus Christ living within the soul, which have made of it, a beautiful and enchanting garden of delights. Love [operating in the Divine Will] has drawn the soul completely into itself, absorbing her in the Light-union of the Most Holy Trinity, as a star is absorbed in the midday sun, yet still exists of itself. This fertile and verdant garden, drenched in celestial Sun-Light, is a boundless place of all abundance; an inviolate space of infinite possibility and potentiality, gushing forth with Life. Other weary and Light-starved souls are revived and nourished by the fragrant flowers, succulent fruits, and new seeds of her life, which encourage them in noble and divine ways.

> *"Who is it who can tell the spark within the fire?*
> *And who, once within God, can perceive what I am?"*
>
> Angelus Silesius.

While before it was enough to know, the now flood-Lit soul sees in the Life-giving splendour of the Mystical Divine Sun. Alas, finding her inner vision true, she beholds before her interior Spiritual eye, this vast and inexpressibly beautiful panoramic garden of wonders and delights. In this transfigured holy land of the soul, full of the most exquisite graces, Father and child are re-united. The celestial Gardener rests from His work, for finally, He is whole-heartedly Loved back [as He can only be Loved, in His own Love and Divine Will] and rewarded for all the countless gifts He has given His beloved child, who is the glory of His creative hand. The Angels and saints stand enraptured, while Satan and his legions recoil and tremble in fear and rage at the invincible Light-presence of God [God-being John 10:34] living within her. For this fulfilment which both Father and child had longed for, is the return of the soul to the Ever-creative and Ever-verdant *living* reality of **Life in the Cosmic and radiant Divine Sun [Most Holy Trinity].** It is the promised place of all safety and divine delights, in which at the consummation of time, she will find the continuous company of all other Light-filled souls [the true Blood brothers, and sisters of Jesus Christ], together with our celestial Mother, the Angels, and all God's living creatures and creation, restored and transfigured in the nuptial Light-ring of the Homeland.

> *"Your pure soul, is untouched by its flesh;*
> *unbounded by its time; exclusively for God;*
> *who is green and flowering, with all joy and power."*
>
> Meister Eckhart.

This is an illustrative account of the Spiritual Love-union that can be achieved between the soul and God [within the ordering of Divine Providence], and which has been described in the lives of Church saints and mystics as the stages of Betrothal, Mystical [Spiritual] Marriage, and Mystical [Spiritual] Incarnation. Bridal Mysticism was first mentioned in the Old Testament, and is continued in the New Testament. Mystical Marriage is vividly expressed in the lives of over seventy Church saints; over three-quarters of whom, have been stigmatists. More recent faithful souls of the 20th Century, such as St. Elizabeth of the Trinity, Blessed Dina Belanger, Venerable Conchita [Concepion Cabrera de Armida], and most notably, Luisa Piccarreta, have described a Mystical Incarnation in which the Life of Jesus Christ is reproduced within and through the soul. In this work, the co-operative soul is made of, a most munificent [suffering] victim and participator in union with and in Jesus Christ, sharing in and relieving His corporeal and interior sufferings, in order to accomplish His Plan of Love. St John Paul II wrote of a *"new and divine holiness"*, at the dawn of the third millennium, which would *"make Christ the heart of the world"* [John Paul II, 'Letter to the Centenary of the Rogation Fathers']. Souls raised to the state of Mystical Incarnation, first traversed the high state of Mystical Marriage. While the complete gift of the Mystical Incarnation given to Luisa Piccarreta *followed* Mystical Marriage, at the age of twenty-three, *and* three further nuptials. Her private Revelations, are currently under review by the Church, and her cause of beatification and canonisation is progressing.

Journey to Bethlehem

No ordinary travellers; St. Joseph – a model man; characteristics of the all-good Life, in perfect fidelity to the divine Blueprint; thorns and roses -discovering who we are in the trials and tests of life; God asks for a place to be born; sanctifying the ordinary and the everyday; primacy of the interior life, and continuity between interior and exterior life; the souls whom God entrusts Himself to; the self-styled crucifixion of the "old man"; beyond signs, miracles and 'feel good' faith – growing up into Jesus Christ; the Eternal Father is always in charge.

"Now in those days, a decree went out from Caesar Augustus, that all the world [Roman Empire] should be enrolled... Joseph went up from Galilee from the town of Nazareth, into Judea, to David's city, which is called Bethlehem, because he was of the house and family of David, to be enrolled with Mary his betrothed, who was with Child...When they were there, the time came for Mary to give birth."

Luke 2:1,4-6.

We accompany Mary and Joseph, as they set out on their mid-winter trip of some five days, from Nazareth to Bethlehem, to fulfil the requirements of the Census. Joseph, as a descendant of king David, was required to register in Bethlehem, the birthplace of David, reaffirming his, and therefore Jesus lineage, and the fulfilment of the prophesy of Micah: *"But you, Bethlehem Ephrathah, being small among the clans of Judah, out of you One will come out to Me who is to be ruler in Israel; whose goings out are from of old, from ancient times"* Micah 5:2.

Bereft of all modern-day comforts, and in a scene that contrasts with the pageant of life, we find Mary and Joseph as ordinary and obscure travellers, amidst the chill of the elements, and the barrenness of the landscape, assisted only by a strong and gentle little donkey. We can imagine Mary's discomfort as a heavily pregnant woman, and Joseph's anxiety to protect her on this trip, not least because of the religious hostilities of the time, which prompted him to take an indirect route. Finding abatement for natural fears in Divine Providence, and with Heaven invisibly wrapped all around them, guiding and protecting their every step, they make their quiet and unobtrusive passage to Bethlehem. While we may expect that this mid-winter journey was difficult [Venerable Mary of Agreda tells us that], it was not without the added inconveniences, and hardships of rain and snow storms. And while the little party were met with warm hospitality in some inns and places of rest along the way, in others they were met with inhospitable and inconsiderate treatment. This poor treatment came most particularly from the *'worldly well to do'*, on account of the material simplicity of the little party, and their unassuming dispositions. Some places flatly turned them away, deeming them worthless and despicable people. We envisage Mary and Joseph counting the hours, and Joseph giving reassurances to her of fitful rest at the end of their wearying journey, for he had relations, friends, and acquaintances in Bethlehem. From these people, they could expect warmth of welcome and good lodgings.

Yet, at the end of this arduous trip, things do not go according to what Joseph had expected. Rather than finding an open door in even one of the homes and residences of those he relied upon, he found himself going up and down the narrow streets of the town, as door after door was closed upon his face. His barbed sorrow and shame at the same cold reception, surely weighed heavily upon him as he returned to Mary troubled, to tell her that he had found nowhere for them to stay. These were his family and friends; his people.

> *"After a long time, Joseph returned in great dejection. I saw that he was shedding tears, and because he had failed again to find an inn, he hesitated to approach. But suddenly he bethought himself of a cave outside Bethlehem used as a storing place by the shepherds when they brought their cattle to the city. Joseph had often withdrawn thither to conceal himself from his brothers, and to pray."*
>
> From the visions of Blessed Anne Catherine Emmerich.

Joseph's gentle and futile knocking on door after door, in the hope of a place to stay, is not without the most profound mystical meaning. For it symbolises Jesus Christ's knocking on the door of stubborn and hard human hearts, asking for shelter that He may be allowed to be born; silently, obscurely and without publicity, within us. And in the same way that Joseph's asking ends, and he moves on as a stranger to find another place to stay, Jesus does not use His power to insist upon entry to our heart's. Rather, He moves quietly on from those who do not want to open themselves to receive His Life. **There is no argument or insistence upon entry, where there is no welcome.** However, when the time of provision and outreach [the time of Divine Mercy, which is our life on earth] is over, and Jesus Christ returns to consummate His Kingdom, the cold and rejecting soul who then tries to enter, will by the decree of Divine Justice, be met with the same rejection that it meted out to Him while on earth.

> *"Once the Master of the house has risen up and has shut the door, and you begin to stand outside and to knock at the door, saying, "Lord, Lord, open to us!" then He will answer and tell you, "I don't know you, or where you come from.""*
>
> Luke 13:25.

We can expect that Mary did not reproach Joseph for failing to find accommodation among those he knew. Gentle and strong, and humble and wise to the works of Divine Providence, her heart was warm to his best efforts and deep disappointment, and grateful when he found them shelter in the cave. Mary knew that Joseph was no weakling. For her and for us, he represents the exemplary created human man [male]. The most hidden and obscure of all of God's saints, he is a most singular vessel of divine predilection, undertaking the most sublime office that no man could ever dare to dream of. Set apart from his worldly brothers from his earliest days, and drawn to graceful [grace-filled] simplicity of life and prayer [Blessed Anne Catherine Emmerich], Joseph was most certainly filled with the most extraordinary graces, to fit Him for the sublimity and trials of his unearthly, earthly life; standing in place of the Eternal Father, as the foster father of a God-man, and protector of His Mother. In his unyielding steadiness, Joseph is chaste and obedient, and zealously dedicated to knowing God's Divine Will through prayer. In his brave humbleness, he is most just and courageous, and generous and tireless, in his most excellent care of the Holy Family. In everything, he embodies fearless faith, non-resistance, and zealous Love of God.

In the difficulties of Mary and Joseph's journey to Bethlehem, we learn that **higher Life in God, is not about human comforts, ease, and safe bets, which deaden man's higher consciousness, and drive out the Holy Spirit.** Rather, it involves travelling by faith and divine knowing, which operates out of range of human sight. This road is not an easy road, by the standards and illusions of the flesh [carnal ego-self] and the old world, and so those who walk in this way, demonstrate the predilection of God, who draws souls capable of a very great Love of, and trust in Him. Walking perfectly [wholly and all-perfectly] upright in this nakedness of [suffering] Love operating in *living* faith and divine wisdom, Mary, and Joseph, were guided through the testing and purifying difficulties of the old world, and unto infinitely higher things. Their outwardly ordinary lives of labour and learning, bear witness to *living faith as* characterized by persevering [committed], and trusting action, in the must humanly inexplicable circumstances. **By their all-good lives, God the Father reveals to us, that the world is an essential part of His Plan of Redemption and Sanctification. That it is through the trials,**

temptations, and contradictions of the world [when we are not on our own agenda], that He and we ourselves, find out who we really are. For it is through the world that our God-Being [John 10:34] is tried, tested, strengthened, and matured; purified, perfected, and guided to absolute freedom in the Father's Love and Divine Will. From carrying a child unbeknown to Joseph before wedlock, and giving birth to Him in a cave; to fleeing to hide in the unknown land of Egypt, as Herod sought to kill the God-Child; to seeing Him betrayed and crucified, Mary experienced a most rigorous and testing way of life, as she co-operated with and participated in the divine Plan. In the same way, every one of us is called [invited] to accept and co-operate with this Plan; a Plan which - according to the height of sanctity to which our soul is capable of and called to, involves much firmness and forbearance, but which alone transfigures and hallows our human personhood, while reaping rewards far beyond what we can begin to imagine. And so, in perfect fidelity to the divine Blueprint, Mary and Joseph accept both joy and sorrow; consolation and suffering; as the allegiances of those for and against God [Truth, Love, and Life] were uncovered, in the great Cosmic drama of [absolute] good forever overcoming the tyranny of evil.

> *"The divine majesty was determined to create me, in order that I might be the Light of a Love most gentle, compassionate, and tender. That is why He prepared for me, a heart pierced by thousands of thorns, even though it was crowned with roses."*
>
> The Blessed Virgin speaks to Venerable Conchita.
> [María Concepción Cabrera de Armida].

In this way of life, we learn that the work of God is secret and active at a much deeper and higher level than we are looking for with our natural intelligence; sustaining the ordinary and the everyday, while remaining above it. **Mary and Joseph's lives of unparalleled divine service [Charity], did not involve elaborate efforts that purposively called or drew attention to themselves. Rather, in concealing the**

extraordinary in the ordinary, they give witness to the reality that the interior life [quality of being], directed upon the Eternal, is much higher than the exterior life [of doing], while all God Willed outward action, takes its inspiration from the interior Life of the Spirit. Operating in harmony with the Eternal-Now Spirit of God flowing within and through their being, their every motion, and everyday tasks: their breathing, moving, working, eating, mending, weaving, washing, cleaning, cooking, errands, and sleep; together with their self-sacrifice and works of assisting those put in their path by Divine Providence; were offered to God, and became arteries of *living* prayer, and channels of extraordinary supernatural graces.

In this same manner, we are called [invited] to offer our necessary and ordinary everyday acts and works to God in Jesus Christ, because it is in making these acts, and every necessary and upright act holy [whole and all-perfect] in Him, that we set a good example to our neighbour, and discover holiness [whole-hearted fullness of being]. For every such act that is infused with the Light-consciousness of Jesus Christ, is transformed to become a divine practice of the All-presence of God. The small things [acts] become great things [Life-giving acts], as our lives issue from, and reciprocate an interior infinite good, formed by God within and through us. In this new [Ever-new] way of being, we become more than is seen, hear more than is audible, and think more than is manifested in thought form. We become divinely creative vessels that carry and transport Light, which clarifies, heals, elevates, and transmutes the divine Spirit in all suffering creation. See 'Work' in Useful Terms.

"Do not despise the day of small things."
Zechariah 4:10.

The simple and unheralded lives of Mary and Joseph also testify to the reality that Life after God not about self-satisfaction in Spiritual matters. It is not about fleeting supernatural signs and [temporal] miracles without pure Love of God, which pass away. Nor is it about clinging to ideas of [temporal or Spiritual] recognition or reward for our works, or about expecting others to do our holy living for us. Naked Love of [and perfect communion with and in] God in His Divine Will, is the barometer [1 Corinthians 13:1-13]. Sacred Scripture tells us that Jesus did not [could not] entrust himself to the surging crowds who besieged Him because they saw, and experienced His miracles, and believed [John 2: 13-25]. For those who appeared 'good' among men; including the multitudes who walked the roads after Him; those who lingered around Him and benefited from His miracles and proofs, and who spoke eagerly of His teachings and ways - including His apostles [but one]; were the same people who deserted Him during His Passion and Death. Like the nine Lepers - of whom *"Jesus remarked: "Were not ten made clean? And so where are the nine? [Luke 17:11-19],* they were not prepared to drink from the cup of suffering Love from which He drank [Matthew 20:22 and Mark 10:38].

> *"...many believed in His Name, observing that signs that He gave. But Jesus didn't entrust Himself to them, because He knew everyone, and didn't need anyone to testify concerning man; for He Himself knew what was in man."*
>
> John 2:23-25.

Only a few people, perfectly [wholly and all-perfectly] flooded with the primordial strength and stability of God's own Love in His Divine Will, scaled Calvary with Him, and stood at the foot of the Cross. Sacred Scripture names these people as our Blessed Mother, her sister Mary, the wife of Clopas, Mary Magdalene and John, the Apostle [John 19:25]. While after the Resurrection, only a small group of one hundred and twenty believers remained; the remnants of the Kingdom, gathered in a little room in Jerusalem, to receive the outpouring of the Holy Spirit [Acts 1:15].

> *"They laid their hands on him [Jesus], and seized Him…. And they all [His disciples] left Him and fled."*
>
> Mark 14:46,50.

In re-orientating to co-operate with and participate in the work of the Spirit, man must then realize that all growth and expansion, requires suffering and overcoming in passing away from the insular *"old man"* to the Eucharistic *"new man"*. And that, what appears to be a crucifixion in every-day life, is often the self-styled agony [cargo of desires and attachments] of the ego-persona; the only self he 'knows'; but which is nothing but an illusion of his own making. *"All the powers of the soul, intelligence and understanding...lead thee into multiplicity. Therefore, [one] must give them all up, in so far as they lead thee into the life of the senses and of images"* says John Tauler [The Illuminated Doctor]. Those wearing the heaviest cloak of the flesh [carnal ego-self], and caught up in the old world, may find that their eyes take a lot longer to adjust to the Light of Truth, if at all. **For like the worldly 'well to do' who turned away the little party of divine royalty in the taverns and places of rest on their way to Bethlehem, deeming them worthless; those who entangle themselves in lowly ways and things, are [by degrees of estrangement] blind and insensible to their own Spiritual poverty, and in opposition to the unearthly ways of those ['Poor in Spirit'] who God gives Himself [His Spiritual wealth] to.** See Chapter on 'Fiat' and 'Poor in Spirit' in Useful Terms.

> *"For those who are Christ's have crucified their flesh, along with its vices and desires."*
>
> Galatians 5:24.

While we know that we cannot overcome on our own, we must never imagine ourselves so miserable that we tire and give up, because for those who truly desire God, everything works together to secure their good, and fulfil His divine designs upon their soul [Romans 8:28]. If we admit to God our weaknesses, He will give us His strength [Isaiah 40:29 and 2 Corinthians 12:9], in every which way we need it, including those that will only be known and appreciated after mortal death. Like Mary and Joseph, our sorrow should then be gentle, and our peace undisturbed, as we take one more step towards God, and He takes ten steps towards us. For the children of salt and Light

[Matthew 5:13–14], of sorrow and joy, for the sake of the restoration of the Kingdom, are the *"Children of Light"* Luke 16:18; John 12:36; Ephesians 5:8; 1 Thessalonians 5:5, whose flight of faith beyond the narrow range of human understanding, is their supernatural liberation in the realms of Light, Truth, and Life.

Ultimately, the journey to Bethlehem reminds us that God our Father is always in charge. While Caesar's show of worldly power serves as a symbol of Rome's forced control over Israel, and the rest of the world, it ironically serves our Father's greater Plan for His Son-God, the Messiah-King, to be born in Bethlehem of Judah. Despite its smallness and worldly insignificance, Bethlehem's divine appointment from the beginning of time, is called out in Genesis 35:19, at a time when it was called Ephrathah, perhaps referring to the exceptional fertility of the region. This royal appointment is echoed by the Prophet Micah, who linked Bethlehem Ephrathah with his foretelling of a new King, who would re-unite the people of Israel, and reign over all nations. Across the centuries, Bethlehem is a place of momentous happenings in the royal lineage from which Jesus came. Boaz, the great grandfather of David, the earthly Old Testament king of Israel, was from Bethlehem [Ruth 2:4], while David himself was born here, and anointed king by the Prophet Samuel [1 Samuel 16:1-13]. We then ever take heart in the reality that **the ultimate victory of good over evil has already been won**, and that everything ultimately serves God's purpose. He does not fail to protect and strengthen; and to purify and illuminate His faithful ones; healing and re-creating [re-birthing] their souls anew, and drawing them ever upwards from the old world, into the blaze of His own incomprehensible Light.

> *"My Father goes on working, and I am working too."*
>
> John 5:17.

Information on the lives of the Holy Family, sourced from the writings of Church saints, primarily Blessed Anne Catherine Emmerich, and Venerable Mary of Agreda.

King of kings

The lost crown of Spiritual wealth; the anointed lineage and promise of the Father; Jesus Christ the One true King; the price of this Cosmic victory and what it means for us; Light-thorns and rocks along the narrow and sacred pilgrims path; only Love operating in the Divine Will crowns the soul; the Children of Light - the Everlasting crown of the Divine Being.

> "Lift up your heads, you gates; yes, lift them up, you Everlasting doors, and the King of glory will come in. Who is this King of glory? The Lord of Armies is the King of glory!"
>
> Psalm 24:9-10.

The Crown is a vital and central symbol in Sacred Scripture. Chiefly, it represents the glorious and immortal crown of Life [Spiritual wealth] rejected by Adam, the head of the human family, together with Eve. The crown of pain, in the form of a plaited ring of thorns worn by Jesus during His Passion, symbolises the bitter state of fallen man, and His work of restoring to man his lost immortal crown, together with His own divine rights as supreme ruler and King of all.

That the true children of God would be ruled by kings, was prophesied in the Old Testament by the three great patriarchs Abraham, Isaac, and Jacob. Their prophesies came to fulfilment in the New Testament in Jesus Christ, the One final and Eternal King, of whose Kingdom there will be no end [Luke 1:33]. For just as the Old Testament king David, of the anointed lineage from which Jesus proceeds [Matthew 1:1; Luke 1:31; Revelation 5:5] established the earthly Kingdom of Israel with its twelve tribes [1 Samuel 16:1-13; 2 Samuel 5:1-5; Psalm 89:20-21], and which decayed when his son Solomon served other gods; Jesus established His Heavenly Kingdom, which is not of this old world [John 18:36], on the foundation of the twelve apostles. The very first verse of the New Testament, identifies the lineage of Jesus as the *"Son of David, the Son of Abraham"* Matthew 1:1, and goes on to envision the restoration of the Old Testament Davidic Kingdom through Him, who would be born of a Virgin, of David's royal lineage. Then, at the end of the New Testament, Jesus identifies Himself to the Apostle John as *"the true One, who has the key of David"* Revelation 3:7, meaning the keys to the Kingdom, which He received in the work of atonement [at-One-ment]. And so, the promise that God the Father gave to king David of establishing a sovereign and peaceful Kingdom, found its true fulfilment in Jesus Christ. The Psalmist in the opening Scriptural quote, depicts Jesus Christ's triumphant entry into this Davidic Kingdom, which is the Paradisaic New Jerusalem.

> *"He will be great and will be called the Son of the Most High. The Lord God will give Him the throne of His father David, and ...His Kingdom will have no end."*
>
> Luke 1:32-33.

Sacred Scripture tells us that this unearthly and Eternal dwelling place, will bring about a most incredible and spectacular change in reality. *"I saw no temple in it, for the Lord God the Almighty and the Lamb are its temple"* Revelation 21:22. In this mutual dwelling place, God will be our dwelling and we will be His, in the re-established and transfigured Edenic state. We prepare for, and enjoy a foretaste of this new [Ever-new] and humanly unfathomable reality, when we abide in Jesus Christ and He abides in us [John 15:5].

The title *"King of kings and Lord of lords"* 1 Timothy 6:15; Revelation 17:14 and 19:16, confirms the royal dignity and majesty; and power and authority of Jesus Christ. He is the Messianic King and the *"Eternal High Priest"* Hebrews 4:14; 8:1, who is God and man, and whose Kingdom is not of this [old] world. Possessing the full Substance [Essence] and Energies [Actions] of the Godhead, He is both the innocent and spotless Lamb destined for sacrifice before the foundation of the world [1 Peter 1:18-21; Revelation 13:8]; and the mighty and victorious Lion of the tribe of Judah [Genesis 49:9-10; Revelation 5:5], who will pronounce Final Judgement on everyone who has ever lived. He is both the Spiritual root [source of king David's power and kingdom] and offspring [descendant] of David. He is All in All; the true *"Bright Morning Star"* Revelation 22:16, and the purity and promise of the inextinguishable Light, who came to swallow up all [Spiritual] darkness and death, in His own Life, and who has prevailed. He is the fully Divine and Eternal heir to the throne of David, whose Light knows no setting. **His supreme and Eternal authority is Truth, and ultimate reality in the realm of the Spirit; the All and the Only, beyond the temporary physical realm.** A royal Kingdom which could never be built by man, but which could only be gifted by God, and received by man.

Sacred Scripture teaches us that Jesus Christ is *"King of kings"* 1 Timothy 6:15; Revelation 17:14 and 19:16, not only by natural right as our Creator, but also by the right that He has won as our Redeemer. This double claim of Creator and Redeemer is confirmed by St. John, who says that Jesus Christ is *"the ruler of the kings of the earth"* Revelation 1:5. He is rightfully King [in the figurative sense] of our mind [bowed] in our heart, which directs our human will [heart's desire], and the entirety of our being to align with the Cosmic Divine Will, because in Him is the Perfection [Wholeness and All-Perfection] of *real Life and purpose* itself. He is King because as Redeemer, He has freed all people, living creatures and creation from bondage to the kingdom of Satan [old world] and Eternal death, placing [recovering] everything under His power. Jesus Christ therefore rightfully reigns and rules over all things; over nation and society; in the home, school, and workplace; and ultimately in the person; because there is no power or authority, but which comes from God [Romans 13:1]. Therefore, while God permits different systems of earthly government, and can gift earthly leaders with a powerful anointing to serve His purpose, earthly theocracies [earthly governments ruled by religious leaders and the priesthood] are not in His Plan for the old world. Governments however are expected to aid [and not thwart] the Church in fulfilling her divine mission of gathering in God's own true seed and heirs. For when time is consummated in Eternity, there will be One King and Kingdom.

Jesus identity as *"King of kings"* 1 Timothy 6:15; Revelation 17:14 and 19:16, goes together with His title as the 'Suffering Servant' [Isaiah 53:1-12]. He is the One who obediently endures the most awful suffering, but which proves to be the way of salvation [healing]. For the fruit of this Cosmic work is the gifting the keys of the Kingdom to His Church on earth [Matthew 16:19]. It is the authority given over to her, to restore man to his native God-being [John 10:34] and Good-being in Him. It is also the principle by which *living* faith operates, which is by operating in the creative power of His Divine-Human Being. See 'Chapter on 'Prayer'.

In the most appalling and sobering event of the Passion, we discover how this Cosmic victory was finally won, and what it means for us. The extremes of violence used against Jesus [God] by the Roman soldiers on the way to Calvary, represents fallen man's blind agony and fierce rejection of Christ's divinity and Kingship over all, as well as his own crown of Spiritual wealth [God-being, John 10:34]. It represents the magnitude of man's difficulty with the **Paradox of Truth,** which conflicts with his wayward human will, that naturally prefers self-love, and is susceptible to the inspirations of evil. **Yet, in this most grotesque and victorious act of purging, scourging, and destroying the works of evil, and the sins of mankind in the primordial Light-fire of His Love [operating in His Divine Will], we recognize the intense Passion of God for human souls. We also recognize the rebalancing of the scales of Justice, as God's rightful Kingship over all, and man's crown of Spiritual wealth is won back.** No longer our own, we have been recovered from Eternal death, at an immense and unquantifiable price [1 Corinthians 6:20], and our bodies and souls are [rightfully] members of Jesus Christ [1 Corinthians 6:15]. With holy fear [awe-filled reverence], we recognize the prodigious power of Divine Justice, and that there will be no "second death" Revelation 2:11, 20:6,14 and 21:8, for Jesus Christ, but for the souls who would consent to, or seek to crucify and kill Him twice within their own [divided] being, and in that of others.

> *"I hide My divinity – I hide My glory – I hide My power; the sight of them would crush you."*
> Jesus speaks to Sr. Mary of the Holy Trinity.

The crown of thorns [suffering] confirms to us, that the path to Heaven leads not along an easy level path [that slays the Spirit], but upwards along a dark and narrow path, strewn with thorns and sharp rocks, which Jesus has first passed over. Thorns were directly connected with the punishment of Adam and Eve, when the Father commanded that the earth would bring forth thorns and thistles [Genesis 3:18]. While, in requiring us to submit to the pricks and piercings of Light-thorns, Jesus is asking us for self-sacrifice [self-giving] and mortification to overcome the old world, the flesh [carnal ego-self], and the works of the devil [Satan]. Our fidelity in this work, [beyond the natural intellect and sense perception] is One with the work of relieving and undoing His Crucifixion within our soul, and in the souls of others. It requires our unquestionable and zealous co-operation with Him, which means walking by faith and not by sight along the dark and sacred pilgrims path.

> *"For it was fitting for Him, because of whom and through whom all things exist, who had led many children into glory, to complete the authorship of their salvation through His Passion."*
> Hebrews 2:10.

Jesus teaches us that only Love [operating in His Divine Will] crowns the soul, and brings celestial peace to the earth. His royal Kingship and empire can only be fully consummated [implemented], when all things return under His supreme rule. This means not only those marked as His own through the rights of Baptism, but all rulers and nations, and the whole of mankind. In the worship of The Maji, we see the beginnings of the restoration of Jesus Christ's Lordship and authority over all earthly authorities. Only in recognition of the full revelation of His divine majesty as Bridegroom, King, and Judge at all levels of society will **true peace, harmony, and order** prevail. Those who are His true children, are therefore encouraged by the urgency of His desire, to co-operate with and participate in Him, in the restoration of His royal Kingdom within and through our souls; and upon a new earth, which will be ushered in at *"the end of the [present] times"* [Revelation 16]. Then, at *"the [final] end of time"* [Revelation 20:7-15; 21], and upon Last Judgement, when the Kingdom is Perfect [Whole and All-Perfect], Jesus Christ will come in His royal power to deliver it up to the Eternal Father, having first dispossessed every earthly rule, authority, and power [1 Corinthians 15:24].

> *"See, the Lord is Coming with thousands upon thousands of His holy ones, to execute Judgement upon all..."*
>
> Jude 1:14–15.

As we approach the First Coming of Jesus Christ as an infant Child at Christmas, let us embrace the duty and privilege of recognizing our Creator and Redeemer, and give royal place to the Eternal Davidic Kingdom within and through our souls. And as we give the Father our zealous *"Fiat"*; our word of consent to His preparing in us, a worthy dwelling place for the birth of His Son-God, the *"King of kings"* 1 Timothy 6:15; Revelation 17:14 and 19:16; let us place ourselves under the mantle of Our Blessed Queen-Mother. For as no royal Kingdom is complete without a Queen; Mary, as the Mother of Jesus Christ and of all mankind, is the full complement to His supreme Kingship. She is *"the woman of glory"* [Pope John Paul II, Revelation 12:1], who together with her faithful children, united in the All-conquering Jesus Christ, will crush the head of Satan [and all evil] both in time, and in the final act of Divine Justice. Walking upright with her, as salt and Light [Matthew 5:13–14, and abiding in innocence and in justice, these *"Children of Light"* Luke 16:18; John 12:36; Ephesians 5:8; 1 Thessalonians 5:5, will form the Ever-lasting crown [of Spiritual wealth] of God's Divine Being, when Jesus Christ hands back the Kingdom to the Eternal Father [1 Corinthians 15:24; Revelation 11:15; Hebrews 2:5,7-8]. For having willingly and gratefully come to the fullness of being in Jesus Christ [Colossians 2:10], these Heaven-Lit and Love-crowned souls, will be found worthy of forming His royal cortege, and of reigning Eternally with Him, and with our Heavenly Queen-Mother, in the blissful Light-union of the Homeland [Revelation 5:10].

> *"Behold, I am approaching quickly!*
> *And My repayment is with Me, to render*
> *to each one according to his works."*
>
> Revelation 22:12.

The Maji

The entire lost caravan of creation journeying through the dark night of the human will; symbolic material gifts of gold, frankincense, and myrrh; no material gift fit for a God-Child; the expanded New Israel; man - a worshipping being; re-learning to worship; wolves dressed in sheep's clothing; the Feast of the Epiphany.

"They, having heard the king [Herod], went their way; and behold, the star, which they saw in the East, went before them until it came and stood over where the young Child was."

Matthew 2:9-10.

Let us approach the birth of Jesus Christ, in both Bethlehem and our souls, with the assurance of the Maji; the Three kings or Three Wise Men, who followed the star along the way to Bethlehem. This journey, in common expectation over a long distance, and through the vault of night, carries much richness in meaning, in the story of the Nativity. Called Maji on account of being well versed in natural sciences and Sacred Scripture, these were men of noble disposition; their swift, humble, and trusting following of the unknown course of the guiding star, representing the conversion of, and call [invitation] to all nations to come into the Light [of Truth and Life]. The Old Testament Covenant has ended, and all people, living creatures and creation, have entered into a New and Ever-lasting Covenant of Love with God the Father, in His Son-God, Jesus Christ.

We picture the Maji sitting high upon camels, loaded with baggage and hangings, while caravanning through desert land as patriarchs of their own processions of people and animals. In this scene, we see represented the entire lost caravan of creation, weighed down with the cargo of the flesh [carnal ego-self], the old world, and the works of evil, with all existence-ignorance, sin, and suffering. Yet, full of hope and trust, their steady journey is planned and purposeful. For among the pale glittering canopy of stars, their attention is focused upon one particular star, dazzling with peculiar brightness in the night sky. Not by natural reason [light], but by inner divine illumination [Light], they know this to be no ordinary star, but a Heavenly star. As the mighty and radiant pillar of fire that led the Israelites out of Egypt [the land of idolatry - Exodus 13:21-22], and the fulgent scene of the Transfiguration of Christ on Mount Tabor [Matthew 17:1-8], they know this star to be the manifestation of the prophesied Light which has shone out of darkness [Isaiah 9:1-2; Matthew 4:16; John 1:4-5]. They know it to herald the Incarnation of the long-awaited for Messiah and Saviour [healer]; the inextinguishable *"Bright Morning Star"* Revelation 22:16, who has come to expose and dispel the deep night of the sinful world, and reveal the One Eternal Day.

In this moving scene, we see all people called [invited] to journey through the deep, desert night of sin and estrangement, that conceals God's glory [blissful magnificence], towards the gladness of His three-fold Light [of Truth, Love, and Life] in Jesus Christ. For this journey is the echo of the interior divine calling [invitation] planted deep within the human soul [Ecclesiastes 3:11], that desires our return [and the return of all suffering creation] to a bright new [Ever-new] beginning in the Light-embrace of Jesus Christ, who leads us back to the safety and splendour of the Homeland.

And so, bearing their own Spiritual poverty in the presence of the One they had zealously sought, these gilded earthly kings fall down upon their knees [as a gesture of honour and total dependence], and bending their heads [mind] into their chest [hearts], worship the Divine Child with all of their being. With hands wetted with tears of joy and thanksgiving, they offer material treasures from the East [Matthew 2:11], symbolising the highest gift of their being:

- *Gold* - with this 'precious' earth metal, representing a gift fit for a King, the Maji recognize the infant Child as Jesus Christ, the Messiah, and true King of the ages, and offer Him back the *true gold* of their human will [heart's desire].

- **𝓕𝓻𝓪𝓷𝓴𝓲𝓷𝓬𝓮𝓷𝓼𝓮** - with this fragrant incense, both used for worship and added to sacrifices, they represent their recognition of the infant Child as their Creator, and offer Him the *true fragrance* of their *living* prayers and worship, *"in Spirit and in Truth"* John 4:24.

- **𝓜𝔂𝓻𝓻𝓱*** - with this fragrant burial ointment used as an ingredient in embalming spices, and in priestly anointing, they represent their recognition of the infant Child as their Redeemer; the immortal One who dies on the Cross, and rises again in three days. With this gift, they offer Him back, His own complete Self-sacrificial Love, operating in His Divine Will.

   [* Myrrh mingled with wine was offered to Jesus Christ on the Cross, as a painkiller to deaden His harrowing agony, although He did not take it. See Mark 15:23].

In this exchange of gifts, we understand it is not the richness of material gifts that God values or desires, but the purity and whole-heartedness of our soul's desire, because **no lowly material [earthly] gift can be proper or worthy of the divine nobility of God.** The primary acceptable and pleasing gift we can offer Him, is the return of our estranged human will [heart's desire], to allow Him to undertake His work of restoring our soul to its native God-being [John 10:34], and Good-being in Him. And so, while the Maji represent earthly authority, and the shepherds represent the earthly unadorned, who were first chosen and favoured with Angelic visitation; together they represent the divinely wise and prudent souls, who long for and recognize Almighty God in the infant Child. They symbolise the faithful souls caught up in the only actual gold rush; making haste to worship Him, by offering Him first and foremost, the true gold of their human will [heart's desire], in exchange for the Cosmic Divine Will, which carries Love's Paradise.

We would expect the Maji's amazement to find the Divine Child with neither palace nor throne, but lying in utter humility in a cave, with animals for warmth and company. Yet, we can believe that they were unperturbed, because the same illumination of Light that had called them from their countries to this cave, had allowed them to conceive of the mystery. We can expect too, that they were instructed in all manner of Spiritual knowledge and wisdom by our Blessed Mother, bringing away with them the Light of Jesus Christ [the Ever-lasting Good News], to instruct the nations.

In this glorious scene of the Maji's prostration before the Divine Child, is the fulfilment of the great Davidic King, who was expected to come and bring nations together, and earthly kings to His feet. Here is fulfilled the prophesy of Isaiah, who exalts that nations would come to His Light, and kings to the brightness of His rising, bringing to Him gifts of gold and frankincense, [Isaiah 60:3-6]. And here too is fulfilled Psalm 72, which describes the Son of David, who would bring justice and peace; ruling over earthly kings and nations, who would bow before Him and serve Him. In this way, the Maji represent the relativity and temporality of earthly authorities, which will end when Jesus Christ brings every earthly authority and power to an end, and hands back the Kingdom to the Eternal Father [1 Corinthians 15:24; Revelation 11:15]. In this glorious consummation, those who are recognized as *living* members of His Mystical Body, will rule with Him and our Queen-Mother in differing degrees of radiance and glory [blissful magnificence] according to the quality and standard of Spiritual Life, sown during earthly life.

It is particularly significant that although these three kings are upright and just in their rule, their genealogy is not that of the people of the original Israel [Catechism, No. 528]. Referring to Jesus as *"King of the Jews"* Matthew 2:2, rather than their king, they symbolise the expanded New Israel [and the first fruits of the pagan and gentile people], who most readily and willingly recognize, worship, and follow the Messianic King, who will lead all nations. It is a most humbling sign of the Father's providential generosity, that pagan and gentile people disposed themselves to be called [invited] and drawn by His Light, while many among His own divinely favoured people of Israel reject Him [and therefore their own glory in Him].

> *"I say to you, that many shall come from the East and the West, and they shall sit at table with Abraham, and Isaac, and Jacob in the Kingdom of Heaven. But the sons of the Kingdom shall be cast into the outer darkness, where there will be weeping and gnashing of teeth."*
>
> Matthew 8:11-12.

Ultimately, the Maji represent man as a worshipping being, whose purpose is to dwell in continuous awareness of God's blissful presence within him; Loving whole-heartedly as God Loves, and offering himself, and everyone, and everything back to Him, in a spirit of thanksgiving and praise. Man must, because of the fall, re-learn by way of the Cross to worship God again, because **what was wholly [holy and] real and purposeful within him, in the beginning, was lost by the fateful decision [meaning *"to divide" or "cut off"* in Hebrew] to divide against and worship himself** in his own fleshy [carnal-ego] estrangement, in place of centring his [divinized] being in God. This work of healing and re-creation [re-birth] is then first and foremost, an act of remembering our origin, and who we really are [or ever can be] in Jesus Christ, as the living dialogue between our soul and the Father, in the Life-breath of the Holy Spirit. For true worship with the entirety of our being [John 4:24], is God's own worship within us, made possible with the gifts He has first given us. It must be rekindled to flow in our spirit, soul [memory, will and intellect] and body, by the upright governance of our entire way of being. Church saints who demonstrated great fidelity to the Life of the *"Fiat",* with all self-sacrifice, prayer, and penance, as to experience the slightest foretaste of this incommunicable union of Love, attest to man's much limited ability to perceive this higher Life at the natural level. They also attest to man's inability to endure, but fragments of this tide of ecstasy of celestial Love and joy, which is the multi-dimensional and multi-sensory creative reality of Eternal Life, for which man was originally Loved into being.

In this journey of the Maji, we come face-to-face with both the assurance of God's providential care of those who recognize Him and follow Him, and the terrible presence of evil amidst those who do not. For along their journey, the Maji find that the Heavenly star disappears over Jerusalem, which had refused Mary and Joseph a place to stay, and they were in need of direction. Approaching king Herod for advice, they find him greatly troubled, as they put the question to him: *"Where, [they said] is He, who has been born King of the Jews? For we have seen His star in the East, and have come to worship Him"* Matthew 2:2. Attempting to hide his alarm and malevolence, the king attempts to convince them to tell him where the Divine Child was to be born, as though to go and worship Him. In reality, he planned to destroy the threat to his own earthly reign [which led to his most cruel slaughter of the Holy Innocents – all male children of two years or under, in and around Bethlehem]. Here we have the lesson and warning, that **even those who truly conceive the Light [see that guiding star], can be turned back on their course, unless they have sufficient dominion over themselves to honour its meaning and value, by continuously acting upon it.** Like the pagan king Herod, and all of Jerusalem, all those who react with upset and anger at the Ever-lasting Good News of Jesus Christ, and who reject Him, will not perceive and benefit from His Light. We are also to be awake to those who present themselves as shepherds of 'good', but who instead of looking after and tending the flock, feed themselves on their milk and dress themselves [as sheep] in their wool [Ezekiel 34:1-6]. Yet still, we are consoled by the Father's providential care of His faithful children, for Sacred Scripture tells us that when the Maji left Jerusalem, the star appeared again and *"went before them, till it came to rest over the place where the Child was"* Matthew 2:9. And after visiting Him, they were enlightened in a dream not to go back to Herod, and returned safely to their own countries by another way. We therefore know that the days of Herod, and all the enemies of God [of Truth, Love and Life] are numbered, while those who like the

Maji, affix their attention on the inextinguishable Light of Heaven, will pass unharmed through the course of the night.

The Feast of the Epiphany

One of the richest feasts in the liturgical calendar, the Epiphany, [also known as the Feast of Lights], which is celebrated on January 6th, is the revelation of the long-awaited Light of Jesus Christ Coming into the world. Derived from the combined Greek word *"epiphainen"*, meaning *"to manifest", "to shine forth",* or *"to make known"*; the Epiphany is an invitation to every one of us to arise and shine; to grow up into the vigour and brightness of *real Life and purpose* in Jesus Christ.

> *"Arise, shine [be enlightened], O Jerusalem;*
> *for your Light has come, and the*
> *glory of the Lord has risen on you!"*
>
> Isaiah 60:1.

Established in the 4th Century, this great feast focuses primarily on the adoration of the Maji; while also celebrates the manifestation of power of the Most Holy Trinity, in the Baptism of Jesus in the river Jordan; as well as the revelation of His glory [blissful magnificence] in His first miracle at the wedding feast of Cana*, in Galilee. With this miracle, where Jesus turns water into new and better wine [from the same Aramaic root word for *"Blood"*], He represents His One true and Eternal Blood bond with the faithful *"Children of Light"* Luke 16:18; John 12:36; Ephesians 5:8; 1 Thessalonians 5:5; the deathless Spiritual Marriage, realized [made real] at the passing point of the Cross.

[*The presence of Jesus and His Mother at the wedding feast of Cana, also represents God's Sanctification of, and presence in earthly marriage].

As we come to celebrate this great feast, our joy is the joy of the Maji, for the long night of travelling in darkness is over. Our journey begins where the journey of the Maji ends, because the radiant Heavenly star which they followed, is the same living Light that has been shining within us since Baptism. With confidence and with joy, we travel by faith and not by sight, reaping [conceiving and birthing] Light upon Light, safe in the knowledge that this Light we bear, is the Ever-living Light of Jesus Christ, who leads and carries us Home. The gifts offered, are no longer casques of gold, frankincense, and myrrh, but our very self [primarily our human will], together with simple gifts of bread and wine, which in the most wonderful and astonishing divine exchange, are transformed into the *real and living reality* of Jesus Christ, who pours Himself into our souls.

> "[This Light] that led the Maji...also illuminates your soul, and directs your footsteps... It fortifies your spirit with divine affection. Without the soul being aware of it, it continually advances towards the Eternal goal."
>
> St. Padre Pio [Excerpt of letter to a soul].

Gifts

The immensity and mystery of our Creator and Father God; Jesus Christ, the ultimate gift and Living embodiment of religion; the one gift we can give [back] to God; the children for whom God looks; gifts which cannot be stolen, hoarded, or plundered; saints in search of higher riches; soul economy and the Spiritual intellect: the contra commerce of Light-poverty and Light-riches.

"And opening their treasures, they offered Him gifts of gold, frankincense and myrrh."

Matthew 2:11.

All is gift. The being we possess by grace, and the life of every living person and creature, and all of nature. From the air we breathe, to the bright sun and pale moon; from the boundless deep night sky with its glittering canopy of stars and planets, to the limitless triune Universe; everyone and everything, is a masterpiece and messenger of the superabundant works, order, and promise of our Creator God and Father, who is the source of all that is. All speak of a continuous relationship of His Love and Divine Will in the present, which holds everyone and everything in being, in every second of every day.

"Who has measured the height of Heaven, and the breadth of the earth, and the depth of the abyss?"

Sirah 1:3.

The immensity of God our Father is expressed in the Old Testament Book of Job, when in a series of some seventy-seven rhetorical questions, He draws Job's attention to the endless wonders of creation. From the natural sun and the configuration of stars; to His wondrous and varied animal creation; including very large and powerful land and sea creatures [unfamiliar to Job, who lived after the Great Flood], God confirms that as the author of all that is, He creates what He Wills, as He Wills, while everything is under His providential care. His perfect order, purpose, and stability are richly demonstrated in the placing of the sun and planets, the earth's rotation, the moon phase cycles, and the seasons, without which there could be no life [or scientific study] on earth. His questions demonstrate, that even with the very best of his natural intellect, man has but an inkling of the Almightiness of God, and the marvel of his being in Him. Yet, it is tripartite man whom God has placed at the centre of His creation. The greatest Truth and humility is therefore to realize that nothing is due, but all is freely given. There is nothing that we can *really* do, but recognize the prodigious power, majesty, faithfulness, and Mercy of Almighty God, and gratefully co-operate with and participate in Him, in His New Covenant of Love, to receive all that He has prepared for us as Father, in and from all Eternity.

In the double fullness and Perfection [Wholeness and All-Perfection] of His Cosmic Divine-Humanity, Jesus Christ is the ultimate masterpiece and gift of the Father's Love and Divine Will. He is the living Word [John 1:1; 1:14]; the centre, meaning, and Blueprint of all creation, through whom and for whom, all things are made [John 1:1-3]. In winning back for us, our lost place at the centre of all creation, as only God could, He has been gifted by the Father, with every soul, who would desire to be restored and re-birthed in time, to the newness [Ever-newness] of *real Life and purpose* in Him [John 14:6]. **From the Latin word *"religio"* meaning *"bind-back"*, Jesus Christ is the living embodiment of religion. He *is* our binding back to the Father, and the Spiritual state of the Kingdom.** In this dynamic sharing of the Love and Divine Will of the Father, centred in the Son, and moving through the Holy Spirit, all people [who would share His Life] and all creation, are transformed into a communion [community] of purest Love, thanksgiving, and praise of their Beloved Creator God and Father. To this end [fulfilment], the Incarnation and birth of Jesus Christ, sets the stage for God's Plan of restoring the glory [blissful magnificence] of Cosmic order.

We associate gift-giving with Christmas, because it marks the time of arrival of the most long-awaited gift of Jesus Christ, the Messiah and Saviour [healer] of the world. As we turn our thoughts to the memorial of His arrival, and the practice of gift-giving, it is therefore only appropriate to ask ourselves: **What gift do we think to give to this celestial Baby and Three-Fold Light, who first gave us everything, and gifted [won] it back, together with immeasurably more?** While to ponder this question, is to realize that in Truth we have nothing of our own to give, and yet we are in possession of the greatest treasure which He desires more than anything else; our free human will [heart's desire], which flows from our Father's own omnipotence. So, while the Angels offered Him a song, and the animals a cave, there is no greater exchange of gifts and no greater Love, than to exchange the human will [heart's desire] for the Divine Will [God's Cosmic Heart's Desire], and receive the fullness and radiance of *real Life and purpose* in Jesus Christ. It is only if, or when, in the example of the shepherds and the Maji, we gladly return this treasure to Him, that He can begin His work par excellence, of offering us infinitely greater gifts, in the astonishing and Life-giving work of the divine exchange.

> *"All good and perfect gifts descend from above, from the Father of Lights."* James 1:17, *but with all other gifts, He wants to prepare us for One gift, which is Himself."*
>
> Meister Eckhart.

In this work, God empowers us to find our own movement towards Him; to become who we are, as pure, noble, and free **divinely-human beings, in a perfect union of wills.** With our mind and heart re-united as one, in whole-hearted Love of, and desire for God it bestows upon us the gift of our holiness [whole-hearted fullness of being]; the return to original innocence and justice [Eternal Beatitude], given to us by God and returned to Him, in a mutual and Ever-expanding circle of giving and receiving. The gift of our human will [heart's desire] in every moment, is then the only appropriate gift to give [back] to God, and to others, and all living creation in Him. Because **restored to our original and true centre, purpose, and power of being, we can offer everyone and everything, the perfect reflection of themselves in another Christ, who co-operates with and participates in God, to heal and restore all that is destined to be healed and restored in Him.** In this faithful soul, they too can know Jesus Christ-being, the absolute and only reality.

> *"Now there is another Light, and that is the Light of grace... God's presence within the soul by grace, brings in more Light than any intellect. And all the Light that the intellect can give, is but a drop in the ocean beside this Light."*
>
> Meister Eckhart.

The gift of Divine [Eternal] Life, is received in the measure [degree to] which the soul consents to the divine crafting. Mary's total gift of herself was a complete response to God, and is the perfect example for the whole people of God to follow, in the Church hierarchy [order] of holiness [whole-hearted fullness of being]. In the teachings, sacraments, and provisions of the Church, we are gifted with every means we need to fulfil our earthly task and purpose of exchanging our sinfulness and brokenness, with His own Perfect [Whole and All-Perfecting] Divine-Humanity. Every baptised person, has the Light-seed of Jesus Christ planted within their soul. Each has been gifted with a supernatural vocation to religious life, which is nothing less than an invitation to become fully oneself again in the Perfect [Whole and All-Perfecting] Cosmic Personhood of Jesus Christ.

To grow in the knowledge and Love God, and therefore ourselves and all things in God, it is first necessary to be conscious of our exile and self-condemnation [Spiritual poverty]. For it is the aware soul that is inspired by grace to turn way from outward earthiness, and towards inward luminosity, and mirror the Life-giving shape of the Cross in their being. Those who do so, find that they are not disappointed, for they are shown the way of transformation and transcendence, to realize - as far as they are willing and capable, the Divine Ideal within.

> *"But be zealous for the better [Spiritual] gifts.*
> *And I will reveal to you a more excellent way."*
>
> 1 Corinthians 12:31.

Jesus continuously looks around for children who are willing and ready to abandon themselves to His creative hand. Those who are awake to the bitter bondage of the human will; who are capable of acting with astuteness and vigilance over their own soul; and who are ready for co-operation [participation] and perseverance [commitment]. **These souls for whom He looks, are none other than the humble, meek** [positively consenting or assenting, gentle, and balanced in Aramaic and Hebrew], **and divinely wise children [Matthew 10:16],** who are capable of listening to and benefiting from His teachings. Those who are sufficiently honest, sincere, and unaffected, to see through the illusions, wantonness, and evils of the flesh [carnal ego-self] and the old world; while discerning and appreciating the inestimable richness of celestial gifts. Whether by firm faithfulness, or by sincere repentance [meaning *"turning back"* or *"coming back"* to God in Aramaic and Hebrew], they are the souls who strive not to [further] elude or degrade themselves with these perishable spoils and apparent 'successes', which disappear upon mortal death.

> *"The person who abides in solitude and quiet is delivered*
> *from fighting three battles: hearing, speech, and sight.*
> *Then there remains one battle to fight - the battle of the heart."*
>
> St. Anthony the Great.

More determined and disposed to Spiritual and immaterial reality, they are capable of co-operating with and participating in God, in the right operation of His Ever-creative power, while not [further] misusing, or abusing it. They are capable of appreciating God's highest gifts and graces of Crosses and consolations, and of using them wisely, knowing that they belong to the giver. **For God's highest gifts, carry the mark of His Blood-red robe and crown of thorns, bringing great tests and trials of purification [the Spiritual Passion of the dark night of the soul] which deeply purge the soul of every natural sensibility [sense perception] and [unconscious] self-love, while crafting upon it the similitude of Jesus Christ.** And because receiving gifts calls for corresponding gifts, so that the reciprocity of Love may be realized [made real], they can be trusted to Love the giver more than the gifts. They do not idolize the gifts in themselves, but find in them divine tastes, in place of earthly tastes, which they use to Love God [and all people, creatures, and creation] more. **They seek neither this gift nor that, nor become preoccupied or self-satisfied with having received or not received this gift or that, in any measure or at any particular time. For they know it is the Giver [God Himself], and not the gifts that satisfies the nobility of the soul.** Receiving all with thankfulness and gratitude, they recognize that they are all divinely arranged, allowing them to cast off the weight of the flesh [carnal ego-self], the old world and the works of evil, and receive the One ultimate gift, which is God [God-being, 10:34] in Jesus Christ. Their primary occupation, is to remain faithful to God in Jesus Christ, in the present moment. See Chapter on 'Fiat'.

> *"Jesus draws the soul in Love,*
> *Without encroaching on its own free will."*
>
> St. Padre Pio.

Let us then follow the example of the Maji; the Three Wise Men and kings of zealous good will, desiring nothing more than to offer the God-Child, our Spiritual gifts of gold, frankincense, and myrrh, in exchange for His royal gifts. For our most valuable life's work, is the interior work of conceiving and birthing Jesus Christ within and through our soul, allowing Him to be known to our fellow man, and all living creation:

- *Gold* - with Love and confidence, we return to Him, the true [Spiritual] gold of our human will [heart's desire], which contains all the desires and tastes of our inner being. We ask Him to convert our will into the refined and refulgent Spiritual gold of His Cosmic Divine Will; melting and purifying, in self-sacrifice [self-giving] and in suffering, all the dross of the human will, and preparing it for His royal imprint.

- *Frankincense* - as the work of Love involves continuous co-operation, participation, and reciprocity, we offer Him the fragrant incense of our prayers and supplications, fused in the primordial power His own Life and sufferings, in the Divine Will. We trust that this spirit of *living* prayer and worship in and through Him, converts all our internal and external acts into Spiritual gold, for the good of everyone and everything.

- *Myrrh* - as our soul [memory, will and intellect] communicates life to our body, we offer Him the continual mortification of our carnal passions and appetites, and all temptations of spirit, soul, and body, embracing His Perfect [Whole and All-Perfect] Divine-Humanity in ours.

> *"Instead of developing your talents [apart from God], seek rather to welcome the gifts of God, all His gifts: your souls will be loaded with imperishable riches."*
>
> Jesus speaks to Sr. Mary of the Holy Trinity.

In this gift of re-birth [re-creation], which is the purification and re-ordering of our soul, to the divine purpose in Jesus Christ:

- The gold of our human will [heart's desire], lives, moves, and rests in Love, gratitude, and praise of God, in His All-Perfect [Whole and All-Perfecting] Divine Will;

- Our memory rests its hope in God [not in other people, or in fleshy or worldly desires], and in gratitude for all the great gifts received; and
- Our intellect [understanding] comprehends the thirst and zeal of His Love for us, in faith as His beloved child.

In the life of others, we discern only the Father's Divine Will for their transcendent good, and not the operation of their human will.
In this continuous feast of giving and receiving between Father and child in Jesus Christ, the faithful child abounds in all manner of incorruptible and surprising gifts. It discovers and cultivates its true talents and potentialities, not only as His faithful image, but in the true creative power of His divine likeness; as an **active participator in the dialogue of the Life of Love [operating in the Divine Will], for the sake of everyone and everything.** Only in Heaven, will the faithful child be given to understand and appreciate the full effects and enrapturing beauty of this unseen dynamic preparation on earth. For by virtue of its activity in the unseen realm, it is being uniquely endowed with all manner of resplendent Spiritual jewels; of colours, scents, and forms, in the promise of a Spiritualized new body, as befits the [qualitative] state of its healed and glorious soul.

Those fortunate children who are most desirous of, and graced with God's divine gifts are more often unknown, for they Love to speak of God alone in all things. Stable and at peace in the Home-ground of pure being, they are the soundless hymn, who draw away from fleshy [carnal-ego] and old worldly conversations and pursuits, to manifest and magnify God in their being. Upon these courageously faithful souls, God confers the great gift of final perseverance [commitment], by which they are found in a state of sanctifying grace at the end of their earthly pilgrimage. This sublime gift, implies God's special providential care of His faithful child, whom He helps to remain in grace, despite the continuous efforts of the enemy, to the moment of death.

Soul economy: Less is more

All must pray for the special gifts of holy fear [awe-filled reverence] of God; the divine wisdom to see what must be done; and the strength of perseverance [commitment] through life, and to the hour of death; none more so, than those most careless and cold; most dislocated from their true centre, Jesus Christ. For life is nothing other than a continuous consummation of the soul in Light or in darkness. Light draws Light, while darkness draws more darkness. At the reflections of Light, those who see gain a greater vision of higher Life, while those who are blind, become more blinded. While from those who would borrow and plunder the Spirit of God, to misuse His creative power and exist in indifferentism, lukewarmness, or rebellion He silently withdraws. Those who would betray Him with a mortal kiss, He will not entrust His divine treasures. For in His ineffable goodness, God does not desire to add to the child's burden of insensibility, defiance, and ingratitude, which would keep Jesus Christ in agony within the soul. Nor does He desire to expose His celestial gifts to theft, plunder, or hoarding, which turn into offences and chastisements, as the soul plunges deeper into the crippled hellishness of its own fleshy [carnal-ego] pride and waywardness. So, while He does not revoke the gifts already given [Romans 11:29], He gives more and greater gifts to other children, or keeps them within Himself. While those who would insist on taking His gifts - namely the Eucharist, without genuine commitment to being transformed, take of their own will - and not God's Divine Will, the short route to self-condemnation [1 Corinthians 11:27].

> *"O my God, burn up this waxen covering of death-giving life,*
> *I will be patient and acquiesce in this mysterious Life-giving death,*
> *before death, as in One tender-wounding flame, You resume*
> *Your reign and rest in me, and I in You.... O come without delay*
> *you deathless death, in self-forgetting Light. And lead me on*
> *in rising bloom, through Eden's hidden gate!"*
>
> Anon.

The saints who took the heroic path after Jesus Christ, exemplify most radically, what it means to thrive and succeed according to the Paradox of Truth. St. Francis of Assisi is perhaps best known for making 'Poorness in Spirit', and moreover the whole-hearted joy and dynamism of this unworldly way, a Universal principle, symbolising freedom of spirit, in pursuit of blissful Light-union with God [and with all things in Him]. With the flaming fire of God's presence alive within the depths of his being, St. Francis recognized the reaping in the sowing, and lived only for the Ever-Now Kingdom of Heaven [Matthew 6:25-34]. In this blessed life-state, he together with the saints of the ages, keenly recognized the peril of misguided attempts to be someone apart from God [the first sin of Adam and Eve], and which Sacred Scripture identifies as lack of divine wisdom. **Graced with keen Spiritual intellect [infused divine knowledge in a purified heart] and wise with the wisdom of God**, these souls have been alive to the works of dis-ordered sense perception, that adheres to the outer husk of appearances, and manifests in desires and attachments on the surface of life, which bind the soul, and block and scatter the Light of the Kingdom. Courageously discarding such illusions and hinderances, in favour of re-dimensioning their awareness in Heaven's Light, they were thus well-disposed to **cast off the dead weight of mammon [money and materiality] and ego-selfhood**; to become energised and possessed of Truth; and receive abundantly from the divine treasury, while sharing its promise with the world. Moving swiftly with lightness of step in God, who raises mortal feet Heavenward, they could scarcely bear to speak of [out of] themselves, or say the words *'me'* or *'mine'*, knowing that in the Kingdom of God, there is no *'you'* and *'I'*; no *'yours'* and *'mine'*.

> *"When we have tasted the sweetness of the Spirit,*
> *all that is flesh becomes insipid; that is, it profits us no more,*
> *and the ways of sense are no longer pleasing."*
>
> St. John of the Cross.

While this most radical momentum may be the exception rather than the norm, it is only in first arriving at some sense of the **contra commerce of the kingdom of Satan, and the Kingdom of Heaven** that we can conceive of what is required to *live the Life of Jesus Christ* [according to our life-state and mission], **which alone glories Him, and the Father in Him [Matthew 15:8; Luke 14:33].** And so, while everyone has a right to the necessary means to life on earth, God in His All-Perfect and Just Blueprint for Divine Life in the immaterial and All-pure realm of Heaven, has decreed that **man cannot assume to serve both God and mammon [money and materiality] at the same time [Matthew 6:24 and 1 John 2:15-16] and win his soul, because he becomes only that which he freely joins himself to [1 Corinthians 6:17; 15:50].** All [the trappings of] false prosperity; all excess and ungodly fleshy and materialistic comforts, pleasures, and statements of 'status' and 'success' taken [and clung to] in earthly life, God sees as nothing but inert and decaying things [Job 41:27; Matthew 6:19 and Luke 6:24], that soil, weigh down, and cripple the soul, scattering and blocking His Light, while blinding the interior Spiritual eye because *"...he who does not gather [reap] with Me [Jesus Christ] scatters"* Luke 11:23. And so, regardless of outward words, gestures, and appearances, God will not, and cannot, entrust the riches of the Kingdom [Edenic state] to those who would presume to offer Him a stale mixture of worldly vanities, appetites, and gatherings, mingled with false humility, and half-hearted resolve, any more than He would to those who readily turn away from Him. For all duplicity and divisiveness is self-deception; it is the mutation of pure being in the indivisible Godhead, that would crucify Jesus Christ anew within the soul, while scandalizing, deluding, and deterring others, and impeding the Spiritual law of sharing, and the forward multiplication of true good. All ultimately translate into lost degrees of glory; an infinity of divine goods, joys, beauties, harmonies, and contentment's, in and for all Eternity. **Earthly 'goods' are then only 'good', in as far as they are gained fairly and shared gladly, in godly and upright works and ways. Insofar as they assist, and do not incapacitate and derail the soul, from its primary task and purpose as a pilgrim on earth,**

desirous of, and committed to, its restoration to the Spiritual state of the Kingdom. While to the one who lives beyond his essential needs *"the spoils of the poor are in your house"* says Isaiah 3:14.

Those on the other hand, who trustingly take to heart 'Poorness in Spirit', for the sake of receiving the higher [imperishable] gifts of the Spirit [1 Corinthians 12:31], find that they are not disappointed. Moved to *"lay up for [themselves], treasures in Heaven"* Matthew 6:20, and raised to a higher state of being by these immaterial Light-riches; they come to re-see by way of the interior eye of the Spirit [Spiritual intellect], and realize that **all gains and losses are relative to Jesus Christ.** Striving not to admit any despoiling desires and superficiality that would soil them, weigh them down, and take them out of Him, their self-sacrifice [self-giving] becomes sweet release, because they know that in Him, they are already interwoven with, and participating in, [the multiplication of] everything *truly* good [real and beautiful] that will ever exist.

> *"For to everyone who has will be given,*
> *and he will have abundance, but from him who doesn't have,*
> *even that which he has will be taken away."*
>
> Matthew 13:12; 25:29; Mark 4:25; Luke 8:18; 19:26.

In the mystery of our everlasting existence, as two-dimensional beings in time, intended for Eternity, let us remain vigilant over our souls, consenting to return to God, all that has been stolen from Him, which is our God-being [John 10:34] and Good-being; and through us, all His suffering creatures and creation. Let us refuse to be impressable and impressionable by lowly earthly influences and the appearance of Life, by replacing value judgements of temporal good and provisional reality, with Eternal standards of absolute good and Spiritual reality, in Jesus Christ. Let us break beyond the boundaries of that which has gone before, desiring nothing more for ourselves and others, than the lost Light-garment and crown [Spiritual wealth] of Eternal Life; the Ever-fresh and adventurous life of beloved children of a celestial

Father, and brothers and sisters of a celestial King. For when the ancient dust of this old world passes, and this temporary body of soil, water, and air returns to the ground, **our one true 'possession' will be our investiture of Light [Divine Life],** that renders us fit for a glorified place in God; the One absolute reality that ever was, and ever will be [1 John 2:17].

> *"For where your treasure is,*
> *there your heart will be also."*
>
> Matthew 6:21.

Charity

St. Nicholas, the embodiment of Charity; the two sides of poverty; Light-poverty - the absolute ill; misconceptions of a much-used word; giving forward and the multiplication of true good; who is our neighbour? our neighbour's keeper and salvation; Charity begins at Home; does not promote one-sidedness; abides in Truth; it's God's work; discerning secrecy and anonymity; only God knows pure acts of Charity; walking upright in Charity.

"Now someone may say: "You have faith, and I have works." Show me your faith without works! But I will show you my faith by means of works."

James 2:18.

The jolly and beloved Father Christmas or Santa Claus, bearer of gifts to all children on Christmas morning, is the modern adoption of the 4th Century Bishop, St. Nicholas of Myra-Turkey [or Bari-Italy, the place where sailors took his relics]. Born in c.270, in Asia Minor [an area then Greek, and which is now part of Turkey], he is the patron Saint of children and sailors, and of many other causes. His feast day is December, 6th.

Taking to heart Jesus challenging words to *"go, sell what you have, and give to the poor"* Matthew 19:21 and Luke 18:22 [Luke 14:33], as to be His disciple, and have *real treasure* in Heaven, it is perhaps not surprising that St. Nicholas has inspired the legend of Santa Claus, who has become central to the Christmas tradition. In a life of fidelity to the meaning of the name Nicholas, deriving from two Greek words, *"Niki"* [meaning victory] and *"laos"* [meaning people], his was the victory of a radically saintly life, of inner and outer union with God, and with all His people and living creation in Him.

Raised well in a faithful family, in a seaside town in Licia, in southern Turkey, Nicholas' life from his earliest days, was marked by **living and active faithfulness** to God. When orphaned at a young age, he remembered the parable of the rich young man in the Gospel, who Jesus advises to sell everything and share with the poor, if he *really* wants to be perfect [whole and all-perfect], and have incorruptible treasure in Heaven. On this advice, Nicholas answered the high calling of a priestly life, and used his whole inheritance to assist the needy, the sick, and the suffering. It was his willingness to be **'Poor in Spirit'**; to detach from the things of the flesh [carnal-ego self] and the old world – from possessions, people, and places – in pure zeal for becoming fully himself in Jesus Christ, that equipped him to totally dedicate his life to **the two sides of human need: that of Spiritual [Light-] poverty, and material poverty [in the sense of abject, and essential need].** For while Light-poverty is ultimately the greater ill, and the root cause of all lack [and lack of sharing], and ultimately Eternal death, Light-poverty and material poverty are inextricably linked.

Made Bishop of Myra while still a young man, Nicholas lived an authentically Eucharistic and unfettered life. His, was a life of very great prayer and fasting, and of self-giving [sacrificial] works, in pure divine service of God. This whole-hearted commitment to a Life of Charity, meant that he quickly became known throughout the land for his generosity to those in need; his dedication to protecting children, and his concern for sailors. Yet, he suffered greatly for his *living* faith, and found himself exiled and imprisoned. Upon his release, he attended the Council of Nicaea in 325, where he heroically defended the Church against heresy. Upon his mortal death, in c.343 in Myra, Bishop Nicholas was buried in his Cathedral Church, where a unique liquid relic called *"Manna"*, formed in his grave. Widely recognized as having extraordinary healing powers, this mysterious liquid [which the Greeks called *"Myron"*], is extracted every year on May 9th, which is the 'Feast of the Translation' of his relics from Myra-Turkey to Bari-Italy. Due to the very many miracles attributed to his intercession, Bishop Nicholas, who was canonised a Saint within one century of his death, continues to inspire great devotion, and is also known as 'Nicholas the Wonderworker'.

As we look forward to the Christmas season, St. Nicholas helps us to understand the true and perennial [supernatural] Christmas Spirit, in the Life of Charity. For although Charity is a much-used word [or concept], current day conceptions are much impacted by its wide application to organisations that help others; a practice which began in the late 18th century. Because of this familiarity, when we think of Charity, we tend to think about *"giving back"*, giving *"to Charity"* or doing something *"for Charity"*, in the manner of formal, periodic, and sporadic acts of alms-giving and benevolence; by way of money [fund-raising and donations]; food or other material goods; and time. While all such genuine efforts are necessary, and express man's intrinsically positive desire to give and to share, all express a misplaced and atrophied view of what Charity is, as described in Sacred Scripture; most particularly in Jesus own Life and teachings. For all intellectual, emotional and third person conceptions and expressions, in terms of individual acts of sympathy, service, and otherness; express Charity as something apart from God, and ourselves [undivided] in God. All are caught up with some degree of self-love and sentimentality; with self-esteem and conquests; and with weighing and measuring possession, gains, and losses in the flesh [the carnal ego-self], and the old world. All inspire man to look primarily to himself for the answer to problems, rather than firstly and continually turning back to *"God [who] is Charity"* 1 John 4:8,16, and who is the One source and supply of all that is truly good.

Appearing over three hundred times in the New Testament, the word Charity was originally demarcated with the Greek word *"Agape"* meaning *"Divine Love"*. This Greek word became *"Charity"* in the 4th century, when St. Jerome translated the bible from Greek to Latin, and used the Latin word *"Charitas"* in his translation. It is here in its more original context, that the richness of all that Charity is, is appropriately articulated, in fidelity to Jesus Christ's own Wholeness [Holiness] of Life. For **Sacred Scripture identifies Charity as God's**

own All-pure and highest Love, operating in His Divine Will [Cosmic Heart's Desire]. God is Spirit and action, and Charity is His Whole-Hearted and Self-less Love in action [in His Divine Will], made manifest in His Son-God Jesus Christ. The Charity of God says St. Hildegard of Bingen, is expressed in His offering us salvation [healing] and restoration to His Kingdom, by sending us His *"Only-Begotten Son" John 1:14,18,* as the atonement [at-One-ment] for our sins. He does this, not because we Loved Him, but because He has first Loved us [1 John 4: 9-10]. Our only right response to God's Charity, is therefore to receive and return His Love [in His Divine Will]; Loving Him above all things for His sake, and Loving our neighbour as ourself [not by the light of natural reason, feelings, and emotions, but] as Truth. **This is the full and complete expression of Charity [Love in action], which is nothing less than who we really are, as creatively Eucharistic beings *living* the Mass, by way of our healing and re-creation [re-birth], in the Divine-Human Personhood of Jesus Christ.**

This perfect [whole and all-perfect] cruciform pattern of interior and exterior life, is nowhere better demonstrated than in the unearthly, earthly life of our Blessed Mother. Ever-attentive to knowing and promptly responding to the Divine Will, Sacred Scripture tells us that upon finding herself the bearer of God, she hurried a long distance over mountainous terrain to visit her cousin Elizabeth. A journey undertaken for the purpose of first sharing Him [the Ever-lasting Good News] with her, as well as helping her [for a period of three months], both with household chores and responsibilities, and with Spiritual preparations for the birth of her child [John the Baptist]. Church mystics [such as Blessed Anne Catherine Emmerich and Venerable Mary of Agreda], tell us that this state of Heavenly-mindedness and attentiveness to earthly good, was all-pervading in her life, as she whole-heartedly communed with God, and engaged in acts of Charity towards the Spiritually and materially poor, whom He put in her path.

Walking in our Blessed Mother's perfect example, Bishop Nicholas, also understood that even the smallest act of Charity fused in Jesus Christ, such as a sip of Spiritual or actual water to someone who is thirsty, nourishes the receiver while being of immense Eternal value to the giver. Rather than fettered with the prideful notion of giving of one's own, he, like Mary, understood that every pure, creative act of Charity united in Jesus Christ [as with the multiplication of the loaves and the fish] is never diminished, but rather multiplied [in Him] when shared. Gifted with Spiritual wealth, and a maternal Love for souls, he embodied in his being while on earth the transformational multiplication of good. **Like Mary, Charity was the very substance of his being [in Jesus Christ].**

> *"For as the body apart from the spirit is dead, even so faith apart from works is dead."*
>
> James 2:26.

To understand the **cruciform pattern of Charity**, the Church identifies earthly moral virtues, as completion of the three Heavenly [theological] virtues of faith, hope, and Charity, While the theological virtues perfect our direct [vertical] relationship with God in our interior being, the moral virtues perfect our [horizontal] relationship with our neighbour [in God]. The chief earthly moral virtues of prudence, justice, fortitude, and temperance [continence], together with other moral virtues, oppose the Spiritual poverty of the capital sins [pride, avariciousness, lust, sloth, greed, anger, and envy], which are the source and cause of other sins. They guide, strengthen, safeguard, and perfect the human will [heart's desire], in accordance with the inviolable Truth of Jesus Christ.

- Prudence, as opposed to avarice for earthly gains;
- Humility, as opposed to pride;
- Gentleness and patience, as opposed to anger;
- Brotherly Love, as opposed to envy;
- Chastity [holy purity; wholeness and wisdom] as opposed to lust, and dis-orderly use of the five senses;
- Zeal and diligence [in good], as opposed to laziness and slothfulness; and
- Temperance, as opposed to gluttony.

Further guidelines are offered by way of the seven chief Spiritual and Corporeal Works of Mercy, which operate together for the good of man, and all things through him. Man has a divine calling to practice both the Spiritual and Corporeal Works of Mercy, in order to learn to eliminate Light-poverty and material destitution, by walking upright in Jesus Christ. This means relinquishing the desires and ways of the flesh [carnal ego-self], and the old world, and the works of evil, to establish the standards of the new world [new earth], by praying for, and sharing what is required for Spiritual [Eternal] as well as bodily [temporal] life.

The Chief Spiritual Works of Mercy, are seven:

- To admonish the sinner*;
- To instruct the ignorant**;
- To cancel the doubtful;
- To comfort the sorrowful;
- To bear wrongs patiently;
- To forgive all injuries; and
- To pray for the living, and the dead.

The Chief Corporal Works of Mercy, are also seven:

- To feed the hungry;
- To give drink to the thirsty;
- To clothe the naked;
- To visit the imprisoned;
- To shelter the homeless;
- To visit the sick; and
- To bury the dead.

[* and ** In these Spiritual works, we must keep in mind that Jesus always holds perfect balance between Truth and grace; between Mercy and Justice. He speaks only Truth, but forces no one to return to Him. Even when approached, He asks people what they *really* want from Him (e.g., Matthew 20:32; John 5:6). He advises His disciples to *"let the (Spiritually) dead bury the (Spiritually) dead"* Matthew 8:22, and to *"shake the dust off (their) feet"* Matthew 10:14, and move on, when faced with those who will not hear or receive (conceive) Truth. He allows people to come or walk away in the freedom of their own human will (heart's desire), because human freedom to move towards Light or darkness flows from the Father's own omnipotence. And as Satan pulled one third of Angels with him to earth, not all human souls are destined for (desirous of) the Kingdom. Never therefore is He found campaigning, fighting, or lobbying for change. For to misrepresent the Light by passive or active insistence is to embody force, unrest, and fighting. It is to drive those mired in darkness, into greater darkness or uselessly (by egoic guilt or fear) towards (but not towards) Light. It is to disturb the peace of God within our own soul. Therefore, while the Spiritual works of Mercy are essential to the mission of the Church on earth, we are advised to exercise discretion, and not be overkeen to instruct others, because we are all at fault in different ways (James 3:1). We speak the Truth in Love as to grow up into Jesus Christ (Ephesians 4:15), and channel persistence (only) into Spiritual works of *living* prayer and reparation, for the sake of everyone and everything].

Who is our neighbour?

Living the Life of Charity means Loving our neighbour as ourself. Jesus emphasized Love of God and of neighbour for God's sake, as the entire law, while St. Paul counsels us that of the three theological virtues [of faith, hope, and Charity], it is Charity which is greatest. Sacred Scripture also tells us, that any gift [from God such as healing, prophesy, or speaking in tongues] or helpful or heroic deed, exercised without the Light-freedom of authentic Charity [Love in action] is empty [1 Corinthians 13:1-13], because **faith receives Life only from, and by way of, Charity.** Only the Light of faith made operative by Charity [Galatians 5:6] can justify us, says St. Paul and St. John.

> *"Each one, according to his condition,*
> *ought to exert himself for the salvation of souls,*
> *for this exercise lies at the root of a holy will."*
>
> God the Father speaks to St. Catherine of Siena.

To this end [fulfilment], and guided by the Spiritual and Corporeal works of Mercy, we understand that this means more than the sharing of mammon [money and material goods]. It means sharing our time, as well as our forgiveness, prayers, fasting and self-sacrifice [self-giving] for the good of all. **We give not only what we have [been given], but who we are, [from what we have first received] in Jesus Christ,** because in the sacrament of Baptism, we entered into union with all souls [past, present, and future] in Him. **We are all members of one another in the Mystical Body of Christ, and holiness [wholehearted fullness of being] is not for oneself alone, but for all God's people and creation which** *"groans and travails in pain"* Romans 8:22 **and** *"waits with eager expectation, for the children of God to be revealed"* Romans 8:19. It is therefore the Father's Divine Will that we operate as salt and Light [Matthew 5:13–14]; ever-preserved in Truth, and acting with integrity; in conscious awareness of the weaknesses in ourselves and in others. For as our brother's and sister's keeper and salvation [Genesis 4:9; Leviticus 19:17; Matthew 16:23, 25:40], we are required not to dispose, tempt, or expose others to sin and corruption, or abide, or keep company with those who do. We are rather, to take the part of Mary, placing the Christ-Child which longs to be born within our souls, in safety. While to resist awareness of our own and others conception and birthing struggle, and our responsibility to act with integrity, is to take the part of the enemy [Matthew 16:21-23].

When we consider who or what our neighbour is, we might be inclined to think of those people around us, and the people that come into our path in life. While this conception is not incorrect, it is in looking to the Hebrew, and more particularly the Aramaic language, in the context of the first two [and greatest] commandments, that we can arrive at a much more complete appreciation of all that is our *"neighbour"*. For while the Hebrew conception of the word means *"a person that is near or close"*, the Aramaic [*"kareb"*] goes further, to encompass anyone who is physically present to us, as well as anyone that we think of, or focus our attention upon. In this frame, our neighbour also includes those who have passed from this world* and even those who have yet to come. Further still, by looking to the Hebrew and Aramaic meaning of the word *"self"* as written in the commandment to *"Love your neighbour as yourself"* Matthew 22:39; Mark 12:31, as inseparable from the first commandment to Love God above all else, and with the entirety of our being [Matthew 22:37; Mark 12:30], we arrive at a yet more full and integrated view. For the word *"self"* [*"nephesh"*] in Hebrew, used interchangeably to mean *"soul"* or *"spirit"*, speaks of the living Spirit [and Soul] of God in all living beings, with life in the blood. While the same word in Aramaic [*"nafsha"* or *"naphsha"*], used interchangeably to mean *"soul"* or *"being"*, speaks of *"self"* as the *"breath of life"*. In these constructs, **to Love our neighbour as our *"self"*, and to Love God above all else with the entirety of our being, is to Love the living Spirit [and Soul] of God in all living beings in the One Cosmic Life-breath [or consciousness] of the Holy Spirit.** This includes not only ourselves, and all people, but all living creatures, who were committed to man's care and keep [meaning *"to exercise great care over"* in Hebrew] in the garden of Eden [Genesis 1:26,28; 2:15; 9:1-2].

[*The souls in Purgatory depend entirely upon our assistance, while our prayers and good works for their deliverance, makes powerful their intercession for us (Catechism, No. 958)].

> *"Oh, if you only knew the torments, they [the souls in Purgatory suffer], you would continually offer them the alms of the Spirit, and pay off their debt to My Justice."*
>
> Jesus speaks to St. Faustina [Divine Mercy].

To conceive of Life as Charity [Love in action] in full realization of who our neighbour is, and in the ordering of all creation, is to be aware that this means firstly the human person who is created in the image and likeness of God [Genesis 1:26-27], and in whom the Kingdom of God is seeded, centred, and restored. And as all living creatures were declared *"good"* Genesis 1:21,25,31, and blessed by God, the healthfulness of our relationship with God, cannot be separated from the healthfulness of our relationship with His living creatures. All share in the Father's Covenant of Love. All are imbued with a beating heart, and living soul [memory, will and intellect], and with intelligence and purpose. All are part of the One living Spirit and beating Heart of creation - albeit not in the same way as man. All have life in Jesus Christ through whom, and for whom all things are made [John 1:1], and all have a future in the new Heaven and new earth where *"No hurt shall be done; no life taken* Isaiah 11:9. Sacred Scripture tells us that after the fall - because of man's sin, God had to make clothing for Adam and Eve out of animal skins [Genesis 3:21]. And while He relates His heart-ache in foreknowledge of the awful hurt and damage caused by man's failure to live up to his true task, privilege, and purpose of being, He undertakes to gradually teach man again about the sacredness of life, and right treatment of His living creatures.

Among Old Testament Mosaic Covenant directions to the Israelites, is the instruction not to turn a blind eye to a stray animal, or an animal in distress, regardless of who owns it, and to avoid overworking or unduly straining or muzzling them [Exodus 23:4-5; Deuteronomy 22:10, 25:4]. Noah is commanded to take two of each animal into the Ark to avoid the Flood [Genesis 6:19-20], and after the Flood, he is instructed not to eat meat with blood in it [Genesis 9:4 and Leviticus 7:26]. Animals are the first creatures to give glory to the God-Child upon His delivery to earth, while Jesus teaches about God's Love and providential care for His living creatures [Luke 12:6; Matthew 6:26;10:29], and man's caring responsibility towards them [Luke 13:15; 14:5]. A duty which requires not only avoiding passive neglect and mistreatment, but proactively stepping up to assist them. **Man's restoration to the Kingdom, must then involve aliveness to, and living up to his responsibility for God's living creatures, who share in its promise, as well as the plant life and ecological systems on which all life depends.**

> *"I will weep and wail for the mountains, and lament for the pastures of the wilderness, because they are burned up, so that no one passes through; men can't hear the voice of the livestock. Both the birds of the sky and the animals have fled." They are gone."*
>
> Jeremiah 9:10.

To co-operate with God, as a dynamic participator in the undoing of evil, and the restoration of the Kingdom, must begin with [Spiritualized] Love of ourselves; which involves reverence of, and fidelity to, the image and likeness of God within our being. For while it is the passions and appetites of the pleasure, comfort, and esteem-seeking *"old man"* [less willing and disposed to receive the higher imperishable gifts of the Spirit], that thoughtlessly and mercilessly violates, poisons, and desecrates life on earth; it is the healthfulness of the **self-forgetting and aware** *"new man"* that recovers and restores it, by way of returning to his primordial way of God-being [John 10:34], rooted in the complete I AM of Jesus Christ. This seeing all that is our neighbour in Jesus Christ, is the reverse of seeing them as a means to glorify our own ends. It is the continuous act of receiving and sharing His Light [Life-consciousness], which flows within and through our healed and re-generated [re-birthed] soul.

In the most excellent example of **graceful [grace-filled] simplicity of desire, and glad sharing in the everyday life of the Holy Family of Nazareth**, let us take to heart our responsibility and high purpose during our fleeting gift of days on earth. Let us desire for ourselves and for all, the imperishable Light-riches of the Spirit, while treading most lightly upon the earth, and in harmony with all of God's people, living creatures and creation. For all that we have done to all that is our neighbour, we have done to Jesus Christ [Matthew 25:40].

Charity begins at Home

In its simplest form, Charity means a continuous attitude of thoughtfulness and respect. Issuing from the Home-ground of our being, it means continual awareness of, and respect for, the presence of God in ourselves and in others. It means continual aliveness to the *true* Spiritual and material needs and conveniences of others, and our example to, and influence on them, beginning with those who God puts in our lives, and on our path. And as both sin and Charity arise in every thought, we must immediately renounce sinful and uncharitable thoughts, which judge, tempt, expose, and increase others' struggles and limitations without Charity. We must renounce thoughts which put our self-centred opinions ahead of the needs and good of others; and which obstructs the good that God wants to do. Charity to all, is also Charity to ourself, because to withhold Charity from one's neighbour is to withhold it from oneself [be in bondage]. It is to be Light-poor, and to deprive others of the Light, because **man cannot be *truly* blessed by God, if he is not willing to be a blessing to all that is his neighbour [2 Corinthians 9:6-8].** Each and every act against true Charity, causes a human and Cosmic ripple effect, affecting [limiting, or derailing] what others think, say, and [can] do, thus blocking the propagation of the Kingdom of God, while propelling the kingdom of Satan. Charity then means continual awareness that everything depends upon our personal state of God-being [John 10:34] and Good-being [as tried, tested, and perfected in relation to our neighbour], which alone allows us to *validly* co-operate with and participate in God, in a dynamic circle of self-giving and healing, that includes everyone and everything [past, present, and future] in Jesus Christ. See 'self-forgetting' in Useful Terms, and Chapters on 'Fiat' and 'The Scales of Justice'.

> *"To act against Charity is an incalculable misfortune...*
> *for every act of Charity honours God, and*
> *makes Him known, and makes Him Loved."*
>
> Jesus speaks to Sr. Mary of the Holy Trinity.

An ever-expanding circle of giving and receiving

In its reciprocal operation of giving and receiving, Charity does not promote one-sidedness; nor is it an end in itself. Rather, **Charity commands that everyone give, as to be drawn into the circle of giving and receiving. For everyone is poor in their estrangement from Light-union with God, and everyone is needy in their need to receive from, and give out of, the abundance of God's goodness, who is the One true source and supply of all that is *truly* good.** In confessing our need for *"our daily bread"* in the Our Father prayer, we recognize God our Father as the source of all [good] supply. We confess our collective need for daily Spiritual and material sustenance, which He provides by way of his own Perfect [Whole and All-Perfecting] example of dynamic work and rest [in His work]. And as it is more blessed to give than to receive [Acts 20:35], we wisely and gladly share [what we have received, and who we are in Him] with others, starting with those in our lives and our parish, knowing that what counts before God, is the good will with which we give what we know, and what He knows, we can, in the sheer Light of Truth. For on the irreversible Day of Judgement, **Charity is the standard by which**

every life will be judged [Matthew 25:31-46 and 1 Corinthians 13:13].

"It is more blessed to give than to receive."
Acts 20:35.

In matters of material Charity, we recognize that work and effort is laid out in the beginning of the Old Testament: *"You will eat bread by the sweat of your face until you return to the ground"* Genesis 3:19. A frank teaching that is affirmed in the New Testament, most notably in Jesus own Parable of the Talents [Matthew 23:14-30]. With this parable, Jesus exhorts active and responsible use of our gifts, talents, and resources, according to what we have received, as well as God's vital interest in our motivations and intentions, and the results of our efforts. An instruction which is reaffirmed by St. Paul, who advises us to work for the bread that we eat [2 Thessalonians 3:10], and in so doing, *"work heartily, as for the Lord and not for [the esteem of] men"* Colossians 3:23. The book of Proverbs carries strong warnings about laziness, and slothfulness [from the Greek word *"nothros"* meaning an interior state of sluggishness, monotony, and lack of zeal]. All speak of the absence of discipline, and the wakeful dynamism of the Spirit of God. All speak of unwillingness to enter in to the circle of giving and receiving the blessed life of Charity, for the good of all, and for the sake of the Kingdom. Every man, unless genuinely prohibited [e.g., by mental or physical sickness or infirmity, age, caring responsibilities, or other circumstances], must then be responsible for themselves, and for those under their care. They must work to earn a living, and partake in everyday tasks and responsibilities. They must avoid a sense of entitlement, and making of themselves a burden to, or user of others, for the sake of ease or advantage. St. Paul instructs the faithful to step back from idle or opportunistic people - not counting them as the enemy, but admonishing them as brothers [2 Thessalonians 3:15], that the consequences of their actions teach them what they will not otherwise learn. For God finds guilty not only evildoers, but those who abide, or keep company with them [Ezekiel 3:17-21, 33:7-9; 2 Corinthians 6:14-18 and Ephesians 5:11-12].

> *"He looked up and saw the rich people who were putting their gifts into the treasury. He saw a certain poor widow casting in two small brass coins. And He said, "Truly I tell you, this poor widow put in more than all of them, for all these put in gifts for God from their abundance, but she, out of her poverty, put in all that she had to live on.""*
>
> Luke 21:1-4 [Mark 12:41-44].

Charity abides in Truth

Pure acts of Charity abide in Truth, and manifest only Truth [1 Corinthians 13:6]. One with the Love and Divine Will of God, they oppose encouraging the singular or collective waywardness of wrong-thinking, wrong-doing and ultimately wrong-being. For the purpose and goal of Charity, in a motive of *true* compassion [from the Greek word *"splagna"* meaning guts], and *true* kinship, is fidelity to God in Jesus Christ. **To** *"walk in Charity, which is the bond of perfection"* **Colossians 3:14 is to** *"put on Jesus Christ"* **Romans 13:14 and Galatians 3:27 [Ephesians 4:13-16 and Colossians 3:14-16].** This is the fulfilment of God-being [John 10:34] and Good-being, because the healed and re-generated soul is drawn into the Light-circle of giving and receiving the Life of Love in the Divine Will, by way of conceiving and birthing the fullness of *real Life and purpose* in Jesus Christ.

Man must then keep right balance between Truth and grace, because on the Day of Judgement, everyone is personally judged, not only on what he did wrong, but on what he could have done, and what he could have done better [sins of omission] in himself, and for his neighbour. A state of equilibrium, which also requires co-operation with and participation in the circle of receiving forgivingness for our sins, while offering forgiveness to others for their sins. In this divine work made possible by grace [in sacramental Confession], everyone is gifted with the opportunity to be set free from the bondage of sin and evil, and return to their original state of glory [blissful magnificence] in God. See 'Sin' in Useful Terms and Chapter on 'The Scales of Justice'.

> *"But speaking Truth in Love [Charity], we may grow up in all things into Him, who is the Head, Christ."*
>
> Ephesians 4:15.

Supernatural grace makes perfect [whole and all-perfect] acts of Charity possible. This is because pure exterior action done by God, and for God, can only flow from the interior guiding action of the Holy Spirit within the disposed soul [John 16:13]. Man, naturally tends towards outward appearances, and to perceiving human standards of good [as they relate to the flesh and the old world], while Charity must be discerned and ordered to Eternal standards of absolute good and Spiritual reality [as they relate to the Oneness of Jesus Christ-consciousness]. Only the Holy Spirit knows the nature and extent of anyone's true needs [in respect of both giving and receiving] and how they should be fulfilled [in the right way, and in right timing], which beyond the immediate and categorically obvious, is not always what we imagine them to be, according to appearances. Sacred Scripture warns us too, that **the Children of the Kingdom [wheat], can be so similar in appearance to those of Satan's children [chaff], that they will only be known and separated at Judgement [Matthew 13: 25-28].** The smiling face and friendly countenance may conceal the worst inner torment, self-centredness, or seething malice. Judas Iscariot's deceitful attempts to manipulate Mary Magdalene's use of perfumed ointment, demonstrates the appearance of good works for wrong motives [John 12:3-8], while his kiss of betrayal that marked Jesus for execution, demonstrates the most hideous treachery and deception of which the human heart is capable. This also teaches us that man's attempts to do greater works according to his own human will [heart's desire], but without God, and therefore not for His glory [in Jesus Christ], are without value in the Spiritual realm and perish.

For the sake of true Charity, the Holy Spirit allows us to discern between **remedial and redemptive suffering** [See Chapter on 'Prayer']. Remedial suffering, which manifests in all manner of mental and physical afflictions, dis-eases, and calamities, points to something that needs to be resolved in one's way of life, or ancestral bloodline [Exodus 20:5, 34:7; Deuteronomy 5:9], and may involve the need for release from the works of evil spirits. Let us therefore always call upon the guidance of the Holy Spirit, who alone can reliably determine anyone's soul-condition, as well as what is [ultimately] needed, in the right way, in right timing, and in harmony with the measure [degree] of Light-union to be realized, in the ordering of Divine Providence. See pp. 237-238 in Chapter on 'Agape'.

The freedom of pure Charity

In the hiddenness of St. Nicholas [and Santa Claus, who comes and goes in the night], we also learn to avoid, as far as is practically possible, outward displays of Charity. Sacred Scripture tells us, that the celestial reward from our Father is given only if we *willingly* bypass [are disinterested in] the earthly reward. This is because true Charity is divine service to God, for His pleasure and glory alone, in a state of aliveness to the operation of sanctifying grace. Purposively or carelessly outward works, for personal advantage; for familiarity, esteem, or creating fleshy [carnal-ego] alliances and investments, although validated by the flesh [carnal ego-self] and the old world, cannot bear the fragrance of the Spirit, but rather carry the odour of pride and vainglory. These works, which give the name of being alive to those who are dead [Revelation 3:1], are found worthless in the Spiritual realm.

[*While the human conscious naturally works on the principle of contradiction - that something cannot be true and untrue at the same time, this is not the case at the Spiritual level. The hidden and public Life of Jesus maintained perfect continuity of Charity. While He did not call out 'doing Charity', He did not avoid doing what needed to be done for the good of souls, and to fulfil His mission. So, although He often went to quiet places to pray and His interior Life was unknown, in His public ministry He was (in a sense) known. While, by adopting the anti-title *"Son of Man"*, and referring all glory to the Father, He remained free. In this way He taught us secrecy in the interior life (as superior to the exterior life), as well as how to 'get out of ourselves' in the exterior life; allowing ourselves and each other to be free, as all glory is returned to the Father in Jesus Christ. Charity then requires discernment according to the act involved. We may opt for anonymity while sharing money and materiality, but we do not forsake helping others as inspired by the Holy Spirit. Nor do we avoid attending Church – e.g., Holy Hour or additional Masses for the good of our souls, and all souls].

> *"But when you do merciful deeds, don't let*
> *your left hand know what your right hand does,*
> *so that your merciful deeds may be in secret, then*
> *your Father who sees in secret will reward you openly."*
>
> Matthew 6:3-4.

With heart's purified by the action of the Holy Spirit, we can recognize the giving in the receiving. We honour the reality that **true Charity is the full *substance and depth* of God's work of grace within and through us, and not our own;** *"…freely you received…so freely give"* Matthew 10:8. All has already been done [enabled] by Jesus Christ, who is present in every pure act of Charity, done in Him, in the creative power of the Holy Spirit. God has first given to [blessed and provided for] us, that we may give to [bless and provide for] others. The charitable giver, having first received from God in order to give, is blessed in giving, while the receiver is blessed in receiving, and having given the giver the opportunity to give. The receiver is inspired to give, and the giver is inspired to receive, and to give more. In this dynamic circle of giving and receiving, the giver and receiver remain dis-interested [non-attached] towards one another, knowing that all is the operation of God [Philippians 2:13], without whom we can do nothing [John 15:5]. **Both giver and receiver remain free ['Poor in Spirit'], as all praise and thanksgiving is ordered and returned to God the Father, in Jesus Christ.**

Knowing what Charity is, we avoid the pitfall of judging others according to what they are perceived to do or not do outwardly, and therefore according to the deceptive standards and appearances of the flesh [carnal ego-self] and the old world [Romans 14:3; Matthew 6:1-18; Luke 22:25-26]. **Only God knows our soul-condition. Only He knows what genuine Charity we have done or omitted, as well our purity of motivation and intention in any act of Charity.** Further, as some souls are called [invited] to a more exterior life, and others to a more interior life, in the Father's Cosmic ordering, He requires more [interior or exterior self-giving], of some and less of others, which means that even the lowest degree of divine service can be a soul's highest degree of Light-union [Fr. Johannes Tauler]. True Charity is not then subject to faulty fleshy [carnal-ego] standards, projections, and judgements, that perceives more or less in oneself or in another; or that flatters or criticises another.

True charity cancels:

- The self-centredness of weighing, measuring, and hoarding, and unwillingness to give or receive freely and graciously;
- The self-glorification of wanting to be seen to be doing good in oneself; in violation of the Truth of our being in God, or to the detriment of another's healing and transformation;
- The presumption of expecting to attain to sanctity by personal prayers and pious acts, apart from our neighbour;
- The inverted pride of seeking to, or acting only in, anonymity; not recognizing or exemplifying all good work as God's work in and through the soul;
- All thanklessness, expectation, and unwillingness to be responsible and accountable for using and sharing the gifts, talents, and resources we have received.

True Charity is stable and does not flourish in one instance [by human emotions and standards of sympathy, concern, guilt, need, and gratitude], and disappear in the next. For to learn to live the Life of Charity, is to conceive, and learn to live in the unimpeded Light-flow of the One community [family] of Heaven, where there will be no *'yours'* and *'mine'*. Like the natural sun, which freely gives Light, warmth, and life to all, without calling attention to its works; all is free and all is given.

> *"The purer and more refined the soul is in faith,*
> *the more infused Charity it possesses...the more the Holy Spirit*
> *illuminates it, and communicates His gifts, because Charity*
> *is the means by which they are communicated."*
>
> St. John of the Cross.

Walking upright in Charity

To this glorious end [fulfilment], the One absolute and most pleasing act of Charity, is the interior work of conceiving and birthing Jesus Christ [the Spiritual state of the Kingdom] within and through our soul. This Eucharistic work, is grounded in the everyday work of pure redemptive suffering, bearing with ourselves, and with others in the trials and contradictions of life [which test our selflessness and purity of heart], while silently uniting our every act [thought, word, and deed], with those of Jesus Christ. It is the work of drawing and sharing Light; being the shield and mirror eye that is the perfect reflection of another in Jesus Christ, through whom they [and everyone and everything] can too know Him, the One absolute reality. It is the work of abolishing Light-poverty - the ultimate source of all lack [and lack of sharing], while building up the Kingdom of God. It is the greatest gift we can receive from God, and give to others, and to all suffering creatures and creation.

Let us then celebrate the Life-giving freedom of Charity, which unites God and man, in the dynamic Life of Love in action. Let us relish also, the spirit of joy and Charity in the tradition of Santa Claus's gift-giving at Christmas time, keeping before our minds the excellent example of St. Nicholas, who points us to the fullness of Charity. For Charity as the continuous 'breaking the bread' of our being as a way of Life, is God's personal Love for us in action, by way of Jesus Christ; the One

Life of All. It is the liberated Life, and the ultimate [complete circle of] worship that God desires from us, because it means carrying and *living* the Mass as an entire way of being. It is the Light-bearing life that makes the boundless I AM of Jesus Christ, not only the Heart of our soul, but the Heart of the world, as we are restored to the complete *living* expression of who we really are in Him. That's the true and perennial [supernatural] Christmas Spirit, that never ends!

> *"God in His wisdom, has [decreed]*
> *that He will reward no work but His own."*

Fr. Johannes Tauler [The Illuminated Doctor].

The Holy Angels

Glory, peace, and goodwill; earthly peace vs celestial peace; the divine purpose and effects of music, singing and all creativity vs the devastating impacts of ungodly works; the scent and music of the soul; the splendour and extraordinary offices of the three Spheres and nine Choirs [Armies] of Angels.

"And suddenly, there was with the Angel, a multitude of the celestial Army praising God and saying, 'Glory to God in the Highest, and on earth, peace to men of good will!'"

Luke 2:13-14.

As the time of the great and wonderful, prophetic fulfilment draws near, the choirs of Angels assemble with faithful souls, to keep watch for Christmas morning. Together with them, we are struck with wonder that Bethlehem in the land of Judah, is preparing to offer a humble cave to contain the One whom nothing can contain; the Pre-Eternal infant God.

The Gospel tells us of the Father's divine intervention, making known to the world the birth of His Beloved Son and our Saviour [Healer], Jesus Christ. We anticipate the amazement and terror of the shepherds abiding in their fields, and keeping watch over their flocks, when suddenly the vault of Heaven opens before their eyes, and shining all around them is a host of the most pure, gracious, and resplendent Spirits, making display of their rapture and delight. In a burst of vaulting song, the jubilant and upshift sound of the Gloria fills the night air, and resounds beyond the furthest star.

To understand the theme of the Angels exultant hymn of praise, is to understand the key tenets of our *faith as* Children of God. For in the words of this hymn, we are given to understand the reasons that the uncreated God became man, and that all glory [blissful magnificence] and honour belongs to Him. The birth of the Divine Child, fulfils God's glory and brings peace to all men, because Jesus Christ who is the cause and centre of the Angelic world, came to *"unite all things in Himself, those in Heaven and those on earth"* Ephesians 1:10. It is therefore right that we come together always in fellowship with the Angels, in prayer, song and adoration.

> *"For in Him was created everything in Heaven and on earth, visible and invisible, whether thrones, or dominations, or principalities, or powers. All things were created through Him and in Him."*
>
> Colossians 1:16.

- **Glory** indicates the divine splendour and power of our Creator God and Father, as well as the glorification which He finds in His works of Creation, Redemption and Sanctification, centred in the faithful and true *"Children of Light"* Luke 16:18; John 12:36; Ephesians 5:8; 1 Thessalonians 5:5. As His created beings, existing upon His Life-breath, we are to give glory to Him [and our being in Him], by gladly offering back to Him our human will [heart's desire], and Loving Him like the Angels, as our Beloved Life-source and destiny.

- **Peace** at the natural level, denotes a deep interior rest within our soul in this earthly life. It is that which frees us from fear, distress, and conflict, and which requires a demonstration of goodwill on our part. Distinct from the counterfeit peace offered by the old world and Satan, and which is pleasing to the flesh [carnal ego-self], but detrimental to the spirit, it means the forgiveness [releasing] of sin, which restores our relationship with God, and with our neighbour in God. However, Sacred Scripture as well as the Aramaic [*"shlama"*] and Hebrew [*"shalom"*] words for peace, point to a celestial peace, which is much more profound. In these frames, it carries meaning that is akin to that which contains all possibilities and potentialities; all surrender, deliverance, and fulfilment. And so, when we speak of peace, we really speak of the transfigured Edenic state, realized [made real] in the Cosmic Divine-Human Personhood of Jesus Christ: *"for He [Christ] is our peace"* Ephesians 2:14. This is *"...the peace of God, which passes all [human] understanding, [and] will guard your hearts and your minds in Christ Jesus"* Philippians 4:7. This is the peace which the Angelic hymn extols, and which is gifted to those with whom God is well-pleased. See 'peace' in Useful Terms.

- **Good will** is the first cause of the Father's actions and blessings, which is His own Love [*"Agape"*] operating in His Divine Will. It is offered to all men, and is received through the Light of sanctifying grace. We share this good will from the treasury of Heaven, through fidelity to the Life of the *"Fiat"*, and with those whom God puts in our lives.

As we join in company with the Angels, in singing the Gloria on Christmas morning [or on any morning], we look forward to the union of praise at the end [fulfilment] of time, when man and the Angels will stand together around the throne of the Lamb, to joyfully acclaim His Divinity: *"Worthy is the Lamb who was slain, to receive power, and divinity, and wisdom, and strength, and honour, and glory, and blessing!"* Revelation 5:12.

Contemplating the beauty of Angels singing, allows us to appreciate and reverence the divine meaning and purpose of music and singing. For the original purpose of all music and singing, was for God's ear; for His joy, and for His honour and glory. In this way, it was also to serve the healthfulness of man, whose life was originally issued from the divine harmonies of God, and was ordained to uphold those harmonies, in its fully Spiritualized state.

Man's attempts to outwardly replicate these harmonies date back to the earliest times, as music and singing have continued to play a vital role in his praise and worship of God. The book of Genesis speaks of stringed [lyre harp] and wind [flute] instruments [Genesis 4:21], while all during the history of the Israelites, music featured in the celebration of victory over enemies; in religious feasts and occasions of joy; and after the building of the Temple of Jerusalem. Music, as an expression of creativity, was also held in high regard by the Hebrews. Church music was first introduced by St. Ambrose in Italy the 4th Century, in the style of simple melodies and chanting, which he learned during his residency in Antioch. The Church music that emerged thereafter, sought to retain the qualities of sanctity, that promoted an atmosphere of pure devotion. Stringed and wind instruments, offering light and upward sounds were eventually included, while percussion instruments, with their heavy and base sounds were forbidden. These methods were eventually superseded, as understanding of, and therefore the purpose of music changed, although attempts have been made to restore earlier traditions.

Across the history of time, it is perhaps among the world of the ancient Greeks, that we discover a people who had [documented] a broad and deep conception of, and reverence for, the divine purpose of music. Derived from the Greek *"mousike"*, the word *"music"* is understood to have embraced any of the arts governed by the nine Muses or *"mousa"*. These mythical daughters of Zeus, were personified creative forces, which included poetry and dance because *"mousike"* was perceived to encompass the synergistic interaction of all [musical, linguistic, visual, and kinaesthetic] art. And so, with a vital moral and ethical role in society, **music was much more than amusement. It was properly understood to be a higher power, that upheld the order and harmony of the Universe**. Its primary role, was not to please and stir up the dis-ordered carnal senses and appetites [sensuality], but to convey Truth, and draw man upwards and out of himself, inspiring him to realize the divine quality and mystery of his being in God. Taken seriously, in terms of word and sound, as affecting and imitating the character or state of our entire being [spirit, soul, and body – including the mind and heart] it had a vital, ethical role to play in helping man manage his health and passions, and mould his character. Bestowing glory and illumination in song, it is said that as the nine muses performed their *"mousike"*, great waves of Light-energy brighter than the sun, poured out. The sun itself shone brighter as they sang; the plants grew, and the leaves even reached towards them, because their Light was brighter than the sun. Even songbirds paused their own song to listen.

Wherever we look to for inspiration, to conceive of the true purpose and power of music and singing, is to conceive of the true purpose and power of our being, and the operation of the Universe. For in its authentic expression, music and singing is Spiritual in substance [essence] and in energies [action]. It is God's presence by sanctifying grace within and through the soul, that creates the song and melody of praise, to be returned to Him as His own creation, in and through all living creation; in a spirit of joyful praise and thanksgiving. Adam, in a state of sanctifying grace, began life in blissful union, with and in these divine harmonies and freedom songs. Comprising both sound and beyond sound, they united his being with the voices of all creatures, and the Angels, to sing and to uphold the hymn of his existence steeped in God. **Each and every human person, living creature, and all creation was ordained to find its home in this One '[primordial] rhythm of Life'**, **that carries the full power and melodic sound of the voice of the *Ever-living* Spirit of God.**

Upon withdrawing from Light-union, man however lost his primordial state of innocence and justice [Eternal Beatitude], and with that, he lost his ears. He lost the blessed sound of these harmonies emanating from pure joyfulness of heart and soul, in [the All-ness of] the One Life-breath and Heartbeat of God. Over the centuries, his ears have become ever more congested, if not blocked off from these divine harmonies, by the clashing din and calamity of the 'modern' world.

Immersed in selfhood and all sensuality, he also lost appreciation for all people, living creatures and creations primordial need and desire for the healthfulness of this same harmony. The twentieth century has seen a vulgarization, and debasement of music and creativity, that has served to propel a climax of existence-ignorance, perversity, and Spiritual demise. Sounds of flesh [carnal ego-selfhood] and dust, as though in unity with the fateful decision of our first parents [to divide against themselves in God] that sent us into exile, have flourished. A desperation and absurdity that reflects the dark voids in the human soul, and the sardonic works of the spirit of darkness. Making its way into every public and private space, it has served to dis-orientate and cripple, the [likewise] vulnerable and lost, while betraying the divine purpose of music, and the dignity and divine purpose of our being in God [John 10:34].

Man must first realize the magnitude of what He has lost, as to co-operate willingly and gladly with God, in the recovery of the healthfulness of his being in Him. He must appreciate that while all human creativity is the expression of man as a creative being, this innate desire [when not essentially corrupted] to bring into being something better than the reality around him, is his desire for the Kingdom of Heaven. It is a desire to return to **divinely creative activity**, that can only be realized by the continuous act of abandoning back [giving the consent of] his human will [heart's desire], to the operation of the Divine Will in every moment. This seismic re-orientation may seem difficult at first [by degree of estrangement], and especially so, amidst the commotion and rushing sounds of the old world that withhold Truth. Yet, **there ever remains within his "enfleshed" soul, a whispering Cosmic song, that is the imperishable substance-essence of his being in the Father, echoing and resounding through all His creation**. This meeting place within the soul, with the One Cosmic Heart's Desire [Divine Will] of the Father, is a place of mutual longing; the virgin space and nuptial chamber, where the child who would re-hear and re-see, would come to answer His upward call [invitation] to return Home, in the Light-embrace of Jesus Christ. Every soul in touch with the Light within, however dim, knows of this mutual desire in the rhythmic silence and sounds of nature, where it finds rest. For this desire for stillness and sacred sensing, confirms that it is not of the old world, and longs for the Homeland.

> *"Don't be drunken with wine, in which is dissipation, but be filled with the Spirit, speaking to one another in psalms, hymns, and Spiritual songs; singing and making melody in your heart to the Lord."*
>
> Ephesians 5:18-20.

In conceiving of Life as music, and music as the Life of the soul, we recognize that every human person carries Spiritual resonance [vibration] or atmosphere, relative to the inner state of Light-union or dis-union with God in Jesus Christ. Every act [thought, word, and deed] of the human person, is an emanation that carries Eternal resonance, and either positively or negatively affects everyone and everything. And **while the emanation of the soul living in union with Jesus Christ, touches Christ in other souls and in all living creation, drawing them upwards towards the Fatherland; the emanation and gravitational pull of a dis-integrated soul creates disharmony, and draws [further] darkness and chaos.**

As the most perfect [whole and all-perfect] created human person that ever lived [or will ever live], the Blessed Virgin Mary is the unparalleled exemplary of the perfect harmony of the fully Spiritualized state. An exalted state of being, expressed beautifully in her exultant hymn of praise known as 'The Magnificat' [Luke 1:46-55]. This perfectly [wholly] Spiritual song [and *living* prayer], stands as a most beautiful ode of wonder and gratitude as to the mystery and majesty of God. Extolling the excesses of His unfathomable Love for her, and for all His people, while linking His First Coming on earth, for the purpose of His Second Coming within and through our souls, it is also a most powerful battle cry for God's glory, and the restoration of His Kingdom in consenting souls.

> *"The whole world is filled with sound,*
> *and every creature has a tone."*
>
> St. Hildegard of Bingen.

A prolific composer of music, musical dramas, and liturgical plays, drawn from her *"inner ear"*, St. Hildegard's experience of what she called *"celestial harmony"*, was the privilege of tapping into *"the trumpet sound of the living Light."* Equally remarkable, she was given to understand that the Choirs [Armies] of the Lord [the Angels] *"sing with marvellous voices about the wonders that God works in blessed souls, by which He is magnificently glorified."* While, together with the Angels, those who are Love's elect among men on earth are made perfect [whole and all-perfect] again in Spiritual music and singing. For God's glorious Light-presence flowing within and through their acts [of thoughts, words, and deeds] creates the notes, the melody, and the harmony of praise. A dynamic preparation on earth, which according to the soul's degree of Light-union, will be the perpetual unfolding and flourishing of its hymn of existence in the Ever-lasting Life of Song, that is the Heavenly Homeland.

> *"The melody of a pure in heart rings so beautifully*
> *before God, that God so wounded by these earthly notes that*
> *echo in the divine spheres, flows into the soul in currents of*
> *fire and Light, raising her into His own celestial radiance,*
> *and clothing her with Ever-lasting Life."*
>
> Anon.

Through the witness of the Old and New Testament's, we can learn much about the glory [blissful magnificence] of hallowed reality, from the glory and offices of the Angels. These immaterial and incorruptible celestial beings, stand [serve] in maximum closeness to the Eternal Father, in the Light-union of the Most Holy Trinity, together with our Blessed Mother; who are honoured, praised, and blessed in them, and by them. Yet, while continuously enjoying the ecstasy of God's Light-presence, they are engaged in interpreting perfectly, and carrying out the Father's Cosmic Divine Will. All are ministering Spirits, employed in the divine service of man, even the highest and most exalted. **Organised in three Spheres and nine Choirs [Armies], according to Sacred Scripture, all are mighty and glorious beings, engaged in overthrowing Satan's kingdom of chaos and ruin, and restoring the Kingdom of Heaven.** Mentioned some one hundred and ten times in the Old Testament, and some one hundred and seventy times in the New Testament, Sacred Scripture demonstrates that God sends His Angels to announce His Divine Will; to teach, console and protect; and to correct, and punish. All receive the power of the nine Choirs [Armies], and are by way of God's Justice, not unequal in power, but different in its kind and means of expression and execution. Job tells us that the number of Angels is without number. Only God knows, and knows personally, the countless multitudes of Angels.

In the Old Testament, Angels appeared to Moses in the burning bush on Mount Sinai, and gave him the law. They appeared to Elijah, and they miraculously lead the Israelites through the Red Sea. A Spirit from the highest heights of the Seraphim, purified the lips [tongue] of Isaiah with a hot coal, and the Cherubim appeared to Ezekiel. In the New Testament, we learn of their key role in Jesus Messianic mission, and as part of God's Divine Providence over His faithful people; the New Israel. Jesus speaks personally of the Angels some twenty-one times in Sacred Scripture, and always in plural form. They play a crucial role throughout His earthly life; at His Incarnation and Nativity; when He is tempted by Satan in the desert, and on His return from the desert; in His agony in the garden of Gethsemane; and at His Resurrection. Angels intervene personally at the most challenging times in the lives of St. Peter and St. Paul. They reveal the law of God, and guide and bring messages from Him; and they provide for, admonish, and protect God's people from the works of fallen Angels.

Across the centuries, they have continued to perform extraordinary works in the lives of those who would be saints and martyrs. A Seraphic Spirit imprinted the sacred sigma on the body of St. Francis of Assisi, and wounded the heart of St. Teresa of Avila with a golden dart. Angels on occasion intervene directly in the lives of ordinary people. They minister to the souls in Purgatory, and inspire those on earth to offer them prayers, penances, and all good works.

We should therefore be clear that Angels are different beings from humans, with a different purpose in God. They do not receive the Eucharist, suffer, or co-operate with and participate in the Redemption of God's people [living creatures and creation] by way of the Cross, because they are not fallen, and they are not called to assimilate into the Divine-Human Personhood of Jesus Christ [Colossians 1:15-20]. And while we are divinely guided, protected, and comforted by them, we are not to be stirred to sentimentality. In almost every record of Angelic visitation in Sacred Scripture, their first words to the human person, including the Blessed Virgin Mary are: *"Fear not...Be not afraid"* confirming the soul's terror of holy fear [awe-filled reverence] and joy, as the All-blazing magnificence [glory] of God flowing within them, approaches the nothing-ness of created man. In the work of the Angels, we are also given to understand that the unseen world, is eminently more real, wonderful, and perilous, than the much-limited part of reality that we do see, while *"enfleshed"* on earth. Angels are responsible for works of Divine Justice, harnessing the elements, from fire and wind, to thunder and lightning, to carry out the works of God. In books such as Chronicles and Samuel, they undertake mighty military roles, slaying the enemies of God for the sake of His Kingdom. The plague over Israel when David numbered the people, through to the earthquakes at the Death and the Resurrection of Jesus Christ, was the work of Angels. Angels will take a central role in smiting and purifying the earth of wickedness [evil and ungodliness] at *"the end of the [present] times"* [Revelation 16], and then again at *"the [final] end of time"* [Revelation 20:7-15; 21], when all men will be called to Final Judgement. Sacred Scripture tells us, that in the final act of Divine Justice, the Angels will carry out

God's commands to banish the wicked [the evil and ungodly] to the infernal flames of Hell, and conduct the good to their place in the Heavenly Homeland.

> *"And I saw another strong Angel, descending from Heaven... And a rainbow was upon his head, and his face was like the sun, and his feet were like columns of fire. And he held in his hand, a small open book. And he stationed his right foot upon the sea, and his left foot upon the land. And he cried out with a great voice, in the manner of a lion roaring."*
>
> Revelation 10:1-3.
> [Matthew 16:27; 24:31; 2 Thessalonians 1:7-9].

All Churches and altars have appointed Angels, who continuously honour and reverence the continuous presence of Jesus Christ in the Blessed Sacrament, as well as guard and defend them. Persons who carry out extraordinary offices for God while on earth; from our Blessed Mother, St. Joseph, and the apostles; to popes and saints throughout the ages; all receive particularly powerful assistance from the Angels. Other holy places may also be appointed Angels from the three Spheres. It is then with great awe and joy that we salute the splendour of the three Spheres and nine Choirs [Armies] of Angels therein, in their most eminent God-like energies and extraordinary governing offices, as the formidable Armies [Choirs] of Almighty God.

The Seraphim [Isaiah 6:2,6], **the Cherubim** [Genesis 3:24, Sirach 49:8; Ezekiel 10:1-22;11:22], **and the Thrones** [Colossians 1:16], **form the first Sphere and highest rank of Angels, and adore God directly in His presence:**

❖ The **Seraphim** hover around the throne of God, tending to Him as bright blazing Light-fire, which signifies their immutable rapture of purest Love for God in Himself. Enjoying the most perfect [whole and all-perfect] unity with Him, they are full of celestial mysteries, and of zealous desire to contemplate Him, while their sacred brightness irradiates to the eight other hierarchies. This rank of Angels has many wings which like mirrors, show all the Church ranks arrayed in order.

> Let us have recourse to these most excellent Spirits, and ask them for the reign of ardent Seraphic Love of God in our hearts, and in all hearts.

❖ The **Cherubim** took up place with the flaming sword at the gates of Paradise, *"to guard the way to the Tree of Life"* Genesis 3:24, after Adam and Eve's expulsion. They are the power by which God's chariot or throne mystically takes flight [Ezekiel 1:14-28]. They also take position above the Ark of the Covenant, where God promised to dwell among His people. Full of eyes to represent their vast intelligence, and of wings, they primarily adore God in His Divine Providence, and communicate Light to the other Choirs [Armies], thus signifying their depth of knowledge of God, by which they see celestial secrets. This Choir [Army] foresees all the human souls who will consent to know the true God; nobly and justly directing their human will [heart's desire] like wings towards Him. Satan, once known as Lucifer [meaning 'Light-Bearer'] is understood to have been originally among this rank [Ezekiel 28:16 and Saint Thomas Aquinas, Summa]. This is why he is so very influential and treacherous, and is the cause of all manner of Spiritual and physical afflictions, and dis-eases. Jesus counselled His closest disciples, that they would need to both pray and fast, to drive out the most virulent of demonic spirits [Mark 9:17–29].

> Let us ask the Cherubim, to teach us to renounce the faulty maxims and ways of the flesh [carnal ego-self] and the old world, and all transitory things, in favour of raising our heart's desire [human will] to knowing and Loving the purity, splendour and excellence, of the infinite and Eternal.

❖ The **Thrones** [Seats of Authority] sit under God in the area of the Cosmos where material form begins. Also filled with celestial mysteries, they primarily adore God in His power and Judgement, and through them Judgement is administered. They shine red like the dawn, signifying the Divinity of Jesus Christ - as superior to His Humanity, bending down to all people, and being conceived in the Holy Spirit in the dawn; which is in the all-perfect purity of the Blessed Virgin Mary. These blessed Spirits, are called 'Angels of Peace', bringing calm and tranquillity to our souls, which is the fruit of a pure conscience. They are arrayed like a crown around two other Choirs [Armies], meaning that they assist the faithful in overcoming natural passions and appetites, and re-ordering and re-directing the five senses to celestial things, knowing that they have been redeemed by the five wounds of Jesus Christ.

> Let us intreat the Thrones for zealous co-operation with our Father's Cosmic Divine Will, and for that celestial peace and tranquillity of heart and soul, that surpasses all human understanding [Philippians 4:7].

Nothing human can be seen in the appearance of these first three hierarchies of Angels, because of the many celestial mysteries that humans cannot understand, while living as mortals on earth.

The Dominations [Colossians 1:16; Ephesians 1:21], **Virtues** [1 Peter 3:22; Ephesians 1:21], **and Powers** [Ephesians 1:21; 3:10; Colossians 1:16; 1 Peter 3:22], **form the second Sphere, and fulfil God's providential Plan for the Universe:**

❖ The **Dominations** [Lordships] regulate the duties of the Angels closer to the fallen material world. They too are consumed with zealous Love for the glory of God, while their primary office is to manifest His Cosmic Divine Will to man. These Angels do have forms and feet like humans, and wear marble tunics and helmets on their heads. They demonstrate Truth as the imitation of Jesus Christ our Head, in a life of *living faith as* "Children of Light" Luke 16:18; John 12:36; Ephesians 5:8; 1 Thessalonians 5:5.

> We invoke these blessed Spirits, that we may have dominion over our natural carnal passions and appetites, and the operation of our five senses.

❖ The **Virtues** [The Shining Ones] receive orders from the Dominations. Representing energy and strength, they govern the elements and Heavenly bodies, and assist with miracles. They may raise or pacify tempests, lightening and storms etc., because all nature is under their control. These blessed Spirits also have human forms that shine with great splendour, from their shoulders down.

> Let us desire to be enlightened and fortified with the Virtues; the seal that enables our souls to battle against the forces of evil, displaying to God our honourable motivation and intention of growing in holiness [whole-hearted fullness of being], and worshipping Him, as He can only be worshipped, *in Spirit and in Truth"* John 4:24.

❖ The **Powers** [Warrior Angels] serve the Virtues, by battling against the evil forces that oppose God's divine Plan. Shining with dazzling brightness, and endowed with prodigious intelligence, these splendid Spirits represent God's unfailing and unfathomable power. Ever in the act of defending us from the enemy, they can discover the schemes and plots of evil spirits, that seek to bring about our destruction. The immensity of their powers is such, that one of them alone could destroy the infernal enemy.

> May we call upon these Spirits who are defenders of our peace and security, to assist us against the malevolent efforts of evil spirits; and to overcome all temptations and inclinations to evil.

The Principalities [Colossians 1:16; 2:15 Ephesians 1:21; 3:10], **Archangels** [1 Thessalonians 4:16; Jude 1:9], **and Angels** [Matthew 18:10; Hebrews 13:2], **of the third Sphere, directly order human affairs, and in exceptional cases, assume visibility to man:**

❖ The **Principalities** carry out the orders of the upper sphere, to guide and protect [from the effects of Divine Justice], the Catholic Church and other institutions, as well as nations, provinces, cities, dioceses, religious communities, and groups of people, etc. These splendid Spirits, have the appearance of white marble and human heads, over which torches burn. From the shoulders down, they are surrounded by an iron-grey cloud. These Angels communicate to the Angels of the last two Choirs [Armies], the orders of God. They show that those who are true rulers of the people, must assume the strength of Divine Justice, according to the immutable law of God. They should imitate their Head who is Jesus Christ, and direct their government according to His Love and Divine Will.

> Let us ask these Spirits to assist us with purity of motivation and intention, and to teach us self-governance; drawing us into whole-hearted co-operation with and participation in God's Perfect [Whole and All-Perfect] divine Plan for our lives.

❖ The **Archangels** [Chief Angels] are fervent in their Love and care for the good-being of man; primarily ministering indirectly, but bringing direct messages in times of great need. Arrayed in the shape of a crown, around five other Choirs [Armies], this Choir [Army] of Angels are described as having wings on their breasts, which display forms like human forms, in which the image of Jesus Christ shines. Continuously intuiting the Divine Will in their perfect Spiritual intellect, they display within themselves, the beauty of divine reason, and magnify Jesus Christ in the purest way, because of their knowledge of celestial mysteries. This demonstrates that the human body and soul, must by way of its co-operative strength, purify and re-order the five senses by the five wounds of Jesus Christ, leading to upright and stable self-governance.

> These Angels are distinguished from the Angels of the first Choir [Army], by their higher function, and are understood to be the guardians of the Pope, of bishops, and all those with offices of authority in the Church, and state. Among the Archangels, are St. Michael [meaning *"who is like unto God?"*], St. Gabriel [meaning *"God Is My Strength"*], and St. Raphael [meaning *"God Heals"*]. Sacred Scripture indicates that these are three of seven Archangels appointed to stand [serve] before the throne of the Eternal Father. St. Michael is the 'Prince of Angels', because of

His most zealous response to Lucifer's rebellion against God, although he is denominated an Archangel.

<u>St. Michael</u> the literal translation of whose name [*"who is like unto God?"*], is a battle cry, shield, and weapon; is the most zealous leader of the victorious Armies [Choirs] of good Angels, who opposed the proud and rebellious battle cry of Satan [and his legions of fallen Angels]: *"I will be like the Most High!"* Isaiah 14:14. Leading the confrontation of Satan [Lucifer], and the fallen Angels before the creation of the world, [Revelation 12:7-9], St. Michael took his place as guardian of the glory [blissful magnificence] and honour of Almighty God. Surpassing all Angels in the intensity of his zealous [Seraphic] Love of God, he is the most splendorous 'Prince of Angels', and is commander and chief over all nine Heavenly Armies [Choirs], continuously engaged in the fierce battle to protect the *living* Church on earth. St. Michael will again lead the final war with the anti-Christ, who by way of false lights and miracles, and false prophets and teachers, will seek to seduce and deceive, even God's elect [Matthew 24:24; Mark 13:22 and Revelation 13:14;19:20]. The many times St. Michael has aided the faithful, is recorded in Sacred Scripture [Daniel 10:13,21; 12:1; Jude 1:9; and Revelation 12:7-8], and in the testimonies of saints such as St. Padre Pio and St. Faustina. We should frequently invoke his assistance, and with him, all the Armies [Choirs] of Heaven. For as it was Eve's direct engagement [or dialogue, meaning *"relationship"* in the early Greek form of the word] with Satan that initiated the fall, it is the intercession of Heaven by the merits of Jesus Christ, and never direct human engagement with Satan or his demons, that the battle is both fought and won.

<u>St. Gabriel</u> is the messenger Angel, who communicates God's messages on earth. St. Gabriel announced the Incarnation of the Son-of-God to Mary, and was sent to the Prophet Daniel, and to Zechariah [father of John the Baptist]. It is assumed that he oversaw the Holy Family, and that he was the one who brought

"good tidings of great joy" Luke 2:10, to the shepherds keeping watch over their flock, the night the Christ-Child was born. It was he who warned Joseph to flee into Egypt with Mary and the Divine Child, and who consoled Jesus in the Garden of Gethsemane. We should invoke his assistance in growing in knowledge and Love of God in His Divine Will, in the everyday trials and circumstances of our lives.

St. Raphael is known to have conducted the young man Tobias safely on his journey into another country; while teaching him how to recognize, and overcome the attacks of the enemy [Tobit 5-12]. He also miraculously healed his virtuous Father, old Tobit of his blindness. We should have recourse to him in his health-giving ministry, and call upon him for guidance during our earthly pilgrimage.

❖ **Angels** [Guardian Angels] are placed nearest to the material world, and minister directly to human beings. Loving us fervently, they are always by our side, waiting for our calls for [consent to] assistance, for their zealous purpose is to render us more glorious in Paradise. Guardian Angels have wings on their breasts, with forms like human forms in front of them, on which human features show, as if in clear water. They are swift to know and accomplish God's Divine Will, and display in themselves the beauty of divine reason, by which God examines all deeds. They ever pay attention to God's Loving Divine Will for the soul under their care, and show Him human actions in themselves.

> Let us gladly call upon our personally appointed Angels often, to guide, protect and console us; and to ever enliven our faith. Let us correspond with their assistance, and have a particular devotion to, and reverence towards them.

*"Ever at our side, is a being living a golden Life.
His work, is a work of Love…he knows to be, a part of God's
Eternal, creative Love, towards our particular soul."*

Fr. Frederick Faber.

Let us be encouraged and invigorated by the example of the luminous and incorruptible Spirits of the nine Choirs [Armies] of Angels, who know and manifest perfectly, the incomprehensible and exhilarating worship of our Creator God and Father, in the Light-union of the Most Holy Trinity. While Sacred Scripture warns us not to worship Angels [Colossians 2:18; Revelation 22:8-9] but God alone, let us endeavour to Love them in Him, and call upon their assistance, while remaining vigilant, as not to offend their most pure gaze. Let us be devout to them, and appreciate their maternal care and friendship, most particularly our Guardian Angels, appointed to our side on earth. For they are all in Loving divine service of us, while looking unceasingly upon the face of God, in the company of Heaven. Let us offer *living* prayers, together with all self-giving good works, observing chastity [holy purity; wholeness and wisdom] above all, for in correspondence with our sincerity and purity [cleanliness and clarity] of heart [heart's desire], they will share the Light of God with us. They will come to our aid and defence, including at the hour of our death, if we have persevered in holy living. When in company with, or thinking of others, let us too salute and revere the radiant presence of *their* Guardian Angel who stands beside them, working continuously for their good regardless of their soul-condition. For they know that God Loves each of us infinitely more than any human person is capable of loving one another, while our fidelity allows all manner of divine graces, favours, and blessings to be rendered to us all.

We whole-heartedly thank God, for the countless multitudes of good Angels, who unceasingly serve to defend us from the fallen Angels, and lead us in our flight of faith back to the celestial heights of the Homeland. We resolve to become One with them in music and song; in prayer, praise, and adoration of the Most Holy Trinity; letting the rhythm and harmonies of praise at the birth of Jesus Christ, rise up and ring forever in our being *"Glory to God in the highest!"* Luke 2:14.

Information on the nine Angelic Choirs [Armies] of God, are drawn from Sacred Scripture, and the writings of Church saints, namely St. Gregory the Great, St. Thomas Aquinas, and St. Hildegard of Bingen.

The Nativity of Jesus Christ

In pursuit of fallen man; the triple Nativity; Satan bewildered at the glory scene in the cave; the mystery and paradox of God's immaterial and unearthly ways; a Life of paradox and untold suffering; living Light vs. false lights; recovering second sight and receiving the Kingdom like a child; godly celebration; we are all innkeepers, and everything depends upon us.

"While they were there, the day had come for her to give birth. And she brought forth her Firstborn Son. And she wrapped him in swaddling clothes and laid Him in a manger, because there was no room for them at the inn."

Luke 2:6-7.

+

"O Come, all ye faithful" and let us go to Bethlehem this day, *"joyful and triumphant"* to behold the celestial Baby; the God-Child, who is born in a cave! Let us join the Angels, the shepherds, and the Maji who journey with the star, together with the full assemblies of Heaven and earth, as we joyfully proclaim the well-known words of the Latin hymn, *"Adeste Fideles."* For today, in the little town of Bethlehem [meaning *"House of Bread"* in Hebrew], Jesus Christ *"The Bread of Life"* John 6:35,48, has come to re-open Paradise!

We could not come Home to God, and so He, in His unfathomable divine Charity, has come for us! Today, the Son-of-God and *"King of Angels"*, has become the *"Son of Man"* [recorded in the Gospels of Matthew, Mark, Luke, and John]. He who is the Life of all life; who masterminded the billions of stars and galaxies, lays down His boundless glory, and lies helplessly in a manger, gazing up at His own creation, as though back to the [Spiritual] heights from where Adam and Eve first fell. Today, human existence has been deified by an infant God-Child, ablaze with the living Light of the Heavenly star. Heaven and earth are re-united, and man has been anointed with divinity, because God who is, has become what He is not, in every way but sin [Hebrews 4:15], to give His Perfect [Whole and All-Perfecting] Divine-Humanity to our souls, and re-create us anew in Himself. Christmas is God's supreme gift of Himself to man. All creation leaps for joy!

On this most hallowed and exuberant of feast days, we who delight in Jesus Christ, celebrate the triple Nativity of:

- His **Eternal** generation as God, in the Light-Womb of the Father;
- His **Temporal** birth from the purest womb of the Blessed Virgin Mary, in Bethlehem of Judah; and
- His **Spiritual** birth in our hearts [heart's desire] and souls, as our Redeemer.

Christmas is both a festivity of the joy of man, and of God's joy in the Most Holy Trinity, because in Jesus Christ, the Father's creative works reach fulfilment. In this most wondrous mystery, He who is without beginning or end; the Whole and All-Perfect expression of God the Father's knowledge of Himself, begins to be as man, in the power of His own divine fecundity. The original Virginal Light-seed [Light-consciousness of God] is Now a Child, born of a Virgin Mother. Today, the *"Sun of Justice"* Malachi 4:2, has shone Light into the darkness, and the Father no longer asks: *"On whom shall I look?"* Isaiah 66:2, because He looks and finds Himself among men, and in the company of His own most holy [whole and all-perfect] Mother.

> *"He has come down to earth, to take you to Heaven,*
> *He became mortal, that you might become God,*
> *and put on your original beauty."*
>
> St. Romanos Melodos.

On this hallowed day, when Heaven comes to earth, the ancient seducer [Satan] is laid low. Struck with bewilderment and terror at the scene before his eyes, this brazen minister of death dare not approach again, as he once did in the garden of Eden. For where he had deceived the original Eve in Paradise, he now sees another woman; the incorruptible New Eve [the new Ark of the Covenant, and Heaven and earths Queen-Mother] transcend nature, to become the Mother of her own Creator made Incarnate, and in the most unexpected of conditions. Giving perfect Love and safety to Him, in the chariot of her most pure womb, and birthing Him in a manner past human understanding, she has become more spacious than the firmament, while her sublime purity is blessed and sealed, in and for all Eternity. For by virtue of her Son-God, this most Blessed among women, is the noblest created person that will ever breathe, and her feet are already upon the head of the serpent [Satan]. There are no rich earthly garments, jewels, or crowns in this cave; no worldly comfort, luxury, or prestige, as in the palace of king Herod, but the serpent yet knows, that this cave is the most exalted place on earth, supernaturally protected by the flaming fire of the sword of the Spirit.

> *"At the twelfth hour, her [Mary's] prayer became ecstatic, and I saw her raised so far above the ground, that one could see it beneath her. Her hands were crossed upon her breast, and the Light around her grew even more resplendent. I no longer saw the roof of the cave. Above Mary, stretched a pathway of Light up to Heaven, in which pathway it seemed that one Light came forth from another, as if one figure dissolved into another, and from these spheres of Light, other Heavenly figures issued. Mary continued in prayer; her eyes bent low upon the ground.*
>
> *At that moment she gave birth to the infant Jesus. I saw Him like a tiny shining Child, lying on the rug at her knees and brighter by far, than all the other brilliancy…. Mary's ecstasy lasted some moments longer. Then I saw her spread a cover over the Child, but she did not yet take Him up, nor even touch Him.*
>
> From the visions of Blessed Anne Catherine Emmerich.

In the most beautiful situation of the little town of Bethlehem, and in the humble seclusion of a cave, the mystery and paradox of Jesus Divine-Human Life is illuminated. For here upon a hill that overlooks Jerusalem, this timeless Babe in a manger, is at once the Crucified Messiah on Calvary, and the Resurrected pre-Eternal God on the Mount of Olives. **In the littleness of His Self-emptied frame [Philippians 2:7], is contained the boundless power and bright joys of His Three-Fold Divine Being. While in the cry of His infant voice that breaks the cold night air, is carried the primordial cry of God's Heart for the recovery of human souls.** This is the most joyous of all of God's acts in creation, and still the most sober, because as the All-powerful One lies powerless, and the untouchable lies subject to the hands of created man; the unfathomable abyss of Divine Mercy is already fulfilling the balancing rights of Divine Justice.

The lowly conditions of the cave, hide the terrifying magnificence [glory] and majesty of Almighty God, delivered to earth, and into the sight of fallen man. And while deprived of every other human comfort, this Holy Family find every contentment in communion with God, in the fullness of His living Light in one another, for they are perfectly [wholly and all-perfectly] governed by higher Life in the Spirit. To the Eternal Father, the atmosphere of this divinely royal little party, offers infinitely more warmth and illumination, than the midday natural sun. Their humility, gentleness, and trust in Him is more pleasing than a glistening golden palace; and their all-pure *living* prayers and *living* silence, a more fragrant hymn of joy-filled worship, than the exhortation of throngs.

> *"Truly you are a God who hides Himself,*
> *O God, and Saviour of Israel!"*
>
> Isaiah 45:15.

While it may be tempting to be captivated by a romantic vision of this glorious night in Bethlehem, the deep humility of this cave scene has much to teach us about the unsentimental and Universal Charity of the Supreme Being, who came to create a new [divine] world order, and transform the being of man into a higher form [Ephesians 4:24]. For although this Divine Child was Marys; carried in her heart and in her womb for the course of her [divine] maternity; on His arrival on earth, she freely places Him in the manger. An act symbolising highest Love [*"Agape"*], which is His total Self-giving, as the gift and promise of all. With His little arms outstretched and His mouth thirsty, our suffering God begins His work on earth of begging for our hearts [desire], in order to exchange the lowly human will with the Light, power and sanctity of the Divine Will, which carries Paradise. **With this gesture, He replaces old worldly inward-looking group and family solidarity with outward-looking person-to-person solidarity in Himself;** thus, forming the Ever-lasting celestial Blood family [community] of the justified and recognizable brothers and sisters of Light [Luke 16:18; John 12:36; Ephesians 5:8; and 1 Thessalonians 5:5, Revelation 22:14].

The humility of this scene also teaches us about the contrast between the heights of [spirit-bearing] sanctity from which man fell, and from which the God-Child descends, to recover human souls. The coarse swaddling rags in which He is wrapped, symbolise the impoverished and perishable rags [Spiritual poverty] of the human will [heart's desire], from which He comes to untangle us, in exchange for the imperishable and refulgent Light-garment and crown [Spiritual wealth] of Eternal Life. The cold, hard bed of straw on which His tender skin lay, represents the remoteness and hardness of human hearts, into which He seeks to descend, and find a welcoming and safe dwelling place. Yet, while the innocent animals in silent and serene adoration, fulfil their calling of warm hospitality and honour, by providing Him with a room, man for the most part, is an absent and inhospitable vessel of strangeness, commotion, and coldness. A state of being, which has run through the centuries, especially in disregard and ingratitude for Jesus sacramental Life [in the Eucharist] on earth.

> *"An ox knows his owner, and*
> *a donkey knows the manger of his Lord,*
> *but Israel has not known me, and*
> *my people have not understood."*
>
> Isaiah 1:3.

The mystery of God [and our God-being, John 10:34] is a most challenging Paradox for natural man, because it sets before us the glory [blissful magnificence] of the graciously [grace-filled] simple way. Raised in a little house in Nazareth, while refusing earthly riches, indulgences, and honours; and all human preferences; then finally laid to rest in a borrowed tomb, Jesus verifies that His Kingdom [glory] is not of this [old] world [John 6:14 and 18:36]. And while he did not promote or encourage lack of vital necessities, severe austerity, or destitution, neither did He offer 'assistance' with a worldly life, or instruct people on how to appear to 'prosper' amidst flesh [egoism] and fallen [material] matter. **For while the Supreme Being lends**

Himself to matter, giving expression to, blessing, and embracing all of creation; it is for the *sole purpose* of our Redemption and Sanctification, and passage to Ever-lasting Life in the immaterial [and incorruptible] realm of the Spirit.

> *"I dominate matter and merely lend Myself to it....*
> *It is by freeing yourselves from matter,*
> *that you will discover the world of the Spirit."*
>
> Jesus speaks to Sr. Mary of the Holy Trinity.

And so, while life on earth is about creativity, expansion, and gain, it is to be directed upwards, and upon the Eternal [Luke 6:20,24], in the knowledge that **God's Light illuminates only that which is God** [Matthew 6:24 and 1 John 2:15-16]. The soul must take to heart, the Holy Family's exemplary way of life, characterized by **voluntary ungrasping simplicity, humility, and Charity,** because it is in His I-dentifying with the authentically 'Poor in Spirit', that Jesus Christ recognizes those who are more disposed to the higher realms of celestial knowledge, wisdom, and refinement. Only of these more discerning and willing souls, can He make of His temple and His Home. See 'Soul economy' in Useful Terms.

> *"For My fruit is better than gold and precious stones,*
> *and My progeny [yield] better than choice silver."*
>
> Proverbs 8:19.

As lights and decorations are put to illuminate and dress homes and gatherings during the Christmas season, or at any time, let us think of Joseph's skilful and patient hands making the best of the meagre cave, to prepare a safe sanctuary for a God-Child, who enjoys the fullness of the Beatific Vision [direct and immediate sight of God]; while yet suffering the defects of hunger, thirst, cold and fatigue, brought about by Adam and Eve. Let us consider the inexpressible difference between man-made light, and the artificial lights [desires] of the flesh [carnal ego-self] and the old world, set against the supernatural power, vigour, warmth, and effects of God's Ever-living Light, that lives and moves, and wants to be birthed within and through our immortal souls.

On the glorious feast of the Nativity, we celebrate the divine innocence [apparent weakness] overcoming [apparent] human strength; the Light of divine knowledge and wisdom, dispelling the dark clouds of existence-ignorance, indifferentism and evil. For to know God as an infant, arrayed in the gracious simplicity and humility of the cave, is to know Him as a man. Lying helplessly in the manger, He is the Heart that Loves [with highest Love], and the Child that takes [receives] our Love [in Him]. To receive the Kingdom like a child [meaning an *"embodiment"* or *"emanation"* that was only potential before in Aramaic] means to give up all the paralysing fear, pride, and pretence, and bring to our return to knowing and Loving God [and everyone, and everything in Him], the fresh qualities of child-like innocence, trust, and simplicity. For to realize the fullness of Spiritual growth, maturity, and vigour [Eternal youthfulness], and return to our original state of innocence and justice [Eternal Beatitude], is to be liberated from the wantonness and staidness; and the anxieties, and projected purposes of the *"old man"*, which bind us, and everyone and everything around us. **It is to relinquish straining forward, and rest in abandoning back [consenting] to that glory [blissful magnificence] which wants to be born within and through us.** It is to be willing to unlearn by letting go of what we think we know; letting be without questioning; and letting God take the initiative; in order to unlearn and re-learn, by the higher ways of the Spirit. For God's Love acts only on the free human will [heart's desire], surrendered to Him; only trusting abandonment [consent] leads to real release and breakthrough. Like the Maji and the shepherds, we must cultivate a pure [clean and clear] heart that re-sees, and re-hears as a child, in order to be able to receive and return God's own highest Love in His Divine Will. And where the Spirit of God is, there is the freedom of childlike wonder, playfulness, joy, and enjoyment that relies on Divine Providence. **We do not ask why, for those who ask why at the human level, are not open to receive at the higher Spiritual level, the glory [blissful magnificence], which wants to be born from within.**

> *"Let the little children come to Me…*
> *For the Kingdom of Heaven belongs to one's like these."*
> Matthew 19:14 [Mark 10:14 and Luke 18:16.]

To receive the Kingdom of God as a child, means living a life of *true* celebration. God wants nothing more than for each of us to cultivate a *living* personal relationship with Him, characterized by a life of celebration. We know that He Loves celebration, because from the honorary feasts given by Him to Israel; to the celebratory gifts, prayers, music, and singing of the Angels, shepherds, and Maji at the birth of Jesus Christ; to the feast of the Mass, and the sacraments; and the ultimate celebration of 'The Wedding Feast of the Lamb'; the Old and New Covenants of Love, are filled with celebration. **This celebration is expressed as joy-filled worship of who God is [the Supreme Being]; what He has freely done for us [sent His Son]; and who we truly are in Him, because of His super-abundant Love for us.**

Rooted in, and governed by, the higher ways of the Spirit, this gracious and wholesome festivity, has nothing to do with the fleeting revelries and disordered rejoicing of the flesh [carnal ego-self] and the old world. Indeed, Sacred Scripture carries particularly strong warnings about such base and idolatrous practices, fashioned as celebrations, but which do nothing to glorify God, or the Truth and purpose of our being in Him. *"I hate and have rejected your festivities; and I will not accept the odour from your gatherings"* Amos 5:21. *"For the customs of the people are vanity… they will all be proven to be unwise and foolish"* Jeremiah 10:3,8. **Only at the bottom of human** culture, do the crowds go wild with noise and parties, says the poet, for these transient endeavours of the flesh [carnal ego-self] and the old world, attempt to, but can do nothing to fill the hunger and emptiness in the ground of our being, that cries out for deep blessedness and satisfaction, found only in *"the fertile embrace of God"* [the Aramaic meaning of the word *"satisfaction"*].

Authentic celebration, is nothing other than the expression of the fullness of Truth. It is the mark of creative realization of our God-being [John 10:34], and Good-being in Jesus Christ. It involves a fully alive and re-integrated [re-centred] view of our human existence; of our soul's simultaneous two-dimensional reality as created beings in time, and as immortal beings, in and for all Eternity. In this mystery of our existence, as Spiritual beings having a finite human experience, our joy is inextricably mingled with *"godly grief [that] produces a repentance, that leads to salvation [healing] and brings no regret, [unlike] worldly grief [which] produces death"* 2 Corinthians 7:10. The Church embodies and expresses this reality in her calendar of celebratory feast days, of joy and of sorrow, which lead the lives of the faithful in rhythms of inner preparation. This *"joy-creating sorrow"* [St. John Climacus], restores our souls to the fullness of overcoming joy, which is our true release, in the holy [whole and all-perfect] Light-freedom of Jesus Christ. And so, with hearts raised above earthly things, and set upon the promise of the festival of the *living* Church in the Heavenly New Jerusalem [Hebrews 12:22-24], let us discard vain, coarse, and empty customs and entertainment, contrary to the Life of the *"Fiat"*, in favour of those given for the intention of honouring and glorifying God [and our being in Him].

> *"I have called you by your name;*
> *you are Mine."*
>
> Isaiah 43:1.

From that Holy Night came the dawn of a new day, and the Holy Family's forty-day sojourn in Bethlehem, where they nursed and cared for this new-born with basic provision, before moving on again. Going out to be circumcised at eight days old, according to the custom of the Jews, Jesus first sheds His Sacred Blood for man, joining the Old Covenant of Israel, and the promise to Abraham [to whom God had sworn an oath, that Israel would be delivered from its enemies] to the New and Ever-lasting Covenant of Love realized [made real] in Himself. Going out again at forty days old [known as the Feast of the Presentation, or Candlemas Day], to be presented to the holy priest Simeon, in the temple at Jerusalem, is represented the public profession of His Messianic mission as *"the Light of the world"* John 8:12 and 9:5, as well as His first public invitation [calling] to all people, to come back to the fullness of being in Him. In Simeon's prophetic words, this is identified as **the Life-giving work of the Cross**, which is the victory of the Kingdom within and through our souls. A **heroic victory, which must be birthed in labour and in pains; in arrivals and in departures, and in joy and in tears during our sojourn on earth.** And so, following the presentation, Mary and Joseph flee together with Jesus during the night, travelling silent-footed like hunted fugitives through the Judean mountains, on a journey of three days to hide in the land of Egypt [the land of idolatry], until it is safe to return to Nazareth. There were no stars, songs, comforts, nor royal entourage on this journey, while danger pressed all around them, as king Herod plotted to kill the Divine Child.

"So, the last will be first, and the first last."
Matthew 20:16.

This state of paradox in the earliest days of Jesus Life on earth, is the mark of the entirety of His Life [God's Life among created man] on earth. For from His arrival here on earth, on the comfortless bed of the manger, to His departure on the forbidding bed of the Cross, He led a Life of untold, silent suffering as He embraced the life of the first man, Adam, to the last man, carrying us in His interior, and re-doing [re-creating] every act [of thought, word, and deed] that we should and would have done, had we remained in Light-union. A continuous act of Living and Dying of unutterable Love for man, and requitting the Love of the Father for us all, as He worked, walked, taught, prayed, rested, and journeyed towards the centre, Jerusalem [representing the New Jerusalem], for the full and final confrontation with, and victory over Satan and his earthly kingdom of ruin. Finally, wrapped in nothing but the Blood-red raiment of His own Sacred Being, He left Himself with us in the most sublime sacraments and provisions of His Church on earth, so that whoever truly desired to return to the Spiritual state of the Kingdom, could realize it in Him.

True to the wonderful excesses of the Father's Love for us, we know that this New Jerusalem [new Eden] will be a fresh departure from the original; where the last things will be greater than the first. For by the fruits of the Cosmic Divine-Humanity of Jesus Christ, we are invited [called] to be transfigured and lifted up above where Adam and Eve first fell. In dying and rising again with and in Him, by way of the Eucharistic [self-sacrificial, self-giving] life, is the promise of the exchange of our lowly earthen body, with a Spiritualized and sinless body of Light [Philippians 3:20-21], which is the imperishable and refulgent Light-garment of Eternal Life.

> *"Those who are wise, shall shine like the brightness of the expanse."*
>
> Daniel 12:3.

As we journey through the days of our life, we recognize that Jesus Christ is not just one more thing; something or someone for appointed times of the day, week, month, or year, while we otherwise 'get on with our lives'. He is God; He is the only One who knows what *real Life and purpose* can offer. He is the only One with the right optics, and He is the only One with an Eternal Plan. In John 8:14, Jesus tells us that only He knows where He has come from, and where He is going, because only He is from Heaven, while all other people are of the earth. In the outpouring of the Father's own paternal Heart, He came with deep and hallowed designs upon our lives, set from long Eternity. **He came to win back for us, the second [Spiritual] sight, and the right [Spiritual] optics for the deep healing, blessedness, and quality of living, that only God [God-being, John 10:34] can deliver.**

> *"Jesus answered them, "Even if I testify about Myself,*
> *My testimony is true, for I know where I came from,*
> *and where I am going.""*
>
> John 8:14.

Everything depends upon us.

These are the days of knowing and of full provision; all is done, all is given, and the fields are *already* shining for the harvest [John 4:35-36]. We are all innkeepers, free to co-operate or not co-operate in offering clean and safe shelter and lodgings within our soul, to this Christ-Child and King, who has preferred nothing in this fallen world to us. We have each been invited, but we will never be forced to consent to realizing [making real] His second return [Advent] within and through our souls.

> *"The Christian mysteries are an indivisible whole...*
> *Thus, the way from Bethlehem leads inevitably*
> *to Golgotha [Calvary], from the crib to the Cross....*
> *In His company, the way of every one of us,*
> *indeed, of all humanity leads through suffering*
> *and death, to this same glorious goal."*
>
> St. Edith Stein. [4]

For those who recognize this mortal life as precious working time; as our appointed time of Spiritual battle and triumph; of washing and dressing for the wedding feast of the Lamb, *"while it is day"* John 9:4, Jesus Christ is the inextinguishable Light [Exodus 4:22; Isaiah 41:8, Galatians 3:16 and Colossians 1:15], who shines ever more brightly within and through our souls, in the unfolding of our gift of days on earth. **For to requite His Love by whole-heartedly carrying Him as He first carried us, is to know and Love God our Father as He is, and as He wants to be known. It is to purify and know ourselves as we really are, and to give purity to others, by being true to who we really are in God. This is the work of the healing and re-creation [re-birth] of our uniqueness of being, in the One Truth of Jesus Christ.** While in the measure in which we have Loved and carried Him in our being during our earthly pilgrimage, will be the measure of our re-birth in God, in the Ever-new and revealing splendour of the Homeland. This New Advent, is the ultimate meaning and purpose of the mystery of Christmas, and of our life on earth.

Let those then among us, who live on earth to receive the privilege and splendour of *real Life and purpose* in Jesus Christ, learn not only to bear with temporal life and death, but let us leap into flame. With hearts lifted Heavenward and feet on the ground, let us keep festival with the Angels and saints among men, knowing that our consumption in Love's own fire, is our ascension in Jesus Christ, into the nuptial Light-ring of the Heavenly Homeland; the One glorious [blissfully magnificent] Spiritual and immaterial reality for which we are created. And as we live on earth to *"lay up for [ourselves], treasures in Heaven"* Matthew 6:20, let us everywhere and in everything, celebrate and glorify [only] God, and the astonishing free gift of our being in Him. Let us spread among all His people, living creatures and creation, the glad tidings of the star, the joy of the Angels, the amazement of the shepherds, and the worship of the Maji, because the bright increase of this new Life flowing within and through us, is [Eternal] Life in the Cosmic and radiant Divine Sun. It is the Life that fulfils the mystery of Christmas; of *"Emmanuel: God-with-us"* Old Testament: Isaiah 7:14; 8:8-10 and New Testament:

Matthew 1:21-23; John 1:14; 14:8-11; Colossians 2:9, which is *"Christ's Mass"* living within us. And for the one who is healed and re-created [re-birthed] anew in Jesus Christ, it is Christmas every day!

> *"To finish, I must be Eternal, like You."*
> Psalm 139:18.

New Advent

The sounds of voices and steps from the darkness,
Were faint at first,
But the signs and steps grew stronger,
And separation began, where shadows fell.
The voices became louder, quickened now,
And I followed the steps that others were following,
Others whose appearances were not unlike my own.
I learned to walk among tangled shadows, but hardly moved.
It seemed there was no need to turn around.
Yet an attraction unknown, called out,
Within the hush of my heart,
A fragile spark of Light glimmered,
Steeped in from somewhere high above, and deep within.

Against the chill of the night and shivering involuntarily,
I took a single step beyond the drift of time,
Anonymously.
As men's voices grew low, and the shadows dimmed,
Fear, delight, and sadness mingled.
At first, the darkness grew deeper, and the silence more intense,
And for a moment, I was lost between worlds, and beyond the flow of time.
But this was the last I would know of loneliness,
As from a distance beyond reach of the furthest star,
A blazing brightness, incomprehensible, pierced the darkness within.
Here everything was suddenly clear,
No stains, nor shadows to spoil my inner vision.

As the sound of up-swift harmonies mingled with portents of Light,
The surge of a sweet New Advent moved across my heart.
Drawing in pulses of joy that could not entertain fear,
My soul swirling in circles of burning Light,
Widened to catch the chords that stirred the Angels.

But in this deepest bliss, I at once understood,
The need for at-One-ment.
I could not stay above His Cross, and find Him echoed in me,
For to be the bearer of His Life, I must be the bearer of His death and resurrection,
A victory up-mounted in submission to His beloved Cross.

O how pleasing are the hymns that flow from the suffering soul,
That wills to share in the privilege of His bitter-sweet chalice!
That toils naked and upheld, amidst the unplumbed depths of frenzied mortal frailties and desires,
To be burned and dissolved in the purest flame of incomprehensible Light!
Only then, to rise again in the blazing splendour of the Eternal sphere.

And so, there was nothing to do Now, but to sink back down,
Through the deepest darkness, of space and time,
With a new mind, bowed in a new heart,
To wait on no-one, `
But to carry everyone and everything in Him,
Taking the first trembling steps of genuine movement,
Along the dark and sacred pilgrim's path,
The silent ascent, where I and the old world shall be no more,
Footprints burned and consumed forever, in the greeting Light-blaze of hallowed reality,
The glory-fire of the Womb-Heart, of our Eternal Father God.
Ever-Now awakening, remembering, Home.

Appendix 1: Paradise Lost

At the beginning of history, man was best disposed to the All-greening power of God's Spirit.

> *"In the beginning, all created things turned green.*
> *In the middle period [of history] flowers bloomed,*
> *but afterwards, the greening power of life lessened."*
>
> St. Hildegard of Bingen. [5]

Over the centuries, and increasingly disconnected from the Light-flow of the Godhead, the generations that have followed Adam and Eve, have grown ever more exposed to the ancestral wounds of Light-separation, and more susceptible to the works of the enemy [Satan]. With a dark veil of forgetfulness of God drawn across his heart, and ever-occupied with man-made prisms of selfhood; of fragmentation, duplicity, and multiplicity in time and in space, he finds it hard to recognize what God is offering [1 John 2:16], which seems to clash with 'modern' ideals. God remains silent amidst the clamour and confusion, while the pathway Home grows ever-faint, if not vanishes under earthen feet [Romans 1:18-25].

The book of Job tells us that no natural force on earth is comparable to the ferocious evil of Satan and his demons. Church saints tell us that so incredible and countless is the number of fallen Angels, that should God permit them to assume human bodies, their thickness upon the air would blot out the light of the natural sun. Most hideous and frightening in their fallen forms, and intruding everywhere, while remaining invisible, it is an act of God's Mercy, says St. Padre Pio, that humans cannot behold their infestation before our bodily eyes.

To conceive of the gift of God, is to recognize the works of the traitor [Satan], and to render him powerless [in his direct and indirect assaults] against our souls. For from that fateful day when he surreptitiously defrauded our first parents, the all-consuming attention and resolve of this malignant and self-deceived seducer and persecutor, is **i-dentity theft**. It is the fatal work of warping man away from the **power, beauty, and nobility** of his Spiritualized-self in perfect Light-union with and in God, and with all things in Him. Knowing that despite the best of intentions, man cannot restore his relationship with God by his own efforts, because of natural conflict between the dark heat of the flesh [carnal-ego self], and the spirit [Galatians 5:17], as well as the vast chasm between the natural and Spiritual intellect; he is ever-vigilant and relentless in seeking to strike at *"an opportune time"* Luke 4:13, with the intention of diminishing man to an ego-shadow mutation of his divine-human being, and ultimately destroying his Eternal soul.

> *"Satan, compared to us, is like a 25-year-old man, looking down at a 3-month-old baby."*
>
> St. Père Lamy.

Keenly aware that to come to the Light, man must abide in vital awareness of what darkness [sin] is, and therefore what Light [Truth] is, as well as what grace requires; this most subtle and shrewd minister of death [Genesis 3:1] is, in his best disguise, a charming gentleman who 'inspires' man to live a death and name it Life. Cloaked in death, while masquerading as an **'Angel of Light' [2 Corinthians 11:14]**, he is one of warm countenance, stirring words, and appealing ways, who stands ready to make a difference by killing with counterfeit kindness, the Light-seed of immortality, if not the Divine Child re-birthing within the human soul. False compassion, kinship, peace, and safety in the flesh [carnal ego-self] and the old world are his way, because with his greatly superior intelligence, he recognizes man's natural struggle [inner division] between Light and darkness, made all the more testing by the entanglement of all shades of good and evil, in a world deeply severed from the *Living Light* of God's Spirit. He knows too, that without this Light, man's naturally carnal and finite mind can no more detect the inertness of pure evil, than the dynamism of pure good. And so, with emotionally resonating half-Truths wrapped up in outwardly pleasing words and ways, he works with great zeal, to offer man a close parody of Truth, by preying upon what is highest in him, and using it to send him on a smooth path of downward transcendence. So convincing is his work of **soft tyranny, distraction, and delusion; of 'uniting' and 'divinizing' all errors and heresies; and administering a painless death to the realities of the origin and destination of the soul, and the doctrine of the Cross [Divine Life]**, that were it possible, even God's elect would be deceived [Matthew 24:24; Mark 13:22; and Revelation 13:14;19:20].

> *"It is the mark of the evil spirit, to take on the appearance of an 'Angel of Light'. He begins by suggesting thoughts that are suited to a devout soul...Afterwards, he will endeavour little by little, to end by drawing the soul into his hidden snares and evil designs."*
>
> St. Ignatius – Spiritual Exercises.

To this diabolic end, the everyday work of Satan and his demons, is that of ascertaining the quality of man's soul-condition, as well as God's designs upon his soul. While they cannot read his thoughts, they work continuously to determine his way of seeing and being, by watching his external behaviour; what he pays attention to and talks about; what [and how] he values, what [and how] he judges; and ultimately what he calls living. An exacting work of identifying his weaknesses, naiveties, and all duplicities, for the purpose of thwarting his correspondence with God's Plan upon his soul. It is their business to look for unrepented sin, and signs of soul-slumber and struggle; to bring accusations against him in the Courts of

Heaven, and gain a [firmer] foothold in his soul, and the souls of others through him. They work tirelessly to render him impressible and impressionable by the false and degrading perceptions, trends, ideals, and fleeting satisfactions of the flesh [carnal ego-self] and the old world; **hurrying him along** with useless and ungodly interests and works, that run down the clock on his precious time on earth. Masterfully and stealthily, **they quietly execute the death of the soul, by crowding out, deadening, and detaining in deadness, the interior Spiritual sight [intellect]**; preventing him from recognizing the primordial might of Eternal Life, seeded within his being.

> *"How narrow is the gate, and how straight [upright and unencumbered] is the way, which leads to Life, and few there are who find it!"*
>
> Matthew 7:14.

One of the more obvious signs of the works of evil today, is the delicate work of benumbing human thinking, as the meaning of words are changed, and language is misused and drained of real meaning. For the alteration of man's hearing and heart results in his greater confusion, and inability to understand or express himself truthfully or adequately. In this gently woven state of soul-slumber, he may have the misappropriated 'spiritual' language, but he has neither the Spiritual sight nor the will to identify the designs of the destroyer upon his soul. Under the influence of an increasingly casual and libertine freedom, together with declining Church and sacramental life, man is rendered susceptible to flattering himself with the worthiness of his soul-condition [and that of others]. He may think that Heaven is won by **cheap grace** [without repentance on God's terms], or that God, Purgatory and Hell don't exist, and Divine Mercy is not required. For **in not knowing God [in Jesus Christ], he cannot know himself [in Him], nor recognize the subtle and treacherous works of Satan**, whose bloody claws work furiously to pull the temple of his soul to the ground. In this Light-vacuum, counterfeit Spiritual 'gold' fanned by half-Truths and humanistic appeal [Matthew 7:15-20] abounds, bringing about a contemporary Spiritual 'revival' and 'consciousness' that insinuates itself everywhere. The true gold of the Cross is substituted with an enthralling brand of **'best of both worlds' soulish 'spirituality'** by which the spirit operates through the dis-ordered and dis-integrated fleshy [carnal-ego] soul, that tosses man *"to and fro"* Ephesians 4:14. True Spiritual healthfulness [healing and transformation] is replaced with all manner of 'positive' devitalizing words, beliefs and practices; treatments, experiences, and influences, that offer nothing but conciliatory care for the *"old man";* while opening the door to the works of fallen spirits*, and manifesting 'fruits' that speak of nothing but the culmination of the present times. For **as in the Garden of Eden, where All-unity [God-being, John 10:34 and Good-being] in God, was substituted with false [God-empty] 'all-unity' and 'good-being' apart from Him;** false inspirations, and the doctrines of demons [1 Timothy 4:1] are found in subtle and soft whisperings, that would sweep away discernment, and attempt to deceive even the elect [Matthew 24:24; Mark 13:22; and Revelation 13:14;19:20].

[*Church saints and mystics teach us that the Spiritually charged realm of the under-Heaven in the earth's atmosphere, is inhabited by countless multitudes of demons; of fallen and wandering spirits, cloaked as spirit guides; as well as countless straying earth-bound souls. To those who would of their own will, propose to experience this unseen world for the sake of curiosity, pride, or self-satisfaction, fallen spirit beings can offer a most alluring and convincing parody of Truth by way of 'spiritual' words, teachings, signs, and miracles; apparent experiences of 'grace' and the 'Holy Spirit' that delight the self-appeasing *"old man"*. Truly exalted experiences contrast sharply with these 'spiritualistic' experiences, and require the soul to be led by the Holy Spirit, and conducted and protected by the Angels, and the powers of Heaven, because man cannot navigate outside of this world by himself, and ward off the fallen ariel realm.]

> *"If anyone loves the world, the Father's Love [Charity] isn't in him. For all that is in the world; the lust of the flesh, and the lust of the eyes, and the pride of life, isn't of the Father..."*
>
> 1 John 2:15-16.

With a warm, convivial night of blindness stretched over a dark underbelly of all soul-crushing suffering, slumber and dis-ease, greater offences against our Creator God and Father go unrecognized, or are carelessly disregarded. Evil spirits are granted free reign to crawl in and invade everywhere, because without the true Jesus Christ of God-avowed Sacred Scripture [Deuteronomy 4:2, Revelation 22:18-19], salvation [healing] is torn from its proper context. Man's once reverential mind is reduced to functionalism; to clutching at life, and coveting and acquiring more and 'better' things and experiences on the surface of life, as though to shield and distract himself from reality of his fallen state in a fallen world. Sensuality replaces sensibility; appearance replaces the substance-essence of things; and projecting, acting and all restlessness, replaces simple, stable presence in Light-union with God. Identity issues and crusades proliferate in a blind and baseless pursuit of false freedom, that is the very destruction of freedom; that mis-creates, re-creates, and compounds chaos and human suffering. The health of the immortal soul is suffocated, if not extinguished by the exaggerated vain care of, and superficial improvements to a mortal body interchangeable with earth. All manner of crude hilarity, innuendo and infantilization is 'glamourized'; or treated as harmless fun. The innocence of children is disregarded, and intentional virgin souls for Love of God and the sake of the Kingdom [Matthew 19:12], become increasingly rare. Yet, **man's disregard for God and for the glory [blissful magnificence] of his own and others being in God, is nothing other than Satan's mocking of the dying agony of Jesus Christ in the *"old man"*;** entangled in the grueling chains of old world slavery, and cut off from the Light of Truth [divided against Himself]; and the peril in which his immortal soul exists.

> *"You cannot drink the cup of the Lord and the cup of demons.*
> *You cannot be partakers of the table of the Lord,*
> *and partakers of the table of demons."*
>
> 1 Corinthians 10:21.

Increasingly absorbed in a virtual web of shadows, man's challenge is ever greater. For with over-exposure to fast-changing superficiality, the deep-reading and multi-sensory [qualitative] human brain becomes impaired, and less capable of thinking, and thinking deeply [qualitatively] for itself. While the intensity of exterior images, thoughts, ideas, and narratives soak into his subconscious mind; confusing, benumbing, and corrupting his way of thinking, doing and being. Caught up with shallow connections, instant gratification, and self-service, he finds it increasingly difficult to be centred and present to himself, or anyone else in any real way. Satan and his demons rejoice, as vast swathes of precious time is swallowed up in his entanglement in a web of dead-end curiosities and pursuits; of casually consuming information and cultural cues, trends, narratives, and amusements without substance. A state of **soul-buffering**, that blocks Spiritual discernment, and prevents him from assuming the heart's desire [will], or the time to do what must be done.

> *"Console My agonizing Heart...*
> *for I am overwhelmed with sadness."*
> Jesus speaks to Blessed Dina Belanger.

The alarming success of Satan's work, has been called out over and over again, in the pleading words of our Blessed Mother, and the saints of the ages. *"Do not offend the Lord our God any more, because He is already so much offended"* warned our Blessed Mother at Fatima, Portugal in 1917. **Less than fifty years later in Garabandal, Spain, she warns us that** *"Few will see God."* **While in Akita, Japan in 1973 she says:** *"As I told you, if men do not repent and better themselves, the Father will inflict a terrible punishment on all humanity. It will be a punishment greater than the deluge, such as one never seen before."* **The** voices of the saints echo down through the ages with similar stark warnings. Speaking of those baptised in the Church: *"The number of the elect is so small; so small that, were we to know how small it is, we would faint away with grief"* says St.

Louis de Montfort; while St. John Vianney [the Cure of Ars] **warns us that** *"The number of the saved is as few as the number of grapes left after the vineyard-pickers have passed."* These deeply aggrieved words, paint the shocking reality that **precious few are the souls who *truly* listen to God and His Blessed Mother. Few and far between, are those *truly* stirred up to know and Love God [in His Divine Will], not only by words and gestures, but by their *whole way of being and living*; their inner and outer life.**

> *"I know that the best way to get hold of souls, is to rouse their desire for enjoyment... Put me first...no humility for me!!... but let me enjoy myself!! This sort of thing assures victory for us... and they tumble headlong into Hell!"*
>
> A demonic vision of St. Josefa Menendez.

The everyday reality of this dis-integration is seen in the myriad of problems that invade **man's Light-starved and ill-defined being, which is the casualty of more breakdowns than breakthroughs**. For when he lies to [misrepresents] himself, he makes a decision *"to divide" against himself* [in Hebrew], in the indivisible Godhead. The resulting cycle of unrest is the mark of interior Spiritual turmoil, originating in the violation of the One Truth of his being [God-being, John 10:34] in Jesus Christ. All manner of fears, anxieties and stresses are mis-created within him and transmitted to others, while his immunity to sin and debility is [further] weakened. This is because every thought creates chemical processes in the body, as well as a Cosmic odour and vibration, impacting his way of thinking, understanding and being; as well as everyone and everything. This is the dis-ease of the [dis-ordered and dis-integrated] false self, which hardens the shell of the ego-mould and works against divine reason, and all true healthfulness, peace, freedom, and fulfilment. Yet, not only does man lack the interior sight and strength of will [heart's desire] to turn back to God, but when he is fraught and unwell, good [Spiritual] food [teaching] appears sickening to him.

This most tragic breakdown of man's relationship with God, is the worst that evil can do, because the violation of the law of Divine Life [Truth], is the direct violation [crucifixion] of his own divine-humanity in the Cosmic Divine-Human Personhood of Jesus Christ. God cannot come to him in this state less he changes, because *"flesh and blood cannot possess [inherit] the Kingdom of God; neither will corruption possess [share in the Life of] incorruption"* 1 Corinthians 15:50. Discontent, suffering, and destruction abound everywhere, for as spirit governs matter, **all that is wrong in man, in his dire poverty of Light-separation from God [God-being, John 10:34], is revealed in the exterior world.** This unrelenting disturbance and chaos [in all its degrees] between Heaven and earth, is man's fate when God's Light is driven out, and the spirit of Satan takes over.

*"Who is the wise man who understands this...
why the land has perished, and has been scorched
like a desert, so much so that no one passes through it?"*

Jeremiah 9:12.

Hell: The Infernal Fire

Many Church saints give shocking testimony to the colossal successes of demonic spirits in the cruel harvest of souls, who continuously fall into Hell as silently, abundantly, and anonymously, as snowflakes on a mid-winter's day.

"The destiny of those dying in one day is that very few; not as many as ten went straight to Heaven...And those cast into Hell, were as numerous as snowflakes in mid-winter."

St. Anna María Taigi.

"I saw souls falling into Hell like snowflakes."

St. Teresa of Avila.

> *"I was watching souls going down into the abyss,
> as thick and fast as snowflakes falling in the winter mist."*
>
> St. Benedict Joseph Labre.

In this stark imagery, is set before us the devastating fate of lost souls, whose hearts [heart's desire] congealed in frozen hardness against Jesus Christ [Truth, Love and Life], and which finds them sinking and fading into deepest darkness, as Christ and the promise of the Beatific Vision [direct and immediate sight of God] seeded in Baptism, dies forever within them. The penalty of Hell, confirms the most sobering reality, that in mortal life and in death, we become that which we freely give ourselves to. While Sacred Scripture affirms that God predestines no one to go to Hell, but rather desires nothing more than His child *freely* turn back to Him and Live; God is effectively 'powerless' before human freedom [to Love in His Divine Will], which flows from His own omnipotence. And so, **as we are, God is to us [1 Corinthians 13:12].** Those who in time, wilfully committed, and persisted in sin, without sorrow or repentance [meaning *"turning back"* or *"coming back"* to God in Aramaic and Hebrew], are those self-condemned to the *"second death"* Revelation 2:11, 20:6,14; 21:8. This state of the complete absence of God within the soul, is its collapse into the realm of death; the *"lake of fire"* Revelation 20:14-15; 21:8; of unquenchable passions and appetites [Mark 9:48], in which it remains forever dead to Eternal Life, but yet cannot ever die [extinguish].

> *"For I have no pleasure in the death of him who dies,"*
> says the Lord. *"Therefore, turn yourselves, and Live!"*
>
> Ezekiel 18:32 [33:11].

In her terrifying vision, permitted by the Mercy of God, and meant to warn souls, St. Faustina [Divine Mercy], a Saint of more recent times, describes Hell as a *"fire that will penetrate the soul without destroying it - a terrible suffering."* **Seeing seven tortures and** different degrees of torture, depending upon the state of the soul, she adds: *"I would have died at the very sight of these tortures, if the omnipotence of God had not supported me."* These souls, now together with demons who assume a hideous and frightening form that befits their state of rejection of, and revolt against God, carry the scalding realization of their gift of days and span of years on earth, which was misspent in ungodly deeds, and the omission of *true* good. They can see [recognize] their wayward 'friends' and 'loved ones' with them, but continue to turn in on themselves, in denial and hatred of God [Truth, Love and Life].

> *"The devils and the souls of the damned see each other, and all the evil, both of others and their own."*
>
> St. Faustina [Divine Mercy].

In describing Hell as the soul's final, most bitter, and excruciating tearing away from God, St. Robert Bellarmine, a 16th Century Italian Jesuit and Church Cardinal, similarly confirms two terrible penalties.

The first penalty, is the Eternal loss of God [and our God-being, John 10:34, and Good-being in Him]. This is the loss of the glorious [blissfully magnificent] enrichment's and contentment's of Divine Life, with all healthfulness and rest from suffering and struggle; traded for the incessant torments and taunts of body and soul, by wicked [evil and ungodly] spirits, amidst unbearable stench and chaos, and alternating extremities of heat and freezing cold. For here, where *"nothing else but everlasting horror, dwells"* Job 10:22; *"fire and brimstone and windstorms will be the portion of their cup"* Psalm 11:7. Here, there will be no provisions of prayer, sacraments, Holy Water or other sacramentals to drive away the attacks of evil spirits, because the soul's Light-reaping time [and time of Divine Mercy] on earth is over. In utter contrast to the inextinguishable Light of Heaven, where *"its gates shall not be closed throughout the day, for there shall be no night in that place"* Revelation 21:25 [Isaiah 60:11], Hell is its own community, where the gates are bolted on the inside, by those who closed the gate of their soul to God when on earth. The second penalty, is of both the internal faculties of the soul [memory, will and the intellect], and the external senses [sight, hearing, taste, smell, and touch]. Capacities, which instead of being purified and re-ordered to God as channels of Light [grace] during earthly life, were used for useless, ungodly, and corrupt purposes, and without sincere repentance, and purpose of amendment.

> *"...we saw, as it were, a sea of fire. Plunged in this fire were demons and souls in human form, like transparent burning embers... without weight or equilibrium, amid shrieks and groans of pain and despair ... The demons could be distinguished by their terrifying and repellent likeness to frightful and unknown animals, black and transparent like burning coals."*
>
> From the First Secret of Fatima – The Vision of Hell.

[The reality of Hell, is confirmed in both the Old and New Testaments. First mentioned and epitomised in the Old Testament (e.g., 2 Kings 23:10; 2 Chronicles 28:3; 33:6 and Jeremiah 7:31;19:2,6; 32:35) as a place of detestable practices, the valley of Hinnom (*"Gai-Ben-Hinnom"* in Hebrew), meaning *"Gehenna"* in Greek, was also known during Jesus earthly Lifetime. Located on the south and west side of the walled city of Jerusalem, this was a place of idolatry and of ill repute; a gruesome and foul-smelling place where trash was constantly thrown and burned, together with the bodies of the crucified, and those who had died of diseases. Jesus refers directly to Gehenna eleven times (in the Gospels of Matthew 5:22,29,30;10:28;18:9;23:15,33, Mark 9:43,45,47, and Luke 12:5), while some apostles refer to it as well. In Matthew 5, Jesus issues strong warning, that it is far better for the body to endure temporary pain, loss, or affliction on earth, than to suffer an Eternity of self-destruction in Hell].

If we find ourselves immersed in the ways of the flesh [carnal ego-self] and the old world, and struggle to be stirred up to Love of God, let us ask ourselves: **whose eyes are truly wet, for the silent and unrelenting cries of purging and ever-lost souls**? Let us remember, that each and every one of us must eventually stand before our long-suffering Creator God and Father, in the All-penetrating and All-determining white fire of Truth. Presenting alone, and in silence before the One who has Loved us with *"an Ever-lasting Love"* Jeremiah 31:3, and whose [divine] thoughts and ways are not ours [Isaiah 55:8], everything sought amidst the clamour and commotion; and the rust and dust of earthly life, will have perished. While what remains, will be our state of being, in or apart from Him.

The magnitude of our opportunity to be healed and raised to the native **purity, nobility, and freedom** of our being in Light-union with Him [and all things in Him], will be revealed, together with Satan's relentless [direct and indirect] attempts to derail us at every turn. Set before us will be the measure of our victory in battle; our fidelity to conceiving and birthing, or rejecting the Spiritual state [and relationship] of the Kingdom within our souls. Also, before us, will be the reality of our example to others; our work of assisting, or of thwarting them with their conception and birthing struggle. And as it is the way of Perfect and immutable Justice, that how we treated Jesus Christ within our soul, and in the souls of others during earthly life determines the company and destination that befits us, in and for all Eternity, there will be nothing else to do, but learn whether we are destined to rise forever in glory, or sink forever, quenched in our own cloak of darkness.

> *"A wise man sees the way of life stretching upwards, leading away from the abyss beneath."*
>
> Proverbs 15:24.

Appendix 2: Spiritual Discernment

The lives of the saints testify to the need for great humility and discernment in the Spiritual life. Sacred Scripture demonstrates by way of parable that hallowed reality is multi-layered, and depends upon the state of readiness and refinement of the soul to receive the Light [of Truth, Love and Life]. There are no shortcuts to the Kingdom, but by and in Jesus Christ [Matthew 7:13; John 10:1; 14:6], which means being willing and able to drink from the cup of suffering that He first drank [Matthew 20:22 and Mark 10:38]. This means that the entirety of man's interior and exterior way of being must be transfigured, and in harmony [Matthew 23:25-26; Luke 11:39-40] with Jesus Christ. A narrow, unknown path to union, that the saints [notably St. John of the Cross] teach us, is travelled in nakedness of [suffering] Love, enabled by *living* faith, knowledge, and divine wisdom; and which means freedom from every perception or attachment [self-interest] at the natural level, including the fruits of our Spiritual works.

The challenge of this way, is demonstrated during Jesus Life on earth, where most of those who followed Him around, eagerly listening to, and discussing His enigmatic teachings; who prayed with Him; and who administered and benefitted from His gifts and healing miracles, deserted Him during His Passion [Mark 14:46,50]. **Only a very small party travelled with Him, and stood at the foot of the Cross, representing the precious few who accept the royal way of the Cross.** Those who are truly willing to commit - by fearless faith and Charity [Love in action], and not by sight - to a God whose [divine] thoughts and ways are not ours [Isaiah 55:8]; and whose invitation into His glory, means sharing in His Cross. And so, while direct interventions of God by way of signs and apparitions, are extraordinary acts of grace to be welcomed in all humility [as not to oppress the Spirit and spurn prophesies, 1 Thess 5: 19-20], they are not intended to excite curiosity about, desire for, or attachment to, other-worldly experiences. They are given rather, to excite the faith; to alert man to the *'signs of the times'*, and to emphasize his task and privilege of committing himself to holiness [whole-hearted fullness of being] of living*. The same can be said of supernatural abilities and miracles [e.g., tongues, or prophesy, as distinct from the One singular gift of the Holy Spirit], which may or may not be carried out in the power of God. [In Acts 16: 1-18, for example, we learn about a girl with a divining (fortune-telling) spirit which **speaks words that are true, yet not from God**, and which St. Paul calls out of her in Jesus Name]. While, even when genuine charismatic gifts from God for good purpose [1 Corinthians 12:3-7], they are not necessarily evidence of sanctity in those bearing them [Romans 11:29], nor an end in themselves. For all God's works, are for the purpose of [further] inspiring man to an authentically holy [whole and all-perfect] way of life, marked by the gold standard of the Cross. A dynamically Eucharistic way of being, which alone determines the healthfulness, and final destination of his soul.

[*Over the last century, messages from Heaven have grown all the more urgent, in calling for repentance, prayer and penance; warning man about the grave sinfulness of the world, and the imminent rebalancing of the Scales of Justice.]

> *"If I speak in tongues of men and of Angels…*
> *If I have the gift of prophesy, and know all mysteries and all knowledge, and if I have all faith…If I give away all…*
> *and hand over my body to be burned,*
> *yet not have Charity, it offers me nothing."*
>
> 1 Corinthians 13:1-3.

Sacred Scripture warns against putting God to the test [Numbers 14:22; Deuteronomy 6:16], by asking for signs and proofs, which is what Satan attempted to provoke Jesus to do in the desert [Matthew 4:7; Luke 4:12]. Indeed, **Jesus severely admonished the Pharisees and Sadducees as wanton and evil, for asking for signs and miracles, while failing to *live by Truth already given* [Matthew 16:4; Luke 11:16].** While to the doubting apostle Thomas, He says: *"Blessed are those who have not seen, and yet have believed"* John

20:29. He declares that many will come to Him on Judgement Day, calling out works of [prayerful non-] prayer, healing, and prophesy and all manner of pious practices; but He will command them to depart, saying: *"I never knew you"* Matthew 7:23 and Luke 13:25-27.

Many Church saints testify to Satan's endless battery of works to deceive and derail souls. From offering ideas of libertine love; of worthiness and false security with no real sense of the origin and destination of the soul - even suggesting the absence of original sin and God's Judgement; to false signs and visions, and ideas of visionary perfection. From false peace [See Meditations on the Song of Songs, Chapter 2, by St. Teresa of Avila], and oppression under the guise of good [e.g., Spiritual complacency or encouraging severe aesthetic practices]; to intellectual or knowledge arrogance, self-reliance, Spiritual gluttony, indiscretion, and ideas of cheap grace, *"he [Satan] gives to everyone according to his condition"* says God the Father to St. Catherine of Siena. **Sacred Scripture warns us to** *"Be aware of false prophets [teachers]... in sheep's clothing"* Matthew 7:15; **because** *"many false prophets have gone out into the world"* 1 John 4:1; 2 Corinthians 11:13–15. **In the last days,** *"some will fall away from the faith, paying attention to seducing spirits and doctrines of demons"* 1 Timothy 4:1. **For as in the Garden of Eden, the works of the master seducer take on very many guises, and emerge in unexpected places,** attempting to deceive and derail even the elect [Matthew 24:24; Mark 13:22; and Revelation 13:14;19:20].

> *"Most certainly, I tell you, one who doesn't enter by the door into the sheep fold, but climbs up some other way, is a thief and a robber...I AM the door."*
>
> John 10:1,9.

Despite the works of the enemy, man yet instinctively knows that **experience expires**; that everything has a relative measure of value and reality, which depends upon his perceptions and emotions at any point in time. While the more appetites and pursuits he chases and showcases, the more he becomes aware that impressions, desires, and successes, oriented to disordered selfhood and the material world, offer diminishing returns, and eventually exhaust themselves. This is because **life is a perpetual becoming in constant need of renewal**; of fresh hope and newness, which only co-operation with and participation in the All-Good Life of the Spirit can offer. *"You have made us for yourself, O Lord, and our hearts are restless until they rest in You" says St. Augustine.*

We are therefore urged to focus on our primary task of abandoning back [consenting] to the ***real work* of transformation of being**, powered by the sacraments and provisions of the Church, as we take up the work of the Cross, to attain to the state of sanctity to which we are called [invited]. A work which requires aliveness to the reality that **authentic growth necessitates great purity of being**, which means detachment from [non-attachment to] all vain [from the Latin word *"vanus"* meaning empty] self-interest and self-satisfaction, in both Spiritual and material matters. It requires holy prudence in the testing of spirits [1 John 4:1-6], and more rarely the assistance of a Priest. Souls of exemplary sanctity and orthodoxy of faith, who through very great Love of God attained to a state of Spiritual Union or Spiritual Incarnation, demonstrate the reality of the narrow way. Most generous in all self-giving, and graced with keen Spiritual intellect, they express great fear [awe-filled reverence], and the most sobering sense of their own no-thing-ness, before the ineffable majesty and magnificence [glory] of God. They are given to radical humility and heightened prayer and penance, together with intense zeal for souls. And they do not speak about such things [which can scarcely be reduced to human language, and which offers inspiration to demons], unless instructed by God for the good of souls.

> *"If you seek to know more than you should know,*
> *you will be deceived by the ancient seducer...*
> *The first man [Adam] sought more than he should have sought,*
> *and was deceived by him, and went to perdition."*
>
> God speaks to St. Hildegard of Bingen. [3]

Appendix 3: The Golden Maxims of St. John of the Cross

To overcome the *"old man"* and find his movement towards God [God-being, John 10:34], man must co-operate with the Holy Spirit in the work of detachment from [non-attachment to] the lower desires, gratifications, and standards of the old world, the flesh [carnal ego-self] and the works of evil.

This is accomplished by being inclined:

- *Not after that which is most easy, but that which is most difficult;*
- *Not after that which is most pleasant, but that which is most unpleasant;*
- *Not after that which gives pleasure, but that which gives none;*
- *Not after that which is consoling, but that which is unconsoling;*
- *Not after that which gives repose, but after that which requires labour;*
- *Not after great things, but after little things;*
- *Not after that which is elevated and precious, but that which is lowest and most despised*;*
- *Not to desire anything, but rather nothing.*

> [The Ascent of Mount Carmel, Book 1 Chapter 13.6]

St. John of the Cross explains this positive self-offering [including being inclined to go *unnoticed or unrewarded], in both earthly and Spiritual matters, as the essential means of exchanging our no-thingness, with the unfathomable All-ness of God. Man's **self-emptying from** the ways and works of the old world, the flesh, and the devil, is not an end in itself, but is **for the sake of** peace and freedom, and ultimately the creative realization, of the Spiritual state of the Kingdom [the Life of Jesus Christ], within the soul.

Appendix 4: The Three Stages of Spiritual Growth

Church theologians, saints and mystics describe the Spiritual Life as three stages of progress or realization, traversed by the soul:

1. **The Purgative Way:** as its name indicates, involves establishing habits of prayer, reparation and distaste for coarseness and sin, as the awareness and attention of natural man [the beginner], is drawn above the old world, the flesh [carnal ego-self], and the works of evil, and on to higher things.

2. **The Illuminative Way:** is that of steady growth in prayer, and purity of heart [heart's desire], motivated by pure Love of God alone. In this intermediate or adolescent stage of creative re-orientation, the soul sincerely strives to move towards God, by *'putting on Jesus Christ'*. Every act [of thought, word, and deed], is mediated more so by a pure act of the human will [heart's desire] in co-operation with and participation in the Divine Will, than by reason, feelings, or emotions at the natural level.

3. **The Unitive Way:** once the soul has been sufficiently purified [purged] of fleshy [carnal-ego] and worldly interference [desires], and is re-ordered and re-integrated [re-centred] in the Spirit, it is can grow strong and stable enough to re-birth in God. In this higher state, the spirit most perfectly [as is possible on earth] illuminates and re-unites the mind in the heart, to govern the soul [memory, will and intellect], which informs the body [Ephesians 4:22-24], through the five senses. This state of transforming union, is known as the Spiritual Life or the Mystical life.

There are many degrees of progress [dimensions of creative awareness] within the three ways, which can operate concurrently, engaging the three levels of man: corporal man;

interior [inner] man and supernatural man. Growth is then not usually characterized by completely stable or sustained 'advancement' as perceived by the human mind, but by authentic co-operation with, and perseverance in [commitment to] the higher Life of the *"Fiat"*. All growth depends upon the soul's disposition; including vigilance, perseverance, stability, and sincere correspondence with grace. While many of the benefits of its Life-giving acts [in union with Jesus Christ] will only be shown to it after mortal death, when it will experience its unique and Eternal flowering within God, at *"the wedding feast of the Lamb"* Revelation 19:9. Union with and in God is God's creative work within and through the soul. It is His gift to man, co-operating with and participating in Him, in graceful [grace-filled] simplicity of being; the human will [heart's desire] acting in harmony with His Love and Divine Will.

Souls of the 20th Century, who describe a state of Mystical [Spiritual] Incarnation, *first attained* the extraordinary state of transforming union or Mystical Marriage. The exceptional degree self-renunciation and fidelity required to first reach the state of Mystical Marriage, is taught, and exemplified by Carmelite saints, St. John of the Cross, and St. Teresa of Avila.

Appendix 5: The Three Degrees of Prayer

Church theologians, saints, and mystics, describe various degrees or levels of prayer, that move us towards spirit-bearing union with God. One such account by Blessed Angela Foligno [an Italian mystic and Third Order Franciscan], describes three modes of prayer which the soul must traverse, to enter into the Life of Jesus Christ.

Corporal prayer: is that which is always accompanied by the sound of words, and by devout bodily exercises, such as kneeling, genuflecting, folding one's hands and bowing one's head. Kneeling reminds us of our total dependence on God, and folding our hands together, reminds us of the necessity of bringing the human will [heart's desire] into harmony with the Divine Will [the Father's Cosmic Heart's Desire]. Intentional and alert bodily posture, is a mark of absolute dependence on God, and of honouring Him, while serving to increase the vigour of our spirit, [against lower sensual tendencies], because **the body must take its part in the work of the spirit.** Sacred Scripture tells us that Jesus knelt to pray, and stretched out his arms in the form of a Cross. He also prayed prostrate forward on the ground. Effective prayer however, depends first and foremost, upon our heart's desire [human will], and can be achieved when completing tasks, or even when lying down, if necessary. As prayer is gently repeated on the lips, and focused in the mind, we are brought to the meaning of what we are saying. In this way, the prayer flourishes and flows inwardly, to become something of the mind [the seat of knowledge and wisdom] in the heart [the seat of emotions], as well as of the lips.

Mental prayer: in mental prayer, meditation on God fills the soul so entirely, that it thinks of nothing else but God. In this state, it becomes mentally absorbed in God, and does not want to think of anything else but Him, in all things. Exterior bodily movements, works and ways of being, come into unison with interior motives, as we begin to learn to pray instinctively with our whole being. The bending of our heads into our chest, reflects the lowering of our mind into our heart, to venerate the divine presence within. While genuflection of the knee is one with the prostration of our hearts. In an atmosphere of higher alertness and awareness, we learn to guard the operation of our soul [memory, will and intellect] and five senses, as our heart's desire [human will] is healed and drawn by Love, into the Cosmic Heart's Desire [Divine Will] of Almighty God.

From mental prayer, the soul proceeds to **Supernatural prayer,** which is when the prayer descends completely from the mind into the heart, which is the centre of our being in Jesus Christ-consciousness. With both united, prayer becomes in the fullest sense, *living* prayer, and pervades every act [of thought, word, and deed] of our being. This is the mark of God's own praying within and through the soul. The soul is uplifted above its own nature and understanding, knowing more about God, than it can know naturally. It is brought to a hidden place of not-knowing or not understanding at the human level, but to a profound and nameless encounter of God, in the deepest mystery of its being. In this wordless state of elevated awareness and creative realization, the soul is strong in darkness, and glimpses in wonder and joy, the wholeness [holiness and all-perfection] and splendour of hallowed reality, that transcends human thinking. In being drawn upwards to know God, it grows to truly Love Him [back], with and in His own Love operating in His Divine Will. In Loving Him, it desires ever more to be consumed and transfigured in Him, in order to be united more closely with Him, who it recognizes as its life-source and absolute contentment. *"Praying at all times in the Spirit, and being watchful to this end [fulfilment] in all perseverance"* Ephesians 6:18, **a**part from any apparent or sensible effects [that is to say, obvious to the natural senses], is the threshold of unceasing prayer. This is the transformation of the soul into a living benediction during its earthly life, and which, if maintained, will be fully realized [made real], and enjoyed, in its Ever-flowering in Eternal Life.

In these three degrees of prayer, man gradually learns to know both God and himself, and to Love all that is his neighbour as himself. To progress, he must proceed from awareness of God, to purity of heart's desire [human will] for God, and finally the Spiritual [Mystical] Life, which is the state of Light-union. This appears to be an effort to the soul, until it forgets the forgetfulness, ingratitude, illusion, and evil into which it has fallen. Ever in a necessary and inseparable state of ascending [retreat from the old world], and descending [into the old world], it must continuously co-operate with God by exercising diligent awareness, good will [heart's desire] and perseverance [commitment] in the Life of grace, in order to strengthen and proceed to attain higher degrees of prayer; of purification, illumination and Sanctification, in a continuous circle of learning, sharing, and maturing.

Such is the return to *real Life and purpose* in Jesus Christ, ordered in God's infinite wisdom, that we must rise far beyond prayer as a mental or vocal exercise, separate from all our acts [of thought word and deed], We must grow and mature beyond prayer for personal intentions, and passing acts of concern, sympathy, and benevolence towards others, to take an active part in the undoing of evil, and the triumph of the *living* Church [the Coming of the Kingdom] on earth. An extraordinary transfiguration of reality, achieved only by whole-heartedly and dynamically co-operating with and participating in God, in His Love and Divine Will. The magnitude of difference in the soul's rapturous glory [blissful magnificence] and bliss, with every additional degree of Light-union [communion of relationship] is such, that many Church saints declared their willingness to accept any suffering, to attain but one more degree of glory-union.

Description of the three degrees of prayer adapted from 'The Book of Divine Consolations of the Blessed Angela of Foligno'.

.

Appendix 6: Suggested Reading

Garabandal and its Secrets, by Ted Flynn.

God's Creative Power for Healing, by Charles Capps.

Revelations of St. Bridget: On the Life and Passion of Our Lord and the Life of His Blessed Mother, by St. Bridget of Sweden.

Saints who battled Satan, by Paul Thigpen.

Sayings of Light and Love, by St. John of the Cross.

Self-abandonment to Divine Providence, by Jean-Pierre de Caussade.

The Book of Wisdom [The Wisdom of Solomon], Holy Bible.

The Dialogue of St. Catherine of Siena, by St. Catherine of Siena.

The Miracle Ship, by Brian O'Hare.

The Spiritual Legacy of Sister Mary of the Holy Trinity, edited by Rev. Silvere Van Den Broek, O.F.M.

The 24 Hours of the Passion of Our Lord Jesus Christ, from the writings of the Servant of God, Luisa Piccarreta.

Your Healing is Within You, by Cannon Jim Glennon.

The Garden of Eden, and the Life of Jesus vintage gallery.

Acknowledgements

General:

Alba House, St. Pauls USA, publisher of the writings of Venerable Conchita - María Concepción Cabrera de Armida. www.stpaulsusa.com

Congregation of Marians of the Immaculate Conception, Edge Hill, Stockbridge, Massachusetts, USA, Copyright © *Diary of Saint Maria Faustina Kowalska*, published by Marian Press.

Convent of Jesus and Mary, Quebec, Canada, Copyright © *Autobiography of Marie-Cecile de Rome, R.J.M (Blessed Dina Belanger)*.

Imprimerie St. Francois, Malines, Belgium Copyright ©1981 *The Spiritual Legacy of Sister Mary of the Holy Trinity,* published by Tan Books and Publishers Inc, Rockford, Illinois. www.tanbooks.com

San Giovanni Rotondo, www.vocedipadrepio.com Padre *Pio of Pietrelcina Letters I, II and III*, Copyright © Edizioni "Padre Pio da Pietrelcina".

In-text citations:

1 (p. 212), 2 (p. 247), 3 (p. xvii). Excerpts from *Scivias*, from The Classics of Western Spirituality, translated by Mother Columba Hart and Jane Bishop, Copyright © 1990 by Abbey of Regina Laudis: Benedictine Congregation Regina Laudis of the Strict Observance Inc, Paulist Press, Inc., New York/Mahwah, N.J. Used with permission of Paulist Press. www.paulistpress.com

4 (p. 345) Excerpt from *Writings of Edith Stein*, translated by Hilda Graef, published by Peter Owen Limited: London. 1956.

5 (p. i) Excerpt from *Hildegard of Bingen's Book of Divine Works, with Letters and Songs* Edited by Matthew Fox, published by Inner Traditions International and Bear & Company, ©1987. All rights reserved. www.innertraditions.com Reprinted with permission of publisher.

www.ingramcontent.com/pod-product-compliance
Lightning Source LLC
Chambersburg PA
CBHW070757020526
44118CB00036B/1807